Ecosystem Approaches to Fisheries

A Global Perspective

Inspired by the work of the renowned fisheries scientist Daniel Pauly, this book provides a detailed overview of ecosystem-based management of fisheries. It explores the complex and interdisciplinary nature of the subject by bringing together contributions from some of the world's leading fisheries scientists and conservationists.

Combining both research reviews and opinion pieces, and reflecting the breadth of Pauly's influence within the field, the book illustrates the range of issues associated with the implementation of the ecosystem approach and the challenge of long-term sustainability. Topics covered include global biodiversity, the impact of human actions on marine life, the implications for economic and social systems, and the role of science in communicating and shaping ocean policy to conserve resources for the future.

This book provides a complete and essential overview for advanced researchers and for those just entering the field.

VILLY CHRISTENSEN is Professor and Associate Director of the Fisheries Centre at the University of British Columbia. He is a leading expert in ecosystem modeling, and has led courses and workshops throughout the world on developing ecosystem approaches to fisheries management.

JAY MACLEAN is a former Acting Director General and Director of the Information Program of the International Center for Living Aquatic Resources Management (ICLARM) in the Philippines. He is currently a consultant for several international organizations and is based in Manila.

Ecosystem Approaches to Fisheries

A Global Perspective

Edited by

VILLY CHRISTENSEN
University of British Columbia, Vancouver

JAY MACLEAN
Manila, Philippines

CAMBRIDGE
UNIVERSITY PRESS

CAMBRIDGE UNIVERSITY PRESS
Cambridge, New York, Melbourne, Madrid, Cape Town,
Singapore, São Paulo, Delhi, Tokyo, Mexico City

Cambridge University Press
The Edinburgh Building, Cambridge CB2 8RU, UK

Published in the United States of America by Cambridge University Press,
New York

10 0673 1948

www.cambridge.org
Information on this title: www.cambridge.org/9780521113052

First published 2011

Printed in the United Kingdom at the University Press, Cambridge

A catalog record for this publication is available from the British Library

ISBN 978-0-521-11305-2 Hardback
ISBN 978-0-521-13022-6 Paperback

Contents

III.   Managing living resources

IV.   The human side

V.   Impacting policy

Contributors

Nicolas Bailly
WorldFish Center, Biodiversity Informatics Office, Khush Hall, IRRI College, Los Baños, Laguna, Philippines

Andrew Bakun
Rosenstiel School of Marine and Atmospheric Science, University of Miami, 4600 Rickenbacker Causeway, Miami, FL 33149, USA

Nancy Baron
SeaWeb, c/o National Center for Ecological Analysis and Synthesis (NCEAS), 735 State St., Suite 300, Santa Barbara, CA 93101, USA

William W. L. Cheung
School of Environmental Sciences, University of East Anglia, Norwich, NR4 7TJ, UK, and Fisheries Centre, University of British Columbia, Vancouver, Canada, BC V6T 1Z4

Villy Christensen
Fisheries Centre, University of British Columbia, 2202 Main Mall, Vancouver, Canada, BC V6T 1Z4

Ratana Chuenpagdee
Department of Geography, Memorial University of Newfoundland, St. John's, Newfoundland, Canada, A1B 3X9

Andrés M. Cisneros-Montemayor
Fisheries Centre, University of British Columbia, 2202 Main Mall, Vancouver, Canada, BC V6T 1Z4

Andrew J. Dyck
Fisheries Centre, University of British Columbia, 2202 Main Mall, Vancouver, Canada, BC V6T 1Z4

Rainer Froese
IFM-GEOMAR, Düsternbrooker Weg 20, 24105 Kiel, Germany

Marah J. Hardt
OceanInk, Kailua Kona, HI 96740, USA

Gotthilf Hempel
Centre for Tropical Marine Ecology, Alfred Wegener Institute for Marine and Polar Research, Bremerhaven, and Institute for Polar Ecology, Wischhofstr 1–3, Geb.12, D-24148 Kiel, Germany

Michael F. Hirshfield
Oceana, 1350 Connecticut Ave., NW, 5th Floor, Washington, DC 20036, USA

Jeremy Jackson
Center for Marine Biodiversity and Conservation, Scripps Institution of Oceanography 0202, University of California, San Diego, 9500 Gilman Drive, La Jolla, CA 92083-0202, USA

Jennifer Jacquet
Fisheries Centre, University of British Columbia, 2202 Main Mall, Vancouver, Canada, BC V6T 1Z4

Sherman Lai
Fisheries Centre, University of British Columbia, 2202 Main Mall, Vancouver, Canada, BC V6T 1Z4

Vicky W. Y. Lam
Fisheries Centre, University of British Columbia, 2202 Main Mall, Vancouver, Canada, BC V6T 1Z4

Jessica J. Meeuwig
Centre for Marine Futures, Faculty of Natural and Agricultural Sciences, University of Western Australia, Plant Biology, M090, 35 Stirling Highway, Crawley WA 6009, Australia

John L. Munro
242 MacDonnell Road, Eagle Heights, Queensland 4271, Australia
Dr Munro died December 13, 2009

Cornelia E. Nauen
International Scientific Cooperation, DG Research, European Commission, 8 Square de Meeûs, 1049 Brussels, Belgium

Maria L. D. Palomares
Fisheries Centre, University of British Columbia, 2202 Main Mall, Vancouver, Canada, BC V6T 1Z4

Roger S. V. Pullin
7A Legaspi Park View, 134 Legaspi St., Makati City, Philippines

Joshua S. Reichert
Pew Environment Group, 901 E St. NW, Washington, DC 20004, USA

Kenneth Ruddle
Professor, School of Policy Studies, Kwansei Gakuin University, Kobe-Sanda Campus, Japan

Carl Safina
Blue Ocean Institute, School of Marine and Atmospheric Sciences, Stony Brook University, Stony Brook, NY 11794, USA

Konstantinos I. Stergiou
Aristotle University of Thessaloniki, School of Biology, Department of Zoology, Box 134, Thessaloniki, 54124, Greece

U. Rashid Sumaila
Fisheries Centre, University of British Columbia, 2202 Main Mall, Vancouver, Canada, BC V6T 1Z4

Carl J. Walters
Professor, Fisheries Centre, University of British Columbia, 2202 Main Mall, Vancouver, Canada, BC V6T 1Z4

Reg Watson
Fisheries Centre, University of British Columbia, 2202 Main Mall, Vancouver, Canada, BC V6T 1Z4

Dirk Zeller
Fisheries Centre, University of British Columbia, 2202 Main Mall, Vancouver, Canada, BC V6T 1Z4

Foreword

Less than two centuries ago, it did not seem silly for Byron to write "Man marks the earth with ruin, his control stops with the shore." Today, as this volume makes clear, the situation is grimly different.

Byron's observation about human impacts on terrestrial species and ecosystems was brought into sharp scientific focus by Vitousek *et al*'s (1986) analysis, suggesting that roughly 35–40% of the products of photosynthesis on land were taken, directly or indirectly, for our use. The corresponding careful analysis for fisheries came 10 years later, finding that although the overall fraction of aquatic primary production required to support all fisheries was around 8%, this did not really capture the essentials. Essentially all the fish we eat comes from fresh water or from oceanic upwelling or shelf systems, and here we took 24–35% of primary production in the years just before 1995 (Pauly and Christensen, 1995); significantly more is taken today.

Even more important was Pauly's emphatic recognition that most fisheries are managed – if you can call it that – on a single stock basis. The present volume is largely devoted to the many and varied developments in fisheries science, subsequent to the recognition that single species management is ultimately nonsense. To take just one example, if you sought to maximize sustainable yield of krill in the Southern Ocean, you would eliminate krill-eating whales, and conversely if you wished to maximize sustainable yield of whales you would not harvest krill at all (the first draft of the Treaty of the Southern Ocean entirely failed to realize this!). Daniel Pauly has played a central role in putting the management of multispecies fisheries on a rational basis, and this volume is a fitting tribute to him.

Not only is Daniel a hugely influential scientist, but he is also a most thoughtful person who expresses himself – both in speech and prose – with clarity and force. I particularly remember his epigrammatic illumination of the contrast between the essential adequacy of our scientific understanding of fisheries and the often distressing inadequacy of our machinery for translating this understanding into effective action: to pursue excellent research that is then disregarded is, he said, like "using a large, modern hospital only for diagnosis, and not for treatment."

In short, this book is timely and important both in itself, and as appropriate recognition of Daniel Pauly's contributions to fishery science.

Professor Lord Robert May of Oxford
OM AC Kt FRS
Department of Zoology, University of Oxford

REFERENCES

Pauly, D. and Christensen, V. (1995) Primary production required to sustain global fisheries. *Nature*, **374**, 255–257.

Vitousek, P. M., Ehrlich, P. R. and Ehrlich, A. H. (1986) Human appropriation of the products of photosynthesis. *BioScience*, **36**, 368–373.

Preface

The need to move from a sectoral to an ecosystem approach in the management of fisheries has become compelling in recent years. Many elements of ecosystem-based management (EBM) of fisheries have been identified but implementing them has proven to be elusive. Management of the oceans' fisheries on an ecosystem basis entails ecosystem-based management of the oceans themselves and, given the diversity of fisheries and marine ecosystems, there is no single recipe toward this end. In this book, we present a broad collection of the elements and some of the recipes for ecosystem-based management. We believe it is one of the first books to deal with this approach to management of the oceans.

This book was inspired by a founding father of research on ecosystem-based management, Daniel Pauly. When he was awarded the 13th International Cosmos Prize late in 2005, Amanda Vincent and Villy Christensen obtained support from the University of British Columbia (UBC) – where Pauly was Director of the Fisheries Centre – for a symposium to honor him for receiving the Cosmos Prize and to be held at the Fisheries Centre on the occasion of his 60th birthday, May 2, 2006. With UBC's generous support, we were able to invite a number of prominent scientists and policymakers with whom Pauly has worked during his career to give presentations at the one-day symposium, which was titled, "Thinking Big: A Global Look at Fisheries Science."

Presenters were asked to write an essay related to their contributions, and to do so without it becoming "an ode to Daniel," while a focus on aspects that related to his work was preferable. The intention was to provide an overview that combined research reviews and opinion pieces. We realized that Pauly's career has spanned many of the elements that are involved in conceptualization, methodology development, and implementation of ecosystem-based management of living resources, and that we were covering a large part of this at the "Thinking Big" symposium. Therefore, we decided to frame the book around the concept of ecosystem approaches to fisheries management, and invited additional contributions to provide a more complete coverage of the topic.

The various chapters describe global biodiversity, the impact we have on life in the oceans, how we evaluate fisheries impact, what consequences these impacts may all have for economic and social systems, what is needed in terms of communication and in scientific capacity building, and how science can influence ocean policy in order to ensure that there may be ocean resources for future generations to enjoy.

We intend the book to give readers a broad view of the elements required for successful implementation of ecosystem-based fisheries management and the long-term sustainability that is implied. Managing at the level of the ecosystem calls for considering a wide range of issues, and it is impossible for any one person to be an expert in all. One can be deep and narrow, or less deep but wide ranging. We hope that the chapters in the book together will give the reader the more wide-ranging perspective on the topic.

Acknowledgments

The editors wish to thank the authors in this book for their contributions and patience during the production phase. The University of British Columbia (UBC) funded and hosted the symposium "Thinking Big: A Global Look at Fisheries Science" on which most of the essays herein are based. We thank UBC, and especially Vice President John Hepburn, for support as well as for opening the symposium. The "Thinking Big" symposium was held as a tribute to Daniel Pauly's achievements, his 60th birthday, and winning the 13th International Cosmos Prize.

We wish to note the passing of one of the authors contributing to this book, John Munro, the pioneer of tropical fisheries science. John Munro was a colleague and great friend of ours for many years, and he will be dearly missed.

VILLY CHRISTENSEN

1

Introduction: toward ecosystem-based management of fisheries

Fisheries have always been important to humanity. In the last century we have, however, witnessed how industrialization of fisheries leads to widespread overexploitation of fish populations. Our general reaction has been to strengthen the call for fisheries management, even if opinions of what this requires differ.

The idea of managing at the ecosystem level has been around for years (McIntosh, 1985), and numerous international agreements make it clear that this is the way forward for management for fisheries as well as for many other resources, such as forestry. Yet, there is considerable uncertainty in the minds of most scientists, environmentalists, managers, and policymakers, of what the term actually implies. Many definitions have been put forward, and we are slowly and gradually getting a clearer picture of what is involved in implementing ecosystem-based management of fisheries.

Pikitch *et al.* (2004) stated that approaches to ecosystem-based management of fisheries should avoid degradation of ecosystems while minimizing the risk of irreversible change therein, consider how to obtain and maintain long-term socioeconomic benefits, and in the process gain an understanding of the likely consequences of human actions. Clearly, area-based management has to be an integral part of ecosystem management, and it must be carried out so as to balance conflicting trade-offs and ensure long-term economic and social sustainability. Implementing ecosystem-based management requires going beyond traditional management and business-as-usual, and this is, in essence, what has dictated the content selection for this book.

We have shaped this book around elements required for ecosystem-based management of fisheries, beginning with how developments in fisheries science over the last three decades have led to the present ecosystem view. Fisheries science has evolved very much in

Ecosystem Approaches to Fisheries: A Global Perspective, ed. V. Christensen and J. Maclean. Published by Cambridge University Press. © Cambridge University Press 2011.

synchrony with the research focus of our main subject (Nauen and Hempel, this volume), and we exemplify this in a series of essays describing some essential elements for ecosystem-based management.

The other parallel focus of this book is on how an influential scientist, Daniel Pauly, has shaped the field and helped to kick-start the science and communication of ecosystem-based management of fisheries.

When fisheries science became a quantitative field, it was with a focus on population dynamics (Beverton and Holt, 1957; Pauly, 1998). Populations are units of a single species, which are not a natural locus for ecosystem-based management, where it is more important to study trade-offs for management – we cannot optimize exploitation of all species separately and simultaneously (Walters *et al.*, 2005). Daniel Pauly realized this when, as a young graduate, he was posted by the German Agency for Technical Cooperation (GTZ) to Indonesia. There, the catches in their trawl surveys included hundreds of species. How was a budding young scientist educated in the era of age-based population dynamics going to assess the fisheries for all those species when there was no way to even age them, let alone derive population parameters for the important ones? Ray Hilborn later said of him "the Prophet Daniel ... must toil in infernal heat, deprived of holy catch-at-age data, armed only with a thermometer" (Hilborn, 1992).

Daniel Pauly took on the task to develop simple assessment methods for use by scientists in developing countries, and to conduct training on how to use them properly. Hilborn was not quite right in his prophet statement; population dynamics in the tropics calls for a ruler in addition to a thermometer. The name of the game was length-based assessment and, through the 1980s, Pauly became the dominant figure in this field, introducing and developing suitable methodologies (Munro, this volume). More than anything, the training that was needed for length-based methods to become part of the applied toolbox in developing countries made it clear that the focus had to be on capacity building as well; methods alone were not enough (Nauen and Hempel, this volume).

The 1970s led to another realization: fish eat fish. This was not explicitly considered in classical population dynamics, but is an essential consideration when working at the ecosystem level. Do you want tuna or herring, predator or prey? You cannot expect to have plenty of both; there are trade-offs to be considered and management decisions influence the options.

Andersen and Ursin (1977) and Laevastu and co-workers (e.g., Laevastu and Larkins, 1981) knew this, but were building complex models calling for data way beyond what was conceivably of use in a developing country context. The breakthrough in realizing that methods for "multispecies management" (as it was called then; Pauly, 1979) could be developed for use in the tropics came when Daniel Pauly visited Jeff Polovina in Hawaii in the mid-1980s. Polovina had made a simplified version of Laevastu's gigantic ecosystem model, and used it to predict "missing" parameters for the part of the ecosystem where information was sparse to nonexisting. As an example, Polovina would predict biomasses for a prey based on how much production was required to meet the combined demand of all predators. Importantly, it did not require individual species data, nor age groups within species (as fisheries biologists of the time were indoctrinated to believe). Instead, the unit of analysis could be the "functional group," consisting of a variety of species.

The neatness of the approach led Pauly to tell Polovina: "If you publish this model, I will ensure that it is applied throughout the (tropical) world." They both met these challenges (Polovina, 1984; Pauly *et al.*, 2000). The result was that the model, Ecopath, was further developed and supported to the degree that it has become the de facto world standard for ecosystem modeling of marine resources (Christensen and Pauly, 1992; Christensen and Walters, this volume), and to the extent that it was nominated by the US National Oceanic and Atmospheric Administration in 2007 as one of the ten biggest scientific breakthroughs in the organization's 200-year history.

Methodologies for ecosystem-based management, while necessary for successful implementation, do not constitute a sufficient condition. For one, we also need details about the resources to be managed. Daniel Pauly recognized this early on, and became increasingly frustrated when expert after expert, expatriated to develop fisheries in some developing country, invariably would start their project document with the argument "We do not know anything about the key species occurring in the area, so we have to start by studying the biology of ... " How many times do we need to establish length–weight relationships for *Rastrelliger kanagurta*?

What caused such repetitive research was the lack of an easily accessible repository for basic information from previous research in developing countries. Development projects rarely end up being published in scientific journals. The best source at the time was the library in Rome of the Food and Agricultural Organization of the United Nations (FAO), where project reports and other grey literature by many fisheries experts was stored. The eventual solution to the problem of accessibility was FishBase, a database initiated by Daniel Pauly and Rainer Froese, and designed to supply "everything you ever wanted to know about fish" as Froese phrased it. FishBase has collated a vast amount of published information (Froese and Pauly, 2006; Froese, this volume).

Still, fish are not the only living beings in the sea, and while FishBase has become the model for how to develop class-specific databases, showing the way for later initiatives, such as Species 2000 and OBIS, similar information is needed for the rest of the ecosystem. Recently, this has been facilitated through the comprehensive SeaLifeBase, which parallels FishBase and, when used jointly with it, will supply much of the global biodiversity information required for ecosystem-based management, especially for modeling (Palomares and Bailly, this volume).

Given methods, given biological and ecological information, what else is needed? We certainly need to understand more about the natural processes that control life in the ocean (Pauly et al., 1989; Bakun, this volume), and we need to incorporate such understanding in the models we make of the oceans. What makes this especially important is the speed with which ecosystems are changing due to human impact, be it through fisheries or climate change.

As ecosystems change there is an inherent danger that we and future generations may forget what has been, and importantly, what could be. We have lived off the oceans for millennia, and, in so doing, we have had an ever-increasing impact. Even when we deal with seemingly unexploited systems (Warne, 2008), we have to question if such systems really are pristine; what about the mega-predators? Yet each (human) generation comes to accept an increasingly degraded state as natural. The shifting baselines syndrome, a term coined and described by Daniel Pauly (1995), has had profound implications on how we think about what is natural in the field of ecology (Jackson and Jacquet, this volume). The symptom of this societal illness is the ability of the collective human psyche to create new impressions of what is pristine; how big is a big fish? The treatment of the illness includes incorporation of historical anecdotes as data and an emphasis on historical ecology in environmental education and ecosystem management.

In the oceans, exploitation greatly expanded after the Second World War when industrialization spread, and when fisheries, especially in the developing world were "developed," soon to be devastated (Pauly, 1979). Worldwide, fisheries catches peaked in the 1980s and have since been declining (Watson and Pauly, 2001; Watson and Sumaila, this volume). Such, at least, is the common perception now, based on reported catch statistics. Yet, catch statistics only paint part of the picture; United Nations member states send their official statistics every year to the FAO where they are compiled and disseminated, e.g., to the Sea Around Us project (Pauly, 2007). This project then combines the information with estimates from other sources, seeking ways to improve it notably with regard to taxonomic and spatial resolution. We know from experience that the official statistics focus on traded products, while extraction for local consumption tends to be underestimated or neglected. Accounting for such has, in the more severe cases, resulted in catch estimates that exceed the official figure by a factor of six or more (e.g., Zeller *et al.*, 2007; Watson *et al.*, this volume).

The increase in landings brought about by industrialized fisheries has had a large impact on ocean resources (Pauly and Christensen, 1995; Pauly *et al.*, 1998; Stergiou and Christensen, this volume), in the process marginalizing the small-scale sector (Pauly, 1997; Chuenpagdee, this volume). Combined with the decline in capture fisheries production, this has led to a widespread belief that future fisheries production should come from aquaculture. While aquaculture clearly has a role to play, much of it is focused on high-trophic-level species, which can only be reared on diets that are based on feeds made from other fish. Given the efficiency of this, more fish are used than produced, and aquaculture of this sort ("farming up the food web"; Pullin, this volume) cannot lead to increased, sustainable fish supply (Liu and Sumaila, 2008). Alternatively, low-trophic-level farming is more likely to contribute to the world's food supply. Food supply is indeed a major part of what we seek in the oceans; just like fish, we eat fish and we have to consider how we best obtain and treat our food (Pullin, this volume; Jacquet, this volume).

Given the generally dismal state of the world's fisheries, it is appropriate to ask how the increased demand for fish products as predicted by the International Food Policy Research Institute (Delgado *et al.*, 2003) is going to be met. Our answer may be "it probably is not" (Alder *et al.*, 2007) because we indeed may be reaching a global state of "Malthusian overfishing" (Pauly, 1994; Ruddle, this volume). The only real hope we see for meeting future demand for fisheries products is through better management and utilization of fisheries resources (Jacquet, this volume). We are also convinced that this implies ecosystem-based management because it is impossible to extract maximum sustainable yield from all the resources all the time

(Walters *et al.*, 2005), and considering options calls for evaluating ecosystem-level trade-offs.

One form of trade-off that needs to be considered, and which has created heated debate in scientific and conservation circles, relates to the role of protected areas. Some view them as highly valuable tools to secure healthy breeding populations; others believe that they are doing more harm than good by increasing fishing pressure in smaller areas, endangering local, weak populations. One thing is clear, however, we need large-scale information about how protected areas can contribute to ecosystem-based management, and we may need to protect vast parts of the oceans (Jackson and Jacquet, this volume).

We also need to understand how ecosystem-based management of fisheries may be affected by future climate change. Modeling this calls for thorough analysis of how populations have changed in the past, relating such changes to climatic factors. This calls for expanding ecosystem modeling with information about species vulnerability and productivity patterns, while building on global databases of biology, ecology, and fisheries of marine organisms (Cheung *et al.*, this volume).

Better management calls for thorough analysis of the resources (Christensen and Walters, this volume) and appropriate methods to ensure that the analyses build on all available, relevant data. Further, we need to understand how human behavior in fisheries is influenced by economic and social factors (Sumaila, 2005) and how this leads to trade-offs between alternative uses. To evaluate such trade-offs, policy-makers need to understand the ecological and economic benefits (Sumaila *et al.*, this volume) as well as social issues, such as those related to small-scale versus large-scale fisheries (Chuenpagdee, this volume).

With better management, we may indeed be able to increase the world's fish production sustainably, not by increasing effort, but by fishing less. That should be a win–win situation, one would think. In the long term, it certainly makes sense economically, but reality is different. Increased fishing pressure will be unavoidable as long as there is a race for the fish and no efficient means or willingness to curtail effort. Changing this mindset calls for a way for scientists to influence ocean management policies more directly. This is not an area that traditionally has been frequented by scientists. There is a deeply rooted skepticism concerning the role of advocacy. "Science should stay pure." We question this, as have many of the scientists who were behind the Intergovernmental Panel for Climate Change, and the Millennium Ecosystem Assessment. It is far better that policy decisions are science-based and with due consideration for environmental impact, than driven primarily by commercial and political interests (Safina and Hardt, this volume).

For this to happen, science has to be conducted in a way that will be of use for policymaking (Hirshfield, this volume), though this by no means is a sufficient condition. There also needs to be communication between policymakers and scientists (Reichert, this volume; Nauen and Hempel, this volume), and while this may seem obvious, it rarely occurs. It is not without cause that scientists often are accused of hiding in their ivory towers.

This may be because of a deep mistrust by many scientists with regard to the role of the press when it comes to communicating science. Too many have been burned, having produced their masterpiece and delivered lengthy speeches, only to be surprised by the seemingly odd and irrelevant tidbits chosen by the journalists who interviewed them. Few scientists excel as communicators, Daniel Pauly being one of the rare exceptions (Baron, this volume). We may ask of course, if the reaction of scientists should be to start thinking like journalists. As scientists, we are good at communicating with fellow scientists. How do you deal with people who are not used to communication based on tables and figures? One possibility is to rethink how we communicate science, and make it more targeted for policymakers. There is no better way of ensuring communication than to talk the language of those you are trying to reach.

REFERENCES

Alder, J., Guénette, S., Beblow, J., Cheung, W., and Christensen, V. (2007) Ecosystem-based global fishing policy scenarios. Fisheries Centre Research Report 15(7). Vancouver, Canada: Fisheries Centre, University of British Columbia.

Andersen, K. P. and Ursin, E. (1977) A multispecies extension to the Beverton and Holt theory of fishing, with accounts of phosphorus circulation and primary production. *Meddelelser fra Danmarks Fiskeri og Havundersøgelser*, 7, 319–435.

Beverton, R. J. H. and Holt, S. J. (1957) *On the Dynamics of Exploited Fish Populations*. London: Chapman & Hall, facsimile reprint 1993.

Christensen, V. and Pauly, D. (1992) Ecopath II: a software for balancing steady-state ecosystem models and calculating network characteristics. *Ecological Modelling*, 61, 169–185.

Delgado, C. L., Wada, N., Rosegrant, M. W., Meijer, S., and Ahmed, M. (2003) *Fish to 2020: Supply and Demand in Changing Global Markets*. Washington DC: International Food Policy Research Institute.

Froese, R. and Pauly, D. (2006) FishBase. Available at www.fishbase.org.

Hilborn, R. (1992) Current and future trends in fisheries stock assessment and management. *South African Journal of Marine Science*, 12, 975–988.

Laevastu, T. and Larkins, H. A. (1981) *Marine Fisheries Ecosystem: Its Quantitative Evaluation and Management*. Farnham, UK: Fishing News Books.

Liu, Y. and Sumaila, U. R. (2008) Can farmed salmon production keep growing? *Marine Policy*, 32, 497–501.

McIntosh, R. P. (1985) *The Background of Ecology: Concept and Theory*. Cambridge, UK: Cambridge University Press.

Pauly, D. (1979) *Theory and Management of Tropical Multispecies Stocks*. ICLARM Studies and Reviews 1. Manila, Philippines: ICLARM.

Pauly, D. (1994) On Malthusian overfishing. In Pauly, D., ed., *On the Sex of Fish and the Gender of Scientists*. London: Chapman & Hall, pp. 112–117.

Pauly, D. (1995) Anecdotes and the shifting baseline syndrome of fisheries. *Trends in Ecology & Evolution*, 10, 430.

Pauly, D. (1997) *Small-scale Fisheries in the Tropics: Marginality, Marginalization, and Some Implications for Fisheries Management*. Bethesda, MD: American Fisheries Society.

Pauly, D. (1998) Beyond our original horizons: the tropicalization of Beverton and Holt. *Reviews in Fish Biology and Fisheries*, 8, 307–334.

Pauly, D. (2007) The Sea Around Us project: documenting and communicating global fisheries impacts on marine ecosystems. *AMBIO: A Journal of the Human Environment*, 36, 290–295.

Pauly, D. and Christensen, V. (1995) Primary production required to sustain global fisheries. *Nature*, 374, 255–257 [Erratum in *Nature*, 376: 279].

Pauly, D., Christensen, V., Dalsgaard, J., Froese, R., and Torres, F., Jr. (1998) Fishing down marine food webs. *Science*, 279, 860–863.

Pauly, D., Christensen, V., and Walters, C. (2000) Ecopath, Ecosim, and Ecospace as tools for evaluating ecosystem impact of fisheries. *ICES Journal of Marine Science*, 57, 697–706.

Pauly, D., Muck, P., Mendo, J., and Tsukayama, I., eds. (1989) *The Peruvian Upwelling Ecosystem: Dynamics and Interactions*. ICLARM Conference Proceedings 18, Callao, Perú; Eschborn, Federal Republic of Germany; Manila, Philippines: Instituto del Mar del Perú; Deutsche Gesellschaft für Technische Zusammenarbeit; International Center for Living Aquatic Resources Management.

Pikitch, E. K., Santora, C., Babcock, E. A., Bakun, A., Bonfil, R., Conover, D. O., Dayton, P., Doukakis, P., Fluharty, D., Heneman, B., Houde, E. D., Link, J., Livingston, P. A., Mangel, M., McAllister, M. K., Pope, J. and Sainsbury, K. J. (2004) Ecosystem-based fishery management. *Science*, 305, 346–347.

Polovina, J. J. (1984) Model of a coral reef ecosystem I. The ECOPATH model and its application to French Frigate Shoals. *Coral Reefs*, 3, 1–11.

Sumaila, U. R. (2005) Differences in economic perspectives and implementation of ecosystem-based management of marine resources. *Marine Ecology Progress Series*, 300, 279–282.

Walters, C. J., Christensen, V., Martell, S. J., and Kitchell, J. F. (2005) Possible ecosystem impacts of applying MSY policies from single-species assessment. *ICES Journal of Marine Science*, 62, 558–568.

Warne, K. (2008) An uneasy Eden. *National Geographic*, July.

Watson, R. and Pauly, D. (2001) Systematic distortions in world fisheries catch trends. *Nature*, 414, 534–536.

Zeller, D., Booth, S., Davis, G., and Pauly, D. (2007) Re-estimation of small-scale fishery catches for US flag-associated island areas in the western Pacific: the last 50 years. *Fisheries Bulletin*, 105, 266–277.

Section I   Life in the oceans

ANDREW BAKUN

2

The oxygen constraint

In trying to understand processes and mechanisms regulating ocean ecosystems, we humans, being terrestrial mammals, naturally rely on intuitions and common sense notions formed by our terrestrial experiences as well as on our inherent terrestrial-mammalian evolved capacities and inclinations. As a result, many aspects of life that may be unique to organisms evolved and operating within marine situations may tend to elude our intellectual grasp and even our notice.

In the early 1980s, I worked with Daniel Pauly and other colleagues on developing an international collaborative "Ocean Science and Living Resources" (OSLR) program (Bakun *et al.*, 1982). This experience presented me with, among other things, an exposure to Pauly's developing theory on the special role of oxygen in the marine situation (Pauly, 1979, 1981, 1984, 2010). The interest was on individual-organism-scale biological issues, such as growth rate and maturation timing. Not being a biologist, but rather an oceanographer habitually focused on regional population-scale issues, I found the notions intriguing while not yet beginning to apprehend their significance to the particular questions that were consuming my own attention.

But, the "seeds" were planted in my mind. Daniel's early insights on the size-related oxygen issues faced by fishes in the ocean led me over the years to the notions outlined here, and are an example of how my own joy in the "ocean quest" has been enriched by his influence.

In the decades that have followed the OSLR program, as I have continued to encounter questions and conundrums in my own views of marine ecosystem operation as well as in the sometimes contrasting views of my community of colleagues, these seeds have occasionally suddenly sprouted forth, rewarding me with delicious flashes of

Ecosystem Approaches to Fisheries: A Global Perspective, ed. V. Christensen and J. Maclean. Published by Cambridge University Press. © Cambridge University Press 2011.

unanticipated recognition and satisfaction. These and other intermittent brief glimpses have, over time, congealed into a sort of unifying conceptual "glue" capable of holding together a personal logical framework within which I am more or less able to rationalize the function, and even the very existence, of marine ecosystems as I have known them.

In this brief chapter, I try to impart an essence of what has become to me a fascinatingly evocative point of view regarding the oxygen constraints faced by marine organisms that must absorb respiratory oxygen in its dissolved form directly from the liquid medium in which they live, and how these constraints may control behaviors and survival mechanisms that, in turn, may act to determine form, function, and the very viability of the ecosystems in which these organisms function.

WHY DON'T PELAGIC ECOSYSTEMS COLLAPSE?

In the ocean, where most organisms are nearly neutrally buoyant, the law of gravity becomes essentially inoperative, being replaced by the laws of hydrodynamics (Bakun, 1996). Turbulent frictional drag replaces the pull of gravity as the major constraint to active movement. In a turbulent liquid environment, size offers distinct advantages. This, for example, is why length rules are so important in sailboat racing. All other things being equal, a longer boat will move through the water faster than a shorter boat. Similarly, a larger fish can generally swim faster, while using relatively less energy, than can a smaller fish. And because photosynthesis in the ocean takes place mainly within microscopic cells, it tends to impose a sequential size progression on trophic flows: predators are nearly always larger than their prey.

Thus, from the point of view of raw speed at least, a predator is generally capable of catching a smaller prey of the same body form and relative muscularity. Furthermore, except in specialized shallow water habitats, such as reefs, mangroves, and seagrass beds, the productive upper ocean layers offer scant cover or safe refuge. In the pelagic realm, there is no refuge at all for a slower prey that has come into a faster-swimming predator's field of view. This leads to the intriguing question as to what it is that prevents predator fish populations from simply growing in abundance until they are able to hunt the populations of their prey to extinction, thereby destroying their own food base and, in the process, their populations and ultimately themselves.

OXYGEN SHIFTS THE ADVANTAGE

The concentration of oxygen even in well-oxygenated seawater is only a few percent of that in air. Thus, acquiring adequate oxygen for metabolic needs presents a distinct problem for marine organisms that do not break the sea surface to breathe air directly, but must absorb oxygen in its dilute dissolved form through membrane surfaces, i.e., gills.

With increasing body size, surface area increases slower than body mass. For example, in simple solid three-dimensional forms the surface area increases as the square (2nd power) of the linear dimension, while volume (and therefore enclosed mass) tends to increase as its cube (3rd power). Thus, larger organisms have a smaller surface-to-volume ratio and therefore have more difficulty in acquiring adequate oxygen to support the metabolic requirements of their body mass than do smaller organisms. It is a simple fact of geometry that as fish grow in size, retaining the same general body form, their gill surface area increases slower than their metabolically active body mass, even if they manage, as they frequently do, to grow gills whose surface increases faster than their length squared (Pauly, 1981).

Large fish, particularly those that operate in warm zones where oxygen demand is high, must either be quite inactive, breathe atmospheric air, or deploy an exaggeratedly large gill area. As examples, Pauly (1979, 1981) has cited (1) the largest fish in tropical (fresh) water, the Amazonian *Arapaimas gigas*, which is an obligatory air-breather; (2) large tunas, which have the largest gill areas of all teleosts as required to satisfy the elevated oxygen requirements of their particularly active lifestyle; and (3) the world's two largest fishes, the basking and the whale shark, which have evolved to become essentially "swimming gills" and, as a result, obligate filter-feeders.

Another example is the Dover sole (*Microstomus pacificus*) of the northeastern Pacific, which has developed a remarkable adaptation to extremely low oxygen availability. After spending their juvenile stages as active predators in the oxygenated upper ocean layers, adult Dover soles sink into that region's severe oxygen minimum zone where their muscle mass undergoes a medusa-like transformation to a rather inert, gelatinous material that requires minimal metabolic maintenance (Hunter *et al.*, 1990). Also, the daily structures on hard parts of diurnally active fishes and invertebrates that allow precise age determination are due to the daily alternation of inactivity at night and oxygen-requiring activities during daytime, which produces pH fluctuations in their bodies (Lutz and Rhoads, 1977; Pauly, 1998).

WHY DON'T FASTER-SWIMMING PREDATORS SIMPLY STAY WITH THEIR PREY?

Since predator fish, being larger, have size-related hydrodynamic advantages that allow them to swim faster and more efficiently than their prey, one may find it puzzling that they don't merely follow the prey schools, continually maintaining contact, and simply snatch a meal whenever they are hungry. Instead, they lose contact with the school, and then proceed to search large water volumes, or to wait in ambush for long periods in hope that a prey may come along, in order to locate their next meal. One could be thankful that they do act this way. Otherwise, the predators would eventually wipe out the entire school, and then wipe out other remaining schools, ultimately rendering nonviable that particular predator–prey pairing.

Importantly, evolution acts to benefit the individual, not to benefit the entirety of a group of individuals in a Darwinian world. Accordingly, the benefit for a behavior must accrue directly to the individual that practices the behavior. Benefits to other individuals in a population are irrelevant. Otherwise, natural selection would quickly weed that behavioral tendency out of the populations.

From the balcony of the Rosenstiel School's cafeteria at the University of Miami, one can sometimes watch small barracuda stalking the schools of small mullet that course through the shallows of the channel separating Virginia Key and Key Biscayne. The barracuda are slim, long, muscular, and streamlined. An individual barracuda would seem obviously capable of swimming faster than a much smaller mullet. But the barracuda do not swim directly toward a moving mullet school. Rather, they repeatedly try to work themselves into an ambush position along some possible path of a mullet school that has come within its sensory view, even though one sees them usually frustrated as the mullet schools continuously abruptly change swimming direction and suddenly split into smaller school segments that later form other school combinations with segments of other schools, rendering rather tenuous the very idea of an identifiable autonomous school. So why do the barracuda not, for obtaining the food necessary to fuel their life, take the more direct path of using their superior speed to directly pursue and approach the schools to prey on the individuals contained within them?

Simply, when following the same path as a smaller mullet, the barracuda would fall more rapidly into oxygen deficit due to its smaller surface-to-volume ratio. And once a fish falls into significant oxygen deficit, it cannot recover quickly and easily in the way an air-breathing organism can. Because large amounts of oxygen are needed to support flight and evasive actions, a fish that has squandered its oxygen reserves has placed itself in mortal danger should its own predator appear. Accordingly, evolutionary selection would have tended to implant a particularly strong aversion to oxygen depletion in active non-air-breathing organisms, even those that as adults operate as top predators (essentially all, in their earlier life stages at least, being prey to predators of some sort).

Thus, hydrodynamics dictates a "bigger is better" rule. But from the point of view of the inescapable oxygen constraint faced by a fish, a contrary "smaller is better" rule prevails. Although both food and oxygen, the two essential material needs of life in a watery medium, must be jointly met, oxygen is the more constant need and, being the most difficult element to store, the most immediately experienced (Pauly, 1979, 1981). Moreover, it is crucial to another immediate need, that of avoiding predation. To reiterate, surface-to-volume ratio constraints mean that larger predators tend to reach a state of oxygen deprivation quicker than do their smaller prey.

Accordingly, even to obtain the basic food that fuels their life, predatory fishes can afford to expend only the minimal required amount of oxygen. This offers an offsetting advantage to smaller prey, preventing predators from freely employing their size-related advantage in swimming speed to maintain continuous direct contact with a group of prey until that group may be entirely eliminated. This serves not only to preserve the prey base, but also the predators that depend on it, the characteristic structuring of the planktonic trophic levels below, and ultimately the entire marine ecosystem.

WHY HAVE MARINE SPECIES NOT DEVELOPED MORE EFFECTIVE OXYGEN-GATHERING APPARATUS?

If oxygen access represents such a constraint, why haven't fish evolved even better ways to collect available oxygen? As mentioned, evolution by natural selection acts to benefit the individual not the group, and contains no mechanism to ensure that an overall ecosystem community structure benefits, even if the continued existence of the species in question ultimately requires it. Accordingly, why hasn't there been an "evolutionary arms race" among marine species leading to bigger, better gills, or even to very extensive, elaborately reticulated gill-like structures contained entirely within the body cavity? (A normally functioning lung of a human being, for example, may contain a total oxygen-absorbing surface area as large as the surface area of a standard tennis court.)

The answer, of course, must be that they would have, if they could have, and that the associated disadvantages must have ultimately outweighed the advantages. Organisms like medusas, which have very limited active muscle mass in need of oxygenation relative to body surface area, may represent one class of solution to the problem. But for a fish or invertebrate species with sufficient active muscle mass to provide substantial speed and agility, the decrease of gill surface area to body mass with increased body size, and hence of oxygen supply per unit body mass, is inescapable (Pauly, 2010). Evidently, the detriment to hydrodynamic streamlining, etc., compared to the benefits with respect to oxygen access, etc., must place effective limits on practical gill sizes for given lifestyles (for example, the large-headed body form of a tuna may represent an adaptive sacrifice of maximum burst speed in favor of increased gill area to support its incessantly moving life-style, in contrast to the smaller-headed body form of a more ambush-oriented predator, such as a grouper or a billfish, for which sudden, short-distance burst speed may be the higher-priority consideration).

The alternative idea of a water-containing lung-like organ in the body cavity of an active fish is unworkable for simple mechanical reasons. To contain an equivalent number of oxygen molecules, an internal lung-like organ containing liquid seawater rather than gaseous air would have to enclose a mass of water thousands of times more massive than that of the air enclosed in the corresponding lung of an air-breathing mammal (water being more than 800 times as dense as air, with only a few percent of the oxygen concentration per unit volume). Obviously, a fish with a large mass of water in its body cavity would require an enormous amount of oxygen-consuming muscle mass in order to provide a reasonable degree of acceleration and agility. The oxygen demand of this amount of muscle mass would probably far outweigh the increase in oxygen uptake capacity.

This is probably why air-breathing mammals, and before them, the air-breathing ichthyosaurs, developed to be highly successful as the largest class of marine animals, in spite of obvious detriments inherent in the necessity to surface at short time intervals to obtain oxygenated air directly from the gaseous atmosphere. It would also seem to be the reason that marine mammals can afford the option of expending oxygen in mere playful activities, whereas fish are not observed to engage in such pursuits. A marine mammal can very quickly restore an oxygen deficit simply by surfacing and gulping in a good lungful of air. But for a fish, restoring an oxygen deficit by means of absorbing dissolved oxygen, available in water only in quite dilute concentrations, through a limited available area of membranous gill surface, is a much more time-consuming, limiting, and potentially dangerous proposition.

THE "LOW-ABUNDANCE REFUGE"

Populations of small pelagic forage fishes are notorious for sudden massive expansions and abrupt collapses. An example is the million-ton explosion of tiny snipefish (*Macrorhamphosus scolopax* and *M. gracilis*), probably representing at least a hundred billion individual adults at peak of abundance, that appeared off the coast of Morocco in the 1970s (Arístegui *et al.*, 2005). During the episode, the snipefish profusion often so completely jammed fishing nets as to make fishing for more desired species impossible. But within a few years the numbers of snipefish fell precipitously, and in recent years they have been rarely seen. However, we do not worry much about their becoming extinct. Other examples of radical population gyrations include the famous triggerfish explosion in the Gulf of Guinea (Caverivière, 1991), and the well-known oscillations of a number of sardine and anchovy populations around the world's oceans (Bakun and Cury, 1999; Chavez *et al.*, 2003).

During a period of high abundance of such a population, the abundant food source represented may be assumed to have allowed its predators to increase their own populations somewhat, and to orient feeding behaviors toward that dominant prey source. Since predators are nearly always longer-lived than their smaller prey, they would tend to vary in abundance less rapidly. Accordingly, one would expect that predation pressure per unit prey biomass should rapidly intensify during an episode of steep population decline. Indeed, it has been a common pattern that once a steep decline has become established, it is not arrested until the population has nearly vanished as a major factor in the regional ecosystem. Nevertheless, such radical collapses have not continued to outright extinction, even though in the marine pelagic situation predators enjoy substantial hydrodynamic advantages in pursuing and capturing their prey. Some sort of low-abundance refuge evidently must exist, such that predators may eventually cease hunting down vanishing remnants of a prey population before outright extinction results (Walters and Juanes, 1993; Walters and Martell, 2004).

But this refuge aspect cannot be attributed to any sort of voluntary "conservation" response on the part of the predators; the "prudent predators" of lore (Slobodkin, 1961) do not exist. Altruistic propensities that would impel an individual to disadvantage itself in order to benefit conspecific individuals not sharing precisely identical DNA are quickly weeded out by natural selection. Accordingly, failure to cease efforts to consume the last remaining prey must convey some disadvantage that falls directly on the individual predator involved.

As discussed above, once a predator is prevented by the oxygen constraint from tracking and remaining in continual contact with potential prey, it is forced to continually expend energy and oxygen to search large water volumes or to lie in ambush for long periods. It is an unavoidable fact that the energy expended by a predator in encountering and gathering prey (plus that expended for physiological maintenance, growth, and reproduction) must be matched by the caloric content of the ingested food or it must soon either switch its choice of prey, migrate to a location of greater prey density, enter an energy-conserving inactive state to await better feeding conditions, or starve (Bakun, 1996). So, at some point, in one way or other, the predator must relax its efforts.

However, this sort of refuge can be effective only if there are no other prey available to sustain the predator's activity, even as the species at issue may continue to decline. Of course, different prey types may require somewhat different searching tactics, perhaps different "training" background, etc. This might well provide at least some relative refuge.

But beyond this, in terms of conceiving the sort of truly robust refuge needed to explain the continued viability of vulnerable pelagic prey species, it is interesting that many predatory species in the sea appear to be adept at employing cooperative prey-herding behaviors (cover photo and Figure 2.1). Observers of such behaviors often describe a scene where at any moment a majority of the predator group appears to be presenting mainly a relatively inactive encircling threat. This allows individual predators to maintain their oxygen reserves, while taking occasional turns in mounting attack forays through the interior of the corralled prey school. These forays may keep the prey embroiled in continual frenzied oxygen-consuming evasive behaviors as each individual tries frantically to position itself such that fellow members of its school are always between itself and a predator (another example where benefit to the individual may disadvantage the group as a whole). At some point, the members of the prey school may be rendered effectively immobile and helpless due to oxygen deprivation, whereupon the predators can proceed to consume

Figure 2.1 Copper sharks gulp mouthfuls of sardines. Illustrates prey herding, similar to cover photo. Photo: © Doug Perrine/Seapics.com.

them with minimal expenditure of their own oxygen resources. In this way, the predator species has effectively obviated the size-dependent oxygen advantage enjoyed by the prey species.

But when abundance of a particular prey species becomes too low for such cooperative herding activities to be effective, the oxygen advantage of the prey species may be reestablished, rendering predators unable to afford the oxygen expenditures required to continue to exert focused predation pressure on it. In this way, the dual necessities of (1) deriving sufficiently favorable trophic energy return relative to energy expended in predatory activity, while (2) dealing with the oxygen disadvantage that a larger predator fish suffers compared to its smaller prey, may combine as a *low abundance refuge*, or at least a component of one, sufficient to preclude outright extinction of the prey by hydrodynamically advantaged predators. This may be the crucial barrier that serves to keep an ocean ecosystem from collapsing inward on itself and transforming itself to something very different from its traditional form and function (Bakun and Weeks, 2004, 2006).

OXYGEN DEFICIT IS A PAIN

Evidently, falling into a state of oxygen deficit in a medium where replenishment is a slow, activity-restricting process presents a distinct set of problems and could even constitute a grave danger to the survival of a fish. Thus, it would seem important to evolutionary fitness that a state of oxygen deficit should continually be strongly avoided. It might be expected that, as in all animals, a fish's nervous system would generate an urgent sensory signal (i.e., physical pain) that would have turned, over evolutionary time, a voluntary aversion into a compelling involuntary response.

Accordingly, lower limits of acceptable dissolved oxygen levels as often measured by laboratory fish physiologists (e.g., concentration levels at which a fish may begin to exhibit active distress symptoms or behaviors) may not be the relevant ones in provoking evident responses. Rather, a fish endowed by evolution with a pain-like aversion to depleting its oxygen reserves may be very hesitant to engage in vigorous physical exertion, even in situations where there would be entirely sufficient oxygen available in the water to support respiration and replenishment while a fish is in a resting, or cruising, state. (An analogy is human visitors from the lowlands to Cusco, Peru, high in the Andes Mountains, who are reasonably comfortable while sitting in the hotel lobby on the ground floor, but when they try to carry baggage upstairs, the growing painful pounding in their heads due to lack of oxygen may well bring them to a halt on the stairs – and if they have access to a gulp of pure oxygen from a portable supply, they might well at that moment be very happy to take it.) Similarly, fish finding themselves in the throes of oxygen deficit might be impelled to move temporarily to a depth zone of higher oxygen concentration if that option is available, or to a cooler depth where oxygen usage is less, in order to achieve more rapid relief. Rapid switching between food-rich, but warm surface waters, and less productive, but cooler waters is known to occur, e.g., from studying tuna behavior through telemetry (Block *et al.*, 2001).

THE PEACEABLE KINGDOM

When one is underwater in a fish-profuse setting (e.g., on a pristine Indo-Pacific coral reef, such as I repeatedly had the opportunity to experience when working in the early 1960s on the multi-year International Indian Ocean Expedition), one may be astonished to see multitudes of predatory fish and prey fish hovering in apparent peaceful proximity. John Kennedy was then the newly inaugurated President of the United States. It was a time of global optimism. Our purpose was to produce an initial marine species catalog as a basis for fisheries development in that protein-starved region. Accordingly, we staff divers, with an abandon that now seems profligate to my present-day sensibilities, were busily engrossed in collecting samples of every living thing we encountered.

When a spear shot went awry such that a targeted fish was injured but not captured, and the injured fish gyrated off in frantic distress behavior, it was often immediately chased down and consumed by a larger fish that moments before had seemed entirely uninterested. If we were collecting the fish in a particular area by stunning them with an application of rotenone (a chemical that inhibits oxygen absorption through gill membranes), a less quickly affected larger fish might be seen to suddenly dart forward to capture an evidently distressed smaller fish. This could release a sudden feeding (and fleeing) frenzy among fish of different sizes, ceasing as the spreading rotenone progressively took effect and started to immobilize larger and larger species.

What could be the explanation for such sudden radical changes in behavior? Imagine the situation to be one in which every fish is involved in avoiding falling into an oxygen deficit that could render it easy prey to a nearby predator. Meanwhile, it is obliged at some point to obtain food for itself. If it can identify a prey that may already be in a state of relative oxygen deficit, it could be expected to be able to capture that prey with lowered resulting expenditure of its own oxygen reserves. This is important because there would always be some probability that any fish could be in the sensory view of an even larger predator that may likewise be seeking some sign of an analogous oxygen deficit-related opportunity. This chain of circumstances could play out over the size ranges, not as any conscious process, but as automatic conditioned responses in which aggressive predatory action may be triggered by any radical oxygen-consuming activity of a potential prey, tempered of course by whatever sense of danger to itself may have been engendered by perceived proximity of its own potential predators and by avoidance of the sensory pain response that would be generated by overly rapid oxygen expenditure.

According to this view, the "peaceable kingdom" tableau that such an undersea community may at any instant present is merely an illusion, an uneasy Garden of Eden (Warne, 2008). Underlying the static composition of the serene snapshot is a tenuous equilibrium between two urgent needs: food and safety. Only when the need for food becomes sufficiently urgent to temporarily outweigh safety concerns can reckless oxygen expenditures be risked. Anything that tends to reduce oxygen expenditure, such as waiting for the moment when a potential prey may have fallen into a state of relative oxygen deprivation, lowers the risk of falling into the same trap as well as the inevitable unwelcome sensory pain response. If all players are playing the same game, the "peaceable kingdom" impression can be the result.

REFERENCES

Arístegui, J., Alvarez-Salgado, X. A., Barton, E. D., Figueiras, F. G., Hernandez-Leon, S., Roy, C. and Santos, A. M. P. (2005) Chapter 23: Oceanography and Fisheries of the Canary Current/Iberian Region of the Eastern North Atlantic. In Robinson, A. R. and Brink, K., eds., *The Sea*, Vol. 14B. Cambridge, MA: Harvard University Press, pp. 877–931.

Bakun, A. (1996) *Patterns in the Oceans: Ocean Processes and Marine Population Dynamics*. La Jolla and La Paz, California: Sea Grant and Centro de Investigaciones Biologicas del Noroeste.

Bakun, A., Beyer, J., Pauly, D., Pope, J. G. and Sharp, G. D. (1982) Ocean sciences in relation to living resources. *Canadian Journal of Fisheries and Aquatic Sciences*, 39, 1059–1070.

Bakun, A. and Cury, P. (1999) The "school trap": a mechanism promoting large-amplitude out-of-phase population oscillations of small pelagic fish species. *Ecology Letters*, 2, 349–351.

Bakun, A. and Weeks, S. J. (2004) Greenhouse gas buildup, sardines, submarine eruptions, and the possibility of abrupt degradation of intense marine upwelling ecosystems. *Ecology Letters*, 7, 1015–1023.

Bakun, A. and Weeks, S. J. (2006) Adverse feedback sequences in exploited marine ecosystems: are deliberate interruptive actions warranted? *Fish and Fisheries*, 7, 316–333.

Block, B. A., Dewar, H., Blackwell, S. B., Williams, T. D., Prince, E. D., Farwell, C. J., Boustany, A., Teo, S. L. H., Seitz, A., Walli, A. and Fudge, D. (2001) Migratory movements, depth preferences, and thermal biology of Atlantic bluefin tuna. *Science*, 293, 1310–1314.

Cavérivière, A. (1991) L'explosion démographique du baliste (*Balistes carolinensis*) en Afrique de l'Ouest et son évolution en relation avec les tendaces climatique. In Cury, P. and Roy, C., eds., *Pêcheries Ouest-Africaines Variabilité, Instabilité et Changement*. Paris: ORSTOM Editions, pp. 354–367.

Chavez, F., Ryan, J., Lluch-Cota, S., and Niquen, C. (2003) From anchovies to sardines and back: multidecadal change in the Pacific Ocean. *Science*, 299, 217.

Hunter, J. R., Butler, J. L., Kimbrell, C., and Lynn, E. A. (1990) Bathymetric patterns in size, age, sexual maturity, water content and caloric density of Dover Sole *Microstomus pacificus*. *CalCOFI Report*, 31, 132–144.

Lutz, R. A. and Rhoads, D. C. (1977) Anaerobiosis and a theory of growth line formation. *Science*, 198, 1222–1227.

Pauly, D. (1979) Gill size and temperature as governing factors in fish growth: a generalization of von Bertalanffy's growth formula. *Berichte des Instituts für Meereskunde an der Universität Kiel*, 63, 156.

Pauly, D. (1981) The relationships between gill surface area and growth performance in fish: a generalization of von Bertalanffy's theory of growth. *Meeresforschung*, 28, 251–282.

Pauly, D. (1984) A mechanism for the juvenile-to-adult transition in fishes. *Journal du Conseil International pour l'Exploration de la Mer*, 41, 280–284.

Pauly, D. (1998) Why squid, though not fish, may be better understood by pretending they are. *South African Journal of Marine Science/Suid-Afrikaanse Tydskrif vir Seewetenskap*, 20, 47–58.

Pauly, D. (2010) *Gasping Fish and Panting Squids: Oxygen, Temperature and the Growth of Water-breathing Animals*. In Kinne, O., ed., *Excellence in Ecology*, 22. Oldendorf/Luhe, Germany: International Ecology Institute.

Slobodkin, L. B. (1961) *Growth and Regulation of Animal Populations*. New York: Holt, Rinehart and Winston.

Walters, C. J. and Juanes, F. (1993) Recruitment limitation as a consequence of natural selection for use of restricted feeding habitats and predation risk-taking by juvenile fishes. *Canadian Journal of Fisheries and Aquatic Sciences*, 50, 2058–2070.

Walters, C. J. and Martell, S. J. D. (2004) *Fisheries Ecology and Management*. Princeton, NJ: Princeton University Press.

Warne, K. (2008) An uneasy Eden. *National Geographic*, July.

MARIA L. D. PALOMARES AND NICOLAS BAILLY

3

Organizing and disseminating marine biodiversity information: the FishBase and SeaLifeBase story

INTRODUCTION

In the 1970s, data manipulation in fisheries science relied on paper and pencil methods aided by programmable calculators and, in some sophisticated laboratories, on huge computer systems with punch cards (see Munro, this volume). Thus, assembling large amounts of data was limited by the availability of paper copies of peer-reviewed publications, the "reprints" of lore, and grey literature. This was the environment in which Daniel Pauly found himself, struggling with how he could test his hypothesis on the relationship between gill size and the growth of fishes (Pauly, 2010; Bakun, this volume; Cheung, this volume). Testing such a hypothesis needed a large amount of empirical data, which might be available in principle, but if so, not at one's fingertips.

Inspired by Walter Fischer's work on the Food and Agriculture Organization of the United Nations (FAO) species identification sheets in the mid-1970s, Daniel believed that assembling data from already published literature was essential for a timely response to the needs of fisheries management, which, at the time, used analytical models requiring growth and mortality estimates (Munro, this volume). And index cards, he found, were ideal for recording the specific data required for assessing size at age, maximum sizes and ages, and growth and natural mortality parameter estimates, as well as temperature and other environmental variables and their sources.

The index card collection provided data for his widely used compilation of length–growth parameters (Pauly, 1978), which served as a basis for investigating the role of gills in fish growth in his doctoral thesis (Pauly, 1979) and subsequent papers, and for his now classic

Ecosystem Approaches to Fisheries: A Global Perspective, ed. V. Christensen and J. Maclean. Published by Cambridge University Press. © Cambridge University Press 2011.

paper on natural mortality (Pauly, 1980). With such a collection, one does not have to create and validate a new dataset every time a new hypothesis is to be tested (see also Froese, this volume).

FISHBASE IS BORN

In 1987, working at the International Center for Living Aquatic Resources Management (ICLARM; Manila, Philippines[1]), Daniel suggested the transfer of these index cards into a standardized and updated format through the ICLARM Software Project (Pauly et al., 1995). In early 1988, Daniel recruited Rainer Froese, then working on identification of fish larvae using artificial intelligence, and computer and video systems, at the Institut für Meereskunde, Kiel, Germany (Froese and Schofer, 1987). His task was to develop "a self-sufficient database implemented on standard microcomputers" to fill the information gap in tropical fisheries science (ICLARM, 1988).

The prototype of FishBase Rainer created was fine-tuned with the help of ICLARM scientists and programmers and was ready for encoding in late 1988 (Froese, 2000). Daniel and Rainer visited the FAO and worked out an agreement on the use of FAO products (species synopses, images, etc.), which has lasted to this day. Cornelia Nauen of the European Commission assisted in making funds available from that institution, allowing the building of the FishBase team in the Philippines. Also, early reviews by fish taxonomists led to rapid improvements of the original design (Froese, 2000).

The first FishBase was released on floppy disks in 1993 and on CD-ROM in 1994 (with data for 2500 commercially important species), and received positive reviews (Matsuura, 1995; McCall and May, 1995). FishBase was heavily used at a workshop jointly organized by the FAO, ICLARM, Marine Sciences Institute of the University of the Philippines, and the Norwegian Agency for Development Co-operation (NORAD), held on October 1-10, 1995, in the Philippines: it gathered renowned fish taxonomists in order to prepare the new version of the FAO species identification guide for fisheries purposes of the Western Central Pacific (Carpenter and Niem, 1999).

---

[1] Renamed 'WorldFish Center' and based in Penang, Malaysia, since 2000. The FishBase team remained in Los Baños, Philippines, sharing office space with the SeaLifeBase team.

FishBase is one of the founding global species databases contributing to the Species 2000 Federation (Bisby, 2000), and later to the Catalogue of Life (Bisby *et al.*, 2002), both being efforts to document global species diversity, at least in terms of species lists. FishBase released CD-ROMs annually between 1994 and 2000 with increasing numbers of species covered, from 2500 in 1994 to 17 500 in 1997 and 25 000 in 2000. FishBase went online in late 1998 and, as a consequence, CD-ROM releases were limited to users without Internet access, with the last CD-ROM update and release being in 2004 (28 506 species).

THE FISHBASE STRATEGY

Data quantity and quality

When the FishBase shell was ready for encoding in 1988, the first task was to identify a strategy to fill it with large amounts of quality data in the shortest possible time. Priority was (and still is) given to encoding the data in scientific monographs presenting information on taxonomy, species descriptions, habitats, and ecology for a large number of species, and emphasis was initially given to covering the FAO species catalogs. This "science first" approach assures the recording of large amounts of expert-reviewed data.

Another area of emphasis has been, particularly in the early years, the incorporation into FishBase of large datasets assembled by specialists (for example, of fish respiration, brain weight, and growth and mortality of larvae), which would have been less used had they not been made readily available in this manner. Though quality criteria were still applied to such data – and datasets supplied by colleagues that did not cover at least 100 species were not considered – this also made the growth of FishBase "opportunity-driven" and, therefore, extremely rapid.

Standards

FishBase provides "hooks" that link information for a species to its valid scientific name. This strategy requires a standard taxonomic hierarchy and a taxonomic authority. In the early years of the FishBase development, an overall and standard taxonomic authority was not available; the encoders used published reviews, monographs, and reports by fish experts (e.g., the FAO species synopses and identification guides to assemble scientific names, synonyms, and common names). In 1998, the release of the three-volume "Catalog of Fishes"

(CofF) by Eschmeyer provided FishBase, and indeed the world, with a standard "nomenclator" and taxonomic authority list. Thus, FishBase can now compare its scientific names with those from the Catalog of Fishes and a continued collaboration between the two teams ensures the quality of the scientific names provided by both data-bases. FishBase also applies the taxonomic hierarchy proposed in J. Nelson's "Fishes of the World" (Nelson, 2006) for higher order taxa and some subfamilies.

Most of the information attached to species names in FishBase (and SeaLifeBase, see below) is in the form of numeric or choice fields, both of which allow quantitative analyses of the encoded information (contrary to the free text used in many other databases). While numeric fields are easy to specify, choice fields are less so, as they demand that the database designers offer choices that cover the possible options, but not in such detail that encoding is slowed down by having to consider very unlikely options (see the example of fish occurring at abyssal depths below).

Collaboration

FishBase follows three main principles in encouraging collaboration with colleagues and users: (1) FishBase gives credit to both the original author(s) of each piece of information entered in the database (through one or several references) and to the person(s) who provided this infor-mation (through a special "stamp" or a reference, if the information was included in a citable document), and this often gives more credit than is expected; (2) FishBase invites, accepts, and acts quickly on critical com-ments; (3) FishBase, though initially conceived to service the fisheries science community for the purpose of improved management of fish-eries, has since evolved to cover many aspects of the life history of fishes, often in response to comments from members of other research com-munities, such as ichthyologists, marine biologists, and aquatic ecolo-gists. In fact, collaborators are so important to FishBase that each has a page as part of the database; for many scientists, notably in developing countries, this is also their only presence on the web.

FISHBASE STRUCTURE AND CONTENT

FishBase is a biodiversity information system (BIS). Ideally, a BIS has three components: a database, a website, and analytical tools. The database is relational, which is the most common model and which is easy to use, but has serious limitations (Codd, 1990; Bailly, 1996). It consists of tables (called "relations") containing records (rows) that are sets of predefined fields (columns); the tables are linked by common field(s), usually unique identifier keys, i.e., "meaningless" serial numbers. Bailly (1997) described the properties of a biodiversity database structure (with examples from ichthyology), and what is expected of such databases in terms of data availability, analysis, and dissemination. The core structure of both FishBase and SeaLifeBase, as illustrated in Figure 3.1, exhibits these properties.

The SPECIES table is the central part of FishBase. It contains principal synthetic information on species. When subspecies are valid, the subspecies are recorded, but not the species itself.

The classification and the nomenclature are managed in the FAMILIES and GENERA tables (with some information in the ORDERS, CLASSES, and PHYLA tables) and in the SYNONYMS table, respectively. Synonyms are understood in the widest sense and also include misapplied names (e.g., misidentifications). The STOCKS table is used to link nearly all other topical tables such as ECOLOGY, GROWTH, REPRODUC, etc., in such a way that information on stocks, populations, and strains can be stored separately. Last but not least, almost all information stored is linked to a reference (article, monograph, other database, etc.) recorded in the REFRENS table through the BIBLIO table where names used in the reference, geographic locality, page numbers where the species is dealt with, and other remarks are documented. Some information computed from empirical models is identifiable as such, and the reference to the method is attached to the information.

Finally, the distribution of species is recorded in four different ways: (1) by FAO areas; (2) by countries and, most recently, by states or provinces for large countries; (3) by large marine ecosystems and oceanic provinces; and (4) by occurrence (point data) extracted from the Global Biodiversity Information Facility/Ocean Biogeographic Information System (GBIF/OBIS), other databases, and directly from the literature. For the first three, an authority file defining the geographic area and the species and stock are linked through a joint table with additional information on various statuses (occurrence, protection, abundance, etc.).

SUSTAINABILITY AND MAINTENANCE
OF FISHBASE

FishBase has over two decades of experience in building an information system. One major conclusion is that the quality of data entered

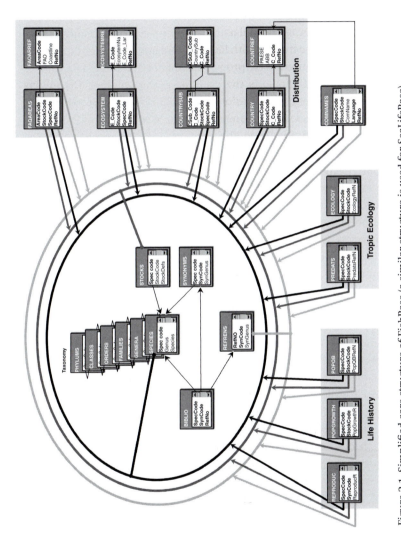

Figure 3.1 Simplified core structure of FishBase (a similar structure is used for SeaLifeBase).

can only be assured by dedicated encoders; modern "mash-up" technology, such as used by the maker of the "Encyclopedia of Life" (http://www.eol.org/) cannot replace human encoding, no matter how smart the technology. "Encoding" does not only imply manual typing of data; rather, it is that aspect of doing science that involves searching the literature for pertinent information, breaking this information down to units of data and finally encoding these into an interface incorporating rules and error traps (as does the FishBase encoding interface). Each step involves decision making, i.e., rejecting or accepting data using a suite of validity and quality criteria (Froese, this volume). The investment that FishBase has made into building this team of expert and dedicated encoders, i.e., the FishBase Team, is what makes FishBase a successful "living" database.

In the first years of its existence, FishBase received large grants, notably from the European Commission, ensuring its rapid growth, and establishment as a de facto standard. However, the change in priorities of many funding institutions from basic research to more policy-oriented initiatives has affected FishBase's ability to maintain its encoding team. In order to assure continuity, Rainer Froese and Daniel Pauly, with the expert help of Cornelia Nauen (then with the European Commission's DG VIII), approached colleagues, mostly frequent users of FishBase, with the idea of setting up a consortium. Members of this consortium were to assure one to two funded FishBase positions within their institutions for its continued support, maintenance, and further development. After preparatory meetings at the European Commission in Brussels and at the Museum of Natural History in Stockholm in 2000, a six-member international consortium accepted and endorsed the FishBase project as one of their permanent activities at a third meeting at the FAO headquarters in Rome. The founding members were the Muséum National d'Histoire Naturelle, Paris, France; Musée Royal de l'Afrique Centrale, Tervuren, Belgium; Swedish Museum of Natural History, Stockholm, Sweden; Institut für Meereskunde, Kiel, Germany; the WorldFish Center, Los Baños, Philippines; and the FAO, Rome, Italy, and with Rainer Froese serving as Scientific Coordinator. A president is elected for 1 year during its annual meeting, which also decides on an annual work plan, including fund-raising strategies. This has led to some funding for the current FishBase team being obtained through collaboration between consortium members. The FishBase Consortium has since accepted three more members: the Fisheries Centre of the University of British Columbia, Vancouver, Canada (2000); School of Biology in the Department of Zoology, Aristotle

University, Thessaloniki, Greece (2005); and Chinese Academy of Fisheries Science, Beijing, China (2008); FishBase continues to receive nominations for new institutional membership.

This new structure has made FishBase itself sustainable, but has not resolved the issue of long-term funding for its encoding team in the Philippines.

FISHBASE'S IMPACT IN SCIENCE

After two decades of bringing the contents of FishBase (Table 3.1) to users' fingertips, we have found that FishBase is very well known among fisheries scientists, ichthyologists, marine biologists, and similar practitioners. Assessing its impact can also be done quantitatively, using web statistics, citation analysis, questionnaires, and links to other online information systems.

Since 1998, when it went online, the number of "hits" received by FishBase on its Internet site has grown exponentially, reaching more than 30 million hits per month in 2009, generated by about 500 000 unique visitors. This combines data from eight mirror sites, in China, France, Germany, Greece, the Philippines, Sweden, Taiwan, and the United States, respectively.

The impact of FishBase in the literature was assessed for 1995–2005 by Stergiou and Tsikliras (2006), who reported a total of 580 citations in Scopus™ and 73 in Google Books™. A query in the ISI Web of Science™ (drawing on over 10 000 journals, books, reports and conferences) yielded 1012 citations showing an exponential increase from 7 citations in 2000 to 245 in 2008, the last complete year (Figure 3.2). Of the citations, 86% were in journal articles and 14% in proceedings, reviews, editorial material, and letters. Over 22% of authors citing FishBase were from developing countries, indicating the importance of such online information systems in areas where hard copies of journals, books, and proceedings are often not available. Moreover, about 31% of citing authors worked in fisheries institutions and about 8% were from developing countries and fisheries institutions, suggesting that FishBase has reached its targeted audience, i.e., fisheries scientists and managers, inclusive of those in developing countries where fisheries-related management issues are most prevalent.

A citation analysis of FishBase was performed in March 2009 in Scopus™, an abstract and citation database covering more than 18 000 peer-reviewed series from more than 5000 international publishers,

Table 3.1 *Contents of FishBase and SeaLifeBase as of July 2009.*

Type of record	FishBase	Comments	SeaLifeBase	Comments
species-group taxa	31 255	192 species have 284 subspecies	105 554	288 species with 502 subspecies; 47 species with 60 varieties
species	30 970	Catalog of Fishes (March, 2009 version) has 30 956 species	105 662	84 261 from the World Register of Marine Species; 23 296 from AlgaeBase
"synonyms"	88 218	81 573 names + 6645 misidentifications	123 032	122 984 names + 311 misidentifications
common names	276 756	291 languages for 252 "countries"	24 295	79 languages for 137 "countries"
country records	171 875	for 291 "countries"	95 821	28 948 species assigned to 292 "countries"
sub-country records	15 594	100 "sub-countries" for 5 "countries"	1926	1014 species assigned to 104 "sub-countries" for 7 "countries"
ecosystem records	118 714	for 437 "ecosystems"	44 011	23 124 species assigned to 158 "ecosystems"
FAO area records	57 126	for 27 areas	57 737	30 590 species assigned to 27 FAO areas
morphology records	14 664	for 7559 species	1516	for 1434 species
identification keys	1486		–	not yet available
images	48 360	for 16 022 fish species	2715	for 1717 metazoan species
bibliographic references	43 076		13 381	
bibliographic citations	290 933		134 691	
total incl. occurrence records	c. 3 million	in 200 tables (more than 60 main tables)	699 481	+2538 occurrence records

FAO = Food and Agriculture Organization of the United Nations.

Note: The terms "countries," "sub-countries," and "ecosystems" are used as follows: FishBase considers overseas archipelagoes and territories, e.g., Canary Islands (Spain) and French Guyana (France) as separate entities, though these are linked to the "main" countries. Sub-countries are administrative country subdivisions, i.e., for Brazil, Canada, China, India, and US. Ecosystems include a varied range of biogeographic areas from coastal rivers or small lakes to large marine ecosystems (LMEs; Sherman and Alexander, 1986), ocean provinces (Longhurst, 1998), and entire oceans (e.g., Pacific Ocean, Atlantic Ocean, Arctic Sea).

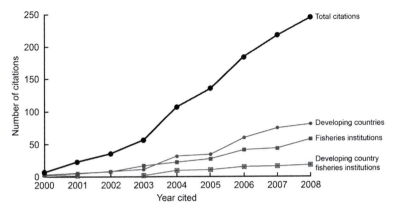

Figure 3.2 FishBase citations on the Web of Science^SM, March 2009. Total number of citations was 1012, using author "Froese R" as senior editor of the FishBase manual (Froese and Pauly, 2000, and its various editions) and keyword "FishBase" (citations to the website as an electronic publication), complemented with additional queries, for 2000–2008.

including coverage of 16 500 peer-reviewed journals, 600 trade publications, and 350 book series. Annual citations to FishBase ranged from 166 in 2006 to 113 in 2008, the decline probably an effect of incomplete coverage in the most recent year. Of 586 Scopus™ citations to FishBase from which the publication type could be ascertained, 520 were journal articles (see Table 3.2), 33 were reviews, and 32 were conference papers. This heavy preponderance of journal articles, though, may reflect more on Scopus™ than on FishBase.

The first two and the fifth journals in Table 3.2 suggest that FishBase has achieved its primary goal by reaching fish and fisheries biologists and ecologists (27% of the authors citing FishBase the most, according to the Web of Science^SM analysis). But it was unexpected that parasitology journals would be in third, sixth, seventh, and eighth positions. Also, in the Web of Science^SM analysis, 50% of the authors citing FishBase the most (n = 52) were fish parasitologists. This was a side effect, demonstrating that BIS are not only required for direct uses in the context for which they were developed, but also by others working in unrelated domains. Another domain where FishBase had an unexpected impact was taxonomy (demonstrated here by the fourth position of *Zootaxa*, and the seventeenth position of *Cybium*), as it was not developed to be a support system for taxonomists. But again, FishBase has become a huge repository of organized information.

Table 3.2 *Journals with most frequent citations to FishBase. These journals published articles most citing FishBase, i.e., first 50% (n = 20) from 586 citations to the FishBase manual (Froese and Pauly, 2000) and FishBase website between 2005 and the beginning of 2009, extracted from Scopus™ on March 4, 2009.*

Journal	Citations	Journal	Citations
Journal of Applied Ichthyology	41	Environmental Biology of Fishes	9
Journal of Fish Biology	34	Aquatic Conservation Marine and Freshwater Ecosystems	9
Systematic Parasitology	31	ICES Journal of Marine Science	9
Zootaxa	23	Estuarine Coastal and Shelf Science	8
Marine Ecology Progress Series	18	Conservation Biology	8
Journal of Parasitology	17	Coral Reefs	8
Acta Parasitologica	14	Cybium	8
Folia Parasitologica	13	Hydrobiologia	8
Fisheries Research	12	Marine Biology	7
Scientia Marina	10	Biological Invasions	7

Finally, the searches revealed that, of the four authors citing FishBase the most in Scopus™, the first three were fish parasitologists, the fourth being Daniel Pauly. A similar result was obtained in Web of Science^SM, where he followed two parasitologists.

The impact of FishBase was further evaluated through a questionnaire sent to 141 fishery biologists and managers from Africa and Asia, who were known to have used FishBase in universities, research institutes, and nongovernment and government agencies. The 36 responses obtained suggested that FishBase was consulted mainly for its species summary pages, pictures, and scientific and common names, in that order, but they also used it for species identification. Nonetheless, the closer users were to research, the more they used other data and analytical tools in FishBase (mainly the "life history" and the "trophic ecology" data and tools).

Another result of this survey was that colleagues from sub-Saharan Africa still appreciate having FishBase on CD-ROMs, due to the continued scarcity and relatively high cost of Internet connections on the continent. This is also the reason why sets of FishBase CD-ROMs are given to graduates of the regular FishBase courses run by the Musée Royal de l'Afrique Centrale.

Finally, FishBase is linked with other biodiversity informatics initiatives and, in some cases, provides them with all or part of their fish-related information, including taxonomy. Examples are the Catalogue of Life, GenBank®, the Barcode of Life, the Encyclopedia of Life, and the Red List database of the International Union for Conservation of Nature (IUCN) (see Appendix 3.1 for Internet addresses).

SEALIFEBASE OR "FISHBASE FOR GROUPS OTHER THAN FISHES"

Given FishBase's success, its makers were often asked why it did not branch out to other aquatic organisms, and the standard response was to invite interested colleagues to develop FishBase-like systems for their groups. In reality, there had been two attempts to develop such databases, by digitizing the FAO's catalog of commercially important crustaceans in one case, and through collaboration with malacologists in the other. Both initiatives failed because of the lack of leaders like Rainer Froese and Daniel Pauly, who acted as "champions" for FishBase and obtained resources for it. The situation was similar for CephBase, a FishBase-like online database for cephalopods, which originated at Dalhousie University in Halifax, Canada, moved to Texas, and then faded for lack of leadership.

In 2004, Daniel Pauly, Nicolas Bailly, and Rainer Froese discussed the Sea Around Us project's need for biodiversity information that could feed life-history information into the project's "database-driven" ecosystem model construction (Christensen *et al.*, 2008, 2009). The objective was not to provide yet another authoritative list of species, but rather, for each species, make available biological information necessary to conduct biodiversity and ecosystem studies, taking advantage of already available electronic and hard-copy species lists, and using the scientific names they provide as "hooks" to organize biodiversity information, as in FishBase. Daniel Pauly convinced the Oak Foundation (Geneva, Switzerland) to provide the start-up funds needed to build what is now known as SeaLifeBase (www.sealifebase. org). In 2006, SeaLifeBase began its operations with Daniel Pauly as the Principal Investigator, Maria Lourdes D. Palomares as its Project Coordinator, and Rainer Froese and Nicolas Bailly as scientific advisers.

SeaLifeBase was built using the FishBase database and website structures as a shell, and progressively modifying graphical charts and adapting fields in tables where some aspects of the taxonomy, biology, and ecology were different from those of fishes. For example, all length type fields for turtles were changed to include straight carapace length as the standard measurement of body length. The most extensive modifications were done to the ecology suite of tables, notably to include habitats, species associations, and life-cycle attributes specific to non-fish organisms, e.g., sessile benthos.

Once the shell was ready for encoding, the next question was which taxonomic backbone to use; this question is pertinent as the proliferation of online systems with marine biodiversity data created much confusion, especially in taxonomy. Several taxonomic groups are covered by global species databases maintained by specialists, 66 of which contribute to the 2009 edition of the Catalogue of Life (CoL), which makes available 1.16 million valid species names and 764 000 synonyms. In spite of this enormous effort, the list of all extant, described valid species in the world, about 1.8 million species, is still not complete, and this is particularly a problem for marine species. Some of these gaps could be tentatively filled by regional, national, or even highly localized databases. However, inconsistent taxonomies make this very difficult. For example, Malacolog, a database of Western Atlantic mollusks, is not compatible with CLEMAM, a database of the Northeastern Atlantic mollusks, and generating a full list for the North Atlantic generates discrepancies, which will have to be checked and verified manually. Fortunately, the World Register of Marine Species (WoRMS), with its network of taxonomists, endeavors to fill these gaps and contributes lists of marine species to CoL.

Thus, with the WoRMS-enhanced CoL as its taxonomic backbone, SeaLifeBase is able to integrate over 100 000 scientific names (of which about 80% are valid species names) of marine metazoans. This collaboration with CoL and WoRMS enabled SeaLifeBase not to have to "reinvent the wheel of nomenclature."

However, neither CoL nor WoRMS has a complete list of all marine species in the world and, in order to go forward, SeaLifeBase resorted to encoding taxonomic data by focusing on specific groups, e.g., tusk shells and stomatopods, that were not completed by these two aggregators. Also, during the first 2 years, SeaLifeBase completed the list of species for smaller marine phyla (Ctenophora, Hemichordata, Priapulida, etc.) from published reviews, catalogs, and checklists and/or with the help of experts. The strategy, which also led to the complete coverage of the known vertebrates (marine reptiles, 362 species; seabirds, 368 species; marine mammals, 184 species) was chosen to avoid large long-term targets (e.g., a complete list of all described mollusks of the world) overlapping with the mandate of other groups, and thus to be eventually available via CoL.

Classification to the class level, and when available to the order level, is primarily based on the higher hierarchy of the CoL (which includes WoRMS); it follows the Tree of Life phylogeny for groups not yet in the CoL.

Full use of published taxonomic literature

There is a huge resource of taxonomic data available in form of published reviews, revisions, monographs, faunal lists, collection catalogs, surveys, and expedition reports, as well as online databases. These jointly form a good part of the resources taxonomists need in order for them to review or revise existing lists. However, not all are encoded in an electronic format and they are often not readily available even in hard copy. Digitized taxonomic data in a database structure (not in a "mashed-up" way) from such literature provides the baseline necessary for the tedious work of taxonomists. Both WoRMS and CoL are progressing with this ambitious task in spite of the hesitations of taxonomists to contribute – mainly due to the common misperception that databases are black holes into which they throw their data, with nothing ever coming back out.

Online reference databases with relevant citations of scientific publications include Zoological Record, Aquatic Science and Fisheries Abstracts, Canada Institute for Scientific Information, among others, and the priorities for extracting data from these databases reflect the short- and long-term objectives for SeaLifeBase. A web crawler was developed to check the updates in these and other important websites, such as the Convention on Biological Diversity, Diversitas, GBIF, IUCN, United Nations Environment Programme (UNEP), UNEP World Conservation Monitoring Centre, and Worldwide Fund for Nature (WWF). Information obtained through this strategy is deep-linked and refers back to the original website.

Data exchange

One of the main goals of biodiversity informatics is to facilitate data exchange. But this goal is also one of the most challenging. In the mid-1980s, botanists, who were ahead of other biologists in using databases, created the Taxonomic Database Working Group (TDWG) to establish data standards to assist data exchanges; their work was partly funded by the Committee on Data for Science and Technology of the International Council for Science, which proposes and sets standards for scientific data. Several working groups were created to develop the required standards, and they progressively adopted the various emerging technologies, such as XML "schemas" and ontologies. Their work resulted in standards that evolved away from centralized databases to separate databases structured around the same schema, to strongly independent databases providing data under a common schema, capable of data exchanges through such wrappers and protocols as Distributed Generic Information Retrieval (DiGIR) and TDWG Access Protocol for Information Retrieval (TAPIR). However, very few databases were developed using these standards, whose systematic application depends, in part, on the incorporation of fuzzy logic.

FishBase and SeaLifeBase are as close as possible to these standards (Bailly *et al.*, 2005), although it was necessary to stretch them to match them to the reality faced by the encoder teams. For example, the term "bathypelagic" used in the SPECIES table in FishBase and SeaLifeBase actually covers "bathypelagic," "abyssopelagic," and "hadopelagic," because for the purposes of FishBase and SeaLifeBase, too much detail can be constraining. In this example, an encoder would have to choose for every deepwater species whether it is bathypelagic, abyssopelagic, or hadopelagic. The information needed to make such a choice is not available for most species, and thus a database with a detailed standard would have a multitude of empty fields.

But even when two databases have adopted the same standards, it does not follow that they can straightforwardly exchange data. Data exchange is easy when a database starts from scratch; in this case, one can import data in one go, as when taxonomic and nomenclatural data were imported from the CoL to SeaLifeBase. Subsequent exchanges are difficult, however, when information is attached to species names, as in FishBase and SeaLifeBase. In fact, even changing names can lead to disaster, because name strings used by different databases may designate two different taxonomic concepts, e.g., in the case of homonyms, or may contain typographical errors. This explains why the "mash-up" technologies used, for instance, by Encyclopedia of Life are unreliable. We perform updates semi-automatically for FishBase with the Catalog of Fishes, and for SeaLifeBase with the Catalogue of Life. After each new release, a set of queries and routines is run to show and verify taxonomic and nomenclatural changes. Some corrections can then be automatically updated, while some others require that we update manually through the encoding interface, because one change may have implications for several fields or tables. In addition, the encoding interface features many integrity controls that are not necessarily taken into account by automatic updates.

Changing a scientific name or correcting a spelling or the authority is not difficult, unlike lumping or splitting species. When splitting, all references cited are reviewed in order to decide which are attached to which taxon. This is a tedious process, which may result in discarding references previously used because the valid taxon cannot be identified. Obviously, the same considerations are true the other way around for partners importing data, e.g., FishBoL or WoRMS, from SeaLifeBase, although the difficulties are fewer when any taxonomic and nomenclature data are considered.

THE HIDDEN PART OF THE ICEBERG: EVERYTHING THAT USERS DON'T REALLY NEED TO KNOW

Biodiversity information systems, BISs, such as FishBase and SeaLifeBase, can be compared to icebergs, whose emerged, shiny part attracts all the attention, but the bulk of whose mass is submerged, attracting attention only when something goes wrong (Mersey, 1912). Some challenges associated with the submerged parts of BISs follow.

The first challenge is the information standards that will meet the maximum of end-users – including in languages other than English, as partly provided by FishBase and SeaLifeBase (Bailly, 2003). Each end-user category and, sometimes, even each user require given scales, different standards, categories and attributes, which explains why there are so many initiatives that are seemingly overlapping, but that present the same data under different interfaces. In other words, users look to express information with the standard that best fits their culture, training, etc. This can be extremely complex in the case of taxonomy where various opinions may be contradictory, and/or if one wants to analyze the history of opinions, and opinions on opinions, as in the case of homologies in phylogenetic analyses (Dettai *et al.*, 2004). This issue becomes critical when the targets are scientific communities. Raw data are less controversial and allow more collaboration, e.g., the occurrence data in GBIF/OBIS. Setting up a website that can be appreciated by the general public, yet retains scientific integrity, is another major challenge, and the Encyclopedia of Life, toward this goal, has started a process where the level of (scientific) detail can be set by the user.

The second challenge is the completeness of information provided. Is it needed? When is it possible to consider that there is enough data/information to create knowledge? How can we measure completeness? Some analytical tools do not require all data and many trends can be depicted, even using some proxies that artificially replace missing data. Establishing thresholds for these tools helps to avoid the never-ending search for comprehensiveness, and users may be satisfied with a given threshold of completeness, although they must be made aware of the possible flaws and biases when using incomplete data. In general, the more global analyses are, the less data need to be complete. On this issue, ecologists may differ from taxonomists, as ecosystem studies can deal better with proxies than can taxonomic studies. In FishBase and SeaLifeBase, the completeness question cannot be solved in an absolute sense.

The third challenge is quality control, i.e., checking the encoding data by identifying mistakes. In FishBase and SeaLifeBase, we use three methods to achieve this: encoding control, alphabetical ordering by field, and queries with null values. The first method is performed by many controls that are set up at the database structure and the encoding interface level. The second is performed by the encoders themselves in their tables of responsibility: ordering one field by alphabetical order allows the depiction of many obvious mistakes. The third is performed by encoders and database managers; here, the principle is to define as many queries as possible that must give a null result. The set of queries is run before each monthly update, and non-null results are corrected before the update if possible.

The perception of the error content is rather contextual: ecologists downloading a dataset with thousands of data would be satisfied even with 20% errors; but a user who looks for one piece of information for one species will find 100% error if there is an obvious mistake for that particular information. Also tricky are species lists in various contexts like country or ecosystem checklists: even with only 1% error globally, when say 200 species are listed, two will be erroneously included or excluded, which will lead many users to consider the entire list to be dubious or erroneous.

Fortunately, numerous users, especially of the well-established FishBase, send feedback for corrections, but we assume that many others do not. For those who do, it is important to have a well-defined and quick procedure to answer their feedback and to show them that it is taken into account (or to explain why not; see below).

The fourth challenge is the validation of information by specialists, which is a necessary process if one attempts to create a scientific BIS. Does the standardizing/encoding method correspond to what the specialists know about the species and/or the topic? Experience shows that specialists are keen to check the entries in a database when the information is organized in a way that is familiar to them, and problems arise when their corrections are returned to them under a format different from the one they used to perform the corrections.

Another question is: how frequently can we ask specialists on the different taxa to validate data? As mentioned above, large parts of FishBase and SeaLifeBase were validated shortly after launch, but it is probably expecting too much to assume that specialists would want to re-validate a database year after year. Indeed, the sustained participation of specialists in the maintenance of databases, especially when they are otherwise not directly involved in them, requires considerations beyond the scope of this chapter – reaching beyond technological aspects into the reward systems of science.

A related question is how to document the validation results. The simple answer is to credit the specialist in the corrected record and in the web page. There are several options for this; the best ones are complex and time-consuming, and the simple ones are misleading. The simplest is to leave the credit as is, and ask the specialist periodically to update his/her validation on the modified records only; in which case, content corrections are separated from the data structure. Moreover, we may encode incorrect information that will be by default (but erroneously) "credited" to the specialist for a while. At the other extreme, the entire history of all changes and checking and their respective types may be stored (like spelling corrections, added or changed information in text fields, etc.), which makes data management extremely complex. It will be noted that this is similar to the errors in source publications. However, we do keep a tag for such changes to avoid their being re-entered by a subsequent encoder.

FISHBASE AND SEALIFEBASE AS SOURCES OF DISTRIBUTION AND ECOSYSTEM INFORMATION

Data and information from FishBase and SeaLifeBase are currently heavily used for two types of research: the mapping of distribution ranges of species, as used by the Aquamaps and Sea Around Us projects;

and ecosystem modeling, mainly using Ecopath with Ecosim (EwE; Christensen and Pauly, 1992; Christensen and Walters, 2004).

Aquamaps uses the environmental characteristics – especially temperature and depth – associated with the occurrence records provided by FishBase or SeaLifeBase to define the environmental "envelope" of a species, then projects it as an expected distribution range via maps of temperature, depth, etc. (Kaschner *et al.*, 2007). The various steps of this procedure are automatic in practice, i.e., the occurrence records and environmental characteristics are picked up from various databases, and several general linear models are run, until one generates a stable global distribution map of probabilities of occurrence (by cells of 0.5 degree latitude/longitude). The map then needs to be trimmed because the procedure cannot distinguish by itself, say, tropical shallow habitat in the Indo-Pacific from the same habitat type in the Atlantic. Presently, about 10 000 maps, mainly for marine fishes, have been produced using this approach, enabling various meta-analyses (see Froese, this volume).

The Sea Around Us project has developed a method for mapping distribution ranges wherein available information (in FishBase, SeaLifeBase, or in the literature) is first used to draw the smallest possible polygon encompassing all non-zero probabilities of occurrence. Then, ecological rules are used (e.g., for equatorial submergence, Ekman, 1967) and an array of characteristics of the habitats in the polygon (e.g., upper continental shelf, lower shelf, shelf slope, seamount, upwelling, etc.) to assign 0.5 degree, cell-specific probabilities of occurrence, such that all cells within a polygon sum to one. One advantage of this scheme, originally devised by Watson *et al.* (2004), then extended to consider habitat associations (Cheung *et al.*, 2005), is that qualitative information on characteristics of certain habitats can be used to derive distributions (Close *et al.*, 2006; Cheung *et al.*, 2008). This method has been applied to over 1000 species of commercial fishes and invertebrates, i.e., species for which at least one of the member countries reports a fishery catch to the FAO.

The development of these biogeographic modeling systems is analogous to the development of cladistics in phylogeny, in that, by using increasing amounts of data, they produce results (here, maps) that are gradually independent of subjective (or expert) opinion. Before cladistics, phylogenies and classification were highly sensitive to specialists' opinions. Today, with the same datasets and the same methodologies, the results for phylogenies and distribution maps are the same from one researcher to another. But just as molecular phylogenies require a huge amount of sequences to be available, such as through GenBank, biogeographic modeling systems require huge and diversified datasets, which, in the case of the aquatic environment, are provided by and through FishBase and SeaLifeBase.

The contribution of FishBase and SeaLifeBase to ecosystem modeling is well established, particularly for FishBase, which has a routine for extracting and exporting data for use in constructing Ecopath models ("Ecopath data," "Species Ecology Matrix," "Trophic pyramids" tools under the "Information by Country/Island" and "Information by Ecosystem" searches). The Ecopath manual documents numerous concepts shared between Ecopath and FishBase (Palomares and Pauly, 2000a, 2000b, 2000c; Palomares and Sa-a, 2000a, 2000b; Pauly and Christensen, 2000; Pauly *et al.*, 2000; Pauly and Palomares, 2000; Pauly and Sa-a, 2000). The traffic between FishBase/SeaLifeBase and Ecopath has been intensified (e.g., Pauly and Palomares, 2007; Pauly *et al.*, 2009) by a new approach for constructing thousands of EwE models rapidly, i.e., as embodied in the "database-driven model construction" of Christensen *et al.* (2008, 2009). This approach will allow the generation of, for example, maps of the global biomass of functional groups (e.g., large predators, small demersal prey, etc.) at 0.5 degree resolution as used for mapping other products of the Sea Around Us project and, hopefully, the completion of the greatest integration of biodiversity and fisheries data ever achieved.

ACKNOWLEDGMENTS

We thank Daniel Pauly and Rainer Froese for their crucial input in initiating FishBase and SeaLifeBase, and our colleagues and friends from the FishBase and SeaLifeBase teams in the Philippines, two of whom helped with this contribution: Elijah Laxamana, FishBase web master and developer, who provided current web statistics; and Kathleen Reyes, who provided the questionnaire results.

APPENDIX 3.1   INTERNET LOCATIONS OF THE DATABASES AND OTHER RESOURCES MENTIONED IN THE TEXT

Aquamaps	www.aquamaps.org
Catalog of Fishes	www.calacademy.org/research/ichthyology/catalog
Catalogue of Life	www.catalogueoflife.org

CLEMAM	www.somali.asso.fr/clemam
Creative Commons	www.creativecommons.org
Ecopath with Ecosim	www.ecopath.org
Encyclopedia of Life	www.eol.org
FishBase	www.fishbase.org
Malacolog	www.malacolog.org
Scopus™	www.scopus.com
Sea Around Us databases	www.seaaroundus.org
SeaLifeBase	www.sealifebase.org
Species 2000	www.species2000.org
Tree of Life	www.tolweb.org
Web of Science℠	www.isiknowledge.com/
WoRMS	www.marinespecies.org

REFERENCES

Bailly, N. (1996) Systèmes de gestion de bases de données en systématique. *Biosystema*, 23, 19–36.

Bailly, N. (1997) Structure et bases de données en Ichtyologie. *Cybium*, 21, 169–181.

Bailly, N. (2003) Functionality for satisfying user demand. In Scoble, M. J. S., ed., *ENHSIN: The European Natural History Specimen Information Network*. London: Natural History Museum, pp. 133–148.

Bailly, N., Capuli, E. and Torres, A. (2005) Towards a concept-based taxonomy management in FishBase. In Stergiou, K. I. and Bobori, D. C., eds., *Fish and More*. Thessaloniki, Greece: University Studio Press, pp. 15–18.

Bisby, F. A. (2000) The quiet revolution: biodiversity informatics and the internet. *Science*, 289, 2309–2312.

Bisby, F. A., Shimura, J., Ruggiero, M., Edwards, J. and Haeuser, C. (2002) Taxonomy, at the click of a mouse. *Nature*, 418, 367.

Carpenter, K. E. and Niem, V. H. (1999) *FAO Species Identification Guide for Fishery Purposes: The Living Marine Resources of the Western Central Pacific*. Rome: FAO.

Cheung, W. W. L., Close, C., Lam, V., Watson, R. and Pauly, D. (2008) Application of macroecological theory to predict effects of climate change on global fisheries potential. *Marine Ecology Progress Series*, 365, 187–197.

Cheung, W., Pitcher, T. and Pauly, D. (2005) A fuzzy logic expert system to estimate intrinsic extinction vulnerabilities of marine fishes to fishing. *Biological Conservation*, 124, 97–111.

Christensen, V. and Pauly, D. (1992) ECOPATH II: a software for balancing steady-state ecosystem models and calculating network characteristics. *Ecological Modelling*, 61, 169–185.

Christensen, V. and Walters, C. (2004) Ecopath with Ecosim: methods, capabilities and limitations. *Ecological Modelling*, 172, 109–139.

Christensen, V., Walters, C. J., Ahrens, R., Alder, J., Buszowski, J., Christensen, L. B., Cheung, W. W. L., Dunne, J., Froese, R., Karpouzi, V., Kaschner, K., Kearney, K., Lai, S., Lam, V., Palomares, M. L. D., Peters-Mason,

A., Piroddi, C., Sarmiento, J. L., Steenbeek, J., Sumaila, R., Watson, R., Zeller, D. and Pauly, D. (2008) Models of the world's large marine ecosystems. GEF/LME global project promoting ecosystem-based approaches to fisheries conservation and large marine ecosystems. UNESCO/Intergovernmental Oceanographic Commissions Technical Series, 80.

Christensen, V., Walters, C. J., Ahrens, R., Alder, J., Buszowski, J., Christensen, L. B., Cheung, W. W. L., Dunne, J., Froese, R., Karpouzi, V., Kaschner, K., Kearney, K., Lai, S., Lam, V., Palomares, M. L. D., Peters-Mason, A., Piroddi, C., Sarmiento, J. L., Steenbeek, J., Sumaila, R., Watson, R., Zeller, D. and Pauly, D. (2009) Database-driven models of the world's large marine ecosystems. *Ecological Modelling*, 220, 1984–1996.

Close, C., Cheung, W. W. L., Hodgson, S., Lam, V., Watson, R. and Pauly, D. (2006) Distribution ranges of commercial fishes and invertebrates. In Palomares, M. L. D., Stergiou, K. I., and Pauly, D., eds., *Fishes in Databases and Ecosystems. Fisheries Centre Research Reports 14(4)*. Vancouver, Canada: Fisheries Centre, University of British Columbia, pp. 27–37.

Codd, E. F. (1990) *The Relational Model for Database Management: Version 2*. Reading, MA: Addison-Wesley Publishing Company Inc.

Dettai, A., Bailly, N., Vignes-Lebbe, R. and Lecointre, G. (2004) Metacanthomorpha. Essay on a phylogeny-oriented database for morphology: the acanthomorph (Teleostei) example. *Systematic Biology*, 53, 822–834.

Ekman, S. (1967) *Zoogeography of the Sea*. London: Sidgwick & Jackson.

Eschmeyer, W. N. (1998) *Catalog of Fishes*. San Francisco, CA: Academy of Sciences.

Froese, R. (2000) The making of FishBase. In Froese, R. and Pauly, D., eds., *FishBase 2000: Concepts, Design and Data Sources*. Los Baños, Laguna, Philippines: ICLARM, pp. 7–24.

Froese, R. and Pauly, D. (2000) *FishBase 2000: Concepts, designs and data sources*. Los Baños, Laguna, Philippines: ICLARM.

Froese, R. and Schofer, W. (1987) Computer-aided identification of fish larvae. *ICES CM*, L: 23.

ICLARM (1988) *ICLARM five-year plan (1988–1992)*. Manila, Philippines: ICLARM.

Kaschner, K., Ready, J. S., Agbayani, E., Rius, J., Kesner-Reyes, K., Eastwood, P. D., South, A. B., Kullander, S. O., Rees, T. and Close, C. H. (2007) AquaMaps: predicted range maps for aquatic species. Available online: www.aquamaps.org.

Longhurst, A. (1998) *Ecological Geography of the Sea*. San Diego, CA: Academic Press.

McCall, R. A. and May, R. M. (1995) More than a seafood platter. *Nature*, 376, 735.

Matsuura, K. (1995) FishBase: a biological database on fish. *Japanese Journal of Icthyology*, 42, 342–343.

Mersey, L. (1912) Report of a formal investigation into the circumstances attending to the foundering on 15th April, 1912, of the British Steamship "Titanic" of Liverpool, after striking ice in or near Latitude 41 46' N., Longitude 50° 14' W., North Atlantic Ocean, whereby loss of life ensued. London: HM Stationery Office.

Nelson, J. (2006) *Fishes of the World*. New York: John Wiley and Sons.

Palomares, M. L. D. and Pauly, D. (2000a) The POPQB Table. In Froese, R. and Pauly, D., eds. *FishBase 2000. Concepts, Design and Data Sources*. Los Baños, Laguna, Philippines: ICLARM, pp. 197–199.

Palomares, M. L. D. and Pauly, D. (2000b) The PREDATORS Table. In Froese, R. and Pauly, D., eds. *FishBase 2000. Concepts, Design and Data Sources*. Los Baños, Laguna, Philippines: ICLARM, pp. 199–203.

Palomares, M. L. D. and Pauly, D. (2000c) Trophic ecology. In Froese, R. and Pauly, D., eds. *FishBase 2000. Concepts, Design and Data Sources*. Los Baños, Laguna, Philippines: ICLARM, pp. 176–204.

Palomares, M. L. D. and Sa-a, P. (2000a) The DIET Table. In Froese, R. and Pauly, D., eds. *FishBase 2000. Concepts, Design and Data Sources*. Los Baños, Laguna, Philippines: ICLARM, pp. 188–193.

Palomares, M. L. D. and Sa-a, P. (2000b) The RATION Table. In Froese, R. and Pauly, D., eds. *FishBase 2000. Concepts, Design and Data Sources*. Los Baños, Laguna, Philippines: ICLARM, pp. 193–196.

Pauly, D. (1978) A preliminary compilation of fish length growth parameters. *Berichte des Instituts für Meereskunde an der Universität Kiel*, 55, 200.

Pauly, D. (1979) Gill size and temperature as governing factors in fish growth: a generalization of von Bertalanffy's growth formula. *Berichte des Instituts für Meereskunde und der Universität Kiel*, 63, 156.

Pauly, D. (1980) On the interrelationships between natural mortality, growth parameters, and mean environmental temperature in 175 fish stocks. *ICES Journal of Marine Science*, 39, 175.

Pauly, D. (2010) *Gasping Fish and Panting Squids: Oxygen, Temperature and the Growth of Water-breathing Animals*. In Kinne, O., ed., *Excellence in Ecology*, 22. Oldendorf/Luhe, Germany: International Ecology Institute.

Pauly, D. and Christensen, V. (2000) The Ecopath modeling approach and FishBase. In Froese, R. and Pauly, D., eds. *FishBase 2000. Concepts, Design and Data Sources*. Los Baños, Laguna, Philippines: ICLARM, p. 177.

Pauly, D., Froese, R. and Rius, J. (2000) Trophic pyramids. In Froese, R. and Pauly, D., eds. *FishBase 2000. Concepts, Design and Data Sources*. Los Baños, Laguna, Philippines: ICLARM, pp. 203–204.

Pauly, D., Gayanilo Jr, F. C., Froese, R. and Christensen, V. (1995) Software tools for management of tropical aquatic resources. In Sakagawa, G. T., ed., *Assessment Methodologies and Management. Proc. World Fisheries Congress, Theme 5*. New Delhi: Oxford and IBH Publishing, pp. 90–102.

Pauly, D., Graham, W., Libralato, S., Morrissette, L. and Deng Palomares, M. (2009) Jellyfish in ecosystems, online databases, and ecosystem models. *Hydrobiologia*, 616, 67–85.

Pauly, D. and Palomares, M. L. D. (2000) Preliminary estimation of trophic levels in fish species without food composition data. In Froese, R. and Pauly, D., eds. *FishBase 2000. Concepts, Design and Data Sources*. Los Baños, Laguna, Philippines: ICLARM, p. 186.

Pauly, D. and Palomares, M. L. D. (2007) SeaLifeBase as a support system for modelling marine ecosystems. *Abstracts, 6th European Conference on Ecological Modelling: ECEM '07*, 18.

Pauly, D. and Sa-a, P. (2000) Estimating trophic levels from individual food items. In Froese, R. and Pauly, D., eds. *FishBase 2000. Concepts, Design and Data Sources*. Los Baños, Laguna, Philippines: ICLARM, p. 185.

Sherman, K. and Alexander, L. M., eds. (1986) *Variability and Geography of Large Marine Ecosystems*. AAAS Symposium. Boulder, CO: Westview Press, Inc.

Stergiou, K. I. and Tsikliras, A. C. (2006) Scientific impact of FishBase: a citation analysis. In Palomares, M. L. D., Stergiou, K. I. and Pauly, D., eds., *Fishes in Databases and Ecosystems. Fisheries Centre Research Reports 14(4)*. Vancouver, Canada: Fisheries Centre, University of British Columbia, pp. 2–6.

Watson, R., Kitchingman, A., Gelchu, A. and Pauly, D. (2004) Mapping global fisheries: sharpening our focus. *Fish and Fisheries*, 5, 168–177.

4

The science in FishBase

INTRODUCTION

FishBase is an online information system with key information on all the known fishes of the world, i.e., over 30 000 species. This key information has been extracted, standardized, and evaluated by a team of specialists from over 40 000 scientific publications. The rationale and development of FishBase are presented in Palomares and Bailly (this volume), who demonstrate that FishBase, the successive editions of the book that document it (notably Froese and Pauly, 2000) and individual chapters therein are heavily cited in both grey and peer-reviewed scientific literature. Indeed, such information has been crucial for numerous high profile studies, including in high profile outlets such as *Science* and *Nature*.

Nevertheless, there have been suggestions that FishBase is a laudable exercise in compiling scientific information, similar to a scientific library, but that its creation and maintenance are not "science," or even "research." Using that logic, one could argue that the work done by all scientists who collect and standardize their data prior to analyzing them is not "science." Also, one could argue that the evaluation of published data prior to their encoding and the tagging of some estimates as "doubtful" (as done by the experienced FishBase encoders) is equivalent to the critical assessment performed by the authors of scientific reviews – who undoubtedly do science.

Rather than developing these arguments, however, I suggest that the scientific status of FishBase can be evaluated by establishing that, based largely on data extracted from FishBase, new insights have been made and published, and that the papers in question have been cited by other scientists. In the following, I present three examples, jointly illustrating the science of FishBase.

Ecosystem Approaches to Fisheries: A Global Perspective, ed. V. Christensen and J. Maclean. Published by Cambridge University Press. © Cambridge University Press 2011.

FISHING DOWN MARINE FOOD WEBS

The first and most widely cited study, done with the help of FishBase, and which could not have straightforwardly been done without it, was a team publication in *Science* (Pauly *et al.*, 1998, 937 citations in Web of Science^{SM}, December 2009). For this, we used the Food and Agriculture Organization of the United Nations (FAO) time series of global catch data for over 1000 species and species groups, and assigned each to one of more than 200 trophic level estimates, as incorporated in FishBase from published diet compositions or from Ecopath models. For every year, we calculated the mean trophic level of the catch, weighted by the catch of the respective species or groups. Plotting mean trophic levels of global catches over time showed a continuous decline from 1970 on (and from 1950 when we omitted a single species, the Peruvian anchoveta).

This global trend is now widely known as "fishing down marine food webs," and is verified by many local studies based on more detailed catch data, but mostly using trophic level estimates from FishBase (Stergiou and Christensen, this volume). Figure 4.1, for example, documents "fishing down marine food webs" in the northwestern Atlantic, where it is particularly strong, due to both the complete collapse of a key high-trophic level species – northern cod – and the availability of detailed fisheries statistics (fishing down cannot be

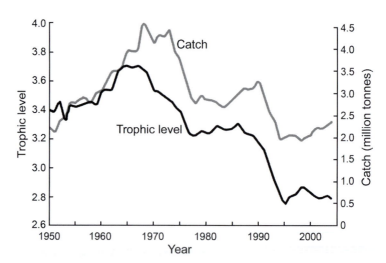

Figure 4.1 Catch and mean trophic level in the northwestern Atlantic.

documented without catch statistics that are well disaggregated). It is a disconcerting finding from the figure that both trophic levels and catches have been declining since the late 1960s. Stergiou and Christensen (this volume) may be consulted for more information on this, the first high-impact paper that used FishBase extensively.

PATTERNS AND PROCESSES IN REEF FISH DIVERSITY

My second example is a study by Mora *et al.* (2003) that examines three hypotheses about the geographic species richness of Indo-Pacific reef fishes. The authors at first used an existing database of Indo-Pacific coastal fishes compiled from published checklists for a previous study (Bellwood and Hughes, 2001). However, in the course of their study, Mora *et al.* (2003) detected that "[m]ore than 300 species were duplicated in the original database as a result of synonymy, misspelled names or misallocations of species to families." After they adopted the FishBase standard for scientific names (i.e., Eschmeyer's *Catalog of Fishes*), and the ensuing corrections to their original list, they then complemented their database with checklists from "the Philippines, Madagascar, Eastern Island, Cook Islands (all from www.fishbase.org)."

Mora *et al.* (2003) then showed that the mid-range points of the species' distributions occur over-proportionally in the Indonesian-Philippine region, thus refuting two hypotheses that proposed that speciation happened outside this area, with the high species richness stemming from the overlapping of the distributions' tails. They conclude that, in contrast to a widely held belief, "the processes of speciation, extinction and dispersal that yield large-scale patterns of species richness also seem to determine which species are present in local assemblages." Their paper was published in *Nature* and had 87 citations in the Web of Science[SM] as of August 2010.

The enormous number of species that must be dealt with when performing analyses of this kind is illustrated in Figure 4.2, which shows the first-ever biodiversity transect across the Indo-Pacific at the equator, derived from the several thousand species in FishBase that have so far been mapped for the Indo-Pacific. Several known diversity patterns are nicely reproduced, such as the lower diversity on the eastern coasts of the Indian and Pacific oceans, the peaks of diversity in shallow waters, and the overall peaks in the Celebes/Halmahera region. The transect is, however, preliminary, as it underestimates the diversity at Celebes/Halmahera because many of the less-common

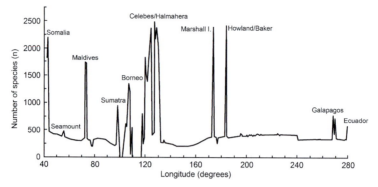

Figure 4.2 Preliminary transect of species richness per half-degree cell along the equator from Somalia to Ecuador, based on several thousand maps of Indo-Pacific fishes, marine mammals, and invertebrates.

species have not been mapped. Also, it overestimates diversity at Marshall and Howland/Baker Islands, because the observed restrictions on species distributions caused by distance from the center have not yet been included properly in the mapping algorithm (Kaschner *et al.*, 2007). Further, the abrupt drop in richness of mostly deep-sea species at 240 degrees latitude is an artifact caused by insufficient sampling of the Southeast Pacific: if no occurrence is reported from an FAO area (here: area 87), then the mapping algorithm prevents the species from spreading there. Despite its preliminary nature, the transect in Figure 4.2 clearly shows the explanatory potential of large datasets, such as those underlying the maps in FishBase.

FISHING ELEVATES VARIABILITY IN THE ABUNDANCE OF EXPLOITED SPECIES

Hsieh *et al.* (2006) explored the temporal variability of exploited versus unexploited fish stocks occurring in the same environment. These authors used larval surveys to estimate the abundance of adults, and FishBase to obtain most of the life-history traits of the adults. They found that exploited species showed higher variability in abundance in the same year and environment than unexploited species. This remained true when differences in life-history traits, such as maximum size, age and size at maturity, fecundity, duration of spawning period, and trophic level were taken into account. They concluded that the increased variability was "probably caused by fishery-induced truncation of age structure, which reduces the capacity of populations to

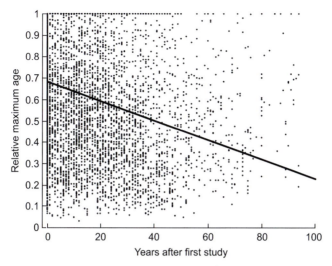

Figure 4.3 Maximum age in exploited fish populations (derived from growth studies as age at 95% of asymptotic length (L_∞), and shown as a fraction of the largest observed value) over years after the first study was done. A robust regression results in relative maximum age = 0.683 – 0.00454 years, with n = 5201 and r^2 = 0.0928.

buffer environmental events" and that "to avoid collapse, fisheries must be managed not only to sustain the total viable biomass but also to prevent the significant truncation of age structure." Their paper was published in *Nature* in 2006 and had received 65 citations in the Web of Science[SM] as of August 2010.

That such truncation of ages occurs in exploited fish stocks can be shown using FishBase. Figure 4.3 shows the maximum ages in various stocks (as fractions of the overall maximum age recorded for the species in question) plotted against the time elapsed since the first study in a given species. While the scatter of these 5201 exploited populations is large, there is a significant decrease in maximum age over time, accounting for 9.3% of the variation in the data.

CONCLUSION

I believe the above examples give an unambiguous answer to the question of whether creating and maintaining FishBase is doing "science." FishBase contains – indeed, consists of – scientific data that were standardized and evaluated by scientists. It is used by numerous scientists to generate new knowledge in the peer-reviewed literature.

The relevance of this new knowledge is shown by the leading status of the journals and the citation record of the papers presenting it.

As an afterthought, it might be the fact that biologists are not yet used to working with large, international datasets that brought up this issue. I have never heard of oceanographers or meteorologists questioning whether their global datasets were part of science.

ACKNOWLEDGMENTS

I thank Daniel Pauly, once the "Science Advisor" of FishBase, for many years of discussing and improving the science in FishBase. Also, I would like to thank the FishBase team for nearly two decades of reliable encoding of data in FishBase. I thank especially Eli Agbayani, Josephine Rius, and Kathleen Reyes for assistance with Figure 4.2, and Crispina Binohlan for assembling the growth/age data shown in Figure 4.3.

REFERENCES

Bellwood, D. R. and Hughes, T. P. (2001) Regional-scale assembly rules and biodiversity of coral reefs. *Science*, 292, 1532–1535.

Froese, R. and Pauly, D. (2000) *FishBase 2000: Concepts, designs and data sources*. Los Baños, Laguna, Philippines: ICLARM.

Hsieh, C., Reiss, C. S., Hunter, J. R., Bedlington, J. R., May, R. M. and Sugihara, G. (2006) Fishing elevates variability in the abundance of exploited species. *Nature*, 443, 859–862.

Kaschner, K., Ready, J. S., Agbayani, E., Rius, J., Kesner-Reyes, K., Eastwood, P. D., South, A. B., Kullander, S. O., Rees, T. and Close, C. H. (2007) AquaMaps: predicted range maps for aquatic species. Available online: www.aquamaps.org.

Mora, C., Chittaro, P. M., Sale, P. F., Kritzer, J. P. and Ludsin, S. A. (2003) Patterns and processes in reef fish diversity. *Nature*, 421, 933–936.

Pauly, D., Christensen, V., Dalsgaard, J., Froese, R. and Torres Jr, F. (1998) Fishing down marine food webs. *Science*, 279, 860.

Section II Evaluating impact on marine life

5

How much fish is being extracted from the oceans and what is it worth?

Any analysis of the impacts of fishing on marine systems, as undertaken by the Sea Around Us project (www.seaaroundus.org), imposes critical demands on fine spatial data documenting the extraction of marine resources. Data sources such as those provided voluntarily from fishing countries through the Food and Agriculture Organization (FAO) of the United Nations are invaluable but have many limitations. Regional datasets are also important in that they provide better detail. Reconstruction of national datasets can also provide great insights into historical catch series (e.g., Zeller *et al.*, 2007), and are important to understand historic baselines (Jackson and Jacquet, this volume). These must be woven into one coherent and harmonized global dataset representing all extractions over time. To provide the necessary spatial detail, the global data are allocated to a fine grid of cells measuring just 30 by 30 minutes of latitude and longitude, resulting in over 180000 such cells covering the world's oceans. The taxonomic identity of the reported catch must be combined with comprehensive databases on where the species occur (and in what abundance) in order to complete this process. This spatial allocation must be further tempered by where countries fish, as not all coastal waters are available to all fleets. After considerable development by the Sea Around Us project, it is now possible to examine global catches and catch values in the necessary spatial context. Like detectives, we have been able to deduce who caught what, where, and when, and how much money they made in the process. Now we can see where fishing has impacted marine resources and examine many other problems such as the potential competition between the diets of marine predators and the insatiable demands of global fishing fleets and consumers.

Ecosystem Approaches to Fisheries: A Global Perspective, ed. V. Christensen and J. Maclean. Published by Cambridge University Press. © Cambridge University Press 2011.

A PROBLEM OF SCALE

To examine the impacts of fishing on the marine environment requires detailed information on what is caught and on how it is caught. Fisheries data sometimes come from the fishing industry on a voluntary basis but are largely obtained as part of the management controls placed on their operations, usually in response to concerns about the sustainability of catches. These data are collected for a variety of purposes. Sometimes they are quite specific, but often the burden of reporting on fisheries is claimed to interfere with their operations if the reporting process is too arduous and detailed. There are often concerns about confidentiality as fishing is a competitive industry and concerns about further restrictions on fishing have engendered much sensitivity about the end-use of this information. Access to these data, often reported in logbooks, some of which are now sophisticated electronic systems, is restricted and often impossible for outsiders to obtain. Nevertheless, generalized information, in which only average locations or total catches per year are reported, are often made available to the public through management agencies. We will talk about "catches" here when generally we mean "landings" – the fish products actually taken ashore and processed – and hence more completely included in the reporting process.

When dealing with questions about the impacts of fishing on global marine environments, the task of attempting to collect public domain data from individual management agencies can be daunting. Often the level of detail in public domain data is not sufficient, as it may not even include details as to where the catches were taken, much less what gear was used or what was discarded. Sometimes more detailed information is available under strict agreements with the agencies that collect the data, but these may also preclude publishing the details that come from the required analysis. Making and managing these arrangements globally would require many teams of multilingual experts and even legal advisors. Fortunately, there are other avenues.

Several major international organizations do publish summaries of fisheries catches. Notably these include regional organizations such as the International Council for the Exploration of the Sea (ICES) and the North East Atlantic Fisheries Commission. There are also summaries reported annually for catches by member countries of the United Nations produced by the Food and Agriculture Organization (FAO). The FAO has also established regional fisheries organizations such as the Fishery Committee for the Eastern Central Atlantic, the General Fisheries Commission for the Mediterranean, and the Indian Ocean Fishery Commission. All of these, suitably harmonized into one non-overlapping dataset, are excellent sources for a complete summary of global catches, but there are several drawbacks for a project that wishes to look at the impacts of fishing on the marine environment.

The first is that the spatial scale is all wrong. Because the FAO's information is not collected for this purpose, it uses very large statistical reporting areas (see Figure 5.1) that generally exceed ecosystem scales (Watson *et al.*, 2003). Some statistics are available from the FAO's regional bodies at slightly smaller scales and are used when possible.

This mismatch in scale poses a significant problem. Much information is available at fine scales, yet is not readily available from management agencies. Other information is available publicly that covers most of the world's fisheries catches, but ironically exactly where the catches were taken is not known. In the worst case, the catch could have come anywhere from within an FAO statistical area in the southeast Pacific with an area of $48\,000\,000$ km^2. This is hardly useful, as it spans many environmental areas, habitats, and national exclusive economic zones (EEZ). There are two approaches to deal with this dilemma. One is very time and resource intensive. This is catch reconstruction, and it must be applied country by country. This is described by Zeller *et al.* (2007) and Zeller and Pauly (2007), and is briefly summarized below. The other approach is to somehow provisionally work with the best of existing data. The question then becomes: how to credibly reverse-engineer the large-scale data into smaller reporting areas so that the potential impacts can be examined at ecosystem-relevant scales? Some detective work is required.

CATCH RECONSTRUCTION

As part of our investigations of the impacts of fishing on marine ecosystems, the Sea Around Us project undertakes "catch reconstructions" that aim to improve upon the data reported by countries. The aim is to estimate total catches, in contrast to officially reported landings, which are usually represented by the data reported by countries to the FAO. In many developing countries, catches related to small-scale artisanal and subsistence fisheries are either missing or under-represented in official fisheries statistics, while in developed countries, recreational and commercial under-reporting are often the missing components. Hence, extractions of marine resources are

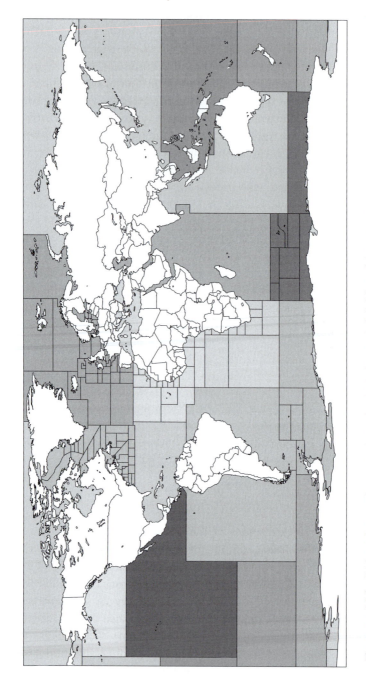

Figure 5.1 Major FAO catch reporting areas shown by shaded areas. Subdivision of these areas represents additional spatial detail available by using records from regional organizations.

usually underestimated in official statistics, as are their economic and social importance (Zeller *et al.*, 2006b). Various approaches can be conceived to retroactively estimate catches in cases where reliable time series data are lacking (Pauly, 1998). The approach used here applies a "re-estimation" methodology to approximate historic catch time series (Zeller *et al.*, 2006a, 2007). Such an approach typically requires assumption-based inferences and interpolations, but is justified, despite data uncertainties, given the less acceptable alternative outcome, namely that subsequent users of the available data will interpret non-reported or missing data as zero catches. Thus, our catch reconstruction approach consists of six general steps:

(1)   Identification of existing nationally reported catch time series, e.g., country-specific catch datasets, and comparison with the equivalent data as reported by the FAO on behalf of the country in question. This allows identification of data transfer efficiencies between national statistics departments and the FAO, and may help identify data uncertainties in the reported data;

(2)   Identification of fisheries sectors, time periods, species, gears, etc. not covered by (1), i.e., missing catch data, via literature searches and consultations;

(3)   Searches for available alternative information sources that contain additional data or qualitative information related to items identified in (2). This may involve extensive literature searches and consultations with local experts;

(4)   Development of data anchor points in time for missing data items, and their expansion to countrywide catch estimates;

(5)   Interpolation for time periods between data anchor points for missing data items; and

(6)   Estimation of final total catch time series for total catch, combining reported catches (1) and interpolated, countrywide expanded missing data series (5).

As countries differ in terms of fisheries sectors, their coverage of reported data, and available alternative information, this general approach has to be adjusted to each country situation, making this approach more resource and labor intensive. However, the final result is a "value-added" accounting that builds on the officially reported data as presented by the FAO on behalf of each country. The differences between estimates of total catch and reported landings vary considerably between cases, and currently range from essentially no missing data in the case of Cuba (Baisre *et al.*, 2003), a 30% underreporting by

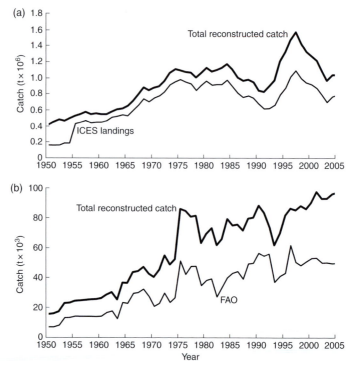

Figure 5.2 Total reconstructed catch (t) for (a) the nine Baltic Sea countries (Denmark, Estonia, Finland, Germany, Latvia, Lithuania, Poland, Russia, and Sweden), being 30% higher then reported landings from the ICES catch statistics database, 1950–2007 (Source: Rossing *et al.* 2010); and (b) the United Republic of Tanzania compared to FAO reported catch, 1950–2005, indicating the missing data from Zanzibar. Source: Jacquet *et al.* (2010).

Baltic Sea countries (Figure 5.2a; Rossing, Booth, and Zeller, 2010), missing whole parts of (nationally recorded and reported) country data as in the case of Tanzania (Figure 5.2b, Jacquet *et al.*, 2010), or underreporting of total catches of 2–7-fold shown for US Pacific Island areas (Figure 5.3; Zeller *et al.*, 2007) or 60 times for Russian arctic fisheries (Pauly and Swartz, 2007).

As part of the continued development of the spatial catch database of the Sea Around Us project, we progressively substitute FAO country data with reconstructed datasets, which amend FAO data by the value-added components as derived through catch reconstruction.

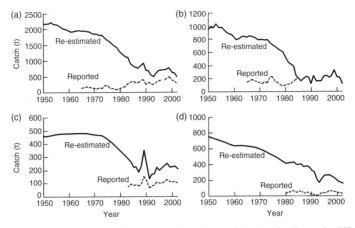

Figure 5.3 Reconstructed catches of small-scale fisheries for the major US flag island areas in the Western Pacific versus the officially reported statistics. Total re-estimated catches (a) summed over all the major US flag island areas of the Western Pacific considered here; (b) for Guam; (c) for the Commonwealth of the Northern Mariana Islands; and (d) for American Samoa. Source: Zeller *et al.* (2007).

WHERE WAS THE CATCH TAKEN?

If we accept that reported catches by the FAO and other bodies, and increasingly reconstructed catches, represent the bulk of catches by fishing countries, and if we further accept that it is reported accurately by statistical reporting areas, however large they may be, then what is required is a way of assigning the catch more accurately within those reporting areas. The first step that came to mind was that many of the records represent the catch of a taxon (usually a species), and that many of these have known limits to their ecological distributions. For example, Atlantic cod (*Gadus morhua*) has a well known global distribution (Figure 5.4), outside of which catches of this species are nonexistent. This would limit where cod could be taken realistically in the FAO's north-eastern and north-western Atlantic statistical reporting area. Though these limits were not documented well for many commercial species when the Sea Around Us project started, there were maps of distributions for several major commercial species of fishes produced by the FAO, and descriptions of ranges of many others available from FishBase (www.fishbase.org). It was necessary to refine these significantly, adding many more commercial species, especially invertebrate species. This became a major work in itself and has led to a range of

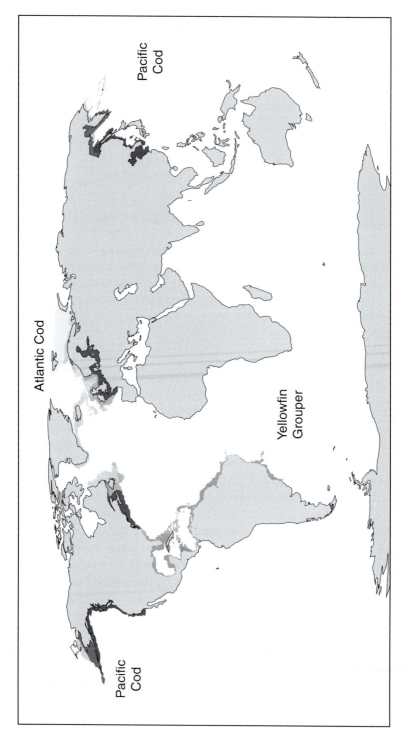

Figure 5.4 The global distributions of a few major commercial species such as are used in the allocation of catches to spatial cells.

publications (e.g., Close *et al.*, 2006), online pages (www.seaaroundus. org/topic/species/), and a body of knowledge that allows us to look at a variety of other research areas, including climate change (Cheung *et al.*, 2008, 2009)

The next important point about determining where a species could be caught is to recognize that fish are caught by fishing fleets, that most fishing is done in inshore and shelf waters currently claimed as national EEZs, and as such, usually requires some agreement to access the resource by other countries. The FAO had the makings of a database of fishing agreements, which we subsequently expanded. We also had to consider that many agreements were confidential or otherwise not documented, and that some fishing is done without agreement, i.e., illegally. Often agreements were for only certain types of fish, and sometimes there were quotas imposed. We had to include all information about fishing patterns. For example, if we did not find an agreement for country *x* to fish in the inshore waters of country *y*, then we may still find evidence of such occurrences through descriptions in trade magazines, etc. By studying where fishing fleets fish, whose waters they access, and when, it is possible to also greatly limit the possible areas where reported catch is taken.

There remains one persistent problem. Too often catches are reported only by vague groupings such as the highly aggregated group "Miscellaneous Marine Fishes" in the global statistics. Without knowing the taxonomic identity of species included, it is very hard to use information about specific distributions or even to use fishing agreements. Obviously more detective work is required.

WHAT KIND OF FISH IS THAT ANYWAY?

Since the beginning of the Sea Around Us project in 1999, we have made several attempts to "disaggregate" the highly aggregated reporting groups used by the FAO and others. Mostly, we deduce the identity of the mysterious individual taxa included in the aggregated group based on what was reported elsewhere, what taxa occur there, and even what taxa are likely not to be specifically named. The most recent attempts are very conservative and require that candidates for the disaggregation process must be taxa that have been previously reported by the reporting country and/or by one of its nearest geographic neighbors. Though this approach does not introduce new taxa to regional catches, it does not necessarily always provide suitable candidates either. Sometimes we are still left wondering. Nevertheless, with the identity of most catches deduced, it is then possible to use taxonomic distribution limits to effectively limit the possible catch areas for most species. Even more useful was the development of measures of habitat suitability within the taxonomic limits (Cheung *et al.*, 2007). For example, it was logical to conclude that many "reef" fishes normally require the presence of reef habitat, and that some areas are richer, and will hence support more abundance than other areas. Many species have a complex range of needs and these can be combined to sculpt gradients of likely abundance for most of them. Our project did much work collaborating with other groups to get detailed global maps of critical habitats such as coral reefs, seagrasses, and mangroves. This allows us to determine that more catch is likely to have come from some areas than others.

WHO IS REALLY FISHING?

It has become a common practice for some fishing companies to save money or increase fishing access by "reflagging" their vessels. This means that, although the vessels or company would normally be considered as nationality *x*, they flag their vessel as if it were from another country, a so-called "flag of convenience." Many countries allow this practice but it causes confusion for fisheries managers and researchers alike. For example, it seems strange that the small nation of Belize would be fishing in European waters, until you determine that these are actually European vessels reflagged with the Belize flag. Determining the real identity of the fishing nation is important to work out which nation is actually getting the benefits from fishing, but more immediately, it is required to know how to apply our knowledge about which countries are allowed to fish where. Reversing the reflagging process is necessary to determine who is really fishing.

HOW WERE THEY FISHING?

Different types of fishing gear have widely varying characteristics. Some gear such as trawl gear has been implicated in much damage to bottom structures and habitats. Some use much more fuel than others. Knowing how the fish were caught can be important in trying to assess the likely impacts. Working with The Nature Conservancy, we were able to determine the common associations between the use of different types of fishing gears and their target species (Watson *et al.*, 2006a). These associations change from country to country, by region, and over time. For example, trawling is more common now than it was in the 1950s. Using this information, we were able to associate catches with the likely gear used to catch it.

HOW MUCH IS IT WORTH?

It is important to determine what the value of the catch is because it motivates the fishing process and determines how decisions are made, and what benefits flow. The price of fish products varies greatly from country to country, by species of fish, and from year to year. Fish products are a true global commodity and are widely traded. Often the catch consumed in one country could have come from huge distances. A global ex-vessel price database was assembled from a wide range of international sources (Sumaila *et al.*, 2007; Sumaila *et al.*, this volume). Subsequently, a process was developed by our project to use this database to provide prices and landed values for all reported global catches.

GLOBAL CATCH DATABASE

A harmonized global catch database of over one million records is prepared from a wide range of data sources. Strictly speaking, the data presented are largely landings, as this database currently includes predominantly retained and landed catches. Increasingly, however, we are replacing reported landings with reconstructed total catch data to more comprehensively account for total extractions of marine resources. Global totals by major grouping per year (including tentative estimates of discards and illegal, unreported, and unregulated [IUU] catches) are shown in Figure 5.5a, while the landed values (in real US$, adjusted for inflation to the year 2000) for the reported catches are shown in Figure 5.5b (excluding discards and IUU).

PUTTING IT ALL TOGETHER

The global catch database is used to allocate the tonnages (as well as landed values) reported to a system of 30-minute latitude by 30-minute longitude cells. These spatial cells were small enough to be used to look at the impacts of fishing in ecosystem models and in other analyses. The allocation process used the taxonomic identity of the catch (after the disaggregation process described earlier) to allocate catch to the system of spatial cells based on our taxonomic distributions. Information about fishing access and fishing patterns of reporting

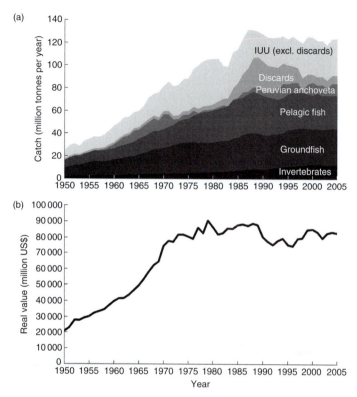

Figure 5.5 Time series of (a) global fisheries catches, adjusted for over-reporting by China (Watson and Pauly, 2001), and including estimates of discards (Zeller and Pauly, 2005) and IUU. Graph modified from Pauly *et al.* (2002). Note that the data for discards and IUU catches are tentative, but their values are likely to be considerable; and (b) real landed value in million US$ (inflation adjusted to the year 2000) for reported global fisheries catches as determined by the Sea Around Us project (note that this excludes discards and IUU). These data are based on the global ex-vessel fish price database described in Sumaila *et al.* (2007).

countries was also used (sometimes after the effects of reflagging were removed) (Watson *et al.*, 2004). This process was successful, as it passed a test of self-consistency. Catches could have come only from the reporting areas, only from areas within this reporting area where the reported taxa are found, and only in locations where the country reporting it can fish. All reported catch was accounted for. Broadly speaking, the dominant pattern that emerges is one where inshore and rich upwelling areas supply most of the global catch (Figure 5.6). Our results also reflected other known patterns in fish catches such as

Catch Rate

t • km²·yr⁻¹

- >15
- <15
- <10
- <7
- <5
- <3
- <1.5
- <1.0
- <0.5
- <0.3

Figure 5.6 Global catches expressed as catch rates for each of more than 180 000 global spatial cells for 2001.

latitudinal gradients. With further work and collaboration, we estimated not only what catch was caught by which country in which spatial cells, but also how much fuel was used in the process (Tyedmers *et al.*, 2005), what gear was likely used (Watson *et al.*, 2006a), what the value of the catch taken was (Sumaila *et al.*, 2007), and how much discards (Zeller and Pauly, 2005) and IUU may likely add to total global catches. We make catch and landed value data taken in the waters of a country and large marine ecosystems widely available on our website (www.seaaroundus.org).

USES OF MAPPED CATCH

How are these mapped catch data used? They have led to maps showing where the use of destructive fishing gear types such as bottom trawl nets is expanding (Watson *et al.*, 2006b; Halpern *et al.*, 2008). They have been used to try to validate national statistics. For example, these data were instrumental in showing that there were problems with reporting of Chinese catches to the FAO, leading to distortions of world trends in catch data (Watson and Pauly, 2001). They have also been used to look at resource competition between fishing and marine mammals (Kaschner, 2004) and nesting seabirds (Kaschner *et al.*, 2007). They have allowed us to examine the ecological footprints of fishing activities (Sea Around Us, 2008), and to present and discuss the impacts of fisheries at the scale of large marine ecosystems (Pauly *et al.*, 2008). These data have facilitated the valuation of global marine resources (Sumaila *et al.*, 2007) and marine biodiversity (Worm *et al.*, 2006), and the impacts of overfishing (Srinivasan *et al.*, 2008). They serve as critical input data in ecological models examining fisheries-induced changes (Christensen *et al.*, 2003, 2009) and even play a role in predicting the likely impacts of global warming (Cheung *et al.*, 2009).

FUTURE IMPROVEMENTS

What is the future of catch mapping and how can its accuracy and usefulness be improved? The key to better mapping is undoubtedly better catch data. To accomplish this requires detailed catch reconstructions for reporting countries. This will not only allow more accurate representations of catch but it will greatly improve our knowledge of historical trends (Zeller *et al.*, 2006a, 2007). Often, catch reports for early periods were only grossly estimated. We also hope to have more comprehensive distribution maps for commercial species based on improved mapping of critical habitats, such as seagrasses and mangroves. We are only beginning to have datasets that include catch that was obtained illegally or was discarded. In the future, we hope that the catch data will prove even more useful in addressing some of the major questions about marine resources such as the impacts of global warming. With more exposure of the products will hopefully come more opportunities to validate and improve the underlying databases and procedures. Work is underway to map global fishing effort, initially as independently as possible from that used to map catch – this will allow cross validation. Fishing catches cannot occur where fishing effort does not happen – moreover the catch rates will hopefully indicate broad trends in the biomass and health of commercial stocks. Assessing and evaluating human impact on global marine environments will always need accurate maps of where fishing occurs.

ACKNOWLEDGMENTS

Without the ideas, continual enthusiasm, support, and guidance of Daniel Pauly this work would not exist. The Pew Charitable Trusts, Philadelphia, have supported these efforts since the beginning through their funding of the Sea Around Us project, a scientific cooperation between the Pew Environment Group and the University of British Columbia. The authors would also like to acknowledge major inputs by Adrian Kitchingman and William Cheung.

REFERENCES

Baisre, J. A., Booth, S. and Zeller, D. (2003) Cuban fisheries catches within FAO area 31 (Western Central Atlantic): 1950–1999. From Mexico to Brazil: Central Atlantic fisheries catch trends and ecosystem models. Fisheries Centre Research Report. Vancouver, Canada.

Cheung, W. W. L., Close, C., Lam, V., Watson, R. and Pauly, D. (2008) Application of macroecological theory to predict effects of climate change on global fisheries potential. *Marine Ecology Progress Series*, 365, 187–197.

Cheung, W. W. L., Lam, V. W. Y., Sarmiento, J. L., Kearney, K., Watson, R., Zeller, D. and Pauly, D. (2009) Large-scale redistribution of maximum fisheries catch potential in the global ocean under climate change. *Global Change Biology*, 16, 24–35.

Cheung, W. W. L., Watson, R., Morato, T., Pitcher, T. J. and Pauly, D. (2007) Intrinsic vulnerability in the global fish catch. *Marine Ecology Progress Series*, 333, 1–12.

Christensen, V., Guénette, S., Heymans, J. J., Walters, C. J., Watson, R., Zeller, D. and Pauly, D. (2003) Hundred-year decline of North Atlantic predatory fishes. *Fish and Fisheries*, 4, 1–24.

Christensen, V., Walters, C. J., Ahrens, R., Alder, J., Buszowski, J., Christensen, L. B., Cheung, W. W. L., Dunne, J., Froese, R., Karpouzi, V., Kaschner, K., Kearney, K., Lai, S., Lam, V., Palomares, M. L. D., Peters-Mason, A., Piroddi, C., Sarmiento, J. L., Steenbeek, J., Sumaila, R., Watson, R., Zeller, D. and Pauly, D. (2009) Database-driven models of the world's large marine ecosystems. *Ecological Modelling*, 220, 1984–1996.

Close, C., Cheung, W. W. L., Hodgson, S., Lam, V., Watson, R., and Pauly, D. (2006) Distribution ranges of commercial fishes and invertebrates. In Palomares, M. L. D., Stergiou, K. I. and Pauly, D., eds., *Fishes in Databases and Ecosystems*. Fisheries Centre Research Reports 14(4). Vancouver, Canada: Fisheries Centre, University of British Columbia, pp. 27–37.

Halpern, B. S., Walbridge, S., Selkoe, K. A., Kappel, C. V., Micheli, F., D'Agrosa, C., Bruno, J. F., Casey, K. S., Ebert, C., Fox, H. E., Fujita, R., Heinemann, D., Lenihan, H. S., Madin, E. M. P., Perry, M. T., Selig, E. R., Spalding, M., Steneck, R. and Watson, R. (2008) A global map of human impact on marine ecosystems. *Science*, 319, 948.

Jacquet, J., Fox, H., Motta, H., Ngusaru, A. and Zeller, D. (2010) Few data but many fish: marine small-scale fisheries catches for Mozambique and Tanzania. *African Journal of Marine Science*, 32(2), 197–206.

Kaschner, K. (2004) Modeling and mapping of resource overlap between marine mammals and fisheries on a global scale. PhD thesis, unpublished, University of British Columbia.

Kaschner, K., Ready, J. S., Agbayani, E., Rius, J., Kesner-Reyes, K., Eastwood, P. D., South, A. B., Kullander, S. O., Rees, T. and Close, C. H. (2007) AquaMaps: predicted range maps for aquatic species. Available online: www.aqua-maps.org.

Pauly, D. (1998) Rationale for reconstructing catch time series. *EC Fisheries Cooperation Bulletin*, 11, 4–7.

Pauly, D., Alder, J., Booth, S., Cheung, W., Christensen, V., Close, C., Sumaila, U., Swartz, W., Tavakolie, A. and Watson, R. (2008) Fisheries in large marine ecosystems: descriptions and diagnoses. In Sherman, K. and Hempel, G., eds., *The UNEP Large Marine Ecosystems Report: A Perspective on Changing Conditions in LMEs of the World's Regional Seas*. The Hague: UNEP, pp. 23–40.

Pauly, D., Christensen, V., Guénette, S., Pitcher, T. J., Sumaila, U. R., Walters, C. J., Watson, R. and Zeller, D. (2002) Towards sustainability in world fisheries. *Nature*, 418, 689–695.

Pauly, D. and Swartz, W. (2007) Marine fish catches in North Siberia (Russia, FAO Area 18). Reconstruction of marine fisheries catches for key countries and regions (1950–2005). Fisheries Centre Research Report. Vancouver, Canada: Fisheries Centre, University of British Columbia.

Rossing, P., Booth, S. and Zeller, D. (2010) Total marine fisheries extractions by country in the Baltic Sea: 1950–present. Report to the Baltic Sea 2020 Foundation, Stockholm, Sweden. Fisheries Centre Research Reports 18 (1). Vancouver, Canada: Fisheries Centre, University of British Columbia.

Sea Around Us (2008) A global database on marine fisheries and ecosystems. Vancouver, Canada: Fisheries Centre, University British Columbia.

Srinivasan, U. T., Carey, S. P., Hallstein, E., Higgins, P. A. T., Kerr, A. C., Koteen, L. E., Smith, A. B., Watson, R., Harte, J. and Norgaard, R. B. (2008) The debt of nations and the distribution of ecological impacts from human activities. *Proceedings of the National Academy of Sciences*, 105, 1768–1773.

Sumaila, U. R., Marsden, A. D., Watson, R. and Pauly, D. (2007) Global Ex-vessel Fish Price Database: Construction and applications. *Journal of Bioeconomics*, 9, 39–51.

Tyedmers, P.H., Watson, R. and Pauly, D. (2005) Fueling global fishing fleets. *AMBIO: A Journal of the Human Environment*, 34, 635–638.

Watson, R., Christensen, V., Froese, R., Longhurst, A., Platt, T., Sathyendranath, S., Sherman, K., O'Reilly, J., Celone, P. and Pauly, D. (2003) Mapping fisheries onto marine ecosystems for regional, oceanic and global integrations. In Hempel, G. and Sherman, K., eds., *Large Marine Ecosystems of the World 12: Change and Sustainability*. Amsterdam: Elsevier Science.

Watson, R., Kitchingman, A., Gelchu, A. and Pauly, D. (2004) Mapping global fisheries: sharpening our focus. *Fish and Fisheries*, 5, 168–177.

Watson, R. and Pauly, D. (2001) Systematic distortions in world fisheries catch trends. *Nature*, 414, 534–536.

Watson, R., Revenga, C. and Kura, Y. (2006a) Fishing gear associated with global marine catches I: database development. *Fisheries Research*, 79, 97–102.

Watson, R., Revenga, C. and Kura, Y. (2006b) Fishing gear associated with global marine catches II: trends in trawling and dredging. *Fisheries Research*, 79, 103–111.

Worm, B., Barbier, E.B., Beaumont, N., Duffy, J.E., Folke, C., Halpern, B.S., Jackson, J.B.C., Lotze, H.K., Micheli, F., Palumbi, S.R. and Watson, R. (2006) Impacts of biodiversity loss on ocean ecosystem services. *Science*, 314, 787–790.

Zeller, D., Booth, S., Craig, P. and Pauly, D. (2006a) Reconstruction of coral reef fisheries catches in American Samoa, 1950–2002. *Coral Reefs*, 25, 144–152.

Zeller, D., Booth, S., Davis, G. and Pauly, D. (2007) Re-estimation of small-scale fishery catches for US flag-associated island areas in the western Pacific: the last 50 years. *Fishery Bulletin*, 105, 266–277.

Zeller, D., Booth, S. and Pauly, D. (2006b) Fisheries contributions to GDP: underestimating small-scale fisheries in the Pacific. *Marine Resource Economics*, 21, 355–374.

Zeller, D. and Pauly, D. (2005) Good news, bad news: global fisheries discards are declining, but so are total catches. *Fish and Fisheries*, 6, 156–159.

Zeller, D. and Pauly, D. (2007) Reconstruction of marine fisheries catches for key countries and regions (1950–2005). Fisheries Centre Research Report. Vancouver, Canada: Fisheries Centre, University of British Columbia.

KONSTANTINOS I. STERGIOU AND VILLY CHRISTENSEN

6

Fishing down food webs

INTRODUCTION

Fishing affects all levels of biological organization, from individuals to populations, affecting their demographic and genetic characteristics, as well as communities and ecosystems, (e.g., Hutchings, 2000; Law, 2000; Jackson *et al.*, 2001; Daskalov, 2002; Pauly *et al.*, 2002). Among the many effects of fishing, those referring to the marine ecosystem (i.e., trophic structure and energy flow within the ecosystem) have received particular attention in recent years.

This attention is in part because of the pioneering work of Pauly *et al.* (1998a). These authors used the world fisheries catch statistics (published annually by the Food and Agriculture Organization of the United Nations, FAO) and the trophic level (TL; Froese, this volume) of all species or groups of species contributing to the catches and showed that the mean trophic level of the catches had declined significantly, by about 0.5 TL, over a 50-year period. This decline was observed for global marine catches as well as for the majority of the different FAO subareas of the Atlantic, Indian, and Pacific Oceans, and the Mediterranean and Black Seas. This process, which, as will be shown here, has had a strong impact on fisheries science, is now known as "fishing down marine food webs" (FDFW). In fact, FDFW gave "flesh and bones" to something that many fisheries scientists intuitively had in their minds, while formal descriptions were few (Christensen, 1996).

FDFW was very enthusiastically received by the media (Baron, this volume) as well as by a large part of the scientific community. It was directly or indirectly conceived to imply a gradual reduction in the abundance of large, long-lived, high TL organisms and a replacement by smaller, short-lived, low TL, more productive invertebrates and fish, for both catches and ecosystems. Indeed, later work by different groups

Ecosystem Approaches to Fisheries: A Global Perspective, ed. V. Christensen and J. Maclean. Published by Cambridge University Press. © Cambridge University Press 2011.

showed that the biomass of high TL fishes drastically declined over different spatial and temporal scales (e.g., Christensen *et al.*, 2003; Myers and Worm, 2003; Rosenberg *et al.*, 2005).

In the following sections we (1) describe the criticisms raised and the elaboration of the FDFW concept as a response; (2) present a review of subsequent studies showing evidence on FDFW at smaller spatial scales; (3) briefly present the ecology behind the FDFW process, which sets the basis for the development of an ecological index; (4) briefly describe the "mental environment" within which FDFW was conceived and realized; and finally (5) present a preliminary history and the impact of FDFW on marine ecology and its teaching using citation analysis.

We limit our analysis to marine ecosystems, but note that fishing down and overexploitation overall is as big or a bigger problem in the inland waters of the world (Allan *et al.*, 2005).

FDFW: THE DEBATE, RESPONSE, AND ELABORATION

An FAO group (Caddy *et al.*, 1998; Caddy and Garibaldi, 2000) responded immediately to the 1998 FDFW paper by identifying a series of biases that might have affected the results of the study. These biases were due to (1) low taxonomic resolution of FAO landings; (2) use of coarse TL estimates and the fact that the original analysis did not account for ontogenetic changes in TL; (3) the fact that landing data do not reflect ecosystem abundances; (4) the fact that fishing technology and prices (especially for low-TL pelagic species) affect landings and provide a distorted picture of FDFW, aggravated by eutrophication of coastal areas, such as in the Mediterranean, which causes an increase in low-TL species and a decrease in high-TL demersal species, lowering the mean TL of the catches; and (5) the fact that aquaculture production was also included in the catch numbers used in the analysis.

The reservations raised and the subsequent debate greatly contributed to the ramification and subtlety of process for analyzing FDFW, and caused refinement of the analysis and the development of a variety of tools for tracking FDFW.

Pauly and colleagues (Pauly *et al.*, 1998b, 2001; Pauly and Palomares, 2000, 2001; Valtysson and Pauly, 2003; Pauly and Watson, 2005) showed that the low taxonomic resolution of the landings (point (1) above) and omission from the original analysis of accounting for fishing-induced ontogenetic TL changes in the implicated species (point (2) above) both had a relatively small effect, (but see Jennings et al., 2001, for the intensity of the effect of ontogenetic TL changes), and contribute to underestimation rather than overestimation of the FDFW trends. Here, it is also worthy of mention that region- and species-specific TL estimates for a variety of species in the Aegean Sea are highly correlated (Karachle and Stergiou, 2008) with the general TL estimates that are available in FishBase (ww.fishbase.org). This also implies that the use of a single TL value for each species causes minimal bias for identification of FDFW trends.

As for the question of whether landings are fair indicators of ecosystem abundances (point (3) above), it is beyond doubt that landings generally are good indicators for many reasons, such as the globalization of fisheries; the recent intense horizontal and vertical expansion of fisheries, which has led to the exploitation of resources in almost all marine habitats (Pauly et al., 1998b, 2002); and, in recent years, total allowable catches of many stocks are set based on some estimate of their biomass. FDFW has also been identified from trawl survey trend data (Christensen, 1998; Jennings et al., 2002; Pinnegar et al., 2002; Gascuel et al., 2007). Also, Coll et al. (2008) found a decreasing trend in the biomass-weighted TL of ecosystem groups in the Catalan Sea during 1975–2003, indicating that FDFW is not just a fishery artifact.

Eutrophication and changes in fishing patterns (e.g., expansion), often price-related (point (4) above), may indeed be more of a problem for FDFW analysis. The effect of eutrophication (i.e., of bottom-up effects) can be detected with the Fishing-in-Balance (FiB) index, which examines an aspect of FDFW.

The reasoning behind the FiB index is, that as we fish down the food web, it should be possible to extract higher catches. Given that the energy transfer efficiency (TE) between trophic levels on the average is around 10% (Pauly and Christensen, 1995), the production will on the average be 10 times higher at the trophic level below a given level. The FiB index as defined (Pauly et al., 2000) for year y of a time series is calculated as,

$$FiB_y = \log\left(\frac{Catch_y \cdot TE^{TL-1}}{Catch_1 \cdot TE^{TL-1}}\right)$$

where $Catch_y$ is the catch of a species in year y, TE is the system energy transfer efficiency (typically ~10% per TL), TL is the trophic level for the species, and the denominator has the same terms for the first year of the time series. The calculation of the FiB index thus calls for time series of catches and their mean trophic levels, as well as estimates of the transfer efficiencies between trophic levels. The FiB index is 0 (= log 1) for the first year of the time series; it does not vary during periods where change in catches is compensated for by a change in TL – the fishing is "in balance" then. Increasing FiB values indicate a geographic expansion (Bhathal and Pauly, 2008), while decreasing values may indicate contraction or collapse of the fishery in question.

The FiB index is based on the finding that productivity is higher at lower trophic levels. Christensen (1996) in a review for the FAO on managing fisheries involving top predators and their prey explored the relationship between fish catches and the trophic levels at which the fisheries operate as part of a FDFW treatise. Based on 36 data-driven models of aquatic ecosystems, he found a strong negative correlation between catch and trophic level. Taking the data points at face value, the indications were that operating one trophic level lower results in a yield 8.3 times higher – surprisingly close to the 10 times that theoretically should be expected if trophic transfer efficiency is around 10% (Pauly and Christensen, 1995).

An example of the use of the FiB index is presented in Figure 6.1 for Greek waters. From the upper panel in Figure 6.1, it is apparent that there was no FDFW in the case of the landings of all species combined; in fact, the mean TL of the landings increased from the late 1970s to 2001 (Stergiou, 2005). This increase was the result of the effect of eutrophication and fisheries expansion, mediated by modernization of the fleet (i.e., larger boats, higher tonnage and engine horsepower, improved gears, use of high-end technology equipment), in open-sea areas, previously largely inaccessible because of strong winds (e.g., in southern waters) and at great depths (Stergiou, 2005). As a result, new "resources" started to be exploited, mostly at TL > 3.5. Yet, FDFW was evident when only the landings of species with TL > 3.5 were considered (Figure 6.1, upper panel). These aspects were nicely captured from the FiB index (Figure 6.1, lower panel), and also have relevance for why Essington et al. (2006) did not find any decline in catches for high TL groups in many areas.

The analysis of Pauly et al. (1998a) did not include aquaculture data; a re-analysis (Pauly et al., 1998b) that specifically excluded taxa likely to be farmed confirmed its main result (point (5) above). However, had aquaculture data been included, it would have masked rather than generated FDFW as an artifact. In fact, the TL of aquaculture is increasing because we are farming up the food web (Stergiou et al., 2009; Pullin, this volume).

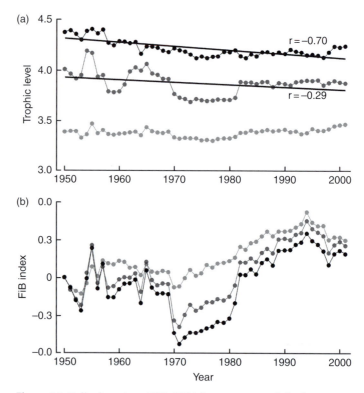

Figure 6.1 Hellenic waters, 1950–2001. Long-term trends in the mean trophic level of landings (a) and in the FIB index (b) for all fish species (trophic levels > 2, light gray) and for fish species having trophic levels > 3.5 (gray) and > 3.75 (black).

In addition to the above-mentioned issues, Pauly and colleagues (Pauly and Palomares, 2005; Freire, 2005) also identified another potential source of bias in the form of spatial aggregation of landings (e.g., when mixing shelf and oceanic fisheries, which often target different species), which can strongly mask FDFW.

In a noted study based on the catch series from the Sea Around Us project for 48 large marine ecosystems (LMEs), Essington *et al.* (2006) found that the FDFW effect could be demonstrated in 30 of the 48 LMEs. The authors emphasized, however, that only 9 of 30 LMEs showed declining catches of the higher trophic level species (TL > 4.0), indicating that the process should be called "fishing through the food web [FTFW]," rather than "fishing down the food web." The study is refreshing in that it questions the widespread assumption that FDFW is associated with fishing down of high TL species, but its finding is contrary to the widespread biomass reductions in high TL species that we have witnessed in ecosystems worldwide. Further studies are called for to evaluate what has happened to the biomasses of high TL species in the world oceans, though indications are that they have declined drastically over the last 60 years, as discussed earlier. We also note that even if the study did not find a decrease in the aggregated catch level of high TL species in many of the LMEs, another study which looked at high TL species in the catches found that within the tuna groups there was widespread FTFW (Pauly and Palomares, 2005). Aggregation tends to mask FDFW, and serial depletions are a part of fisheries, even if rarely documented.

FDFW AT FINER SPATIAL SCALES

Since the appearance of the first FDFW paper, numerous studies have been made to identify FDFW processes at finer spatial scales than the global and regional used for the original study. As an example, a workshop of the Mediterranean Science Commission (CIESM) on "Fishing down Mediterranean food webs?" was held in July 2000 on Corfu Island, Greece, for this purpose, and with the participation of 31 scientists from 12 countries (Durand, 2000).

There have been many similar studies in areas ranging from Icelandic waters in the north to Chile in the south (Table 6.1), based on a variety of catch data (such as FAO or national data, reconstructed FAO or national data, survey data), over different time periods and spatial scales, and on TL estimates derived from either diet or isotope studies. These studies have shown that FDFW is a global phenomenon with TL changes per decade varying between 0.02 and 0.28, and that the trends are stronger than originally suggested by Pauly *et al.* (1998a). We see this as a reflection of the strength of the FDFW concept as an indicator for capturing the ecological effects of fishing.

ECOLOGICAL EFFECTS OF FISHING

It is generally well known that fishing removes the largest individuals, both within and between species, at a fast pace and at a large scale (e.g., Christensen *et al.*, 2003; Myers and Worm, 2003). Large-bodied fish are generally positioned high in the food webs (Froese and Pauly, 2000), and can represent large, rather unproductive biomasses in an unimpacted system (Warne, 2008; Bakun, this volume). In addition, fishing removes the structure-forming benthic fauna (e.g., sponges, bivalves),

Table 6.1 *Studies of marine ecosystems conducted to evaluate fishing-down-food-web (FDFW) effects. "TL decline" lists years with declining TL of catches for the area. BP is year before present.*

Country/Area	Years	TL decline	Source and remarks
Gulf of Thailand	1963–1982; 1963–1997	1965–1982; 1965–1997	Christensen, 1998; Pauly and Chuenpagdee, 2003
Cuban EEZ	1960–1995	1960–1995	Pauly *et al.*, 1998b; Baisre, 2000
Portuguese landings	1923–1999 1970–2005	1986–1999 1970–2005	Coelho, 2000; Baeta *et al.*, 2009; found decrease for mainland
Greek waters	1964–1997	1965–1997	Stergiou and Koulouris, 2000
Eastern Canada	1950–1997	1957–1997	Pauly *et al.*, 2001
Western Canada	1873–1996	1910–1996	Pauly *et al.*, 2001
Chinese EEZ	1950–1998	1970–1998	Pang and Pauly, 2001
Caribbean	1850 BP – 560 BP	1850 BP – 560 BP	Wing and Wing, 2001; found decline in TL between two time periods studied
Celtic Sea	1945–1998	1946–2000	Pinnegar *et al.*, 2002; based on trophic levels estimated from stable nitrogen isotopes
North Sea	1925–1996	Inconclusive	Jennings *et al.*, 2002
Iceland	1900–1999	1918–1999	Valtysson and Pauly, 2003
Ebrie Lagoon, West Africa	1978–1980	1978–1980	Albaret and Lae, 2003
Western Mediterranean	1973–1999	None	Pinnegar *et al.*, 2003; could not demonstrate FDFW
Venice Lagoon	1945–2001	1990–1998	Libralato *et al.*, 2004
Quoddy Region, Bay of Fundy	1700s–	1900s	Lotze and Milewski, 2004
Senegal, Guinea	1981–1998	1981–1998	Laurans *et al.*, 2004
Gulf of California	1980–2000	1980–2000	Sala *et al.*, 2004
Cantabrian Shelf, Spain	1983–1999	1983–1999	Sanchez and Olaso, 2004
Gulf of Maine	5000 BP – now	5000 BP – now	Steneck *et al.*, 2004
Cueva de Nerja, Spain	17000 BP – 4300 BP	Inconclusive	Morales and Roselló, 2004
West Central Atlantic	1950–2000; 1950–2000	1950–2000; 1950–2000	Pauly and Palomares, 2005

Table 6.1 (*cont.*)

Country/Area	Years	TL decline	Source and remarks
World, tuna and billfishes	1950–2000	1950–2000	Pauly and Palomares, 2005
World, all fishes	1950–2000	1950–2000	Pauly and Watson, 2005
North Sea	1973–2000	1973–2000	Heath, 2005
Uruguay	1990–2001	1990–2001	Milessi *et al.*, 2005
Chile, central	1979–1999	1979–1999	Arancibia and Neira, 2005
Mexico	1940–2001	1940–1960	Perez-Espana *et al.*, 2006; steady/increasing TL since 1960
World LMEs	1950–2000	In 30 of 48 LMEs	Essington *et al.*, 2006; concludes that fishing-through-the-foodweb is more common than FDFW
Japan East Sea	1958–2003	1970–2003	Tian *et al.*, 2006; excluding sardine
St. Augustine Florida	3460 BP – 2000	3460 BP – 2000	Reitz, 2004; Quitmyer and Reitz, 2006
Mauretania	1982–2007	1982–2007	Gascuel *et al.*, 2007
Argentina– Uruguay	1989–2003	1989–2003	Jaureguizar and Milessi, 2008
Gulf of St. Lawrence	1985–1995	1985–1995	Morissette *et al.*, 2009
California Channel Isl.	14000BP		Erlandson *et al.*, 2009; Initially low TL, higher after colonization
Alaska	1893–2004	None	Litzow and Urban, 2009; TL increased over time

which are replaced by small benthic animals. Finally, fishing indirectly increases eutrophication of the water column by constantly resuspending sediment. These effects all serve to increase the ecosystem production/biomass ratio. Thus, fishing may initially drive ecosystems to be more productive – this is indeed the foundation for fisheries, that maximum productivity is obtained when biomasses are reduced below their carrying capacity levels. If, or often as, biomasses are reduced to below the level that produces maximum sustainable yield

(Christensen, 2010), productivity declines, a common result of overexploitation.

Fisheries thus eventually cause the system to be less productive, and from an ecological perspective, less resilient, and less mature *sensu* Odum (1971). The fishing pressure induces ecological adaptations and evolutionary trends, and favors species that generally have short longevity, small size, small length at maturity, high growth rates, and high productivity. Such favored species are also generally characterized by low TLs. As a result, fishing increases the relative abundance of low TL species in the ecosystems and, consequently, in landings.

FDFW IN PRACTICE

In 2004, the Conference of the Parties to the Convention on Biological Diversity (CBD), which has 193 countries as parties, adopted the Marine Trophic Index (MTI) as one of eight indicators identified by CBD for "immediate testing" toward reaching the target to "achieve by 2010 a significant reduction in the current rate of biodiversity loss" (CBD, 2004). The MTI is actually the mean TL of fisheries landings above a certain level, which may vary between locations. This restriction is included because MTI puts emphasis on the effects of fishing on the relative abundance of high-TL fishes, which are generally more threatened than low-TL species (Pauly and Watson, 2005).

As described earlier, FDFW trends may be masked by poor quality landing data. It must be stressed here that the FDFW concept is not responsible for the often poor quality landing data and the poor availability of TL estimates (i.e., area–time–length species-specific estimates) in the same sense that an ARIMA statistical technique is not responsible for the low quality of the time series on which it is applied (e.g., see Stergiou *et al.*, 2003). Thus, future research should be directed toward alleviating these two shortcomings in order to fully realize the strength and usefulness of the MTI. The catch reconstruction emphasized by the Sea Around Us project (Watson *et al.*, this volume) should help to resolve these problems.

FDFW: AN IDEA WHOSE TIME HAD COME

The FDFW idea was not born at an arbitrary time: it was an idea whose time had come. In order to show this, we examine the "mental environment" within which the idea was conceived and realized.

The early work of Pauly (e.g., Pauly, 1979, 1980) was related to the collection and analysis of published life-history parameters (i.e., growth parameters, K, L_∞, natural mortality) for a large number of fish stocks. In addition, in the late 1980s, Pauly and colleagues (Pauly and Gaschütz, 1979) developed ELEFAN (later merged with an FAO initiative to become FiSAT; Pauly and Garcia, 1994), a specialized software for the estimation of various parameters of fish from length-frequency data. ELEFAN was widely used by fisheries scientists, mainly in the tropics, but also elsewhere. This also led to an accumulation of a plethora of such data on fishes. In order for the accumulated data from these two sources not to disappear in the grey literature, Froese and Pauly (Pauly and Froese, 1991a,b; Froese and Pauly, 1990) developed FishBase in the late 1980s (see Palomares and Bailly, this volume).

During the same period, Christensen and Pauly started the development of the Ecopath ecosystem modeling approach (e.g., Christensen and Pauly, 1991, 1992), based on Polovina's original formulation (Polovina, 1984). Over the following decade, FishBase and Ecopath both evolved into highly valuable research, information, and ecological modeling tools (e.g., Walters *et al.*, 1997, 1999; Christensen and Walters, 2004, this volume) respectively.

This development had an important impact on fisheries science and marine ecology in general. The more or less synchronous development of these tools, which are strongly related to the TL concept, widened the scope of fisheries science. This is because it led to large-scale (regional or global) studies aimed at exploring status and impact of fisheries (e.g., Christensen *et al.*, 1991; Pauly and Christensen, 1995; Pauly *et al.*, 1998a) in which previously reported pieces of information were transformed into robust scientific knowledge. This made possible the answering of "high-order questions," which refer to large spatial and time scales across many species and/or functional groups, that is, to the most interesting questions in ecology and conservation (Pimm, 1991).

But what has the scientific impact of the FDFW paper been so far in the cold language of citation analysis? This issue is taken up in the next section.

FDFW: SCIENTIFIC IMPACT

The impact of a scientific paper is shown by citations to it in the primary literature by other scientists; if it is cited often, the knowledge is assimilated into reviews and monographs and then into textbooks (Bauer, 1994). We used two indices to measure the impact of the FDFW paper: (1) penetration into the primary "general ecological" literature, and (2) penetration into "general ecology" textbooks (in which the percentage of aquatic references is less than 15%; Stergiou and Browman, 2005).

A search for the FDFW paper in February 2010 revealed 961 citations in the Institute for Scientific Information (ISI) Web of Knowledge[SM] database, 947 citations in the Scopus[TM] database and 1580 citations using Google Scholar[TM]. The following analyses were based on the Scopus[TM] citations.

What do more than 950 citations imply in terms of overall impact? Overall, about 38 million items were published during 1900–2005, half of which had not been cited at all at the end of that period (Garfield, 2006). Of the remainder, only 34 000 items (0.17%) had been cited more than 400 times, and the FDFW paper belongs to this small group of highly cited published items.

The mean impact factor for *Science* in 1998–2006 was about 25. This implies that the average *Science* paper receives 25 citations per year. Based on that, the impact-factor-anticipated citations of the FDFW paper, which appeared in 1998, should have been 275 citations (11 years · 25 citations/year). Thus, the FDFW paper performed about 3–4 times better than the average *Science* paper.

The FDFW paper had a very good penetration into the primary "ecological" and review literature. From the 947 Scopus[TM] citations 45 were self-citations. The remaining 902 citations (i.e., excluding self-citations) were derived from 151 journals more than half of which were "general," mainly ecological, journals (88 journals, 56.1%, accounting for 350 out of the 902 citations, 38.8%). Also, 15 journals (10%) in which FDFW was cited specialize in reviews (i.e., included the word review in the title), accounting for 73 citations (8.1%). Nine out of these 15 journals (6%) were general journals (i.e., not including aquatic or relevant terms in the title), accounting for 25 citations (2.8%).

The FDFW paper was cited in many aquatic or general books (in more than 250 titles, based on a search from Google Books[TM] in February 2010 on the exact title of the FDFW publication). It was cited in many aquatic "ecology" textbooks (Jennings *et al.*, 2001; Walters and Martell, 2004; Sumich and Morrissey, 2004; Bone and Moore, 2008), and textbooks related to environmental sciences and conservation (Gaston and Spicer, 2004; Thompson and Turk, 2004; Lindenmayer and Burgman, 2005; Hunter and Gibbs, 2006; King, 2007; Simmons *et al.*, 2008) and in recent general ecology textbook (Schmitz, 2007; Miller and Spoolman, 2008).

REFERENCES

Albaret, J. -J. and Lae, R. (2003) Impact of fishing on fish assemblages in tropical lagoons: the example of the Ebrie lagoon, West Africa. *Aquatic Living Resources*, 16, 1.

Allan, J. D., Abell, R., Hogan, Z., Revenga, C., Taylor, B. W., Welcomme, R. L. and Winemiller, K. (2005) Overfishing of inland waters. *Bioscience*, 55, 1041–1051.

Arancibia, H. and Neira, S. (2005) Long-term changes in the mean trophic level of Central Chile fishery landings. *Scientia Marina*, 69, 295–300.

Baeta, F., Costa, M. J. and Cabral, H. (2009) Changes in the trophic level of Portuguese landings and fish market price variation in the last decades. *Fisheries Research*, 97, 216–222.

Baisre, J. A. (2000) Chronicles of Cuban Marine Fisheries (1935–1995): Trend analysis and fisheries potential. FAO Fisheries Technical Paper, 394. Rome: FAO.

Bauer, H. (1994) *Scientific Literacy and the Myth of the Scientific Method.* Urbana-Champaign, IL: University of Illinois Press.

Bhathal, B. and Pauly, D. (2008) "Fishing down marine food webs" and spatial expansion of coastal fisheries in India, 1950–2000. *Fisheries Research*, 91, 26–34.

Bone, Q. and Moore, R. (2008) *Biology of Fishes.* New York, NY: Routledge.

Caddy, J. F., Csirke, J., Garcia, S. M. and Grainger, R. J. (1998) How pervasive is "fishing down marine food webs"? *Science*, 282, 1383a.

Caddy, J. F. and Garibaldi, L. (2000) Apparent changes in the trophic composition of world marine harvests: the perspective from the FAO capture database. *Ocean & Coastal Management*, 43, 615–655.

CBD (2004) Annex I, decision VII/30. The 2020 biodiversity target: a framework for implementation. *Decisions from the Seventh Meeting of the Conference of the Parties of the Convention on Biological Diversity.* Kuala Lumpur.

Christensen, V. (1996) Managing fisheries involving predator and prey species. *Reviews in Fish Biology and Fisheries*, 6, 417–442.

Christensen, V. (1998) Fishery-induced changes in a marine ecosystem: insight from models of the Gulf of Thailand. *Journal of Fish Biology*, 53, 128–142.

Christensen, V. (2010) MEY = MSY. *Fish and Fisheries*, 11, 105–110.

Christensen, V., Guenette, S., Heymans, J. J., Walters, C. J., Watson, R., Zeller, D. and Pauly, D. (2003) Hundred-year decline of North Atlantic predatory fishes. *Fish and Fisheries*, 4, 1–24.

Christensen, V. and Pauly, D. (1991) *A Guide to the ECOPATH II Software System (Version 2.0).* Manila, Philippines: ICLARM.

Christensen, V. and Pauly, D. (1992) *A Guide to the Ecopath II Software System (Version 2.1).* Manila, Philippines: ICLARM.

Christensen, V., Trinidad-Cruz, A., Paw, J., Torres, J., Jr. and Pauly, D. (1991) Appendix 6. Catch and potential of major fisheries resource systems in tropical and subtropical areas. In *A Strategic Plan for International Fisheries Research.* Manila, Philippines: ICLARM.

Christensen, V. and Walters, C. J. (2004) Ecopath with Ecosim: methods, capabilities and limitations. *Ecological Modelling*, 172, 109–139.

Coelho, M. L. (2000) "Pandora's Box" in fisheries: is there a link between economy and ecology? In Briand, F., ed., *Fishing Down the Mediterranean Food Webs?* CIESM Workshop Series 12. Kerkyra, Greece: CIESM.

Coll, M., Palomera, I., Tudela, S. and Dowd, M. (2008) Food-web dynamics in the South Catalan Sea ecosystem (NW Mediterranean) for 1978–2003. *Ecological Modelling*, 217, 95–116.

Daskalov, G. M. (2002) Overfishing drives a trophic cascade in the Black Sea. *Marine Ecology Progress Series*, 225, 53–63.

Durand, F., ed. (2000) Fishing Down the Mediterranean Food Webs? Proceedings of a CIESM Workshop held in Kerkyra, Greece, July 26–30, 2000, CIESM Workshop Series No 12. Kerkyra, Greece: CIESM.

Erlandson, J. M., Rick, T. C. and Braje, T. J. (2009) Fishing up the food web? 12 000 years of maritime subsistence and adaptive adjustments on California's Channel Islands. *Pacific Science*, 63, 711–724.

Essington, T. E., Beaudreau, A. H. and Wiedenmann, J. (2006) Fishing through marine food webs. *Proceedings of the National Academy of Sciences of the United States of America*, 103, 3171–3175.

Freire, K. D. (2005) Fishing impacts on marine ecosystems off Brazil, with emphasis on the northeastern region. Ph.D. thesis University of British Columbia, Vancouver.

Froese, R. and Pauly, D. (1990) FishBase: An information system to support fisheries and aquaculture research. *Fishbyte*, 8, 21–24.

Froese, R. and Pauly, D., eds. (2000) *FishBase 2000: Concepts, Design and Data Sources.* Los Baños, Philippines: ICLARM.

Garfield, E. (2006) The history and meaning of the journal impact factor. *Journal of the American Medical Association*, 295, 90.

Gascuel, D., Labrosse, P., Meissa, B., Sidl, M. O. T. and Guenette, S. (2007) Decline of demersal resources in North-West Africa: an analysis of Mauritanian trawl-survey data over the past 25 years. *African Journal of Marine Science*, 29, 331–345.

Gaston, K. and Spicer, J. (2004) *Biodiversity: An Introduction.* Oxford, UK: Blackwell.

Heath, M. R. (2005) Changes in the structure and function of the North Sea fish foodweb, 1973–2000, and the impacts of fishing and climate. *ICES Journal of Marine Science*, 62, 847.

Hunter, M. and Gibbs, J. (2006) *Fundamentals of Conservation Biology*, 3rd edn. Oxford, UK: Wiley-Blackwell Science.

Hutchings, J. A. (2000) Collapse and recovery of marine fishes. *Nature*, 406, 882–885.

Jackson, J. B. C., Kirby, M. X., Berger, W. H., Bjorndal, K. A., Botsford, L. W., Bourque, B. J., Bradbury, R. H., Cooke, R., Erlandson, J., Estes, J. A., Hughes, T. P., Kidwell, S., Lange, C. B., Lenihan, H. S., Pandolfi, J. M., Peterson, C. H., Steneck, R. S., Tegner, M. J. and Warner, R. R. (2001) Historical overfishing and the recent collapse of coastal ecosystems. *Science*, 293, 629–638.

Jaureguizar, A. J. and Milessi, A. C. (2008) Assessing the sources of the fishing down marine food web process in the Argentinean-Urugnayan Common Fishing Zone. *Scientia Marina*, 72, 25–36.

Jennings, S., Greenstreet, S. P. R., Hill, L., Piet, G. J., Pinnegar, J. K. and Warr, K. J. (2002) Long-term trends in the trophic structure of the North Sea fish community: evidence from stable-isotope analysis, size-spectra and community metrics. *Marine Biology*, 141, 1085–1097.

Jennings, S., Kaiser, M. J. and Reynolds, J. D. (2001) *Marine Fisheries Ecology*. Oxford, UK: Blackwell Science.

Karachle, P. K. and Stergiou, K. I. (2008) The effect of season and sex on trophic levels of marine fishes. *Journal of Fish Biology*, 72, 1463–1487.

King, M. (2007) *Fisheries Biology, Assessment and Management*. 2nd edn. Oxford, UK: Wiley Blackwell.

Laurans, M., Gascuel, D., Chassot, E. and Thiam, D. (2004) Changes in the trophic structure of fish demersal communities in West Africa in the three last decades. *Aquatic Living Resources*, 17, 163–173.

Law, R. (2000) Fishing, selection, and phenotypic evolution. *ICES Journal of Marine Science*, 57, 659–668.

Libralato, S., Pranovi, F., Raicevich, S., Da Ponte, F., Giovanardi, O., Pastres, R., Torricelli, P. and Mainardi, D. (2004) Ecological stages of the Venice Lagoon analysed using landing time series data. *Journal of Marine Systems*, 51, 331.

Lindenmayer, D. and Burgman, M. (2005) *Practical Conservation Biology*. Collingwood, Victoria, Australia: CSIRO.

Litzow, M. A. and Urban, D. (2009) Fishing through (and up) Alaskan food webs. *Canadian Journal of Fisheries and Aquatic Sciences*, 66, 201–211.

Lotze, H. K. and Milewski, I. (2004) Two centuries of multiple human impacts and successive changes in a North Atlantic food web. *Ecological Applications*, 14, 1428–1447.

Milessi, A. C., Arancibia, H., Neira, S. and Defeo, O. (2005) The mean trophic level of Uruguayan landings during the period 1990–2001. *Fisheries Research*, 74, 223.

Miller, G. and Spoolman, S. (2008) *Essentials of Ecology*. Pacific Grove, CA: Brooks/ Cole Pub Co.

Morales, A. and Roselló, E. (2004) Fishing down the food web in Iberian prehistory ? A new look at the fishes from Cueva de Nerja (Málaga, Spain). Antibes, Petits Animaux et Sociétés Humaine du complément Alimentaire aux Ressources Utilitaires, XXIVe rencontres internationales d'archéologie et d'histoire d'Antibes.

Morissette, L., Castonguay, M., Savenkoff, C., Swain, D. P., Chabot, D., Bourdages, H., Hammill, M. O. and Hanson, J. M. (2009) Contrasting changes between the northern and southern Gulf of St. Lawrence ecosystems associated with the collapse of groundfish stocks. *Deep-Sea Research Part II-Topical Studies in Oceanography*, 56, 2117–2131.

Myers, R. A. and Worm, B. (2003) Rapid worldwide depletion of predatory fish communities. *Nature*, 423, 280–283.

Odum, E. P. (1971) *Fundamentals of Ecology*. Philadelphia: W. B. Saunders Co.

Pang, L. and Pauly, D. (2001) Part 1 Chinese marine capture fisheries from 1950 to the late 1990s: the hopes, the plans and the data. In Watson, R., Pang, L. and Pauly, D., eds., The Marine Fisheries of China: Development and Reported Catches. Fisheries Centre Research Report 9(2). Vancouver, Canada: Fisheries Centre, University of British Columbia, pp. 1–27.

Pauly, D. (1979) *Theory and Management of Tropical Multispecies Stocks*, ICLARM Studies and Reviews 1. Manila, Philippines: ICLARM.

Pauly, D. (1980) On the interrelationships between natural mortality, growth parameters, and mean environmental temperature in 175 fish stocks. *ICES Journal of Marine Science*, 39, 175–192.

Pauly, D. and Christensen, V. (1995) Primary production required to sustain global fisheries. *Nature*, 374, 255–257 [Erratum in Nature, 376: 279].

Pauly, D., Christensen, V., Dalsgaard, J., Froese, R. and Torres, F. (1998a) Fishing down marine food webs. *Science*, 279, 860–863.

Pauly, D., Christensen, V., Guénette, S., Pitcher, T. J., Sumaila, U. R., Walters, C. J., Watson, R. and Zeller, D. (2002) Towards sustainability in world fisheries. *Nature*, 418, 689–695.

Pauly, D., Christensen, V. and Walters, C. (2000) Ecopath, Ecosim, and Ecospace as tools for evaluating ecosystem impact of fisheries. *ICES Journal of Marine Science*, 57, 697–706.

Pauly, D. and Chuenpagdee, R. (2003) Development of fisheries in the Gulf of Thailand large marine ecosystem: analysis of an unplanned experiment. In Hempel, G. and Sherman, K., eds. *Large Marine Ecosystems of the World: Change and Sustainability*. Amsterdam: Elsevier Science.

Pauly, D. and Froese, R. (1991a) FishBase: assembling information on fish. *Naga*, 14, 10–11.

Pauly, D. and Froese, R. (1991b) The FishBase Project ... or how scattered information on fish can be assembled and made useful for research and development. EC Fisheries Cooperation Bulletin, Commission of the European Communities, Brussels, Belgium, DG VIII/D/5.

Pauly, D., Froese, R. and Christensen, V. (1998b) How pervasive is "fishing down marine food webs"? *Science*, 282, 1383a.

Pauly, D. and Garcia, S. (1994) Announcing the release of FiSAT (version 1.0). *Naga*, 17, 46–47.

Pauly, D. and Gaschütz, G. (1979) A simple method for fitting oscillating length growth data, with a program for pocket calculator. International Council for the Exploration of the Sea. Council Meeting 1979/G: 24. Demersal Fish Committee, 26 pp.

Pauly, D. and Palomares, M. L. D. (2000) Approaches for dealing with three sources of bias when studying the fishing down marine food web phenomenon. In Durand, F., ed., *Fishing down the Mediterranean Food Webs?* Proceedings of a CIESM Workshop held in Kerkyra, Greece, July 26–30, 2000, CIESM Workshop Series No 12. Kerkyra, Greece: CIESM.

Pauly, D. and Palomares, M. L. D. (2001) Chapter 4. Fishing down marine food webs: an update. In Bendell-Young, L. and Gallaugher, P., eds., *Waters in Peril*. Norwell, MA: Kluwer Academic Publishers.

Pauly, D. and Palomares, M. L. (2005) Fishing down marine food webs: it is far more pervasive than we thought. *Bulletin of Marine Science*, 76, 197–211.

Pauly, D., Palomares, M. L., Froese, R., Sa-a, P., Vakily, M., Preikshot, D. and Wallace, S. (2001) Fishing down Canadian aquatic food webs. *Canadian Journal of Fisheries and Aquatic Sciences*, 58, 51–62.

Pauly, D. and Watson, R. (2005) Background and interpretation of the "Marine Trophic Index" as a measure of biodiversity. *Philosophical Transactions of the Royal Society, Biological Sciences*, 360, 415–423.

Perez-Espana, H., Abarca-Arenas, L. G. and Jimenez-Badillo, M. D. (2006) Is fishing-down trophic web a generalized phenomenon? The case of Mexican fisheries. *Fisheries Research*, 79, 349–352.

Pimm, S. (1991) *The Balance of Nature? Ecological Issues in the Conservation of Species and Communities*. Chicago, IL: University of Chicago Press.

Pinnegar, J. K., Jennings, S., O'Brien, C. M. and Polunin, N. V. C. (2002) Long-term changes in the trophic level of the Celtic Sea fish community and fish market price distribution. *Journal of Applied Ecology*, 39, 377–390.

Pinnegar, J. K., Polunin, N. V. C. and Badalamenti, F. (2003) Long-term changes in the trophic level of western Mediterranean fishery and aquaculture landings. *Canadian Journal of Fisheries and Aquatic Sciences*, 60, 222–235.

Polovina, J. J. (1984) Model of a coral reef ecosystem I. The ECOPATH model and its application to French Frigate Shoals. *Coral Reefs*, 3, 1–11.

Quitmyer, I. R. and Reitz, E. J. (2006) Marine trophic levels targeted between AD 300 and 1500 on the Georgia Coast, USA. *Journal of Archaeological Science*, 33, 806–822.

Reitz, E. J. (2004) "Fishing down the food web": a case study from St. Augustine, Florida, USA. *American Antiquity*, 69, 63–83.

Rosenberg, A. A., Bolster, W. J., Alexander, K. E., Leavenworth, W. B., Cooper, A. B. and Mckenzie, M. G. (2005) The history of ocean resources: modeling cod biomass using historical records. *Frontiers in Ecology and the Environment*, 3, 84–90.

Sala, E., Aburto-Oropeza, O., Reza, M., Paredes, G. and Lopez-Lemus, L. G. (2004) Fishing down coastal food webs in the Gulf of California. *Fisheries*, 29, 19–25.

Sanchez, F. and Olaso, I. (2004) Effects of fisheries on the Cantabrian Sea shelf ecosystem. *Ecological Modelling*, 172, 151.

Schmitz, O. (2007) *Ecology and Ecosystem Conservation*. Washington DC: Island Press.

Simmons, I., Brazel, A., Day, J., Keller, E., Gregory, K., Yanez-Arancibia, A. and Sylvester, A. (2008) *Environmental Science: A Student's Companion*. London: Sage Publications Ltd.

Steneck, R. S., Vavrinec, J. and Leland, A. V. (2004) Accelerating trophic-level dysfunction in kelp forest ecosystems of the Western North Atlantic. *Ecosystems*, 7, 323.

Stergiou, K. (2005) Fisheries impact on trophic levels: longterm trends in Hellenic waters. In Papathanassiou, E. and Zenetos, A., eds., *State of the Hellenic Marine Environment*. Athens: Hellenic Center for Marine Research, pp. 326–329.

Stergiou, K. and Browman, H. (2005) Imbalances in the reporting and teaching of ecology from limnetic, oceanic and terrestrial eco-domains: bridging the gap between aquatic and terrestrial ecology. *Marine Ecology Progress Series*, 304, 292–297.

Stergiou, K. I. and Koulouris, M. (2000) Fishing down the marine food webs in the Hellenic seas. In Briand, F., ed., *Fishing Down the Mediterranean Food Webs?* CIESM Workshop Series 12. Kerkyra, Greece: CIESM.

Stergiou, K., Tserpes, G. and Peristeraki, P. (2003) Modelling and forecasting monthly swordfish catches in the Eastern Mediterranean. *Scientia Marina*, 67, 283–290.

Stergiou, K. I., Tsikliras, A. C. and Pauly, D. (2009) Farming up Mediterranean food webs. *Conservation Biology*, 23, 230–232.

Sumich, J. and Morrissey, J. (2004) *Introduction to the Biology of Marine Life*. Ontario, Canada: Jones & Bartlett Publishers.

Thompson, G. and Turk, J. (2004) *Earth Science and the Environment*, Pacific Grove, CA: Brooks/Cole Pub Co.

Tian, Y. J., Kidokoro, H. and Watanabe, T. (2006) Long-term changes in the fish community structure from the Tsushima warm current region of the Japan/East Sea with an emphasis on the impacts of fishing and climate regime shift over the last four decades. *Progress in Oceanography*, 68, 217–237.

Valtysson, H. and Pauly, D. (2003) Fishing down the food web: an Icelandic case study. In Guðmundsson, E. V., ed., *Proceedings of a Conference held in Akureyri, Iceland, on April 6–7th 2000 Competitiveness within the Global Fisheries*. Akureyri, Iceland: University of Akureyri.

Walters, C., Christensen, V. and Pauly, D. (1997) Structuring dynamic models of exploited ecosystems from trophic mass-balance assessments. *Reviews in Fish Biology and Fisheries*, 7, 139–172.

Walters, C., Pauly, D. and Christensen, V. (1999) Ecospace: prediction of mesoscale spatial patterns in trophic relationships of exploited ecosystems, with emphasis on the impacts of marine protected areas. *Ecosystems*, 2, 539–554.

Walters, C. J. and Martell, S. J. D. (2004) *Fisheries Ecology and Management*. Princeton, NJ: Princeton University Press.

Warne, K. (2008) An uneasy Eden. *National Geographic*, July.

Wing, S. R. and Wing, E. S. (2001) Prehistoric fisheries in the Caribbean. *Coral Reefs*, 20, 1.

7

Aquaculture up and down the food web

INTRODUCTION

This chapter celebrates the author's long association with Daniel Pauly, as a colleague in the International Center for Living Aquatic Resources Management (ICLARM) from 1979 to 1999, and as a firm friend and collaborator in aquatic science thereafter. Daniel's prolific contributions to fisheries science have included many that pertain, directly or indirectly, to aquaculture. Growth and reproduction of all fish, wild and farmed, are determined by the same natural laws and this has provided perfect "Pauly territory" for fundamental research and development of new methods.

Daniel and his many collaborators and disciples have also taken concepts and methods developed for capture fisheries management and ecology and have adapted and/or applied them to important areas in aquaculture research and development, for example, fish egg development (Pauly and Pullin, 1988, 1997), food consumption of fishes (Palomares and Pauly, 1996), growth of farmed fish (Pauly and Hopkins, 1983; Hopkins et al., 1988; Pauly et al., 1988; Mair and Pauly, 1993; Prein et al., 1993; Prein and Pauly, 1993; Van Dam and Pauly, 1995; Moreau and Pauly, 1999), industrial fisheries that provide ingredients for fish feeds (Pauly and Tsukayama, 1987; Pauly et al., 1989; Pauly et al., 2005); invasive alien species (Pullin et al., 1997), mortality estimations (Hopkins and Pauly, 1993), predator–prey relationships (Hopkins et al., 1982), tilapia biology and farming (Peters, 1983; Pullin et al., 1996) and trophic modeling (Lightfoot et al., 1993; Ruddle and Christensen, 1993; Van Dam et al., 1993). To this author's knowledge, there is no example of any aquaculture scientist making comparable contributions to capture fisheries science.

Ecosystem Approaches to Fisheries: A Global Perspective, ed. V. Christensen and J. Maclean. Published by Cambridge University Press. © Cambridge University Press 2011.

In this chapter, the main storyline is omnivory. The omnivory of humans is noted first, followed by definitions of aquaculture and of its main types of growout operations (based on feeds and feeding habits) and a brief look at its history from a food web perspective. The diversity of farmed aquatic plants and fish (meaning finfish and aquatic invertebrates) is then summarized and options for feeding farmed fish are reviewed: herbivory and detritivory, farm-based feeds and various fertilizers, low value/trash fish, fishmeal and fish oil, rendered livestock wastes and other sources of protein/energy, and lipid ingredients for fish feeds. The focus throughout is on fish that are fed by farmers in semi-intensive and intensive farming systems, rather than on bivalve mollusks and other invertebrates that filter feed on natural aquatic productivity. Their future is assured, provided that their farm environments are well cared for and their products made safe to eat. The feeding "crunch" in aquaculture concerns not these self-feeders, but rather the farming of fish that must be fed by farmers.

The chapter concludes with speculation about the future of aquaculture and suggestions for further research: pursuit of responsible, ecological aquaculture in partnership and synergy with other sectors; facilitating feed-efficient omnivory in intensive aquaculture; and exploring further and operationalizing, for the domestication and genetic improvement of farmed fish, Daniel Pauly's hypotheses about the constraints to and potentials for fish growth and reproduction, particularly with oxygen as the main controlling factor.

THE SUMMITS OF THE GLOBAL FOOD WEB: OMNIVOROUS HUMAN STOMACHS

The Rev. William Buckland (1784–1856), who has been dubbed the world's first paleoecologist, used to pronounce at his lectures: "The stomach, sir, rules the world. The great ones eat the less and the less the lesser still" (Brook, 1993). The Rev. Buckland's eldest son Frank (1826–1880), who became a famous name in fisheries science, devoted much of his career to research and development for aquaculture. He established a museum of fish and oyster culture, was appointed Fish Culturist to the Queen (Victoria), and pursued a lifetime's ambition of "eating his way through the whole animal kingdom though (having) problems with the blue-bottle and the mole" (Gardner-Thorpe, 2001). His breadth of omnivory would not sit well today with modern consumers who have ethical constraints to their food choices (e.g., the vegan or organic food movement; www.ifoam.org). However, omnivory has undoubtedly contributed much to the success of the genus *Homo*. Eaton *et al.* (1996) mentioned the consumption of some 329 plant and game animal species by paleolithic humans. Fish and other hunted and gathered aquatic species have also figured prominently in the diets of most coastal, floodplain, and island dwellers throughout recorded history; e.g., in ancient Egypt (Brewer and Friedman, 1989). Unfortunately, many modern humans, rich and poor, are now in a nutrition transition to worse health through over-consumption of fats and sugars (e.g., Popkin *et al.*, 2001), and under-consumption of fruit and vegetables, and indeed fish.

Bayvel (2005) estimated that the average UK citizen consumes during her/his lifetime: 550 poultry, 36 pigs, 36 sheep, and 8 cows. Perhaps over a lifetime of 70 years, the average global citizen might eat 13 kg of fish/year (i.e., 250 g/week), which could represent between 1820 and 3640 individual finfish yielding 500 g or 250 g of consumable fish products, respectively. The numbers and weights eaten would, of course, vary greatly among countries and not always according to wealth; for example, average per caput fish consumption in Switzerland is less than 15 kg/year, compared with more than 60 kg/year in Japan (Delgado *et al.*, 2003). However, fish and fish products are vital contributors to food security and well being worldwide, for their contributions to healthy, diversified human diets (e.g., Elvevoll and James, 2000; ADB, 2005; Anon., 2006) and as ingredients for livestock and pet feeds.

AQUACULTURE DEFINITIONS

For the purposes of this chapter, aquaculture is defined simply as the *farming* of aquatic organisms. Aquaculture has two main operational components, which are usually under different management: mass production of seed (eggs, larvae, fry, fingerlings, etc.), usually from broodstock held in hatcheries though sometimes by collection from wild populations; and growout of seed to marketable size in a wide variety of production facilities (artificial or natural substrates in open waters, cages, pens, ponds, raceways, recirculation systems, and rice-fields). The early life-history stages (postlarvae and fry) of farmed fin-fish, including herbivorous and omnivorous species, such as carps and tilapias, are typically carnivorous, with heavy reliance on consumption of zooplankton, benthic meiofauna, etc. However, the amounts of animal protein-rich feeds (mass-cultured live food organisms and arti-ficial feeds) that are used for fish seed production are insignificant compared to those required for growout. This chapter is focused on feeding farmed fish in growout systems, and these are commonly separated into three main categories, based on their main sources of fish feeds: extensive aquaculture, having sole dependence upon the natural production of foods in farm waters, such as plankton and detrital organisms; semi-intensive aquaculture, receiving supplementary feeds and/or enhanced production of natural food by fertilization; and intensive aquaculture, receiving largely or exclusively nutritionally complete feeds.

AQUACULTURE HISTORY, FROM A FOOD WEB PERSPECTIVE

From its earliest history, principally in China (ca. 475 BC) and also in ancient Egypt (e.g., Brewer and Friedman, 1989) and Hawaii (Costa-Pierce, 1987), aquaculture was closely integrated with crop and vegetable husbandry, and with water resources management. Traditional (pre-1949) Chinese inland aquaculture, widely copied in neighboring countries, was essentially ecosystem-based management of carp ponds and their surrounding farmlands. Well-conceived ratios of carp species, having different feeding habits, were farmed as polycultures. Substantial feeds were generated in the fishponds, as plankton and detritus, while vegetation to feed the grass carp (*Ctenopharygodon idella*) and organic fertilizers were sourced on-farm or in the surrounding area. The grass carp was the pivotal species, acting as a "living manuring machine," and was estimated to generate enough plankton to feed two silver carp (*Hypophthalmichthys molitrix*) and one bighead carp (*Aristichthys nobilis*) (Edwards, 2004). Integrated farming systems (crop–livestock–fish and wastewater/excreta-fed) were further developed in China and copied in neighboring countries (e.g., Edwards *et al.*, 1988; Mathias *et al.*, 1994). However, the rapid growth of human populations required ever-higher production per unit area of farmed land and water through intensification. For aquaculture, this meant stocking fish at higher densities and feeding them mainly on externally sourced, formulated feeds. As this trend proceeds, integrated farming systems inevitably lose their integration with other farm enterprises, and polycultures of fish with different feeding habits lose their natural feeding niches and synergisms. The intensively fed fishpond becomes ultimately a feedlot system with its fish, whether farmed in monoculture or polyculture, becoming "feed pelletivores."

This trend is already well advanced in China, where integrated farming peaked in the 1980s (Edwards, 2004). In the main fish farming areas of China, livestock and vegetable farming are usually no longer integrated with aquaculture, though the dominant pond-farmed fish is still the grass carp, fed with grass cut on- and off-farm, supplemented with pelleted feeds. The same trend is also underway in carp farming in Andhra Pradesh, India. There, polyculture of six carp species (three indigenous and three alien) has long been advocated by scientists, but has recently been largely discontinued, on the initiative of the farmers themselves, in favor of farming together just two indigenous carps – the high priced (naturally zooplanktivorous) catla (*Catla catla*) and the lower priced (but relatively omnivorous) rohu (*Labeo rohita*). Over the course of two decades, annual yields from these increasingly intensive carp ponds have grown from about 1500 kg/ha to as much as 16 000 kg/ha, though there is still much variation, with typical yields from 800 to 10 000 kg/ha (Nandeesha, 2001). Here, a semi-intensive polyculture, mainly reliant on inorganic and organic (manuring) fertilization to produce natural feeds, has become a more intensive – though still, strictly speaking, semi-intensive – duoculture. Its fish are fed on natural feeds (green water and detritus) produced by liming (1000 kg/ha/year), inorganic fertilization (2300 kg/ha/year), manuring (20 000 kg/ha/year), and on supplemental feeds (10–20% oilcakes, 80–90% rice bran; 27 000 kg/ha/year).

Apart from ancient carp ponds in monasteries and castles, etc., and some examples of coastal lagoon aquaculture, most aquaculture in the developed world began from the outset as intensive aquaculture. For example, highly unnatural but cost-effective feed sources, such as slaughterhouse wastes, were used for rearing salmonids from about 1860 (Rumsey, 1994). Nutritionally complete formulated fish feeds, based on scientific determinations of the nutrient requirements of fish, have a much shorter, essentially post-1950s history, as reported by Halver (1989). Though natural feeds produced *in situ* have remained important in freshwater pond aquaculture, as described by Hepher (1988), semi-intensive and intensive aquaculture is increasingly based on feeds formulated from any nutritional resources that will yield good fish growth and survival, and profits, irrespective of the extent to which these resources correspond to the natural feeds of the farmed species.

Tacon *et al.* (2006) estimated that in 2003 at least 41.6% of production of farmed finfish and crustaceans was derived from feeding them with farm-based and/or industrially manufactured feeds and reported, citing Gill (2005), that 19.5 million tonnes of the latter were used in aquaculture in 2004, comprising 3% of the global total of industrially manufactured animal feeds (620 million tonnes). The remainder was used for feeding poultry (38%), pigs (32%), cattle (24%), and other animals (3%).

MODERN AQUACULTURE

With the world's capture fisheries in deep crisis, and their restoration in many cases proving to be difficult or impossible, aquaculture has become the main hope of many nations, rich and poor, for increasing and then sustaining their fish supply (e.g., Brugère and Ridler, 2004). FAO aquaculture statistics and the national statistics from which they are derived are beset with uncertainties, including underreporting of production from small-scale farmers and the need to explore further the very large aquaculture production reported from China, which was 30 614 918 tonnes of farmed fish in 2004, comprising 67.3% of the world total. It is clear, however, that the recent growth of aquaculture has been spectacular, especially when compared with other food production sectors. Pullin *et al.* (2007) presented the following analysis of the growth of aquaculture from 1950 to 1997, by reconciling pre-1984 FAO aquaculture data (which were combined with fish catch data) and post-1984 data, which are reported separately (Figure 7.1).

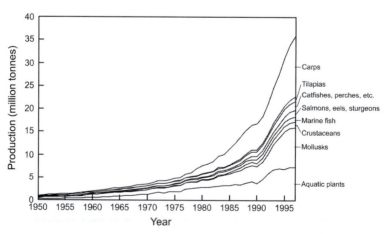

Figure 7.1 Contribution of major groups to aquaculture production, 1950–1997, based on FAO statistics. Source: Pullin *et al.* (2007).

Moffitt (2005), using FAO data, estimated the average percentage annual growth rate (APR) of aquaculture from 1990 to 2002 as 10.2%, compared to the following APRs for other sectors: "oceanic fish catch," 0.5%; beef, 0.8%; mutton, 1.5%; pork, 2.5%; eggs, 3.6%; and poultry, 4.8%. In 1970, aquaculture contributed only about 3.9% of world fish supply. Its contributions in 2006 comprised 47% of the total world supply of 110 million tonnes of food fish (FAO, 2008) and will soon exceed those from capture fisheries.

Global expansion and intensification of aquaculture over the last 150 years, enabled by the increasing application of science, have usually been accompanied by its separation from other forms of agriculture, with respect to administration, institutions, and policy-making. Aquaculture is widely regarded as a separate sector within food production and/or as a separate subsector of capture fisheries, though farming and hunting have very little in common. Similar monosectoral perspectives have, until recently, typified all sectors that depend heavily upon aquatic ecosystems: agriculture, fisheries, forestry, water supply, and waste disposal. This sectoral isolationism remains a major impediment to equitable and sustainable use of natural resources.

Fortunately, intersectoral policymaking and natural resources management are increasing as ecosystem-based management becomes more widely recognized as the key to food security and to the well being of humans and their environment. From this new perspective, farmed aquatic organisms, as well as the food webs in which they are produced, are a part of agrobiodiversity, with aquatic farms and their surroundings recognized as agroecosystems. However, modern semi-intensive and intensive aquaculture, like modern crop and livestock farming, inevitably has ecological footprints far beyond its own boundaries. For example, Folke (1988), cited by Folke and Kautsky (1992), estimated that the sea surface area required for plankton production sufficient to yield the necessary ingredients for feed pellets given to cage-farmed Atlantic salmon (*Salmo salar*) is 40 000 to 50 000 times the surface area of the cages. Moreover, as Pauly and Christensen (1995) have shown, for every inhabitant of planet Earth there are only about 6 ha of sea space, of which only about 0.5 ha are productive waters, sufficient to produce about 12 kg of consumable fish per year. Similarly, Larsson *et al.* (1994) pronounced semi-intensive shrimp farming in Colombia as "one of the most resource-intensive food production systems … an ecologically unsustainable through-put system."

FARMED AQUATIC PLANTS

Farmed aquatic plants, the lowest trophic level in aquaculture, comprise (1) microalgae and cyanobacteria for direct human consumption (e.g., chlorella and spirulina) or for feeding fish seed, (2) marine macroalgae for direct human consumption and for extraction of chemicals for food and other industrial purposes, and (3) a wide diversity of freshwater macrophytes for direct human consumption and as animal fodders and organic fertilizers. With the exception of a few widely farmed seaweed species (e.g., *Laminaria japonica*, *Porphyra tenera*, and *Eucheuma cottonii*), global production of all farmed aquatic plants by species is very poorly documented. This applies particularly to the farming of floating and emergent freshwater macrophytes, which, despite their high importance and potential in developing-country aquaculture (e.g., Edwards, 1980), have yet to be adequately covered in national and FAO aquaculture or agriculture statistics.

FARMED FISH

From major aquaculture compendia published during 1972–95 and from current FAO statistics, Pullin (2007) found the following ranges of numbers of aquatic animals, actually identified to species, that have been farmed principally for consumption as human food: crustaceans, 26–79; mollusks, 20–74; other invertebrates, 4–7; finfish, 130–294; amphibians and reptiles, 3–11; all aquatic animals, 181–400. More species, mainly finfish, are farmed as ornamentals. New (2002) found merit in concentrating future aquaculture research on fewer farmed species, as in the history of domestication and farming of livestock, where about 80 species of livestock are used in farming and ranching and only 14 of these provide most of the world's supply of livestock meat and other products, though with over 6000 recognized breeds (Science Council, 2005). In aquaculture, probably as many as 500 fish species have been farmed experimentally or commercially to some extent, for food and other purposes. About 30 of these contribute probably as much as 90% of world farmed food fish production, but many other species make important contributions locally and nationally. For example, Malawi has a laudable policy of farming only its indigenous species and keeping out or eliminating alien species, in order to safeguard its rich and unique aquatic biodiversity (e.g., Msiska and Costa-Pierce, 1993).

FEEDING FARMED FISH, GENERAL
CONSIDERATIONS

There is a huge literature on the nutrient requirements of fish (e.g., National Research Council, 1977) and on sources of ingredients for the manufacture of feeds for farmed fish (e.g., Tacon, 1993; Tacon *et al.*, 2006). The most important aspect of feeding farmed fish is that all, from herbivores to carnivores, need high protein diets to grow fast; e.g., (as % crude protein in dry feed) grass carp, 23–28%; tilapias, 30–35%; salmonids, 40–55%; penaeid shrimps, 30–57% (various authors, reviewed by Hasan, 2001).

As aquaculture operations intensify, the costs of feeding fish comprise ever higher percentages of total variable production costs. For intensive, open water, cage farming of carnivorous fish, which derive no nutritional benefits from their surrounding waters, feeds typically comprise about 65% of total variable production costs. The key to successful and profitable intensification of aquaculture is least-cost formulation of fish feeds that will supply all necessary nutrient requirements, as well as fast growth with good feed conversion. The history of channel catfish (*Ictalurus punctatus*) pond farming in the US provides an example. Pauly (1974) recorded US catfish pond production at about 1000 kg/ha and predicted that it could increase at least two-fold. The FAO gives its typical current production as 1800 kg/ha, with higher production possible and with feeding costs now comprising about 40–45% of total variable production costs (FAO, 2006).

Farmed livestock are categorized broadly as monogastrics (e.g., pigs and poultry), which are typically opportunistic omnivores, and ruminants (e.g., cows and sheep), which are herbivores. No farmed livestock species is a carnivore, apart from a few minor niche market examples; e.g., dogs in some Asian countries. As an aside here, dogs are a good example of how wrong can be an assumption of obligate carnivory in a domesticated species that has naturally carnivorous wild ancestors. Carnivorous species can often be entrained to plant-rich omnivory under domestication. This author's Labrador dog moved from the Isle of Man to the Philippines in 1979 and rapidly lost condition. She was constrained (on excellent local advice) to change from a meat-rich diet to a rice- and vegetable-rich one and soon recovered well. Here, a carnivore showed its potential to become an opportunistic omnivore.

Farmed fish species naturally exhibit all modes of feeding from autotrophy in giant clams (e.g., Munro and Heslinga, 1983), through herbivory (filter feeding on phytoplankton and grazing on aquatic macrophytes) and omnivory (filter feeding on mixed plankton, consumption of detrital biota, and opportunistic predation on mixed benthic and water column species) to strict carnivory (eating fish). Following the example of livestock farming, and for sound economic reasons, it would make most sense to farm herbivorous/detritivorous fish species that, by inference from their natural diets, could be largely fed quantities of plant or microbial protein.

Gerking (1994) listed 23 families of marine fish and 21 families of freshwater fish as having members in which plants are a prominent part of the diet. Horn (1989) listed about 140 species from 20 families of "shallow water marine fish" as being substantially herbivorous, but most of these are not farmable for various reasons, including one or more of the following: small size, limited acceptability as food fish, and lack of available technology for seed production and husbandry. In this author's opinion, the most promising herbivorous candidates, that have not yet been farmed to large extents for marine and brackish water aquaculture, are the rabbitfishes, *Siganus* spp. (e.g., Duray, 1998) and, despite its small size, the Asian brackish water cichlid *Etroplus suratensis* (De Silva *et al.*, 1984, 2006). In contrast, there are undoubtedly many potential new herbivorous/detritivorous freshwater fish species for aquaculture, especially among the carps, catfishes, and tilapias. Tacon *et al.* (2006) presented 2003 data for four main categories of farmed fish based on their feeding habits (Table 7.1). Figure 7.2 shows the entire trophic pyramid of global aquaculture production in 2003,

Table 7.1 *Production in 2003 and average annual percentage growth (APR) in production (1970–2003) of major groups of farmed fish, by main feeding habits. Source: modified from Tacon* et al. *(2006).*

Group/ main feeding habit	Production in 2003	APR (%)
Filter feeding finfish	7.04 million tonnes (26.0% of farmed finfish)	8.6
Herbivorous/omnivorous finfish	16.02 million tonnes (59.3% of farmed finfish)	9.2
Carnivorous finfish	3.98 million tonnes (14.7% of farmed finfish)	10.3
Omnivorous/scavenging crustaceans	2.79 million tonnes (9.3% of farmed finfish + farmed crustaceans)	18.5

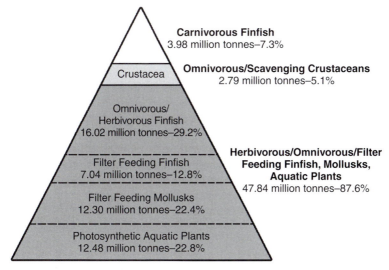

Figure 7.2 Global aquaculture production pyramid by feeding habit and nutrient supply in 2003 (million tonnes). Source: Tacon *et al.* (2006) calculated from FAO data.

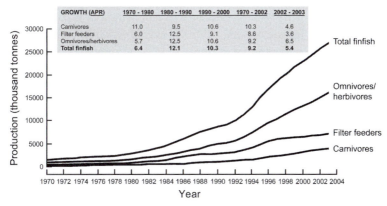

Figure 7.3 Production (thousand tonnes live weight equivalents of farmed finfish by feeding habit), 1970–2003. APR = average percentage annual growth rate. Source: Tacon *et al.* (2006), calculated from FAO data.

including farmed aquatic plants, and Figure 7.3 shows the trends, 1970–2003, in production of farmed finfish by feeding habits.

The two main questions concerning the feeding of farmed fish to produce harvests acceptable to consumers both involve assessments of biological/ecological and economic feasibility: (1) to what extent can feeds for fish on farms differ from their natural feeds; and (2) to what extent can sufficient quantities of natural or unnatural fish feeds be obtained/produced on-farm and/or sourced off-farm? Omnivory is likely to provide most of the answers.

FISHPONDS AND DETRITIVORY

Fishponds merit special consideration here because, unlike most fish cages, raceways, and other flow-through containments, they are not merely "feeds in, feces and uneaten feeds out systems," but act as producers of natural feeds and as processors of fish wastes. Schroeder (1987) conceived the fertilized fishpond as a "sunlit rumen," i.e., a digestion vessel, with autotrophs (mainly phytoplankton) and hetero-trophs (especially detrital microorganisms) at the base of simple food webs from which fish, such as carps and tilapias, could be harvested reliably and cost-effectively. Semi-intensive fishponds receiving supple-mental feeds would also fit this description. Leachates from added feed, as well as uneaten feed, always fertilize a pond to some extent, and the feces of the farmed fish fertilize it more. The sunshine on such ponds is still of immense importance, because the photosynthesis of phytoplank-ton provides much of the oxygen necessary for fish survival and growth.

Detritus is dead organic matter. It makes very important contri-butions to fish nutrition; for example, detrital nonprotein amino acids feed some tilapia populations (Bowen, 1980, 1987). However, detriti-vory in most aquatic ecosystems, especially fishponds, is actually a kind of "micro-omnivory" because detritus also supports living com-munities of bacteria, fungi, microalgae, protozoans, and miscellaneous meiofauna – rotifers, nematodes, crustaceans, etc. Understanding and managing detrital food webs in fishponds has high potential for increasing and sustaining their fish yields. This potential attracted Daniel Pauly to study the detritivorous tilapia *Sarotherodon melanotheron* in Sakumo Lagoon, Ghana (Pauly, 1974, 1976; Pauly *et al.*, 1988) and ICLARM to convene a Bellagio conference to explore detritivory and microbial food webs in aquaculture (Moriarty and Pullin, 1987).

The more intensive aquaculture becomes, however, the more arti-ficial aeration becomes essential and the less becomes its capacity to rely on sunshine and photosynthesis by phytoplankton to produce its oxygen needs. An intensively fed pond or tank, receiving nutritionally complete (or nearly so) feeds, can be conceived as a monogastric stomach rather than a rumen, and an entire intensively fed fish farm as the stomach of a large predator. The important point here is that all such fish containments are digestion vessels. The challenges for aquaculturists are to maximize their options for least-cost fish feed formulation by persuading these fish farm stomachs to be as omnivorous as possible, and to manage the autotrophic and heterotrophic food webs in farm waters for best feed conversion efficiency. For example, shrimp ponds can be inoculated with commercially available probiotics (beneficial bacteria) to improve feed conversion efficiency, shrimp health, and effluent quality (e.g., Moriarty, 1998). In these "fish farm stomachs," probiotics act rather like the cultures of lactobacilli that are ingested by humans.

FARM-BASED FEEDS AND VARIOUS FERTILIZERS

It would clearly be to the advantage of a fish farmer, particularly a resource-poor small-scale farmer, to be able to source most or all of the fish feeds and fertilizers needed for her/his aquaculture enterprise on-farm, from farm-grown resources and wastes or by-products that have no other uses with higher opportunity costs. Farmed-based feeds, such as vegetation, rice bran, and oilcakes, and farm-based fertilizers, such as livestock manure and composts, have been central to the development and success of integrated farming. However, the large literature on this topic (e.g., New *et al.*, 1993; Edwards and Allen, 2004) shows that reliance on feeds and fertilizers derived entirely from within actual fish farm or mixed enterprise/integrated farm boundaries rarely exists. Almost every fish farmer using farm-based feeds also sources some feeds, feed ingredients (e.g., soybean meal, rice bran, fishmeal), and fertilizers off-farm, though most off-farm feed ingredients (with the obvious exception of most fishmeal) are still derived from farming elsewhere. It is hard to supply the organic fertilizer requirements of aquaculture operations entirely from on-farm sources; therefore, farmers rely frequently on purchasing manures off-farm, particularly dried chicken manure, though avian influenza risks could be a future deterrent to use of this resource. Most farmers using green water systems must also lime their ponds and, if they have insufficient supplies of manure, must purchase inorganic fertilizers (especially urea and triple superphosphate) off-farm.

FISHMEAL AND FISH OIL

Intensive and semi-intensive aquaculture is often heavily dependent on feeds based on fish and fish products and this has caused many to

Table 7.2 *Fishmeal content (as % dry diets) of typical feeds given to farmed animals. Source: modified from Tacon* et al. *(2006).*

Farmed animal	Early rearing	Main growth/finishing
Pigs	5–10	3
Broiler poultry	< 3	2–5
Dairy cattle	2.5–10	5–10 (lactating)
Sheep	2.5–10	5–10 (lactating)
Carnivorous fish	35–70	20–50
Omnivorous fish	10–25	2–15
Marine shrimp	25–50	15–35

question their sustainability (e.g., Naylor *et al.*, 2000). There is a large literature on the use of fishmeal and fish oil in aquaculture feeds (e.g., Tacon *et al.*, 2006). Information concerning fishmeal and fish oil production and use is also provided by the International Fishmeal and Fish Oil Organization (IFFO; http://www.iffo.net/). Fishmeal is used to varying extents in livestock and fish feeds (Table 7.2).

Note here the relatively low proportions of fishmeal in livestock feeds. Historically, however, poultry production consumed as much as 60% of world fishmeal production. The 1997–98 El Niño caused the cost of fishmeal to rise to 3.8 times that of soybean meal. Poultry producers were forced to use much more of the latter and by 2000 were using only 24% of world fishmeal production (Jystad, 2001 cited by Tacon *et al.*, 2006). From 1988 to 2002, however, the proportion of world fishmeal and fish oil production used in aquaculture feeds grew from 10 to 46% and from 16 to 81%, respectively, and from 1992 to 2003, the quantities of fishmeal and fish oil used in compound aquaculture feeds grew from 936 000 tonnes to 2 936 000 tonnes and from 234 000 tonnes to 802 000 tonnes, respectively – broadly matching the approximate 3-fold increase (10.9 to 29.8 million tonnes) in production of farmed finfish and crustaceans during this period (Tacon *et al.*, 2006). In 2002, the 54% of world fishmeal production not used in aquaculture was used for feeding poultry (22%), pigs (24%), other animals (7%) and ruminants (1%), while the 19% of fish oil not used in aquaculture was used for direct human consumption (14%) and for industrial purposes (5%) (Tacon *et al.*, 2006). Figures 7.4a and b show how fishmeal and fish oil in aquaculture feeds were used to farm different fish in 2003.

From about 1980 to 2004, fishmeal and fish oil production was relatively constant, apart from a 1997–98 year-on-year decline of 18%

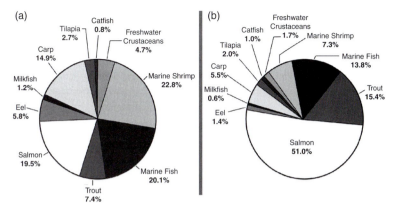

Figure 7.4 Estimated global use of (a) fishmeal, and (b) fish oil (both in % dry as-fed basis) within compound aquafeeds in 2003 by major species. Source: FAO data cited by Tacon *et al.* (2006).

and 28%, respectively, due to the El Niño, which affected particularly the anchoveta fisheries of Peru and Chile. These fisheries produced 35% of global fishmeal and 36.4% of global fish oil in 2003 (Tacon *et al.*, 2006).

Fishmeal production uses a lot of wild fish. Tacon *et al.* 2006 cite data indicating that world production of fishmeal in 2003 (about 5.5 million tonnes) required catches of 22.08 to 27.6 million tonnes of fish, based on multiplication factors of 4 and 5. Asche and Tveterås (2004) concluded that increased demand from aquaculture for fishmeal had not increased fishing pressure on industrial fisheries, mainly because poultry and pig farmers had largely switched to vegetable protein sources for feed manufacture, but they added that increased growth of aquaculture could change the situation, resulting in higher fishmeal and fish oil prices.

Delgado *et al.* (2003) modeled price changes to 2020 for fish, farmed animal products, fishmeal, and fish oil, under a variety of scenarios including most likely, slower, and faster aquaculture expansion, efficient use of fish meal and fish oil, and "ecological collapse." They defined ecological collapse rather gently as "–1% annual growth trends in production, excluding supply response to price change, for all capture fisheries commodities including fishmeal and fish oil." Table 7.3 summarizes some of their findings, which suggest that, under all scenarios depicted there, livestock farming will be largely disconnected from dependency on fishmeal and fish oil, whereas most aquaculture, especially that of high value finfish and crustaceans, will

Table 7.3 *Summary of predicted total % price changes under various scenarios, from 1997 to 2020, for livestock commodities, food fish commodities from capture fisheries and aquaculture, and for fishmeal and fish oil. Source: modified from Delgado et al. (2003).*

Commodity	Most likely (baseline scenario)	Baseline scenario with 50% faster growth of aquaculture	Baseline scenario with 50% slower growth of aquaculture	Baseline scenario with ×2 conversion efficiency of fishmeal and fish oil	Ecological collapse
Low value fish	6	−12	25	5	35
High value fish	15	9	19	14	69
Crustaceans	16	4	26	15	70
Mollusks	4	−16	25	3	26
Fishmeal	18	42	0	−16	134
Fish oil	18	50	−4	−5	128
Poultry meat	−2	−5	0	−3	7
Pig meat	−3	−4	−1	−3	4
Beef	−3	−5	−2	−4	1
Sheep meat	−3	−5	−1	−3	2
Milk	−8	−10	−8	−9	−5
Eggs	−3	−5	−2	−4	3

not and will yield increasingly expensive products. Delgado *et al.* (2003) included another scenario of reduced capture fisheries production by China, based on the analyses of Watson and Pauly (2001) and this scenario, by coincidence, gave price change projections almost identical to those shown here for increased feed conversion efficiency of fishmeal and fish oil.

Tacon *et al.* (2006) reported IFFO expectations that use in aquaculture feeds of total world fishmeal and fish oil production would increase to 50% and 88%, respectively, by 2012. Tacon *et al.* (2006), however, citing various authors, expect that fishmeal and fish oil use in aquaculture feeds will actually decline in the long term because of their high prices; there will be successful substitution with plant and other protein and lipid sources and consumer resistance to eating farmed fish fed on other fish.

Perceptions about food safety could be another constraint. The fishmeal and fish oil industry has been vocal in pointing out that feeding fishmeal and fish oil to farmed fish and livestock cannot be compared to feeding livestock waste products to livestock (e.g., FIN, 1998). However, because of the recent history of bovine spongiform encephalopathy (BSE) in cattle and its potentially horrific consequences for humans, there is now greater public and official scrutiny about what is fed to what in all forms of farming. Processed fish offal has been hailed as an obvious and valuable resource for making processed fish feeds (e.g., Rathbone and Babbitt, 2000). However, the European Commission (2003) has recommended that by-products of *farmed* fish should not be fed to farmed fish and that farmed fish should not be fed on wet diets containing "fresh or frozen but otherwise unprocessed fish by-products."

Ensilage of fish and livestock offal using organic acids has long been recommended to produce a cost-effective ingredient for livestock feeds (e.g., Disney *et al.*, 1978) and has seen use in poultry and pig feeds, though less so in fish feeds. A search through the literature on fish silage use in aquaculture turns up a very wide variety of items; for example, a comparison of dogfish and herring silage in Atlantic salmon feeds (Heras *et al.*, 1994) and silage production from salmon farm mortalities (Lo *et al.*, 1993). Use of fish silage use in aquaculture feeds remains limited, though there are many experimental data and reports of potential and small-scale trial use.

LOW VALUE/TRASH FISH

Low value/trash fish (LV/TF) is a generic term for wild fish catches that may be eaten directly by humans, fed to farmed fish or livestock, processed into fishmeal and fish oil, used as plant fertilizers, etc. Given these potentially conflicting uses, it is not surprising that the future supply of LV/TF was an issue raised in an FAO publication reviewing the future of Asia-Pacific fisheries and aquaculture (Sugiyama *et al.*, 2004). They commented that, despite many uncertainties over most LV/TF statistics, reports have indicated that catches by China of LV/TF rose from 1.3 million tonnes in 1980 to over 5 million tonnes in 2002, that over 60% of the total marine catch in the South China Sea is LV/TF, and that LV/TF comprise 60% of Gulf of Thailand trawl catches, with 18–32% of the fish being juveniles of commercially important species. Funge-Smith *et al.* (2005) pointed out that high demand for LV/TF has made them the target of more small-scale fishers and the basis for the economic viability of many of the latter's vessels, as well as important sources of livelihood and food for the poor. The concern is that many LV/TF fisheries are unsustainable, although catches may actually rise in the short term from ecosystems in which the top predators have been fished out.

There are no reliable data on the overall use of LV/TF for feeding farmed fish. Funge-Smith *et al.* (2005) gave a "conservative estimate" that 25% of the entire LV/TF catch is used for feeding farmed fish and livestock. Despite the paucity of good data, it is clear that the use of LV/TF to feed farmed carnivorous fish is increasing and causing concern. This has stimulated a quest for alternative feed sources and a general thrust to develop compounded feeds rather then feeding wet LV/TF (FAO, 2005).

An example from Hong Kong shows how difficult it is to manage some LV/TF fisheries. Chau and Sadovy (2005) found that a total of 109 LV/TF species from 38 families were in use to feed cage-farmed groupers and porgies, though 89 species from 32 families were only minor contributors. The major LV/TF families used for what these authors call "mixed fish feeding (MFF)," in order of their percentage predominance by numbers in the MMF samples, were: Leiognathidae, 51%; Clupeidae, 18%; Carangidae, 9%; Apogonidae and Engraulidae, 7% each; with other families comprising the remainder. By weight, a similar picture emerged with these five families accounting for 84% of the so-called MFF used as fish feeds, though with synodontid and trichiurid species now accounting for 6% and 4%, respectively. From FishBase (Froese and Pauly, 2000), the maximum and minimum trophic levels of members of these families all indicate carnivory (defined as having a trophic level of > 2.8): Leiognathidae, 3.27–4.42; Clupeidae, 3.18–4.50; Carangidae, 3.88–4.50; Apogonidae, 3.47–4.20; Engraulidae, 3.31–4.20; Synodontidae, 4.18–4.63; and Trichiuridae, 4.08–4.50. This scenario also provides an opportunity to cite the historic bibliography on the Leiognathidae by Pauly and Wade-Pauly (1981), which contains 941 entries on this important family in aquatic food webs.

In summary, although the use of LV/TF as or in aquaculture feeds for carnivorous fish might seem to make economic sense at present, ultimately feeding juvenile and adult wild carnivorous fish to other farmed carnivorous fish cannot be sustainable in the long term or provide significant contributions to world food fish supply. Indeed, although it is providing employment for some poor people, it is also taking away from others LV/TF that they could consume directly.

RENDERED LIVESTOCK WASTES AND OTHER PROTEIN/ENERGY AND LIPID INGREDIENTS FOR FISH FEEDS

There is a wealth of technical and public awareness information on rendered livestock wastes meat and bone meal, meat meal, hydrolyzed feather meal, poultry by-product meal, blood meal, tallows, lard, and yellow grease (e.g., NRA, 2005, n.d.; www.renderers.org). Bureau (2000) reported that blood meal, feather meal, meat and bone meal, and poultry by-products meal have a long history of use in fish feeds, including use as substitutes for fishmeal, and concluded that "it does not appear economically reasonable to avoid using rendered animal by-products in aquafeeds given their cost, probable safety, and relatively high nutritive value." This seems reasonable and it is obviously to the benefit of humans to recycle such nutrient resources efficiently and safely into valuable foods. There has been much research activity in this area (e.g., Bharadwaj *et al.*, 2002; Martino *et al.*, 2003), but mostly from the point of view of fish nutrition. Public perceptions about fish fed on rendered livestock wastes and the possible impacts of dietary constraints (on religious/ethical grounds) to consumption of such fish are under-researched.

Plant meals, plant protein concentrates, and plant oils are the main alternatives to use in fish feeds of fishmeal, fish oil, and rendered livestock wastes. Tacon *et al.* (2006) recorded, from FAO sources, global production in 2003 of 200.5 million tonnes of plant cakes and meals and 105.5 million tonnes of plant oils, and listed some 25 plant meal/ protein concentrates and 10 plant oils that have been incorporated, experimentally or in production systems, in finfish and/or crustacean feeds. Reducing the future use of LV/TF, fish meal, and fish oil in aquaculture is an extensive field of research, including attempts to maximize the acceptability of plant proteins and lipids to farmed fish, and to ensure consumer acceptance and the nutritional value of the resulting farmed fish products. Soybean meal is the most widely used plant-based ingredient for fish feeds and a soybean meal aquaculture database (http://soyaqua.org/) is available online.

Feeding fish with fresh aquatic plant material is not usually an option in intensive aquaculture, even for specialized herbivores, such as the grass carp, and herbivorous tilapias, such as *Tilapia rendalli*

(Pullin, 1986). The energy costs to the fish of ingesting and digesting the large amounts of feed required for good growth also limit that growth. Aquatic macrophytes have very high water content (and sometimes high ash content) and these increase the energy costs of feeding and digestion relative to fish growth; e.g., azolla (Cagauan and Pullin, 1994).

The use in fish feeds of single cell proteins, from mass-cultured bacteria, yeasts, and micro- or filamentous algae has been reviewed by Tacon *et al.* (2006) with mention of six recent studies. These protein sources may have high potential in some areas of aquaculture, especially in seed production, but it is hard to envisage them becoming major contributors to fish feeds in general because of the high costs of culturing such organisms on the scale required. The main exceptions to this could be using fish farm waters and substrates themselves as bacterial culture media to produce bacterial flocs.

THE FUTURE OF AQUACULTURE: SOME SUGGESTIONS FOR RESEARCH

Pursue responsible, ecological aquaculture in partnership and synergy with other sectors

Aquaculture is but one option among the many that can contribute to feeding humans from the global food web, but it is an important option because of its potential to share natural resources, especially water, with other users and to recycle wastes. This applies to both rural and urban settings (Edwards *et al.*, 2002; Costa-Pierce *et al.*, 2005). The report from the first meeting of the FAO's Sub-Committee on Aquaculture (FAO, 2002) stated:

> Aquaculture is an important domestic provider of much needed, high quality, animal protein, generally at prices affordable to the poorer segments of society. It is also a valuable provider of employment, cash income, and foreign exchange, with developing countries contributing over 90% of the total global production. When integrated carefully, aquaculture also provides low-risk entry points for rural development and has diverse applications in both inland and coastal areas.

The FAO Code of Conduct for Responsible Fisheries and its guidelines for aquaculture development (FAO, 1995, 1997) have set the scene for a new era of responsible aquaculture and numerous authors have called for ecosystem-based, "ecological" aquaculture as the only kind of aquaculture that can be in the long term profitable, sustainable, and equitable (e.g., Costa-Pierce, 2002; Lubchenco, 2003). Irresponsible aquaculture has caused many environmental problems (e.g., Pullin et al., 1993), though no more so than irresponsible and unsustainable agriculture, animal husbandry, fisheries, and forestry. Indeed, given the astonishing rate of growth of aquaculture and its increased contributions to human food security, its adverse impacts on the planet have been arguably rather limited compared to, say, the dust bowls created by agriculture, loss of rainforest, coral reef destruction, shrinking of the Aral Sea, etc.

Even the much publicized destruction of mangroves has not always been a simple story with aquaculture as the main or sole culprit (e.g., Lassen, 1997). For example, in Thailand, Fast and Menasveta (2003) reported that the 1961 total area of mangroves (367 900 ha) had been reduced by 1993 to 168 683 ha, with 32% of mangrove conversions attributed to shrimp pond construction and the remainder to other causes; e.g., agriculture, community development, mining, overharvesting for charcoal and other wood products, mining, road and port development, etc. They also reported mangrove forest recovery to 244 160 ha by 2000. Jacinto et al. (2006) cited records that show total mangrove areas in Manila Bay, Philippines, falling from around 54 000 ha in 1890 to only 2000 ha by 1990 and 794 ha by 1995. These Manila Bay mangroves were, of course, converted for human settlements, industry, and other developments, as well as for aquaculture.

The use of alien species and genetically altered farmed types in aquaculture will undoubtedly increase because, as in agriculture and forestry, these are often the most profitable organisms to farm. De Silva et al. (2006) found that alien species contributed over 40% of total freshwater fish production in Asia, excluding production of indigenous carps farmed in China. Casal (2006) found that alien species contributed 72% and 87% of aquaculture production in Indonesia and Brazil, respectively. The farming of alien aquatic species and of all genetically altered farmed aquatic organisms, irrespective of which technology is used to produce them, requires essentially the same precautionary approaches and biosafety provisions (e.g., see ICLARM–FAO, 1999). This constraint provides, however, opportunities for a new approach in which aquaculture and conservation can be co-planned, co-financed, and co-governed, by establishing not only production areas but also conservation areas that are off-limits to aquaculture and other disturbance.

Concerning world fish supply in particular, the question that has often been posed (e.g., by Delgado *et al.*, 2003) – can aquaculture alleviate the pressures on capture fisheries? – is too narrow. A slightly better question could be devised by including, among the possible pressure alleviators on capture fisheries, all farmed animals, pets, and other consumers of wild caught fish and fish products that are not eaten directly by humans. But the much better question is – how can aquaculture of plants and fish contribute most responsibly to world food supply and the well being of humans, in partnership and synergy with all other forms of food production? This means working out the true potentials of aquaculture systems as food producers, waste recyclers, etc., and their economic, ecological, nutritional, and other benefits relative to those of other sectors. For example, Delgado *et al.* (2003) found that income growth and urbanization are fuelling demand for the products of "carnivorous aquaculture." However, it is surely the failure of management of the capture fisheries for the same products (e.g., Sadovy *et al.*, 2003) that is really fuelling this demand, and if such fisheries are indeed to all intents and purposes unmanageable, then aquaculture is probably the only way of sustaining a supply, at any level.

Aquaculture can also make huge contributions to multipurpose use of scarce freshwater resources because it can often merely occupy and share water rather than consuming it. Another area of potential synergy is urban wastewater-fed aquaculture, though there are many attendant problems to be solved, such as the mixing of toxic industrial wastes with domestic wastes, and wastewater reuse through aquaculture has been declining (Edwards, 2005). In theory, well-engineered wastewater-fed aquaculture can facilitate multipurpose use of water and recycling of nutrients to produce fish that are completely safe for human consumption, while providing employment and lessening environmental pollution.

Facilitate feed-efficient omnivory in intensive aquaculture

Tacon *et al.* (2006) concluded that global production of 30 million tonnes of farmed finfish and crustaceans in 2003 consumed 20 to 25 million tonnes of captured pelagic fish and LV/TF. They also pointed out that fishmeal and fish oil are usually "secondary" nutritional resources for the naturally or potentially omnivorous farmed fish, such as carps, many catfishes, tilapias, and some shrimp. These aquatic organisms are becoming the aquatic equivalents of ruminant and monogastric live-stock, whereas most obligate carnivorous fish will remain more demanding, requiring feeds sourced mainly from fish and other animals.

There is much basic nutritional, feed formulation, and food product quality and safety research to be done. There are bound to be biological limits to the extent that fish farmed as omnivores can be pushed further toward herbivory. There are also product quality constraints. Fish feeds that contain only plant oils rather than fish oils will not contain the omega-3 fatty acids that are such a major reason for fish being good foods for humans, unless plants are genetically engineered to produce them, and that will raise other consumer acceptance and environmental issues. The goal is to improve the productivity and profitability of intensive farming of naturally herbivorous/detritivorous/omnivorous fish species, as omnivores.

Managing the microbial ecology of aquaculture systems, and, in particular, pursuing detritivory as a form of "micro-omnivory," can be an important contributor, but clearly has better prospects with farmed carps, catfishes, shrimps, and tilapias than with farmed carnivorous fish. The extent to which they can be farmed as omnivores also merits more research, though the prospects of success are less.

In a list of 67 marine and brackish water finfish species farmed in China, including three seahorse species (Hong and Zhang, 2001), only six food fish species (three mullets, two siganids, and the milkfish) appear to be obvious candidates for on-farm omnivory. To what extent is it worth researching the prospects for weaning the ten farmed grouper, five snapper, and other carnivorous species mentioned by these authors away from carnivory? Maybe this would be a good investment for very high priced and highly prized species. Feeding these as carnivores on-farm looks increasingly unsustainable and, from some perspectives, unethical, though there are plenty of enthusiasts around for farming and eating them. The "superstar" farmed carnivorous fish of the moment is probably cobia (*Rachycentron canadum*), reported to grow to 4–6 kg in 12 months fed on pellets containing 50% fishmeal, at a feed conversion ratio of 1.8 (Benetti *et al.*, 2006).

There is scope for much economic research here as well as biological research. For example, the suggestions of Goodland (1997) to tax production and consumption of the food organisms that are the least efficient converters and worst degraders of the Earth's natural capital could be revisited. He proposed taxing feedlot pork and beef more heavily than poultry, eggs, and dairy produce, with "ocean fish" attracting the lowest taxes. Those positions would now need revision, with most capture fisheries in distress and aquaculture, hopefully of omnivores, set to provide 50% of world fish supply.

Exploring further some of Daniel Pauly's hypotheses

With few exceptions, notably the common carp, domestication of farmed food fish is still at a very early stage. There are huge advances to be made in, for example, food conversion efficiencies of intensively farmed fish. For comparison, Forster (1999), citing Watts and Kennett (1995), described improvements in feed conversion ratios in broiler poultry farming from 1935 to 1994 of 4.4:1 to 1.9:1.

Daniel Pauly's grand hypothesis on fish growth (Pauly, 1981; also explained simply and concisely in Pauly, 1994) is that, given adequate nutrition, it is actually oxygen availability to and transport through fish that limits their growth and largely timetables their maturation and spawning, because their gill surface areas and the capacity of other oxygen pathways cannot grow as fast as the somatic growth that requires oxygen. This hypothesis has potential importance for the further domestication and genetic improvement of farmed fish (see also Pauly, 2010).

Domestication in farmed animals usually means selection for quiet behavior, which in turns spares more oxygen for growth. For example, Bozynski (1998) found that fast growing, genetically improved (GIFT strain) Nile tilapia (*Oreochromis niloticus*) showed significantly quieter behavior than control fish. Therefore, in looking for potential winners among aquaculture species in which to invest heavily in domestication and genetic improvement, it could pay dividends to screen them against indicators developed from the Pauly oxygen hypothesis. This includes use of the broad index of fish "growth ability" ($Ø' = \log K + 2. \log L_\infty$, where K and L_∞ are terms as in the von Bertalanffy Growth Function); for example, as used by Moreau and Pauly (1999) for comparing tilapia hybrids and their parents.

For some fish, domestication for intensive farming will mean progression towards omnivory, and this will involve different oxygen budgets from those in herbivory and carnivory. The main research challenge here is to operationalize Daniel Pauly's oxygen hypothesis in shaping these efforts, rather than just using it to explain past observations.

ACKNOWLEDGMENTS

The author acknowledges with gratitude the immense help and encouragement that Daniel Pauly has given to him over many years of working together. For their help with the preparation of this chapter, the following are also thanked: Aque Atanacio, Christine Casal, Peter Edwards, Mohammad R. Hasan, Grace Pablico, and Albert Tacon.

REFERENCES

ADB (2005) *An Evaluation of Small-scale Freshwater Rural Aquaculture Development for Poverty Reduction*. Manila, Philippines: Asian Development Bank.

Anon. (2006) Diet and the unborn child. The omega point. *The Economist*, January 19, 2006.

Asche, F. and Tveterås, S. (2004) On the relationship between aquaculture and reduction fisheries. *Journal of Agricultural Economics*, 55, 245–265.

Bayvel, A. C. D. (2005) Animals in science and agriculture: a global perspective. *Biologist*, 52, 339–344.

Benetti, D. D., Brand, L., Collins, J., Orhun, R., Benetti, A., O'Hanlon, B., Danylchuk, A., Alston, D., Rivera, J. and Cabarcas, A. (2006) Can offshore aquaculture of carnivorous fish be sustainable? *World Aquaculture*, 37, 44–47.

Bharadwaj, A. S., Brignon, W. R., Gould, N. L., Brown, P. B. and Wu, Y. V. (2002) Evaluation of meat and bone meal in practical diets fed to juvenile hybrid striped bass *Morone chrysops* × *M. saxatilis*. *Journal of the World Aquaculture Society*, 33, 448–457.

Bowen, S. H. (1980) Detrital non-protein amino acids are the key to rapid growth of tilapia in Lake Valencia, Venezuela. *Science*, 207, 1216–1218.

Bowen, S. H. (1987) Composition and nutritive value of detritus. In Moriarty, D. J. W. and Pullin, R. S. V., eds., *Detritus and Microbial Ecology in Aquaculture*. Manila, Philippines: ICLARM.

Bozynski, C. (1998) Interactions between growth, sex, reproduction, and activity levels in control and fast-growing strains of Nile tilapia (*Oreochromis niloticus*). MSc thesis, Department of Zoology, University of British Columbia, Vancouver, Canada.

Brewer, D. J. and Friedman, R. F. (1989) *Fish and Fishing in Ancient Egypt*. Cairo, Egypt: American University in Cairo Press.

Brook, A. J. (1993) The Rev. William Buckland, the first palaeoecologist. *Biologist*, 40, 149.

Brugère, C. and Ridler, N. (2004) *Global Aquaculture Outlook in the Next Decades: an Analysis of National Aquaculture Production Forecasts to 2030*. FAO Fisheries Circular. Rome: FAO.

Bureau, D. P. (2000) Fish feeds: Use of rendered animal protein ingredients. *International Aquafeed*, July 2000, 30–34.

Cagauan, A. G. and Pullin, R. S. V. (1994) Azolla in aquaculture: past, present and future. In Cagauan, A. G., Pullin, R. S. V., Muir, J. F. and Roberts, R. J., eds., *Recent Advances in Aquaculture*. Oxford, UK: Blackwell Science.

Casal, C. M. V. (2006) Global documentation of fish introductions: the growing crisis and recommendations for action. *Biological Invasions*, 8, 3–11.

Chau, G. T. H. and Sadovy, Y. (2005) The use of mixed fish feed in Hong Kong's mariculture industry. *World Aquaculture*, 36, 6–13.

Costa-Pierce, B., Desbonnet, A., Edwards, P. and Baker, D. (2005) *Urban Aquaculture*. Wallingford, UK: CABI Publishing.

Costa-Pierce, B. A. (1987) Aquaculture in ancient Hawaii. *Bioscience*, 37, 320–331.

Costa-Pierce, B. A. (2002) *Ecological Aquaculture: The Evolution of the Blue Revolution*. Oxford, UK: Blackwell Science.

De Silva, S., Maitipe, P. and Cumaranatunge, R. (1984) Aspects of the biology of the euryhaline Asian cichlid, *Etroplus suratensis*. *Environmental Biology of Fishes*, 10, 77–87.

De Silva, S. S., Nguyen, T. T. T. Abery, N. W. and Amarasinghe, U. S. (2006) An evaluation of the role and impact of alien fish in Asian inland aquaculture. *Aquaculture Research*, 37, 1–17.

Delgado, C. L., Wada, N., Rosegrant, M. W., Meijer, S. and Ahmed, M. (2003) *Fish to 2020: Supply and Demand in Changing Global Markets*. Washington DC: International Food Policy Research Institute.

Disney, J. G., Hoffman, A., Olley, J., Clucas, I. J., Barranco, A. and Francis, B. J. (1978) Development of a fish silage/carbohydrate animal feed for use in the tropics. *Tropical Science*, 20, 129–144.

Duray, M. N. (1998) *Biology and Culture of Siganids*. Tigbauan, Iloilo, Philippines: Aquaculture Department, Southeast Asian Fisheries Development Center.

Eaton, S. B., Konner, M. J., and Shostak, M. (1996) An evolutionary perspective enhances understanding of human nutritional requirements. *The Journal of Nutrition (US)*, 126, 1732–1740.

Edwards, P. (1980) Food potential of aquatic macrophytes. *ICLARM Studies and Reviews*. Manila, Philippines: ICLARM.

Edwards, P. (2004) Traditional Chinese aquaculture and its impact outside China. *World Aquaculture*, 35, 24–27.

Edwards, P. (2005) Development status of, and prospects for, wastewater-fed aquaculture in urban environments. In Costa-Pierce, B. A., Desbonnet, A., Edwards, P. and Baker, D., eds., *Urban Aquaculture*. Wallingford, UK: CABI Publishing.

Edwards, P. and Allen, G. (2004) Fish feeds and feeding in countries of the lower Mekong Basin. *World Aquaculture*, 35, 30–32.

Edwards, P., Little, D. C. and Demaine, H. (2002) *Rural Aquaculture*. Wallingford, UK: CABI Publishing.

Edwards, P., Pullin, R. S. V. and Gartner, J. A. (1988) Research and education for the development of integrated crop-livestock-fish farming systems in the tropics. *ICLARM Studies and Reviews*, 16, 53.

Elvevoll, E. O. and James, D. G. (2000) Potential benefits of fish for maternal, foetal and neonatal nutrition: a review of the literature. *Food, Nutrition and Agriculture*, 27, 28–39.

European Commission (2003) *The use of Fish By-products in Aquaculture. Report of the Scientific Committee on Animal Health and Animal Welfare. Health and Consumer Protection Directorate-General*. Brussels, Belgium: European Commission.

FAO (1995) *Code of Conduct for Responsible Fisheries*. Rome: FAO.

FAO (1997) *Aquaculture Development. FAO Technical Guidelines for Responsible Fisheries*. Rome: FAO.

FAO (2002) *Aquaculture Development and Management: status, issues, and prospects. Sub-Committee on Aquaculture, Committee on Fisheries*. Rome: FAO.

FAO (2005) APFIC Regional workshop on low value and "trash fish" in the Asia Pacific Region. Bangkok, Thailand, Regional Office for Asia and the Pacific, FAO.

FAO (2006) *Appendix G, Conference Declaration: Report of the International Conference on Agrarian Reform and Rural Development, Porto Alegre, Brazil.* Rome: FAO.

FAO (2008) *The State of World Fisheries and Aquaculture 2008.* Rome: FAO.

Fast, A. W. and Menasveta, P. (2003) Mangrove forest recovery in Thailand. *World Aquaculture*, 34, 6–9.

FIN (1998) Fishmeal deserves a fair deal: there are no grounds for a ban. No problem feeding fishmeal to farmed fish, says SEAC. Fishmeal Information Network. Peterborough, UK: FIN, The Chamberlain Partnership.

Folke, C. (1988) Energy economy of salmon aquaculture in the Baltic Sea. *Environmental Management*, 12, 525–537.

Folke, C. and Kautsky, N. (1992) Aquaculture with its environment: prospects for sustainability. *Ocean and Coastal Management*, 17, 5–24.

Forster, J. (1999) Aquaculture chickens, salmon: a case study. *World Aquaculture*, 30, 33–40/69–70.

Froese, R. and Pauly, D. (2000) *FishBase 2000: Concepts, Designs and Data Sources.* Los Baños, Laguna, Philippines: ICLARM.

Funge-Smith, S., Lindebo, E., and Staples, D. (2005) *Asian Fisheries Today: the Production and Use of Low Value/Trash Fish from Marine Fisheries in the Asia-Pacific Region.* Bangkok: FAO.

Gardner-Thorpe, C. (2001) Who was … Frank Buckland? *Biologist (London, England)*, 48, 187–188.

Gerking, S. D. (1994) *Feeding Ecology of Fish.* San Diego, CA: Academic Press.

Gill, C. (2005) World feed panorama: disease takes toll, but feed output bounces back. *Feed International*, 26, 4–9.

Goodland, R. (1997) Environmental sustainability in agriculture: diet matters. *Ecological Economics*, 23, 189–200.

Halver, J. E. (1989) *Fish Nutrition.* New York: Academic Press.

Hasan, M. R. (2001) Nutrition and feeding for sustainable aquaculture development in the third millennium. In Subasinghe, R. P., Bueno, P., Phillips, M. J., *et al.*, eds., *Aquaculture in the Third Millenium (Technical Proceedings of the Conference on Aquaculture in the Third Millenium, Bangkok, Thailand, 20–25 February 2000).* Rome: Network of Aquaculture Centres in Asia-Pacific, Bangkok and the Food and Agriculture Organization of the United Nations.

Hepher, B. (1988) *Nutrition of Pond Fishes.* Cambridge, UK: Cambridge University Press.

Heras, H., Mcleod, C. A. and Ackman, R. G. (1994) Atlantic dogfish silage vs. herring silage in diets for Atlantic salmon (*Salmo salar*): growth and sensory evaluation of fillets. *Aquaculture*, 125, 93–106.

Hong, W. S. and Zhang, Q. Y. (2001) The status of marine fish culture in China. *World Aquaculture*, 32, 18–20/67.

Hopkins, K. D., Hopkins, M. L. and Pauly, D. (1988) A multivariate model of fish growth, applied to tilapia seawater culture in Kuwait. In Pullin R. S. V., Bhukasawan T., Tonguthai K., and MacLean J. L., eds., Proceedings of the Second International Symposium on Tilapia in Aquaculture, 16–20 March 1987, Bangkok, Thailand. *ICLARM Conference Proceedings* 15. Manila, Philippines: ICLARM, pp. 29–39.

Hopkins, K. D. and Pauly, D. (1993) Instantaneous mortalities and multivariate models: applications to tilapia culture in saline water. *Multivariate Methods in Aquaculture Research: Case Studies of Tilapias in Experimental and Commercial Systems. ICLARM Studies and Reviews.* Manila, Philippines: ICLARM.

Hopkins, K., Pauly, D., Cruz, E. M. and Van Weerd, J. H. (1982) Recruitment control: an alternative to predator-prey ratios. *Berichte der Deutschen Wissenschaftlichen Kommission für Meeresforschung*, 29, 125–135.

Horn, M. H. (1989) Biology of marine herbivorous fishes. *Oceanography and Marine Biology Annual Review*, 27, 167–272.

ICLARM–FAO (1999) Consensus Statement. In Pullin, R. S. V., Bartley, D. M. and Kooiman, J., eds., *Towards Policies for Conservation and Sustainable Use of Aquatic Genetic Resources*. Manila, Philippines: ICLARM, p. 253.

Jacinto, G. S., Azanza, R. V., Velasquez, L. B. and Siringan, F. P. (2006) Manila Bay: environmental challenges and opportunities. In Wolanski, E., ed., *The Environment in Asia Pacific Harbours*. Dordrecht, The Netherlands: Springer, pp. 309–328.

Jystad, P. T. (2001) Fishmeal and oil or vegetable alternatives: will high volume production spoil premium fish production? IntraFish Industry Report.

Larsson, J., Folke, C. and Kautsky, N. (1994) Ecological limitations and appropriation of ecosystem support by shrimp farming in Colombia. *Environmental Management*, 18, 663–676.

Lassen, T. J. (1997) Environmental extremes versus sustainable policies in aquaculture. *World Aquaculture*, 28, 49–51.

Lightfoot, C., Roger, P. A., Cagauan, A. G. and Dela Cruz, C. R. (1993) Preliminary steady-state nitrogen models of a wetland ricefield ecosystem with and without fish. In Christensen V. and Pauly D., eds., *Trophic Models of Aquatic Ecosystems. ICLARM Conference Proceedings*, 26. Manila, Philippines: ICLARM, pp. 56–64.

Lo, K. V., Liao, P. H., Bullock, C. and Jones, Y. (1993) Silage production from salmon farm mortalities. *Aquaculture Engineering*, 12, 37–45.

Lubchenco, J. (2003) The blue revolution: a global ecological perspective. *World Aquaculture*, 34, 8–10.

Mair, G. C. and D. Pauly (1993) A multivariate analysis of growth in juvenile tilapia (*Oreochromis aureus* and *O. niloticus*; Cichlidae) reared in recirculating systems. In Prein M., Hulata G. and Pauly D., eds., *Multivariate Methods in Aquaculture Research: Case Studies of Tilapias in Experimental and Commercial Systems*. ICLARM Studies and Reviews. Manila, Philippines: ICLARM, pp. 97–104.

Martino, R. C., Trugo, L. C., Cyrino, E. P. and Portz, L. (2003) Use of white fat as a replacement for squid liver oil in practical diets for suribim, *Pseudoplatystoma coruscans*. *Journal of the World Aquaculture Society*, 34, 192–202.

Mathias, J., Charles, A. T. and Bao-Tong, H. (1994) *Integrated Fish Farming*. Boca Raton, FL: CRC Press LLC.

Moffit, C. M. (2005) Environmental, economic and social aspects of animal protein production and the opportunities for aquaculture. *Fisheries*, 30, 36–38.

Moreau, J. and Pauly, D. (1999) A comparative analysis of growth performance in aquaculture of tilapia hybrids and their parent species. *Asian Fisheries Science*, 12, 91–103.

Moriarty, D. J. W. (1998) Control of luminous *Vibrio* species in penaeid aquaculture ponds. *Aquaculture*, 164, 351–358.

Moriarty, D. J. W. and Pullin, R. S. V. (1987) *Detritus and Microbial Ecology in Aquaculture*. Manila, Philippines: ICLARM.

Msiska, O. V. and Costa-Pierce, B. A. (1993) *History, Status and Future of Common Carp (Cyprinus carpio L.) in Malawi*. Manila, Philippines: ICLARM.

Munro, J. L. and Heslinga, G. (1983) Prospects for the commercial cultivation of giant clams (Bivalvia: Tridachnidae). *Proceedings of the Gulf and Caribbean Fisheries Institute*, 35, 122–134.

Nandeesha, M. C. (2001) Farmers as scientists. Andra Pradesh fish farmers go into revolutionary carp research. *Aquaculture Asia*, VI, 29–32.

National Renderers Association (NRA) (n.d.) *The True Story of Meat and Bone Meal, Poultry Byproduct Meal, Feather Meal, Tallow, Poultry Fat, Yellow Grease*. Hong Kong: Asian Regional Office, National Renderers Association, Inc.

National Renderers Association (NRA) (2005) *Pocket Information Manual. A Buyer's Guide to Rendered Products*. Alexandria, VA: National Renderers Association, Inc.

National Research Council (1977) *Nutrient Requirements of Poultry*. Washington DC: National Academy of Sciences.

Naylor, R. L., Goldburg, R. J., Primavera, J. H., Kautsky, N., Beveridge, M. C. M., Clay, J. Folke, C., Lubchenco, J., Mooney, H. and Troell, M. (2000) Effect of aquaculture on world fish supplies. *Nature*, 405, 1017–1024.

New, M. B. (2002) *Trends in Freshwater and Marine Aquaculture Production Systems. Production Systems in Fishery Management. Fisheries Centre Research Report*. Vancouver, Canada: Fisheries Centre, University of British Columbia.

New, M. B., Tacon, A. G. J. and Csavas, I. (1993) Farm-made aquafeeds. Proceedings of the Regional Expert Conference on Farm-Made Aquafeeds. Bangkok, Thailand, Regional Office for Asia and the Pacific, Food and Agriculture Organization of the United Nations, and the ASEAN-EEC Aquaculture Development and Coordination Programme (AADCP).

Palomares, M. L. D. and Pauly, D. (1996) Models for estimating the food consumption of tilapias. In Pullin, R. S. V., Lazard, J., Legendre, M., Amon Kothias, J. B. and Pauly, D., eds., *Proceedings of the Third International Conference on Tilapia in Aquaculture*. Manila, Philippines: ICLARM, pp. 211–222.

Pauly, D. (1974) Report on the US Catfish Industry: Development, Research, Production Units, Marketing and Associated Industries. Neue Erkenntnisse auf dem Gebiet der Aquakultur. Arbeiten des Deutschen Fischereiverbandes, Heft.

Pauly, D. (1976) The biology, fishery and potential for aquaculture of *Tilapia melanotheron* in a small West African lagoon. *Aquaculture*, 7, 33–49.

Pauly, D. (1981) The relationships between gill surface area and growth performance in fish: a generalization of von Bertalanffy's theory of growth. *Berichte der Deutschen Wissenschaftlichen Kommission für Meeresforschung*, 28, 251–282.

Pauly, D. (1994) Growth performance in fishes: descriptions and comparisons. *On the Sex of Fish and the Gender of Scientists (Collected Essays in Fisheries Science)*. London: Chapman and Hall, pp. 61–66.

Pauly, D. (2010) *Gasping Fish and Panting Squids: Oxygen, Temperature and the Growth of Water-breathing Animals*. In Kinne, O., ed., *Excellence in Ecology*, 22. Oldendorf/Luhe, Germany: International Ecology Institute.

Pauly, D. and Christensen, V. (1995) Primary production required to sustain global fisheries. *Nature*, 374, 255–257.

Pauly, D. and Hopkins, K. D. (1983) A method for the analysis of pond growth experiments. *ICLARM Newsletter*, 6 (1), 10–12.

Pauly, D., Moreau, J. and Palomares, M. L. (1988) Detritus and energy consumption and conversion efficiency of *Sarotherodon melanotheron* (Cichlidae) in a West African lagoon. *Journal of Applied Ichthyology*, 4, 150–153.

Pauly, D., Muck, P., Mendo, J. and Tsukayama, I. (1989) *The Peruvian Upwelling System: dynamics and interactions*. Manila, Philippines: ICLARM.

Pauly, D. and Pullin, R. S. V. (1988) Hatching time in spherical, pelagic, marine fish eggs in response to temperature and egg size. *Environmental Biology of Fishes*, 22, 261–271.

Pauly, D. and Pullin, R. S. V. (1997) The Egg Dev Table. *FishBase '97. Concepts, Design and Data Sources*. Manila, Philippines: ICLARM, pp. 154–158.

Pauly, D. and Tsukayama, I. (1987) The Peruvian anchoveta and its upwelling system: three decades of change. *ICLARM Studies and Reviews*, 15, 351.

Pauly, D. and Wade-Pauly, S. (1981) An annotated bibliography of slipmouths (Pisces: Leiognathidae). *ICLARM Bibliographies*. Manila, Philippines: ICLARM.

Pauly, D., Watson, R. and Alder, J. (2005) Global trends in world fisheries: impacts on marine ecosystems and food security. *Philosophical Transactions of the Royal Society B*, 360, 5–12.

Peters, H. M. (1983) Fecundity, egg weight and oocyte development in tilapias (Cichlidae, Teleostei). Translated by Pauly, D. *ICLARM Translations*, 2, 28.

Popkin, B. M., Horton, S. H. and Kim, S. (2001) *The Nutrition Transition and Prevention of Diet-related Diseases in Asia and the Pacific*. Manila, Philippines: Asian Development Bank.

Prein, M., Hulata, G. and Pauly D. (1993) On the use of multivariate statistical methods in aquaculture research. In Prein M., Hulata G. and Pauly D., eds., *Multivariate Methods in Aquaculture Research: Case Studies of Tilapias in Experimental and Commercial Systems. ICLARM Studies and Reviews*. Manila, Philippines: ICLARM, pp. 1-11.

Prein, M. and Pauly, D. (1993) Two new approaches for examining multivariate aquaculture growth data: the "extended Bayley Plot" and path analysis. In Prein M., Hulata G., and Pauly D., eds., *Multivariate Methods in Aquaculture Research: Case Studies of Tilapias in Experimental and Commercial Systems. ICLARM Studies and Reviews*. Manila, Philippines: ICLARM, pp. 32-49.

Pullin, R. S. V. (1986) Culture of herbivorous tilapias. In Chan, H. H., Ang, K. J., Law, A. T., Mohamed, M. I. H. and Omar, I. H., eds., *Development and Management of Tropical Living Aquatic Resources*. Selangor, Malaysia: Universiti Pertanian Malaysia, pp. 145-149.

Pullin, R. S. V. (2007) Genetic resources for aquaculture: status and trends. In Bartley, D. M., Harvey, B. J. and Pullin, R. S. V., eds., *Status and Trends in Aquatic Genetic Resources: a Basis for International Policy*. Rome: FAO.

Pullin, R. S. V., Froese, R. and Pauly, D. (2007) Indicators for the sustainability of aquaculture. In Bert, T. M., ed., *Ecological and Genetic Implications of Aquaculture*. Dordrecht, The Netherlands: Kluwer Academic Publishers, pp. 53–72.

Pullin, R. S. V., Lazard, J., Legendre, M., Amon Kothias, J. B. and Pauly, D. (1996) *Proceedings of the Third International Conference on Tilapia in Aquaculture*. ICLARM Conference Proceedings. Manila, Philippines: ICLARM.

Pullin, R. S. V., Palomares, M. L., Casal, C. V., Dey, M. M. and Pauly, D. (1997) Environmental impacts of tilapias. In Fitzsimmons, K., ed., *Tilapia Aquaculture: Proceedings from the Fourth International Symposium on Tilapia in Aquaculture*. New York: Northeast Regional Agricultural Engineering Service Cooperative Extension, pp. 554–570.

Pullin, R. S. V., Rosenthal, H. and Maclean, J. L. (1993) Environment and aqua-culture in developing countries. *ICLARM Conference Proceedings*. Manila, Philippines: ICLARM.

Rathbone, C. K. and Babbitt, J. K. (2000) Whitefish offals make great fish feeds. *World Aquaculture*, 31, 20–22.

Ruddle, K. and Christensen, V. (1993) An energy flow model of the mulberry dike-carp pond farming system of the Zhuijiang Delta, Guandong Province, China. In Christensen V. and Pauly D., eds., *Trophic Models of Aquatic Ecosystems. ICLARM Conference Proceedings*, 26. Manila, Philippines: ICLARM, pp. 48–55.

Rumsey, G. L. (1994) History of early diet development in fish culture, 1000 BC to AD 1955. *The Progressive Fish Culturist*, 56, 1–6.

Sadovy, Y.J., Donaldson, T.J., Graham, T.R., McGilvray, F., Muldoon, G.J., Phillips, M.J., Rimmer, M.A., Smith, A. and Yeeting, B. (2003) *While Stocks Last: The Live Food Reef Fish Trade.* Manila, Philippines: Asian Development Bank.

Schroeder, G.L. (1987) Carbon pathways in aquatic detrital systems. In Moriarty, D.J.W. and Pullin, R.S.V., eds., *Detritus and Microbial Ecology in Aquaculture. ICLARM Conference Proceedings.* Manila, Philippines: ICLARM, pp. 217–236.

Science Council (2005) *Conservation of Livestock and Fish Genetic Resources.* Rome, Italy, Joint Report of Two Studies Commissioned by the CGIAR Science Council Secretariat, Consultative Group on International Agricultural Research.

Sugiyama, S., Staples, D. and Funge-Smith, S. (2004) *Status and Potential of Fisheries and Aquaculture in Asia and the Pacific.* Bangkok, Thailand, Regional Office for Asia and the Pacific, Food and Agriculture Organization of the United Nations.

Tacon, A.G.J. (1993) Feed ingredients for warmwater fish: fish meal and other processed feedstuffs. *FAO Fisheries Circular*, 856, 64.

Tacon, A.G.J., Hasan, M.R. and Subasinghe, R.P. (2006) Use of fishery resources as feed inputs for aquaculture development: trends and policy implications. *FAO Fisheries Circular*, 1018, 105.

Van Dam, A.A. Chikafumbwa, F.J.K.T., Jamu, D.M. and Costa-Pierce, B.A. (1993) Trophic interactions in a Napier grass (*Pennisetum purpureum*) fed aquaculture pond in Malawi. In Christensen V. and Pauly D., eds., *Trophic Models of Aquatic Ecosystems. ICLARM Conference Proceedings*, 26. Manila, Philippines: ICLARM, pp. 65–68.

Van Dam, A.A. and Pauly, D. (1995) Simulation of the effects of oxygen on food consumption and growth of Nile tilapia, *Oreochromis niloticus (L.). Aquaculture Research*, 26, 427–440.

Watson, R. and Pauly, D. (2001) Systematic distortions in world fisheries catch trends. *Nature*, 414, 534–536.

Watts, G. and Kennett, C. (1995) *The Broiler Industry.* Poultry Tribune, Centennial Edition. Mt. Morris, IL, USA: Watt Publishing.

8

Beyond food: fish in the twenty-first century

The earliest interactions between human beings and the marine environment are through the human appetite. Modern humans, i.e., *Homo sapiens*, began consuming seafood at least 164 000 years ago on the shores of what is now South Africa, as evidenced by shell middens containing the remains of brown mussels, giant periwinkles, and whelks (Marean *et al.*, 2007). Similar remains were found in 125 000-year-old middens along the Red Sea coast of East Africa, in what is now Eritrea, where humans enjoyed meals of oysters, crustaceans, and other shellfish (Walter *et al.*, 2000). They also briefly consumed the flesh of the giant clam *Tridacna costata*, which they collected from the reefs. But their clambakes did not last. Shortly after human arrival, *T. costata* nearly disappears from the fossil record – the first documented case of eradication through overfishing (Richter *et al.*, 2008).

Today, our hunger for seafood continues, and so do its consequences. Seafood consumption is on the rise globally. The US now consumes almost five times more fish than it did 100 years ago (~2.2 million tonnes in 2004 compared to ~500 000 tonnes in 1910, NMFS, 2006), and Chinese consumers are now eating almost five times more seafood per capita than they did in the early 1960s (25.4 kg/person in 2005 compared to 4.8 kg/person in 1961, Halweil and Mastny, 2006). Worldwide, per capita consumption of marine fishes has nearly doubled since the 1960s (9 kg in 1960s compared to 16 kg in 1997, WHO, 2003), while the human population also doubled over this same time period. In addition to humans, pigs, poultry, and carnivorous farmed fish are eating more and more seafood because it is currently an inexpensive protein source for industrial farmers. But turning 36% of fisheries catches into fishmeal – as we do currently – comes at the expense of malnourished humans.

Ecosystem Approaches to Fisheries: A Global Perspective, ed. V. Christensen and J. Maclean. Published by Cambridge University Press. © Cambridge University Press 2011.

Projections show that seafood supply from capture fisheries is decreasing and that, overall, today's marine fisheries are unsustainable (Pauly *et al.*, 2002; Worm *et al.*, 2006). Further exacerbating overfishing is that seafood has become increasingly profitable, markets have been globalized, and technology has facilitated fishing in every dimension of the sea. The impacts of the recent "global" fishing industry are considerable. One trawler today can remove 60 tonnes of fish from the ocean in a single haul, and as a result we have witnessed widespread declines in the biomass of fish in the oceans (Christensen *et al.*, 2003; Myers and Worm, 2003).

As seafood becomes more profitable and local waters become more depleted, fishing fleets travel further, toward the high seas and waters off tropical developing countries, where fish stocks are less exploited. When they take place in distant waters, these industrial fisheries can outcompete many coastal small-scale fisheries. Sometimes, this competition between luxury and subsistence seafood is obvious. In African waters, for instance, shrimp trawlers from distant shores compete with local fishers for the same fishing grounds. Rather than feeding local people who rely on fish for survival, the shrimp is shipped to food-secure markets in Europe, Japan, and the United States.

If the actual boats do not travel to the developing world, the demand still might. In this case, the "invisible hand" of the market shrouds the redirection of fish from those who need it to survive to those who do not. Many developed countries have become net importers of seafood because their fisheries fail to meet national demand due to the historical overexploitation of their fishing grounds. Between 1996 and 2006, world exports of fish and fishery products for human consumption grew 57% (FAO, 2009). In 2006, the top five seafood importing nations were Japan, United States, Spain, France, and Italy, while China, Thailand, Chile, and Vietnam were among the top 10 exporters (FAO, 2009). This redirection is facilitated by non-transparent access agreements (Kaczynski and Fluharty, 2002) and subtle and not so subtle unequal trade patterns. This is an age-old North–South story and it is likely only to worsen as climate change pushes fish out of the tropics and closer to the poles (Cheung *et al.*, 2009).

We currently have a limited understanding of the role fish plays in food security. This is partially because those who rely on fish for food have been marginalized, in part due to the fact that they are (1) often located in the developing world; and (2) catch seafood predominantly to feed their families rather than the market. In Mozambique, women and children glean reefs and intertidal areas for mollusks, crustaceans, and other small fish, primarily for home consumption, but their catches have not been considered in official fisheries catch statistics (Jacquet *et al.*, 2010). Thus, part of understanding food security is in the improvement of fisheries catch data.

Fisheries landings data are compiled by the Food and Agriculture Organization of the United Nations (FAO) and are fed by national statistics. These data have served as the primary tool for many global and regional fisheries studies, and are used to determine fish consumption, the value of fisheries to national economies, and the amount of "surplus" fisheries production. Developing countries eager for foreign exchange will sell what they perceive to be "surplus" fisheries (often driven by reliance on incomplete statistics) in the form of fishing rights.

It is possible that many developing world countries do not indeed have a "surplus" of fish, because those fish are caught by small-scale, subsistence fishers but have gone unrecorded. To obtain a better understanding of fisheries catches around the world, catches can be reconstructed by using historical gray literature to establish proxies (Pauly, 1998) or by biological models (e.g., Watson and Pauly, 2001).

Members of the Sea Around Us project are busy reconstructing catches for small-scale fisheries worldwide and re-examining policy decisions based on the improved catch estimates (see contributions in Zeller and Pauly, 2007). In Mozambique, for instance, access agreements have allowed distant-water fleets to access Mozambican waters – often under the premise that local, small-scale fisheries produce little to no fish. Since the 1950s, Mozambique has reported to the FAO primarily industrial catches and has vastly underreported the country's small-scale fishing sector due to lack of resources and civil war. However, based on reconstructed data for the small-scale sector, the Mozambique fishing sector as a whole has caught between 150 000 and 172 000 tonnes per year since 2000. Overall, reconstructed marine fisheries catches for Mozambique during 1950–2005 were 6.2 times greater than data reported to and by the FAO (Jacquet *et al.*, 2010).

Underreporting of catches does not only undermine issues related to food security but also management of marine ecosystems and protection of wildlife. In today's globalized market, regional demand can result in global pressure on a species or group of species. Asian demand for shark fin soup combined with overfishing in Asian waters has led to an increase in shark finning in distant waters, including those off the coast of South America. Perhaps due to the highly contentious nature of shark finning, shark catches in Ecuador have been underreported. Reconstruction of Ecuador's mainland shark landings for 1979–2004 shows that they reached an estimated 7000 tonnes per year, or nearly half a million sharks, and were 3.6 times greater than those reported by the FAO for 1991 to 2004 (Jacquet *et al.*, 2008).

Overfishing imperils one of the globe's last hunter–gatherer food systems and those humans who still largely rely on seafood for survival. One could argue on moral grounds that we should prioritize fish for those people who rely on them most, and point out the immorality of the fishmeal industry or the discarding of perfectly edible fish as do many industrial fisheries, such as shrimp trawlers. But these ethical arguments have been relegated as secondary to the science.

When it comes to the science, research, like globalization itself, has been largely dismissive of issues pertaining to equity such as food security, cash flows, and the wasteful fishmeal industry. Instead, in the same way that climate research has focused on the natural and physical sciences, the bulk of fisheries research has, to date, focused on the technically rigorous (and therefore often intellectually stimulating) biological and supply-side of the fisheries crisis. Often overlooked is the real culprit: demand led by that small but greedy organ, the human stomach. The conservation movement, however, has considered things differently.

Because it is the appetite that lies at the root of the fisheries crisis, it is unsurprising that many conservation groups believe it is through addressing this insatiable demand that overfishing will be solved. A substantial effort has developed over the last two decades that attempts to affect consumer demand in the Western world through various awareness campaigns (Figure 8.1). These campaigns aim to decrease consumption of overfished species by encouraging demand for sustainably caught ones.

There are major impediments that undermine consumer campaigns, such as the renaming and mislabeling of seafood (Jacquet and Pauly, 2008b) – a type of cheating that is likely to become more prevalent as seafood demand and trade continue to grow. Even the most sophisticated consumers would have difficulty navigating the confusing messages and underhandedness that occur in Western seafood markets.

But changing consumption in the household cannot compete with over-efficient fishing techniques with lax and unsustainable policies. These small changes at the household level would require widespread adoption and, therefore, a lot of time – time we do not

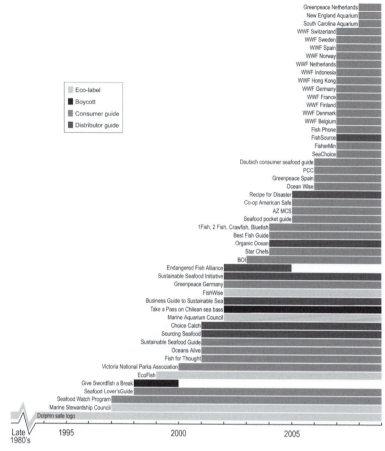

Figure 8.1 Growth in number of awareness campaigns related to seafood consumption.

have – to yield positive effects. This is why consumer efforts, which aim to reform consumer preferences in luxury markets, are largely futile. So far, the consumer campaigns that address "sustainable seafood" have not proved themselves capable of much more than catering to niche desires to "do the right thing" (Jacquet and Pauly, 2007; Jacquet *et al.*, 2010). Furthermore, localized successes in reducing demand for certain species are easily masked by a globalized and increasing demand for seafood.

This certainly does not mean such efforts should not be undertaken. Indeed, one could argue the benefits of marine protected areas are also eclipsed in an ocean where more than 99% of the ocean is open to fishing (Spalding *et al.*, 2008; Wood *et al.*, 2008). However, it does provide an argument that the conservation community must be more strategic in its efforts and its funding strategy (Jacquet and Pauly, 2008a).

Today's conservation movement, like the fishing industry it seeks to revolutionize, must make big changes over small time. It can do this best by working higher in the demand chain, in what can be described as vertical (consumer to mega-consumer or government), rather than horizontal (consumer to consumer), agitation. In a market-based approach, efforts should be directed at eliminating harmful fisheries subsidies (Jacquet and Pauly, 2008a), working with large seafood buyers, and eliminating the use of fishmeal in agricultural feed (Jacquet et al., 2010). The seafood that humans catch should go to humans, not animals.

In North America and Europe, there has been a call to eat lower on the food web (Pimentel and Pimentel, 2003; Pollan, 2008) and this has been echoed for marine food webs (Hall, 2007; Grescoe, 2008). However, humans currently must compete with factory-farmed animals for this meal of small pelagic fish. Currently, about 30 million tonnes of fish (36 % of world fisheries catch) are ground up each year into fishmeal and oil, mostly to feed farmed fish, chicken, and pigs (Alder et al., 2008; Pullin, this volume). Decreasing the amount of fish used for the production of animal feed should be a top priority of the sustainable seafood movement, particularly because pigs and chickens alone consume six times the amount of seafood as US consumers and twice that of consumers in Japan. One premise of sustainable seafood should be that no fishery that catches fish for the production of animal or feed fish oil should be eco-certified.

Finally, the biggest change the conservation community could hope to achieve would be to create an ethical shift that seeks to create mythologies for fish and invertebrates, i.e., to de-commodify them. We were able to achieve this with whales because they are mammals that nurse their young, communicate with one another, and apparently exhibit high levels of intelligence. However, fish are, for the most part, cold-blooded, expressionless creatures. But, in some ways, fish are not that different from birds and, as anyone who has ever been to England knows, there is no shortage of sentiment for avian species. Like the albatross, tunas cover remarkable migratory distances. Like an eagle, an octopus can also build an impressive home. And, like many macaws, the Moorish idol chooses a mate for life. Fish are not only food. When discussing their future, we should engage as citizens concerned about Earth's fellow inhabitants as much as consumers worried only about our appetite.

REFERENCES

Alder, J., Campbell, B., Karpouzi, V., Kaschner, K. and Pauly, D. (2008) Forage fish: from ecosystems to markets. *Annual Review of Environment and Resources*, 33, 153–166.

Cheung, W.W.L., Lam, V.W.Y., Sarmiento, J.L., Kearney, K., Watson, R., Zeller, D. and Pauly, D. (2009) Large-scale redistribution of maximum fisheries catch potential in the global ocean under climate change. *Global Change Biology*, 16, 24–35.

Christensen, V., Guénette, S., Heymans, J.J., Walters, C.J., Watson, R., Zeller, D. and Pauly, D. (2003) Hundred-year decline of North Atlantic predatory fishes. *Fish and Fisheries*, 4, 1–24.

FAO (2009) *The State of the World Fisheries and Aquaculture*. Rome: FAO.

Grescoe, T. (2008) *Bottomfeeder: how to eat ethically in a world of vanishing seafood.* New York: Bloomsbury.

Hall, M. (2007) Eat more anchovies. *Conservation*, 8, 24.

Halweil, B. and Mastny, L. (2006) *Catch of the Day: Choosing Seafood for Healthier Oceans*. Washington DC: Worldwatch Institute.

Jacquet, J., Alava, J.J., Ganapathiraju, P., Henderson, S. and Zeller, D. (2008) In hot soup: sharks captured in Ecuador's waters. *Environmental Sciences*, 5, 269–283.

Jacquet, J., Fox, H., Motta, H., Ngusaru, A. and Zeller, D. (2010) Few data, but many fish: marine small-scale fisheries catches for Mozambique and Tanzania. *African Journal of Marine science*, 32, 197–206.

Jacquet, J., Hocevar, J., Lai, S., Majluf, P., Pelletier, N., Pitcher, T., Sala, E., Sumaila, R. and Pauly, D. (2010) Conserving wild fish in a sea of market based efforts. *Oryx*, 44, 45–56.

Jacquet, J. and Pauly, D. (2008a) Funding priorities: big barriers to small-scale fisheries. *Conservation Biology*, 22, 832.

Jacquet, J.L. and Pauly, D. (2007) The rise of seafood awareness campaigns in an era of collapsing fisheries. *Marine Policy*, 31, 308–313.

Jacquet, J.L. and Pauly, D. (2008b) Trade secrets: renaming and mislabeling of seafood. *Marine Policy*, 32, 309–318.

Kaczynski, V.M. and Fluharty, D.L. (2002) European policies in West Africa: who benefits from fisheries agreements? *Marine Policy*, 26, 75–93.

Marean, C.W., Bar-Matthews, M., Bernatchez, J., Fisher, E., Goldberg, P., Herries, A.I.R., Jacobs, Z., Jerardino, A., Karkanas, P. and Minichillo, T. (2007) Early human use of marine resources and pigment in South Africa during the Middle Pleistocene. *Nature*, 449, 905–908.

Myers, R.A. and Worm, B. (2003) Rapid worldwide depletion of predatory fish communities. *Nature*, 423, 280–283.

NMFS (2006) *Fisheries of the USA, 2005*. Silver Springs, MD: National Marine Fisheries Service.

Pauly, D. (1998) Rationale for reconstructing catch time series. *EC Fisheries Cooperation Bulletin*, 11, 4–7.

Pauly, D., Christensen, V., Guénette, S., Pitcher, T.J., Sumaila, U.R., Walters, C.J., Watson, R. and Zeller, D. (2002) Towards sustainability in world fisheries. *Nature*, 418, 689–695.

Pimentel, D. and Pimentel, M. (2003) Sustainability of meat-based and plant-based diets and the environment. *American Journal of Clinical Nutrition*, 78, 660S.

Pollan, M. (2008) *In Defense of Food: An Eater's Manifesto*. New York, NY: Penguin Press.

Richter, C., Roa-Quiaoit, H., Jantzen, C., Al-Zibdah, M. and Kochzius, M. (2008) Collapse of a new living species of giant clam in the Red Sea. *Current Biology*, 18, 1349–1354.

Spalding, M. D., Fish, L. and Wood, L. J. (2008) Toward representative protection of the world's coasts and oceans – progress, gaps, and opportunities. *Conservation Letters*, 1, 217–226.

Walter, R. C., Buffler, R. T., Bruggemann, J. H., Guillaume, M. M. M., Berhe, S. M., Negassi, B., Libsekal, Y., Cheng, H., Edwards, R. L. and Von Cosel, R. (2000) Early human occupation of the Red Sea coast of Eritrea during the last interglacial. *Nature*, 405, 65–69.

Watson, R. and Pauly, D. (2001) Systematic distortions in world fisheries catch trends. *Nature*, 414, 534–536.

WHO (2003) Global and regional food consumption patterns and trends: availability and consumption of fish. Report of a joint WHO/FAO expert consultation, Geneva, January 28–February 1, 2002, available at http://www.fao.org/docrep/005/ac911e/ac911e05.htm.

Wood, L. J., Fish, L., Laughren, J. and Pauly, D. (2008) Assessing progress towards global marine protection targets: shortfalls in information and action. *Oryx*, 42, 340–351.

Worm, B., Barbier, E. B., Beaumont, N., Duffy, J. E., Folke, C., Halpern, B. S., Jackson, J. B. C., Lotze, H. K., Micheli, F. and Palumbi, S. R. (2006) Impacts of biodiversity loss on ocean ecosystem services. *Science*, 314, 787–790.

Zeller, D. and Pauly, D. (2007) Reconstruction of marine fisheries catches for key countries and regions (1950–2005). Fisheries Centre Research Report. Vancouver, Canada: Fisheries Centre, University of British Columbia.

JEREMY JACKSON AND JENNIFER JACQUET

9

The shifting baselines syndrome: perception, deception, and the future of our oceans

INTRODUCTION

Humans consider the surroundings of their youth as natural and, as they age, recognize the changes to their environment as unnatural. Children repeat the errors of their parents. Thus, as each new generation collectively adopts this perverse perspective, we lose track of the inexorable degradation of native ecosystems. Pauly (1995) coined the term "shifting baselines syndrome" to describe this phenomenon in relation to the problem of fisheries, for which baselines for so-called "pristine" populations are established by managers that ignore the impacts of earlier fishing that had already greatly reduced fish abundance and size. Consequently, expectations change as we shift to eating smaller and smaller fish and invertebrates at progressively lower trophic levels – the phenomenon now commonly referred to as "fishing down the food web" (Pauly *et al.*, 1998). The gradual accommodation of loss applies to a host of other ecological and cultural resources. Pollan (2008) writes on "the tangible material formerly known as food" and notes that many modern food systems would be unrecognizable to people only a few decades ago. Similarly, we are in the process of destroying many indigenous cultures through a combination of genocide and assimilation. We lose one of the 7000 languages remaining on Earth every two weeks (Wilford, 2007). The "future of the past" (Stille, 2002) is grim indeed.

It is not sycophantic to say that the idea of shifting baselines was revolutionary for the field of ecology, for which our limited understanding of patterns of distribution and abundance, food webs, and community structure are based on the assumption that what we can observe today is all that matters (Jackson, 1997, 2006). The folly of this

Ecosystem Approaches to Fisheries: A Global Perspective, ed. V. Christensen and J. Maclean. Published by Cambridge University Press. © Cambridge University Press 2011.

"arrogance of the present" has been clear to historical ecologists since at least the 1980s (Cronon, 1983). No rational person would deny the once fantastically great abundance of bison in North America before European contact (Isenberg, 2000) simply because there are no ecological survey data from the fifteenth century. But in effect this is what most marine ecologists have done until very recently for the former extraordinary abundance of large animals in coastal seas around the world (Jackson, 1997, 2001; Jackson *et al.*, 2001). This is the problem of shifting baselines.

SYMPTOMS

There are three requisite symptoms of the shifting baselines syndrome: change, time, and amnesia. Sáenz-Arroyo *et al.* (2005) captured the complete spirit of shifting baselines after interviewing three genera-tions of Mexican fishers and finding that, compared to young fishers, older fishers named five times as many species and four times as many fishing sites as being once productive but now depleted. Very few young fishers appreciated that large species had ever been common or that nearshore sites had been productive.

Oceanic whitetip sharks (*Carcharhinus longimanus*) were described as the most common pelagic shark in the Gulf of Mexico in the 1950s. Today, scientific papers refer to them as "rare" or dismiss the species entirely because oceanic whitetip sharks in the region have declined by more than 99% and so has their human memory (Baum and Myers, 2004). Fishers off of Canada's east coast, once the center of the cod industry, now fish for formerly discarded hagfish and sea cucumbers (CanWest, 2008), and in Oregon fishers are trading in their salmon fishing gear for gear to catch prawns because the salmon are nearly gone (Yardley, 2008). The "Euro series" spear gun has been introduced in North America to hunt smaller fish. Recently, an east coast US fish-erman in his twenties accosted a fisheries manager and told him he was angry at lowered Atlantic bluefin tuna (*Thunnus thynnus*) quotas because there were more tuna out there than he had ever seen. "Well, you're not very old," responded the manager (Woodard, 2008). In fact, Western Atlantic bluefin tuna are critically endangered (Safina and Klinger, 2008; Safina and Hardt, this volume).

Similarly radical shifts are occurring because of global warming as formerly tropical and subtropical species migrate into higher lati-tudes (Cheung *et al.*, 2009). England's National Marine Aquarium at Plymouth used to have a Mediterranean tank. Today, as temperature and other factors of the North Atlantic have changed, so should the tank's name since so many Mediterranean species are now found off of Plymouth's coast (Mitchell, 2009).

OPTIMISM IS INVERSELY RELATED TO DATA QUALITY

Our optimism or pessimism about our predicament varies as a function of the age and quality of our data. Since baselines for what is natural are reset with every new generation, younger people are allowed to be more hopeful than older people. The gray whale, for instance, is considered an icon of success of the US Endangered Species Act. Gray whale numbers have rebounded from near extinction to 22 000 whales today – a truly great achievement of conservation. But new research using DNA to reconstruct former gray whale abundance suggests that the gray whale population before whaling was more likely 96 000 animals, or three to five times greater than today's estimates (Alter *et al.*, 2007). Humpback whales in the Northern Pacific also have rebounded from 1400 individuals in 1966, after more than a century of whaling, to 20 000 animals today, giving conservationists cause for celebration (Calambokidis *et al.*, 2008). But we have little idea of the actual abundance of humpbacks before whaling. The recovery of the bald eagle tells a similar story. Conservation efforts brought bald eagles back from the brink – 417 nesting pairs were reported in the United States in 1967. Today there are more than 10 000 nesting pairs, causing them to be removed from the federal list of endangered and threatened species (Fahrenthold, 2007). However, the recovery baseline for bald eagles was not the population estimated in 1782, when the United States adopted the bird as its national symbol and when as many as 100 000 nesting pairs (ten times the current population) lived in the continental United States (excluding Alaska, USFWS, 1999). No one is suggesting a goal of 200 000 eagles living in the contiguous United States, but it is important to recognize that the baseline has shifted.

Whales and eagles are great success stories for the likely survival of the species. But there is a darker side to shifting baselines, which manifests itself in misplaced confidence based on far more modest successes, as exemplified by the situation of Caribbean green turtles (*Chelonia mydas*), which were vividly described in the documents of the Columbus voyages and most subsequent explorations (Jackson, 1997). Native Americans heavily exploited green turtles long before

Columbus and had already hunted them to near local extinction in places like Jamaica and the Bahamas (Carlson and Keegan, 2004; Fitzpatrick *et al.*, 2008; Hardt, 2008). But prehistoric depletion of green turtles is trivial when compared to European slaughter that systematically exploited green turtles for their meat and eggs (Jackson, 1997; McClenachan *et al.*, 2006). As a result, green turtles were reduced to less than 1% of their abundance in the sixteenth century and 20% of nesting beaches were entirely eliminated – with nesting populations at half of the remaining beaches perilously close to extinction. An alarming implication for management is that all the examples of local nesting beach recovery are from baselines of less than 40 years duration whereas all longer time series exhibit dramatic decline (McClenachan *et al.*, 2006).

The globally endangered goliath grouper (*Epinephelus itajara*) in Florida provides another even more disturbing example because dramatic decreases in this highly prized fish occurred much more recently and are well documented historically (McClenachan, 2009b). Recent protection resulted in substantial increases in grouper to some 30% of the 1990 baseline of "virgin biomass," which has been used by sports fishers to declare success and urge the reopening of the fishery. However, analysis of historical photographs and newspaper accounts clearly demonstrate dramatic decreases in goliath grouper abundance and size since the beginning of the twentieth century, strongly suggesting that the recent increases do not represent a significant recovery for the survival of the species.

ANECDOTES AND HISTORICAL DATA

Occasionally, we have rigorous, long-term quantitative catch data for commercially important species like cod and herring to confirm shifting baselines and show that our perception of what is "natural" is skewed (Lotze and Milewski, 2004; Rosenberg *et al.*, 2005; Roberts, 2007; McClenachan, 2009a, 2009b). But, far more often, most of the changes occurred before we were there to see them or could record relevant numbers. In these circumstances, we need to exploit geological, archeological, and historical data in addition to more modern ecological records to reconstruct what used to be in the sea (Jackson, 2001; Jackson *et al.*, 2001; Pandolfi *et al.*, 2003; Lotze *et al.*, 2006; Jackson and McClenachan, 2009).

Many of these historical data are qualitative or semi-quantitative, which is why ecologists tended to ignore them. But there is an enormous wealth of historical data if we know how to use them; and confidence in reconstructions of past conditions greatly increases when different kinds of primary data and proxies are in general agreement. Most importantly, failure to incorporate historical information into scientific assessments because the data are imprecise risks ignoring the obvious. As Daniel Pauly (1995) famously said, the anecdotes are the data. Insistence on traditional quantitative population data represents a kind of false "precisionism" that ignores reality and generality (*sensu* Levins, 1968), and we do so at our peril. The oceans used to be dominated ecologically by lots of very large animals that are impossible to study with modern quantitative ecological methods because they are ecologically or biologically extinct (Jackson *et al.*, 2001; Lotze and Worm, 2009).

The sheer multitude of historical observations easily overcomes the issues of subjectivity and quantitative rigor. The data for Caribbean green turtles discussed previously, for example, come from 163 separate records of observations or hunting of green turtles on or around beaches and gathering of their eggs that were highly prized as food (McClenachan *et al.*, 2006). Those data, combined with data for numbers of turtles harvested or surveyed on particular beaches and at different times, provided the basis for the calculation that there were 91 million large adult green turtles in the tropical western Atlantic before Europeans began to hunt them. Allowing for uncertainties in the data and calculations, we can confidently conclude that there was somewhere between 50 and 150 million green turtles – a biomass that at 200 to 300 kg/turtle approaches the biomass of the human population of the United States today! Taking either the upper or lower bound, historical estimates dwarf the present population – fewer than 300 000 much smaller green turtles in the tropical Western Atlantic today. (Seminoff *et al.*, 2002). Using similar techniques, the abundance of hawksbill turtles exploited for their shells was about 11 000 000 compared to fewer than 30 000 today (McClenachan *et al.*, 2006) and the abundance of the now extinct Caribbean monk seal was once between 233 000 and 338 000 (McClenachan and Cooper, 2008).

McClenachan (2009a) used an entirely different approach to determine the decline of sports fish around Key West from the 1950s to the present. Sport fishing logbooks might be sparse but sport fishermen love to be photographed with their catch. Using historical photographs taken in Key West from 1956 to 2007, McClenachan examined the mean individual size and species composition for 13 groups of recreationally caught "trophy" reef fish. Measurements derived from the photographs show that the mean length of trophy fish declined by more than 50% (92 cm to 42 cm), mean weight declined by 90% (19.9 kg to 2.3 kg), and species composition changed from dominance by large groupers and other predatory fishes to dominance by small snappers. The average length of sharks also declined by more than 50% over 50 years. Nevertheless, the price for a fishing trip remains the same adjusted for inflation. Thus, consumers are still paying the same for catching much less fish – a remarkable example of shifting baselines in personal expectations.

Finally, when the kinds of historical data illustrated above are lacking, one can simply code historical observations to reflect categories of abundance, (e.g., what was the most abundant species observed, or classification of species as abundant, common, rare, or absent) and statistically compare their rankings or frequency of occurrence (Jackson et al., 2001; Palomares et al., 2006). All of these approaches have been used to document in considerable detail the varyingly precipitous decline of innumerable species in all the major ecosystems of the oceans (Pauly et al., 1998; Pauly et al., 2003; Jackson, 2001; Jackson et al., 2001; Myers and Worm, 2003; Lotze and Milewski, 2004; Lotze et al., 2005; Lotze et al., 2006; Jackson, 2008). The degradation is so great that entire ocean ecosystems are globally endangered, rather than just individual species. By analogy with the criteria for the Red List of endangered species compiled by the International Union for Conservation for Nature, coral reefs and coastal seas are critically endangered, continental shelves are endangered, and open ocean pelagic ecosystems are threatened (Jackson, 2008).

THE ARROGANCE OF PRECISIONISM

The report by Myers and Worm (2003) that globally 90% of large predatory fish were gone because of overfishing attracted lots of attention but also generated bitter disagreement between fisheries scientists and ecologists, such as Ray Hilborn and Boris Worm, which was captured for posterity in the 2009 documentary film "The End of the Line." Nevertheless, the National Research Council report to investigate the ecosystem consequences of fishing acknowledged declines within the range of 65–80%, which is much more than had been acknowledged by fisheries scientists or the fishing industry before Myers and Worm's article appeared (NRC, 2006).

The intensity of this squabble over what turned out to be a relatively small discrepancy in interpretation of the data is symptomatic of the "precisionism" of fisheries managers who tend to forget the limitations of the scientific data and the simplifying assumptions of the models used to calculate truly sustainable catch. A good example is the case of Alaskan pollock (*Theragra chalcogramma*) in the east Bering Sea that have so far sustained one of the largest fisheries in the world that supplies a great proportion of the fish used for frozen breaded fish products that are a staple of the fast food industry. The US National Marine Fisheries Service (NMFS) intensively manages the fishery, providing impressively detailed annual analyses of abundance and stock structure and highly sophisticated models of past and predicted future abundance to provide the basis for setting ecologically responsible quotas for the fishery (Ianelli *et al.*, 2008). But the road to ruin is paved with good intentions and the fishery has been in decline for several years with increasing rumors of population collapse in 2009. Eastern Bering Sea pollock biomass dropped 65% between 2003 and 2008, fishers are traveling greater distances to find fish, and northern fur seals that feed on pollock are in decline (NOAA, 2008).

If the fishery does collapse and has to be shut down to allow stocks to recover, it will cause extreme economic hardship and loss of jobs on the scale of the collapse of Atlantic cod in eastern Canada in 1992 (Walters and Maguire, 1996). How could this happen in 2009? The problem is that the fishery is managed to the margins of what the models say they can catch, based on models that assume we can safely ignore changes in oceanography, climate, and interactions with other species that may have profound effects on reproduction and abundance. Remarkably, the quotas have been reduced by only a small percentage each year, even though the stock of reproductive females has declined steadily and steeply for the past 5 years, because the *model* predicted that the population would recover a few years out (Ianelli *et al.*, 2008), which so far it has not. This policy is equivalent to giving a very large loan to a very large company that is hemorrhaging money on the basis of a revised business strategy that promises increases in profits several years in the future – a very high risk game indeed.

The pollock story may be an extreme case of overconfidence in models, but we don't think so. Perusal of the NMFS website (http://www.nmfs.noaa.gov/) shows that inadequate data are available for a little more than half of the 528 fisheries for which NMFS is responsible, despite the financial resources of the wealthiest economy in the world. Of the remaining 244 stocks, 41 are "subject to overfishing," 42 are "overfished," and 148 are "fully fished" or "not fished to capacity." Thus, at best, only 28% of US fisheries are believed to be in good shape and NMFS is managing by wishful thinking. Try to imagine how much worse the situation is in the waters of developing countries whose fish are being overfished by the wealthy nations of Europe, North America, and Australasia (e.g., Kaczynski and Fluharty, 2002).

After several years of pedantic disagreement, Hilborn and Worm assembled a team of fisheries biologists and ecologists to try to resolve their differences (Worm et al., 2009). The authors report: "In 5 of 10 well-studied ecosystems, the average exploitation rate has recently declined and is now at or below the rate predicted to achieve maximum sustainable yield for seven systems." The paper is titled "Rebuilding global fisheries," but "well-studied ecosystems" inevitably refers to the relatively small number of data-rich fisheries that occur within the waters of the wealthy, developed nations that can afford detailed quantitative stock assessments and are best equipped to deal with management. Of the 24 ecosystem models considered in the study, there is one considered from all of Africa, one from all of South America, and zero from Asia (Worm et al., 2009, Fig. 2). Moreover, for the ten fisheries stock assessments examined, none of the data extend further back than the 1970s (Worm et al., 2009, Fig. 3). For all of their impressive quantitative rigor and model building, the authors seem to be grasping for examples of success. For an outsider it seems that, even today, quantitative fisheries management is complicit in fisheries collapses.

If the notion of scientists intentionally resetting baselines seems far-fetched, consider the New England Fisheries Management Council's 2007 stock assessment for monkfish (Lophius americanus) in the Northwest Atlantic, which declared that monkfish were not over-fished. The 2007 assessment reversed the scientific community's previous understanding about monkfish, which were considered overfished and in great need of rebuilding. There was a perverse reason for the reversal: the new analytic model ("SCALE") for monkfish used to generate the stock assessment was done considering data using a shorter assessment time frame (1980–2006) rather than the previous time frame (1963–2006) when biomass indices from surveys were approximately two times higher than 1980s estimates (NMFS, 2007). Using similar "smoke and mirrors" techniques of analyzing only fish biomass from, say, 2005 onward, we could erase the problem of overfishing around the globe. In fact, this was effectively done with sport fishing records when, in 1996, the International Underwater Spearfishing Association (http://www.iusarecords.com/about.htm)

reset world records, creating twentieth century records and a new twenty-first century category, likely because fish were getting smaller.

THE CONFOUNDING ROLE OF THE MEDIA

If some scientists are guilty of clouding the issue with false precision, some media outlets are just as guilty of clouding the issue with misleading imagery that strongly shapes the public's belief about the state of our state of our environment. The most popular movie ever made about fish is "Jaws," not "Empty Oceans, Empty Nets." And although the excellent front-page articles by Ken Weiss (2006) in the *Los Angeles Times* were awarded the Pulitzer Prize, they have not had the same impact as the Emmy-award winning Blue Planet television series that glossed over human impacts. Feature films and commercial television have vastly larger audiences than public television and newspapers.

Successful story telling, which explains the success of "Jaws" and other popular media, thrives on tension. But the media often creates tension between the wrong actors. It has been recognized that the so-called "fair and balanced approach" to science news can be detrimental. As Al Gore pointed out in "An Inconvenient Truth," climate scientists, as represented by their peer-reviewed literature, hold a consensus view on the effects of our carbon emissions while the media continues to report skepticism (Boykoff and Boykoff, 2004; Oreskes, 2004). Similar problems inhibit more realistic discussion of the collapse of fisheries and ocean ecosystems. Likewise, consistently bad news does not make for good entertainment, as is clear from the television shows "E.R.," "Chicago Hope," and "Rescue 911" that portray two-thirds of cardiac resuscitations as successful, whereas in reality rates of recovery after patient resuscitation are closer to 15% (Diem *et al.*, 1996). People believe that 70% of CPR patients survive because that is what they see on television, and they believe that the oceans are okay because that is what they see on the Discovery Channel and National Geographic TV.

FUTURE SCENARIOS

Learning about the past is important because it will help us determine our future. We already have glimpses at what could be our "Brave New Ocean" (Jackson, 2001, 2008) – an ocean full of jellyfish, hagfish, and microbes. In the sci-fi novel "The Swarm" (Schätzing, 2006), whales and fish disappear, invasive species foul ships, and jellyfish and toxic blooms take over. People living near the coast move inland and scientists are the only ones thinking about the big picture. This science-fictional future is painfully close to reality. In Florida, when a red tide comes ashore, the barrier island is now evacuated; the emergency rooms fill up with people with congestive problems and acute asthma (Weiss and McFarling, 2006). Nobody can live there for weeks if the red tide lasts. This is "Brave New Ocean" and "The Swarm" and it is real. Imagining future scenarios can be very provocative (think Arthur C. Clarke, Aldous Huxley, or H. G. Wells). Schätzing spent several years researching marine issues and the publication of his book led to a large increase in the profile and funding for marine science in Germany where "Der Schwarm" was first published (Worm, 2006). On the other hand, consistently bad news is depressing and causes people to disconnect and give up hope. So we desperately need examples of successful actions that have reversed the seeming inexorable degradation of the oceans.

Overfishing must be stopped immediately and the mandate to rebuild stocks within a 10-year window strictly enforced (Safina et al., 2005). The establishment and enforcement of vastly more and much larger marine protected areas (MPAs) where most wildlife is protected are a good place to start. MPAs work, as evidenced by the increases in fish stocks on George's Bank after large areas were closed to fishing (Rosenberg et al., 2006). They also have welcome unexpected consequences, including the increased resilience of protected coral reef ecosystems to global warming and disease (Knowlton and Jackson, 2008; Sandin et al., 2008). But MPAs represent much less than 1% of the total area of the oceans while most ecologists agree that we need to set aside a third of all habitats and ecosystems as insurance for the future (Wood et al., 2008).

To protect highly migratory species, we need to zone the entire global ocean including the high seas to internationally regulate protection and resource use. Australia has made a dramatic beginning by rezoning to protect one third of all habitats and ecosystems along the entire 2000 km long Great Barrier Reef, a distance similar to the Pacific coastline of the USA from Seattle to San Diego (Pandolfi et al., 2005). The United States has followed by setting aside vast areas of the Pacific within the exclusive economic zones surrounding the Hawaiian Archipelago and the Pacific Trust Territories. These are areas surrounding wealthy nations where relatively few people are affected. The much harder challenge is to extend protection to the waters of developing nations that cannot afford to simply shut down the livelihoods of their starving poor, and to the high seas that have been traditionally open to plunder by anyone with the resources to do so. Or we can do nothing and wait for catastrophe to knock, as it surely will. The choices are ours.

ACKNOWLEDGMENTS

The authors would like to thank Daniel Pauly for his inspiration and leadership, Loren McClenachan for her excellent work and innumerable conversations about shifting baselines and historical ecology, and Randy Olson for his wit and tireless efforts to communicate the shifting baselines syndrome.

REFERENCES

Alter, S. E., Rynes, E. and Palumbi, S. (2007) DNA evidence for historic population size and past ecological impacts of gray whales. *Proceedings of the National Academy of Sciences*, 104 (38), 15162–15167.

Baum, J. K. and Myers, R. A. (2004) Shifting baselines and the decline of pelagic sharks in the Gulf of Mexico. *Ecology Letters*, 7, 135–145.

Boykoff, M. T. and Boykoff, J. M. (2004) Balance as bias: global warming and the US prestige press. *Global Environmental Change*, 14, 125–136.

Calambokidis, J., Falcone, E. A., Quinn, T. J., Burdin, A. M., Clapham, P. J., Ford, J. K. B., Gabriele, C. M., Leduc, R., Mattila, D., Rojas-Bracho, L., Straley, J. M., Taylor, B. L., Urbán R, J., Weller, D., Witteveen, B. H., Yamaguchi, M., Bendlin, A., Camacho, D., Flynn, K., Havron, A., Huggins, A. J. and Maloney, N. (2008) SPLASH: Structure of Populations, Levels of Abundance and Status of Humpback Whales in the North Pacific. Cascadia Research for U.S. Dept of Commerce.

CanWest (2008) East Coast considers harvesting hagfish, sea cucumber. January 3, 2008, available at http://www.canada.com/vancouversun/news/business/story.html?id=bfe2db86-2c89-4287-9cd9-cfb7b69584d4&k=32751, accessed July 30, 2010.

Carlson, L. A. and Keegan, W. F. (2004) Resource depletion in the prehistoric northern West Indies. In Fitzpatrick, S. M., ed., *Voyages of Discovery: Archeology of Islands*. New York, NY: Praeger Publishers, pp. 85–107.

Cheung, W. W. L., Lam, V. W. Y., Sarmiento, J. L., Kearney, K., Watson, R., Zeller, D. and Pauly, D. (2009) Large-scale redistribution of maximum fisheries catch potential in the global ocean under climate change. *Global Change Biology*, 16, 24–35.

Cronon, W. (1983) *Changes in the Land: Indians, Colonists, and the Ecology of New England*. New York: Hill and Wang.

Diem, S. J., Lantos, J. D. and Tulsky, J. A. (1996) Cardiopulmonary resuscitation on television – miracles and misinformation. *New England Journal of Medicine*, 334, 1578–1582.

Fahrenthold, D. (2007) US declares bald eagles no longer threatened. *Washington Post*, June 29, 2007.

FItzpatrick, S. M., Keegan, W. F., and Sealey, K. S. (2008) Human impacts on marine environments in the West Indies during the middle to late Holocene. In Rick, T. C. and Erlandson, J. M., eds., *Human Impacts on Ancient Marine Ecosystems*. Berkeley, CA: University of California Press, pp. 147–164.

Hardt, M. J. (2008) Lessons from the past: the collapse of Jamaican coral reefs. *Fish and Fisheries*, 10, 1–16.

Ianelli, J. N., Barbeaux, S., Honkalchto, T., Kotzwicki, S., Aydin, K. and Williamson, N. (2008) Assessment of the walleye pollock stock in the Eastern Bering Sea. Alaska Fisheries Science Center and National Marine Fisheries Service. NPFMC Bering Sea and Aleutian Islands SAFE, pp. 47–136.

Isenberg, A. C. (2000) *The Destruction of the Bison*. Cambridge, UK: Cambridge University Press.

Jackson, J. B. C. (1997) Reefs since Columbus. *Coral Reefs*, 16, 23–32.

Jackson, J. B. C. (2001) What was natural in the coastal oceans? *Proceedings of the National Academy of Sciences of the United States of America*, 98, 5411–5418.

Jackson, J. B. C. (2006) When ecological pyramids were upside down. In Estes, J. A., ed., *Whales, Whaling, and Ocean Ecosystems*. Berkeley, CA: University of California Press, pp. 27–37.

Jackson, J. B. C. (2008) Ecological extinction and evolution in the brave new ocean. *Proceedings of the National Academy of Sciences*, 105, 11458–11465.

Jackson, J. B. C., Kirby, M. X., Berger, W. H., Bjorndal, K. A., Botsford, L. W., Bourque, B. J., Bradbury, R. H., Cooke, R., Erlandson, J., Estes, J. A., Hughes, T. P., Kidwell, S., Lange, C. B., Lenihan, H. S. Pandolfi, J. M., Peterson, C. H., Steneck, R. S., Tegner, M. J. and Warner, R. R. (2001) Historical overfishing and the recent collapse of coastal ecosystems. *Science*, 293, 629–637.

Jackson, J. B. C. and McClenachan, L. (2009) Historical ecology for the paleontologist. In Dietl, G. P. and Flessa, K. W., eds., *Conservation Paleobiology: Using the Past to Manage for the Future*. Paleontological Society Special Publications, pp. 81–95.

Kaczynski, V. M. and Fluharty, D. L. (2002) European policies in West Africa: who benefits from fisheries agreements? *Marine Policy*, 26, 75–93.

Knowlton, N. and Jackson, J. B. C. (2008) Shifting baselines, local impacts, and global change on coral reefs. *PLoS Biology*, 6 (2), e54.

Levins, R. (1968) *Evolution in Changing Environments*. Princeton, NJ: University Press.

Lotze, H. K., Lenihan, H. S., Bourque, B. J., Bradbury, R. H., Cooke, R. G., Kay, M. C., Kidwell, S. M., Kirby, M. X., Peterson, C. H. and Jackson, J. B. C. (2006) Depletion, degradation, and recovery potential of estuaries and coastal seas. *Science*, 312, 1806–1809.

Lotze, H. K. and Milewski, I. (2004) Two centuries of multiple human impacts and successive changes in a North Atlantic food web. *Ecological Applications*, 14, 1428–1447.

Lotze, H. K., Reise, K., Worm, B., Van Beusekom, J., Busch, M., Ehlers, A., Heinrich, D., Hoffmann, R. C., Holm, P. and Jensen, C. (2005) Human transformations of the Wadden Sea ecosystem through time: a synthesis. *Helgoland Marine Research*, 59, 84–95.

Lotze, H. K. and Worm, B. (2009) Historical baselines for large marine animals. *Trends in Ecology and Evolution*, 24, 254–262.

McClenachan, L. (2009a) Documenting loss of large trophy fish from the Florida Keys with historical photographs. *Conservation Biology*, 23, 636–643.

McClenachan, L. (2009b) Historical declines of goliath grouper populations in South Florida, USA. *Endangered Species Research*, 7, 175–181.

McClenachan, L. and Cooper, A. B. (2008) Extinction rate, historical population structure and ecological role of the Caribbean monk seal. *Proceedings of the Royal Society B, Biological Sciences*, 275, 1351.

McClenachan, L., Jackson, J. B. C. and Newman, M. J. H. (2006) Conservation implications of historic sea turtle nesting beach loss. *Frontiers in Ecology and the Environment*, 4, 290–296.

Mitchell, A. (2009) *Sea Sick: The Global Ocean in Crisis*. Toronto: McClelland & Stewart.

Myers, R. A. and Worm, B. (2003) Rapid worldwide depletion of predatory fish communities. *Nature*, 423, 280–283.

NMFS (2007) Monkfish assessment summary for 2007. US Dept Commerce, Northeast Fisheries Science Center.

NOAA (2008) NOAA finds decline in pollock; recommends catch cut to council. Washington DC: NOAA, November 20, 2008.

NRC (2006) *Dynamic Changes In Marine Ocean Ecosystems: Fishing, Food Webs, and Future Options*. Washington DC: National Academy Press.

Oreskes, N. (2004) Beyond the ivory tower: the scientific consensus on climate change. *Science*, 306, 1686.

Palomares, M. L. D., Mohammed, E. and Pauly, D. (2006) European expeditions as a source of historic abundance data on marine organisms: a case study of the Falkland Islands. *Environmental History*, 11, 835–847.

Pandolfi, J. M., Bradbury, R. H., Sala, E., Hughes, T. P., Bjorndal, K. A., Cooke, R. G., McArdle, D., McClenachan, L., Newman, M. J. H., Paredes, G., Warner, R. R. and Jackson, J. B. C. (2003) Global trajectories of the long-term decline of coral reef ecosystems. *Science*, 301, 955–958.

Pandolfi, J. M, Jackson, J. B. C, Baron, N., Bradbury, R. H., Guzman, H. M., Hughes, T., Kappel, C. V., Micheli, F., Ogden, J., Possingham, H. P. and Sala, E. (2005) Are US coral reefs on the slippery slope to slime? *Science*, 307, 1725–1726.

Pauly, D. (1995) Anecdotes and the shifting baseline syndrome of fisheries. *Trends in Ecology & Evolution*, 10, 430–430.

Pauly, D., Alder, J., Bennett, E., Christensen, V., Tyedmers, P. and Watson, R. (2003) The future for fisheries. *Science*, 302, 1359–1361.

Pauly, D., Christensen, V., Dalsgaard, J., Froese, R. and Torres Jr, F. (1998) Fishing down marine food webs. *Science*, 279, 860–863.

Pollan, M. (2008) *In Defense of Food: An Eater's Manifesto*. New York, NY: Penguin Press.

Roberts, C. (2007) *The Unnatural History of the Sea*. Washington DC: Island Press.

Rosenberg, A. A., Bolster, W. J., Alexander, K. E., Leavenworth, W. B., Cooper, A. B. and Mckenzie, M. G. (2005) The history of ocean resources: modeling cod biomass using historical records. *Frontiers in Ecology and the Environment*, 3, 78–84.

Rosenberg, A. A., Swasey, J. H. and Bowman, M. (2006) Rebuilding US fisheries: progress and problems. *Frontiers in Ecology and the Environment*, 4, 303–308.

Sáenz-Arroyo, A., Roberts, C. M., Torre, J., Cariño-Olvera, M., and Enríquez-Andrade, R. R. (2005) Rapidly shifting environmental baselines among fishers of the Gulf of California. *Proceedings of the Royal Society B, Biological Sciences*, 272, 1957–1962.

Safina, C. and Klinger, D. H. (2008) Collapse of bluefin tuna in the western Atlantic. *Conservation Biology*, 22, 243–246.

Safina, C., Rosenberg, A. A., Myers, R., Terrance, Q., II and Collie, J. (2005) US ocean fish recovery: staying the course. *Science*, 309, 707–708.

Sandin, S. A., Smith, J. E., Demartini, E. E., Dinsdale, E. A., Donner, S. D., Friedlander, A. M., Konotchick, T., Malay, M., Maragos, J. E. and Obura, D. (2008) Baselines and degradation of coral reefs in the northern Line Islands. *PLoS One*, 3 (2): e1548.

Schätzing, F. (2006) *The Swarm*. New York, NY: Harper Collins.

Seminoff, J. A., Resendiz, A. and Nichols, W. J. (2002) Home range of green turtles *Chelonia mydas* at a coastal foraging area in the Gulf of California, Mexico. *Marine Ecology Progress Series*, 242, 253–265.

Stille, A. (2002) *The Future of the Past*. New York, NY: Farar, Straus, and Giroux.

USFWS (1999) The bald eagle is back! President Clinton announces proposal to remove our national symbol from endangered species list. Washington DC: US Fish and Wildlife Service.

Walters, C. and Maguire, J. J. (1996) Lessons for stock assessment from the northern cod collapse. *Reviews in Fish Biology and Fisheries*, 6, 125–137.

Weiss, K. and McFarling, U. L. (2006) Altered Oceans. *Los Angeles Times*, July 30–August 3, 2006.

Wilford, J. N. (2007) Languages die, but not their last words. *New York Times*, September 19, 2007.

Wood, L. J., Fish, L., Laughren, J. and Pauly, D. (2008) Assessing progress towards global marine protection targets: shortfalls in information and action. *Oryx*, 42, 340–351.

Woodard, C. (2008) Sea captains' logbooks reveal secrets of New England's fishing culture. *Christian Science Monitor*, February 1, 2008. Available at http://www.csmonitor.com/USA/2008/0201/p20s01-usgn.html, accessed July 30, 2010.

Worm, B. (2006) Book review: Armageddon in the oceans. *Science*, 314, 1546.

Worm, B., Hilborn, R., Baum, J. K., Branch, T. A., Collie, J. S., Costello, C., Fogarty, M. J., Fulton, E. A., Hutchings, J. A., Jennings, S., Jensen, O. P., Lotze, H. K., Mace, P. M., McClanachan, T. R., Minto, C., Palumbi, S. R., Parma, A. M., Ricard, D., Rossenberg, A. A., Watson, R. and Zeller, D. (2009) Rebuilding global fisheries. *Science*, 325, 578–585.

Yardley, W. (2008) Salmon gone, fishermen try to adapt on a changing coast. *New York Times*, May 9, 2008.

Section III   Managing living resources

JOHN L. MUNRO[†]

10

Assessment of exploited stocks of tropical fishes: an overview

INTRODUCTION

The basic purpose of work on fish stock assessment is to provide advice on the combinations of gear and fishing effort that will provide sustainable yields from a stock. Technically, the status of an exploited stock may lie between being underfished (a combination of low fishing effort and large age or size at first capture) or overfished (when effort is high and size or age at first capture is small). Additionally, overfishing can progressively reduce recruitment to the fishery, leading to a long-term decline in catches. The actual catch that is taken from any fishing strategy will be proportional to the numbers of recruits to the fishery within the area under consideration. Recruitment rates will be determined by spawning stock biomasses, events in the pelagic phase, and post-settlement dynamics, but only the maintenance of spawning stock biomasses at prudent levels and the protection of nursery areas are realistically within the control of fishery managers.

FIRST STOCK ASSESSMENTS: 1890S–1950S

Stock assessments had their genesis in the late nineteenth century, when scientists first took note of the changes in fish stocks that were induced by fishing. Petersen (1892) observed modes in plots of the length-frequency distributions of various fish species and attributed these modes to successive year classes and noted their variability. Rings in otoliths and scales soon became firmly established as a means to estimate growth rates (Hoffbauer, 1898; Reibisch, 1899; Thompson, 1902). Estimates of mortality rates based on relative abundances of

[†] Deceased, December 13, 2009.

Ecosystem Approaches to Fisheries: A Global Perspective, ed. V. Christensen and J. Maclean. Published by Cambridge University Press. © Cambridge University Press 2011.

successive year classes were developed by Heincke (1913) and the first form of virtual population analysis (VPA) was derived by Derzhavin (1922).

By the start of the Second World War, the foundations of the modern theory of fishing had been firmly established (Graham, 1929, 1935; Hjort et al., 1933) and variability in year-classes was well understood (Hjort, 1914, 1926). The concept of overfishing was established by Russell (1931) and the theoretical and mathematical foundations of stock assessment were laid over the next 50 years. The task of summarizing the development of stock assessment concepts was greatly facilitated by the compilation by Cushing (1983) of a set of 16 "key papers on fish populations" published between 1931 and 1981. These include the papers of Russell (1931) on the overfishing problem, Graham (1935) and Beverton and Holt (1956) on the theory of fishing, Schaefer's works (1954, 1957) on surplus production models as applied to Pacific tuna stocks and Ricker (1954, 1958a) on stock and recruitment.

The early works in stock assessment were consolidated by Beverton and Holt (1957) and Ricker (1958b, 1975), whose works form the backbone of fisheries science. However, the focus remained fixed on temperate gadoids, clupeoids, salmonids, and a few other temperate groups. The von Bertalanffy (1938) growth equation became accepted as the principal means for describing and comparing growth rates in fishes and other aquatic species, if mainly because of its incorporation in Beverton and Holt's yield-per-recruit model.

After the publication of the works of Beverton and Holt (1957) and Ricker (1958a), VPA and cohort analysis were fully developed (Gulland, 1965; Garrod, 1967; Pope, 1972). The generalized stock production model was created (Pella and Tomlinson, 1969) and the Schaefer model applied to Northwest Atlantic stocks by Brown et al. (1976), which appears to be the first published attempt at a multispecies assessment. Papers by Gulland (1968) on marginal yield, by Gulland and Boerema (1973) on scientific advice on catch levels, and by Cushing (1981) on stock and recruitment complete Cushing's set and take us into the age where the availability of personal computers started to facilitate enormously the application of stock assessment models and to turn fish stock assessments into feasible undertakings by small government and university fisheries laboratories with limited funding.

TROPICAL STOCK ASSESSMENTS: 1950–1980

All of the conventional stock assessment methods described by Ricker (1958b, 1975) and Gulland (1969, 1983) can be applied to tropical fishes, given some adjustments. However, the required parameters must be estimated from length-frequency data and not from reading annual rings on scales (see contributions in Pauly and Morgan, 1987). The greatest problem encountered in gathering length-frequency or other biological data for tropical species exploited by artisanal fishers is the relatively low numbers of individual species taken in the catch, or delivered to a landing place, in a single day. Obtaining a satisfactory size-frequency sample or otolith collection can be expensive and time consuming, particularly for the larger and more valuable species. If there are centralized fish markets, data acquisition problems are reduced but getting the cooperation of fishers and traders can still be difficult.

Although a few countries in the tropics gather fairly detailed catch data on a regular basis, these are the exceptions. Most tropical developing countries have no detailed catch statistics apart from periodic sample surveys. Where catch data are collected, they are almost invariably aggregated by families or into even broader groups and, consequently, are of very little value for stock assessment. It would be of much greater value if managers of tropical fisheries identified the top 20 species in terms of value and concentrated on gathering statistics for those species. This subset of species usually represents about 90% of the weight of the total catch (Munro, 1974, 1983; McManus *et al.*, 1992; Trinidad *et al.*, 1993; Jennings *et al.*, 1995; Kahn *et al.*, 1997; Sary *et al.*, 2003). In addition to monitoring the trends in landings of the major species, it would be necessary to include others that are of concern because of their large sizes and high abundances in the past (e.g., large sciaenids, serranids, or lutjanids) or their status as threatened species (e.g., sharks and rays or ornamental species, such as angelfish). The remaining fraction can be aggregated as miscellaneous species "not elsewhere included" or "n.e.i." in the jargon of the Food and Agriculture Organization of the United Nations (FAO).

While advances in stock assessment methodology forged ahead in temperate regions, assessments of tropical species got off to a slow start. The taxonomy and basic biological features of many important species were often unknown and governments and aid agencies were more concerned with fisheries development than with conservation. However, Garrod (1961a, 1961b, 1963) produced a classic series of papers on mesh selection, growth, mortality, and rational exploitation of *Oreochromis esculentus* (previously known as *Tilapia esculenta*, Cichlidae), then endemic to Lake Victoria. This, I believe was the earliest complete stock assessment of any tropical species.

In India, biological studies produced growth parameters for at least 18 species, mostly through the 1950s and 1960s (Banerji and Krishnan, 1973), but no complete assessments had been published for any stock. In the French spheres of influence, Le Guen (1971) estimated growth and mortality rates of the Bobo croaker (*Pseudotolithus elongatus*, Sciaenidae) and other species in Senegal, based on annuli in otoliths. Significant work was done in the Indian Ocean, where Lebeau and Cueff (1975) used scale rings to estimate age and growth of blackeye emperor (*Lethrinus enigmaticus*, Lethrinidae) and made a complete yield-per-recruit assessment of the stocks on the Saya de Malha and adjacent banks. Loubens (1978, 1980) used otolith rings to estimate the growth rates of the 20 principal species taken on handlines in the New Caledonian lagoon.

Pauly and Martosubroto (1980) made a complete length-based yield-per-recruit assessment for red filament threadfin bream (*Nemipterus marginatus*, Nemipteridae) stocks off West Kalimantan, based on field work undertaken in the mid-1970s. This was the first such work completed in Southeast Asia.

In the Caribbean, work funded by the United Kingdom's Overseas Development Administration (now the Department for International Development) in 1969–73 enabled studies to be undertaken on the principal species in the Jamaican coral reef fishery and a first multi-species yield-per-recruit assessment of a tropical fish community (Munro, 1975, 1983). Length-based methods were used; scales and otoliths provided some information for a few species but were considered to be too confusing and labor intensive to warrant the attention of a small team. A fishing intensity surplus yield curve was devised to evaluate catch rates in ecologically similar areas that were subjected to different fishing intensities (Munro and Thompson, 1973).

STOCK ASSESSMENT PROGRAMS FOR CALCULATORS AND PERSONAL COMPUTERS

The earliest stock assessments were made in the times of pencil-and-paper science, when long columns of figures were added mentally, graphs were painstakingly drawn by hand and slide rules and tables of logarithms were kept close to hand. Mechanical calculators appeared in the 1940s and were electrically powered by the late 1950s. Electronic calculators became available in the 1960s, the earliest being expensive typewriter-sized machines with four functions and no memory. Computers became available to many institutions by the 1960s, filling whole rooms, boasting 64 kilobytes of memory, and accessible by the privileged few, under the close supervision of the guardians of these delicate monsters.

Calculators rapidly downsized to become hand-held, with impressive mathematical and statistical functions, but remained quite expensive. In the late 1970s, the first personal computers arrived, expensive and slow and running cumbersome and complicated operating systems. But the electronic revolution had arrived and radically changed the possibilities for fish stock assessment because tasks that were considered to be formidable undertakings in terms of time and person power became ever more feasible.

Abramson (1971), working for the FAO, was able to list 15 stock assessment programs covering age and growth estimation; mortality rates; yield curve computation; generalized stock production model fitting; simulation programs; normal distribution separation; and spawner-recruit, length–weight curve fitting. By 1982, Caddy listed 236 computer programs that were in use at major fisheries institutions and the development of mainframe applications continues in all of these institutions.

Pauly (1984a) provided an almost complete coverage of stock assessment methods based on the use of Hewlett Packard 67/97 programmable calculators. The emphasis was on length-based methods. Vakily *et al.* (1986) adapted the programs for HP 41CV calculators. The calculators and programs were soon outmoded, but the accompanying manuals still provide some of the clearest expositions of stock assessment concepts and equations, and are particularly useful to anyone who wishes to use them in modern spreadsheets.

Collaboration between the FAO and the then International Center for Living Aquatic Resources Management (ICLARM) led to the development of FiSAT (FAO–ICLARM Stock Assessment Tools) (Gayanilo *et al.*, 1996; Gayanilo and Pauly, 1997), a DOS-based suite that incorporated the ELEFAN suite (Pauly, 1987) and the methods presented by Pauly (1980, 1984a) and Sparre and Venema (1992). Both of these works were aimed primarily at the assessment of tropical stocks and made much use of applications based on length-frequency distributions, including length-based VPA and yield assessments. FiSAT II (Gayanilo and Pauly, 2002) is now available in the Microsoft® Windows operating environment (www.fao.org/fi/statist/fisoft/fisat/downloads.htm).

METHODS FOR PARAMETER ESTIMATION

The first step toward obtaining growth and mortality parameters for important species is to simply look in FishBase (Froese and Pauly, 2000; www.fishbase.org), which contains most published estimates. While the estimates reported vary in quality and accuracy, independent estimates exist for many species and if there is general agreement on the magnitude of the parameters they can be taken as first estimates. For example, Ault *et al.* (1998, 2002, 2005) made estimates of the status of 35 fish stocks in the Florida Keys, based entirely on published material.

Growth rates

Simple graphical methods of estimating age and growth by following modal progressions in length-frequency samples date from the early years of fisheries science. The work of Pauly and David (1981) in developing the first computerized method for "the objective extraction of growth parameters from length-frequency data," ELEFAN I, provoked much interest and debate and led to refinements in the original program (Pauly, 1987). The robustness and reliability of length-based methods in general, and of growth parameter estimation in particular, were reviewed in much detail in Pauly and Morgan (1987) and by Gulland and Rosenberg (1992).

The ELEFAN I program prompted the development of Shepherd's Length Composition Analysis (SLCA) (Shepherd *et al.*, 1987) which is conceptually similar to ELEFAN I. A modified version of SLCA (Pauly and Arreguin-Sanchez, 1995) is included in the FiSAT II package and is stated to give improved results.

An alternative system, MULTIFAN was developed by Fournier *et al.* (1990) and derives growth parameters and age compositions from multiple length-frequency samples. It had its genesis in the work of MacDonald and Pitcher (1979), Schnute and Fournier (1980), and Fournier and Breen (1983), who derived growth, age composition, and total mortality estimates from single length-frequency samples.

Comparisons have been made between the length-based models by a number of investigators and the findings were summarized by Terceiro *et al.* (1992). The basic conclusions were that ELEFAN I and SLCA are both sensitive to increasing variation in length at age (which results in multiple age-classes in the larger length groups), that SLCA tended to produce somewhat elevated estimates of the growth coefficient, K, and that ELEFAN I tended to underestimate both K and L_∞.

However, it should be noted that for most tropical fisheries the problem of multiple age-classes in the larger size groups virtually disappears when the stocks are heavily exploited and a few age groups represent the bulk of the stock.

Terceiro *et al.* (1992) compared the performance of the original version of SLCA and MULTIFAN, on simulated distributions of exploited stocks with 3 to 13 age classes. They concluded that "as a quick and simple method to examine length-frequency distributions, SLCA provided a good return for the amount of computational resources invested with limited user input." They considered MULTIFAN a "more complex but more powerful estimation technique with a formalized set of rules for a more objective evaluation of alternative interpretations of the length-frequency data" and suggested that SLCA should be used to obtain initial estimates of the parameter range, followed by application of MULTIFAN. The improved version of SLCA (Pauly and Arreguin-Sanchez, 1995), which gives clearer goodness of fit estimates, should now be used.

No application of MULTIFAN to tropical demersal fish species has been reported to date, but it is routinely used for tuna assessments in the South Pacific fisheries and has also been used for blue shark (*Prionace glauca*, Carcharhinidae) stock assessment (Kleiber *et al.*, 2001).

A new set of stock assessment tools has been released (Hoggarth *et al.*, 2005), intended for use primarily in tropical situations. One of the four parts, length-frequency distribution analysis (LFDA), is very similar to and draws on the ELEFAN suite for estimating growth parameters and mortality rates.

In tropical fish, daily rings in otoliths have been widely reported (Ntiba and Jaccarini, 1988; Szedlmayer, 1998; Robertson *et al.*, 1999; Allman and Grimes, 2002). Counting daily rings in large otoliths is difficult and the system has the greatest utility in determining the ages of juvenile fishes (Ralston *et al.*, 1996). Marks can be detected that indicate the time of settlement from the pelagic phase and can reveal the duration of the presettlement phase, the date of settlement, and the actual age at recruitment to the exploited stocks (Campana and Thorrold, 2001).

Annual rings in otoliths have been reported for tropical fish families, including lutjanids, lethrinids, clupeids, sciaenids, serranids, scarids, balistids, labrids, acanthurids, and pomacentrids (Le Guen, 1971; Loubens, 1978, 1980; Bullock *et al.*, 1992; Davis, 1992; Ferreira and Russ, 1992; McPherson and Squire, 1992; Sadovy *et al.*, 1992; Ferreira and Russ, 1994; Morales-Nin, 1994; Fowler, 1995; Choat and

Axe, 1996; Hart and Russ, 1996; Newman *et al.*, 1996; Cappo *et al.*, 2000; Luckhurst *et al.*, 2000; Marriott and Cappo, 2000; Newman *et al.*, 2000a, 2000b; Pilling *et al.*, 2000; Newman and Dunk, 2002). Most studies have been done in New Caledonia and on the Great Barrier Reef and elsewhere in Australia. These are areas with significant seasonal temperature variations. However, the work of Pilling *et al.* (2000) on lethrinids and lutjanids was based in the central Indian Ocean and included species inhabiting deep water where seasonal changes in temperature would be expected to be minimal.

Following early work by Templeman and Squires (1956) and Fletcher (1991), it has been found that otolith weight is a good predictor of age in Lane snapper (*Lutjanus synagris*, Lutjanidae) (Luckhurst *et al.*, 2000) and in Russell's snapper (*L. russelli*, Lutjanidae) (Newman and Dunk, 2002). Pilling *et al.* (2003) found significant variation in the age–otolith weight relationship in sky emperor (*Lethrinus mahsena*, Lethrinidae) and otolith weight was therefore not a precise indicator age. However, they found that using otolith weights to estimate age frequencies produced distributions that did not differ significantly from distributions derived from counting otolith increments. They concluded that this was a practical and economical method of assessing age structure of this species. Similarly, Strelcheck *et al.* (2003 and references therein) showed a relationship between otolith weight and standard length and age in gag (*Mycteropera microlepis*, Serranidae).

These studies of otoliths have shown that many species of tropical fishes have high longevity. This was regarded with some surprise, but has now been widely confirmed. Unexploited stocks of snappers, for example, have been shown to include around 30 year classes. The consequence has been that the recruitment variability that is a feature of many fish stocks only becomes apparent when the stocks are heavily exploited and the failure of a year class results in a significant reduction in catches.

Methods for deriving growth rates from mark and recapture data are well established and include techniques developed by Gulland and Holt (1959), Fabens (1965), Munro (1982), and Appeldoorn (1988). A tagging program executed within a small marine fishery reserve in Jamaica using Antillean fish traps produced growth estimates for 15 species of reef fish (Munro, 1999). Marked fish that were captured within the reserve were released. Of 6949 fishes marked, 5690 recaptures were made, with the high recapture rate being attributable to repeated catches of individual fishes. This was a very cost-effective exercise and probably worth repeating in a larger reserve.

Mortality rates

Mortality rates can be derived from four sources of data: age-frequency analyses, length-frequency analyses, mark-and-recapture data, and mean lengths or weights of individuals in the catch. All analyses can be confounded by migration from the area sampled unless the full depth and habitat range of the species are covered.

The increasing use of otoliths for estimation of age and growth rates in tropical species has permitted the direct estimation of total mortality rates from age-frequency data. Most results to date are for various Australian snappers (Lutjanidae) (Davis, 1992; Newman and Dunk, 2002; Newman et al., 2000a, 2000b).

In the absence of large samples of aged otoliths or other bony structures, representative annual average length-frequency samples can be used to estimate total mortality rates using length-converted catch curves, developed by Pauly (1984a) and as the computer program ELEFAN II (Pauly, 1984b, 1984c, 1984d). Alternatively, the method of Ault and Erhardt (1991) can be used to estimate total mortality rate from the mean length of fish in a representative sample, given the growth parameters, the length at first capture and the length of the largest fish included in the sample. Both methods are included in the FiSAT II package (Gayanilo and Pauly, 2002). The LFDA program (Hoggarth et al., 2005) also produces length-converted catch curves.

Many estimates of mortality rates based on length-converted catch curves have been published. The plots of catch curves are surprisingly robust and excellent fits of points to the linear descending arm of the catch curve are often obtained from relatively small sample sizes. However, it is essential that sample sizes are adequate and are representative of the annual average length composition of the stock. The same limitation applies to age-structured catch curves and it is probably easier to get a very large representative length-frequency sample than to get an age-frequency sample. However, the accuracy of the estimate of Z is highly dependent on the accuracy of the growth parameter estimates (K, L_∞) (Isaac, 1990). High variability in individual growth rates (common in many species of fishes) also limits accuracy, as do seasonal growth oscillations of short-lived species. A routine in FiSAT II corrects for the latter factor.

The development of accurate ageing of tropical fishes leads to the possibility of combining reliable estimates of K and L_∞ with large length frequency samples to obtain good estimates of total mortality rates from length-converted catch curves. If variability can be shown to be limited, growth parameter estimates obtained in one area can be used to obtain mortality estimates from length-frequency data collected in other areas.

Age-based or length-converted catch curves do not necessarily have linear descending arms. If samples are truly representative of the stock, the descending arm should reflect age- or size-specific mortality rates. For example, if fish become too large to be caught by the most popular size of gill net, the larger fish should have lower apparent mortality rates. Also, if fish migrate out of the exploited habitat at a particular size, the catch curves should show an increase in apparent Z, that reflects the outmigration.

Several empirical methods have been developed to estimate natural mortality rates (M), based on growth coefficients, length at first maturity, maximum size, or maximum age (Rikhter and Efanov, 1976; Pauly, 1980; Hoenig, 1983; Ralston, 1987) and have been widely used. The equation of Hoenig produced estimates of the natural mortality coefficient that were very similar to those obtained from age-structured catch curves for various species of snappers (Newman et al., 2000a, 2000b) and for *Lutjanus russelli* (Newman et al., 2000a), whereas that of Pauly (Pauly, 1980) yielded estimates that were much greater that those obtained from age-structured catch curves. Newman et al. (1996) reported that the empirical equation of Ralston (1987) gave even more divergent estimates of M than that of Pauly. The Rikhter and Efanov equation was based on temperate species and its usefulness has not been verified for tropical species.

Alternatively, when growth conforms with the von Bertalanffy equation, the "Beverton and Holt invariants" state that there are consistent relationships between growth parameters, age and length at maturity and natural mortality rate;

$$M/K = 1.5$$
$$L_m/L_\infty = 0.67$$
$$M \cdot t_m = 1.65.$$

in which M is the natural mortality coefficient, K is the growth constant, L_m is length at first maturity, t_m is age at maturity, and L_∞ is the asymptotic length (Jensen, 1996).

Fish that have not attained the length at first capture in a fishery suffer only natural mortality and the total mortality rate increases progressively as fishes become fully recruited to the fishing gear. Fishery-independent sampling of prerecruits using small-meshed gears should produce length-converted catch curves with a progressive increase in slope within the range of the selection curve. The left-hand side of the catch curve should reflect the natural mortality rate.

Natural mortality rates of stocks of reef fish at unexploited parts of Pedro Bank in the Caribbean in 1969–73 were derived from size frequency analyses (Munro, 1975, 1983). Similarly, estimates of natural mortality rates of unexploited species of snappers were obtained from length- or age-frequency samples by Newman *et al.* (1996), Newman *et al.* (2000b), and Newman and Dunk (2002) in Australian waters. Additionally, Hart and Russ (1996) estimated mortality rates in unexploited stocks of brown surgeonfish (*Acanthurus nigrofuscus*, Acanthuridae) on the Great Barrier Reef. Munro (1999) obtained estimates of natural mortality rate from length-converted catch curves for a variety of species in a small fishery reserve in Jamaica. The increasing development of marine reserves offers opportunities for direct estimation of natural mortality rate, preferably using nonlethal sampling, possibly with fish traps or underwater visual size-estimation methods.

STOCK ASSESSMENTS IN TROPICAL FISHERIES

The stock assessment methods that are embodied in the work of Beverton and Holt (1957) and in the manuals of Ricker (1958b, 1975), Gulland (1983), and Pauly (1984a) can be applied to any tropical fish stock, given the necessary catch statistics and parameter estimates. However, by the start of the 1980s there were very few complete assessments of tropical fish stocks. In an attempt to change this situation, ICLARM launched the Network of Tropical Fishery Scientists (NTFS) and its newsletter, *Fishbyte*, in 1982 (Munro and Pauly, 1982; Pauly and Munro, 1982) as a means for encouraging developing-country scientists to publish their work, to encourage professionalism, and to aid these scientists in accessing the literature. Members in developing countries were provided with copies of any publication that was cited in Fishbyte. *Fishbyte* ran as an independent ICLARM publication for 9 years (1983–91) before being absorbed by ICLARM's quarterly journal, *Naga*, where it continued as a separate section until *Naga* ceased publication in 2006. In its first 9 years as the NTFS newsletter, over 150 papers were published, mostly authored by developing-country scientists. The overall output was summarized and indexed by Cruz-Trinidad *et al.* (1992).

During this period, a lot of effort was devoted to the development of stock assessment instruction manuals and the presentation of specialized courses for fisheries scientists from developing countries (e.g., Sparre and Venema, 1992). An FAO/Danish International Development

Agency (DANIDA) project on "Training in fish stock assessment and fishery research planning" was launched in 1983, coinciding with the development of the ELEFAN suite and with the creation of NTFS and *Fishbyte*. This led to close collaboration between the groups working at the FAO and ICLARM (Venema *et al.*, 1988) and to the FAO/DANIDA project funding the activities of the NTFS for almost a decade.

A different approach to estimating maximum sustainable fishing mortality rate and potential yield, based on the Beverton and Holt invariants and on stock/recruitment relationships, has been suggested by Beddington and Kirkwood (2005). However, our poor understanding of stock/recruitment relationships in tropical fish stocks would appear to limit its utility at present.

The package developed by Hoggarth *et al.* (2005) includes three single-species stock assessment programs: YIELD, CEDA, and ParFish. YIELD is an age-structured model that produces estimates of yield, biomass, and spawning stock biomass either in total or on a per-recruit basis. CEDA, or catch-effort data analysis, is used to fit various surplus production models, given a time series of catch data plus catch-per-unit-effort estimates. ParFish is intended for use in data-limited situations and uses a Bayesian approach to fitting a Schaefer production model.

MULTIFAN was extended and refined as MULTIFAN-CL (Fournier *et al.*, 1998), a model that can be used to estimate age composition, growth parameters, mortality, and recruitment rates, given inputs of a time series of spatially structured data on catch and effort in the fishery and age- or length-frequency data. It provides confidence intervals for the estimated parameters. MULTIFAN-CL is now routinely applied to South Pacific tuna and billfish stocks (e.g., Fournier *et al.*, 1998). It has also been applied to Pacific cod (*Gadus macrocephalus*, Gadidae) and King George whiting (*Sillaginodes punctatus*, Sillaginidae), and to Hawaiian spiny lobster (*Panulirus marginatus*, Palinuridae).

New treatises have been published in recent years (Hilborn and Walters, 1992; Hilborn and Mangel, 1997; Quinn and Deriso, 1999; Punt and Hilborn, 2001) that embody the techniques of modern stock assessment science and a host of new stock assessment programs have emerged in recent years (ADAPT, A-SCALA, CASAL, COLERAINE, FASST, SESAME1, SCALIA), some well established and others in various stages of development. In common with MULTIFAN-CL, there is no reason why they should not be applicable to tropical demersal or pelagic fish stocks, other than the perennial difficulty of obtaining adequate datasets.

MULTISPECIES ASSESSMENTS, NATURAL
MORTALITY, RECRUITMENT AND ECOPATH
WITH ECOSIM

Almost all fishing gears capture many species simultaneously, a fact that was largely ignored in the management of the major commercial fisheries for many decades. In all tropical fisheries, very large numbers of species can be found in the catches. However, as mentioned previously, it appears to be invariably true that a limited number of species, typically about 20, constitute approximately 90% of the weight of the catch.

Multispecies formulations of the Beverton and Holt (1957) yield-per-recruit (B&H Y/R) model have been developed by Munro (1975, 1983), Murawski (1984), Shepherd et al. (1987), Silvestre and Soriano (1988), Polovina (1989), and Munro et al. (2003). In its simplest form, this consists of summing the yield curves, assuming a single price/kg for all species (Silvestre and Soriano, 1988). Alternatively, the yield curves can be expressed in terms of the value of each species to give weighting to the most valuable species in the catch (Munro, 1975, 1983).

Multispecies length cohort analysis or VPA (Pope and Yang, 1987; Christensen, 1995) requires information on diets in addition to size-frequency and catch data and these are precursors to ecosystem models. Multispecies assessments can also be made using the FiSAT II software (Gayanilo and Pauly, 2002), based on an extension of the Thompson and Bell (1934) model. It does not allow for species interactions and requires substantial data, including VPAs for each species.

A fundamental weakness in most stock assessment models is that the natural mortality rate is assumed to be constant. However, there is little basis for this assumption other than to suggest that over the size range that yields the bulk of the catch of a particular species in a relatively stable ecosystem, the value of the natural mortality rate might be relatively constant. This constancy is implicit in the derivation of the Beverton and Holt invariants and the other empirical approaches to deriving M discussed above.

However, being small is very dangerous and it seems evident that the natural mortality rate must change with size and age, particularly when most species in a fish community are exploited and the trophic pyramid is flattened. To take an extreme example, the stocks of most predatory reef fish in Jamaica have been drastically reduced or even eliminated. Consequently, natural mortality rates must be greatly reduced when compared to stocks in unexploited reef areas and, furthermore, must decrease with increasing size as the numbers of predators capable of catching and swallowing a particular fish decrease.

In applying the B&H Y/R model to reef fish stock in Jamaican waters, Munro (1975, 1983) reduced the natural mortality rate from the levels existing in virgin stocks in proportion to the biomass of predators remaining in various exploited areas. This is a fairly simplistic approach and no way has been found of testing this assumption.

Changes in natural mortality rates have been modeled by Appeldoorn (1988), Caddy (1991) and Watson *et al.* (2002) and rates of reduction of the natural mortality rate with increasing age have been obtained for a few species. It seems logical that decreasing mortality rates with increasing age or size should be a feature of most aquatic communities, where the numbers of potential predators decline with increasing size of all potential prey species. Mortality rates would be expected to increase with very high age, but few fish in exploited stocks are likely to attain extreme longevity. Fournier *et al.* (1998) used increasing rates of age-dependent natural mortality to improve the fit of the MULTIFAN-CL model to data for a top predator, the South Pacific albacore (*Thunnus alalunga*, Scombridae).

A final matter concerning the assessment and management of fish stocks concerns the degree of connectivity between stocks of marine organisms. Some stocks that inhabit circumscribed habitats (such as coral reefs, mangroves, and estuaries) can be separated by areas of unsuitable habitat. Oceanic depths can separate neritic pelagic or demersal stocks. In all cases, some degree of genetic exchange *must* occur over the range spanned by a species. It is very likely that some propagules are transferred between adjacent stocks that are separated by modest distances but only occasionally between distant areas. In such cases, the individual stocks are components of a meta-population, linked only by the spread of their propagules. It is also likely that some stocks on the edge of the range of a species are "sinks" that are maintained by upstream "sources." However, in the case of tropical fish stocks there is no agreement on the degree to which stocks are self-replenishing. That some species are capable of self-replenishment is shown by the existence of species that are endemic to the shallows of isolated oceanic islands. The ability to self-replenish will be much dependent on oceanographic features of the area and on biological features of the adults and of the pelagic larvae (Sponaugle *et al.*, 2002). Cowen *et al.* (2000) argued that the wide dispersal of reef fish larvae originating from a single spawning area, combined with high mortality rates, will greatly reduce the chances of significant numbers of larvae reaching reefs elsewhere and that most will die in the open ocean. The same observation would apply to species occupying other circumscribed habitats.

Watson and Munro (2004) have shown that settlement rates of reef fish postlarvae on the heavily exploited north coast of Jamaica are orders of magnitude less than their settlement rates on reefs in the moderately exploited British Virgin Islands. Furthermore, the only postlarvae that settle on Jamaican reefs in relatively large numbers are those of species that mature before recruitment to the local trap fisheries or larger species that have specialized oceanic pelagic larval stages, such as surgeonfishes (Acanthuridae) and goatfishes (Mullidae). Triggerfishes (Balistidae) also have postlarvae that remain in the pelagic zone for extended periods and jacks (Carangidae) can do so opportunistically by associating with drifting objects. The conclusion was that the reef fisheries around a relatively isolated island, such as Jamaica, are very largely dependent on the existence of adequate spawning stock biomasses in local waters; very few recruits will arrive from distant reef areas. The corollary is that overexploitation will lead to reduced recruitment to fisheries and, probably, to more variability in recruitment and that, for most species, the solutions to recruitment overfishing are very much the responsibility of local management

The development of the Ecopath model by Polovina (1984a) and its application to the reef system at French Frigate Shoals in the northwestern Hawaiian Islands chain (Polovina, 1984b) led to the development of Ecopath II (Christensen, 1991; Christensen and Pauly, 1992) and its widespread application to aquatic ecosystems (Christensen and Pauly, 1993; Christensen and Walters, this volume). It is implicit in the structure of Ecopath that natural mortality rates must change as the biomasses of predators change. To date, more than 300 Ecopath models have been developed; some reported in the primary literature, others informally.

The development of Ecopath with Ecosim (Walters et al., 1997), which enables dynamic simulation models to be run on the mass-balance models produced by Ecopath, enable scientists to predict changes in exploited fish communities in response to management measures, to verify the accuracy of such predictions and, ultimately, to advise managers of the likely outcomes and consequences of management decisions. This is reflected in the paper by Christensen and Walters (2005) in which they state that "we are moving towards ecosystem-based management of fisheries" (see also Christensen and

Walters, this volume). This cannot come too soon. In the interim, we must use the available stock assessment models to assess exploited communities, to show managers the degree to which individual species are overexploited and to get governments to accept self-evident conservation strategies (but see Christensen and Lai [this volume] for new approaches in ecosystem-based management visualization).

DISCUSSION AND CONCLUSIONS

With few exceptions, tropical fisheries are directed at the exploitation of entire communities of fish and invertebrates, using a variety of relatively unselective fishing gears. Fishing effort can best be expressed in person–days, with fishers switching gears according to opportunities and season. It is evident that, while tropical fisheries are exceedingly complex, they are amenable to assessment by conventional means. Certainly, it is very easy to demonstrate whether or not the principal species are overfished and to initiate preliminary steps toward developing a set of management strategies in consultation with stakeholders.

Methods for estimating parameters required for stock assessment models have advanced in many areas. All exploited species of reef fish appear to have daily rings in their otoliths that are readable in the early life stages and many have annual rings and can be accurately aged. Such age estimates can be used to validate estimates of growth rates based on length-frequency analyses. Mortality rates can be derived from length-frequency data, particularly when the required growth parameter inputs are derived from otolith analyses.

Sophisticated length-based models have been developed and applied to the assessment of large pelagic species. These should be tested in tropical demersal fisheries for which there are adequate data.

Numerous ways of assessing the status of multispecies fish stocks have been developed but not yet applied to many tropical fisheries. These range from simple assessments of harvests per unit area, through total biomass surplus production models to parameter-intensive yield-per-recruit, VPA and allied models. Although multi-species yield-per-recruit models require the application of some simplifying assumptions about species interactions, they provide a reasonable assessment of the current status of a fishery and a starting point for evaluating changes in response to management measures. There is a wide degree of uncertainty in all fisheries estimation but this should not be an excuse for not exploring assessment methods and improving strategies for obtaining better estimates of the required parameters.

The development of Ecopath provides a route toward ecosystem-based tropical fisheries management and Ecopath with Ecosim provides the means for simulating the changes that result from changes in the fishery. This also applies to spatial issues, which can be addressed with Ecospace (Walters *et al.*, 1999), now a component of Ecopath with Ecosim (Christensen and Walters, this volume). However, additional data on trophic interactions in tropical systems and better knowledge of life-history parameters and of behavioral interactions of tropical fish species are needed before these models can be confidently used for fisheries management in the most complex marine ecosystems.

Data acquisition costs are proportional to the degree of sophistication desired. Herein lies the problem for tropical fisheries managers in developing countries, where governments are reluctant to spend large sums of money on the management of small-scale fisheries that are not perceived to be of great value. This view is erroneous, however, as demonstrated by Sary *et al.* (2003) who showed in 2003 that the cumulative cost of non-management of Jamaica's trap fisheries amounted to US$1.3 billion over the previous 25 years.

Daniel Pauly has played a central role in the development of tropical fisheries science over the past 30 years; based on a combination of enthusiasm, innovation, intellect, and a huge capacity for hard work. This is well demonstrated by the flood of published papers that have had their origins in the methods that he promoted, the training courses that he participated in, and his personal dedication to the advancement of fisheries scientists in the developing, tropical world.

To evaluate the success of these efforts, I performed an Internet search that produced a list of 286 papers published in the primary literature during the 25 years from 1981 to 2005, that had used either ELEFAN or FiSAT for parameter estimation. About 58% (166) of these works were done in 45 tropical developing countries, many of the remainder were done in the Mediterranean, and some were as far removed from the tropics as Antarctica. Over 60 of the works dealt with invertebrates. In addition to the above, there are probably several thousand papers in the non-refereed literature and in the proceedings of conferences, including the ICLARM conference series. And, of course, these are but a small fraction of the total number of citations of Daniel Pauly's work.

REFERENCES ·

Abramson, N. J. (1971) *Computer Programs for Fish Stock Assessment*. Rome: FAO.

Allman, R. J. and Grimes, C. B. (2002) Temporal and spatial dynamics of spawning, settlement, and growth of gray snapper (*Lutjanus griseus*) from the West Florida shelf as determined from otolith microstructures. *Fishery Bulletin: National Oceanic and Atmospheric Administration*, 100, 391–403.

Appeldoorn, R. S. (1988) Ontogenetic changes in natural mortality rate of queen conch, *Strombus gigas* (Molluska: Mesogastropoda). *Bulletin of Marine Science*, 42, 159–165.

Ault, J. S., Bohnsack, J. A. and Meester, G. A. (1998) A retrospective (1979–1996) multispecies assessment of coral reef fish stocks in the Florida Keys. *Fishery Bulletin*, 96, 395–414.

Ault, J. S., Bohnsack, J. A., Smith, S. G. and Luo, J. (2005) Towards sustainable multispecies fisheries in the Florida, USA, coral reef ecosystem. *Bulletin of Marine Science*, 76, 595–622.

Ault, J. S. and Erhardt, N. M. (1991) Correction to the Beverton and Holt Z-estimator for truncated catch length-frequency distributions. *Fishbyte*. Manila, Philippines: ICLARM.

Ault, J. S., Smith, S. G., Luo, J., Meester, G. A., Bohnsack, J. A. and Miller, S. L. (2002) Baseline multispecies coral reef fish stock assessments for the Dry Tortugas. *NOAA Technical Memorandum NMFS-SEFSC*. Washington DC: NOAA.

Banerji, S. K. and Krishnan, T. S. (1973) Acceleration of assessment of fish populations and comparative studies of similar taxonomic groups. *Proceedings of the Symposium on the Living Resources of the Seas Around India*, pp. 158–175.

Beddington, J. R. and Kirkwood, G. P. (2005) The estimation of potential yield and stock status using life-history parameters. *Philosophical Transactions of the Royal Society B: Biological Sciences*, 360, 163.

Beverton, R. J. H. and Holt, S. J. (1956) The theory of fishing. In Graham, M., ed., *Sea Fisheries: Their Investigation in the United Kingdom*. London: Arnold.

Beverton, R. J. H. and Holt, S. J. (1957) On the dynamics of exploited fish populations. *Fisheries Investigations (Series II)*, 19, 533.

Brown, B. E., Brennan, J. A., Grosslein, M. D., Heyerdahl, E. G. and Hennemuth, R. C. (1976) The effect of fishing on the marine finfish biomass in the Northwest Atlantic from the Gulf of Maine to Cape Hattersa. *Research Bulletin of the International Commission for Northwest Atlantic Fisheries*, 12, 49–68.

Bullock, L. H., Murphy, M. D., Godcharles, M. F. and Mitchell, M. E. (1992) Age growth, and reproduction of the jewfish *Epinephelus itajara* in the eastern Gulf of Mexico. *Fishery Bulletin*, 90, 242–249.

Caddy, J. F. (1991) Death rates and time intervals: is there an alternative to the constant natural mortality axiom? *Reviews in Fish Biology and Fisheries*, 1, 109–138.

Campana, S. E. and Thorrold, S. R. (2001) Otoliths, increments, and elements: keys to a comprehensive understanding of fish populations? *Canadian Journal of Fisheries and Aquatic Sciences*, 58, 30–38.

Cappo, M., Eden, P., Newman, S. J. and Robertson, S. (2000) A new approach to tetracycline validation of the periodicity and timing of increment formation in the otoliths of 11 species of *Lutjanus* from the central Great Barrier Reef. *Fishery Bulletin*, 98, 474–488.

Choat, J. H. and Axe, L. M. (1996) Growth and longevity in acanthurid fishes: an analysis of otolith increments. *Marine Ecology Progress Series*, 134, 15–26.

Christensen, V. (1991) On ECOPATH, Fishbyte and fisheries management. *Fishbyte*. Manila, Philippines: ICLARM.

Christensen, V. (1995) A multispecies virtual population analysis incorporating information of size and age. *ICES CM: D*, 8.

Christensen, V. and Pauly, D. (1992) ECOPATH II: A software for balancing steady-state ecosystem models and calculating network characteristics. *Ecological Modelling*, 61, 169–185.

Christensen, V. and Pauly, D. (1993) Trophic models of aquatic ecosystems. *ICLARM Conference Proceedings*. Manila, Philippines: ICLARM.

Christensen, V. and Walters, C. J. (2005) Using ecosystem modeling for fisheries management: where are we? *ICES CM: M*, 19.

Cowen, R. K., Lwiza, K. M. M., Sponaugle, S., Paris, C. B. and Olson, D. B. (2000) Connectivity of marine populations: open or closed? *Science*, 287, 857.

Cruz-Trinidad, A., Torres, F. J. and Pauly, D. (1992) Index to Fishbyte: Volumes 1 to 9 (1983–1991). *ICLARM Fishbyte*. Manila, Philippines: ICLARM

Cushing, D. H. (1981) Stock and recruitment. In *Fisheries Biology: A Study in Population Dynamics*. Madison, WI: University of Wisconsin Press, pp. 142–171.

Cushing, D. H. (1983) *Key Papers on Fish Populations*. Oxford, UK: Island Press.

Davis, T. L. O. (1992) Growth and mortality of *Lutjanus vittus (Quoy and Gaimard)* from the North West Shelf of Australia. *Fishery Bulletin*, 90, 395–404.

Derzhavin, A. N. (1922) The stellate sturgeon (*Acipenser stellatus* Pallas), a biological sketch. *Byulleten'Bakinskoi Ikhtiologicheskoi Stantsii*, 1, 1–393.

Fabens, A. J. (1965) Properties and fitting of the Von Bertalanffy growth curve. *Growth*, 29, 265–289.

Ferreira, B. P. and Russ, G. R. (1992) Age, growth and mortality of the inshore coral trout *Plectropomus maculatus* (Pisces: Serranidae) from the central Great Barrier Reef, Australia. *Australian Journal of Marine and Freshwater Research*, 43, 1301–1312.

Ferreira, B. P. and Russ, G. R. (1994) Age validation and estimation of growth rate of a tropical serranid, the coral trout *Plectropomus leopardus* (Lacepede 1802) from Lizard Island, Northern Great Barrier Reef. *Fishery Bulletin*, 92, 46–57.

Fletcher, W. J. (1991) A test of the relationship between otolith weight and age for the pilchard *Sardinops neopilchardus*. *Canadian Journal of Fisheries and Aquatic Sciences*, 48, 35–38.

Fournier, D. A. and Breen, P. A. (1983) Estimation of abalone mortality rates with growth analysis (*Haliotis kamtschatkana*). *Transactions of the American Fisheries Society (USA)*, 112, 403–411.

Fournier, D. A., Hampton, J. and Sibert, J. R. (1998) MULTIFAN-CL: a length-based, age-structured model for fisheries stock assessment, with application to South Pacific albacore, *Thunnus alalunga*. *Canadian Journal of Fisheries and Aquatic Sciences*, 55, 2105–2116.

Fournier, D. A., Sibert, J. R., Majkowski, J. and Hampton, J. (1990) MULTIFAN: a likelihood-based method for estimating growth parameters and age composition from multiple length frequency data sets illustrated using data for southern bluefin tuna (*Thunnus maccoyii*). *Canadian Journal of Fisheries and Aquatic Sciences*, 47, 301–317.

Fowler, A. J. (1995) Annulus formation in otoliths of tropical fish – a review. In Secor, D. H., Dean J. M. and Campana S. E., eds., *Recent Developments in Fish Otolith Research*. Columbia, SC: University of South Carolina Press, pp. 45–63.

Froese, R. and Pauly, D. (2000) *FishBase 2000: Concepts, Designs and Data Sources*. Los Baños, Laguna, Philippines, ICLARM.

Garrod, D. J. (1961a) The rational exploitation of the *Tilapia esculenta* stock of the North Buvuma Island area, Lake Victoria. *East African Agricultural and Forestry Journal*, 27, 69–76.

Garrod, D. J. (1961b) The selection characteristics of nylon gill nets for *Tilapia esculenta* Graham. *ICES Journal of Marine Science*, 26, 191.

Garrod, D. J. (1963) An estimation of the mortality rates in a population of *Tilapia esculenta* Graham (Pisces, Cichlidae) in Lake Victoria, East Africa. *Journal of the Fisheries Research Board of Canada*, 20, 195–227.

Garrod, D. J. (1967) Population dynamics of the Arcto-Norwegian cod. *Journal of the Fisheries Research Board of Canada*, 24, 145–190.

Gayanilo, F. C. and Pauly, D. (1997) FAO–ICLARM stock assessment tools. (FiSAT). Reference Manual. FAO Computerized Information Series (Fisheries). Rome: FAO.

Gayanilo, F. C. and Pauly, D. (2002) FiSAT II User's Guide. Rome: FAO

Gayanilo, F. C., Sparre, P. and Pauly, D. (1996) The FAO–ICLARM Stock Assessment Tools (FiSAT). User's Manual. FAO Computerized Information Series (Fisheries). Rome: FAO.

Graham, M. (1929) Studies of age determination in fish. Part II. A survey of the literature. *UK Ministry of Agriculture and Fisheries, Fisheries Investigations (Ser.2)* 11 (3), 50 pp.

Graham, M. (1935) Modern theory of exploiting a fishery and application to North Sea trawling. *ICES Journal of Marine Science*, 10, 264–274.

Gulland, J. A. (1965) Estimation of mortality rates. Annex to Arctic fisheries working group report. *ICES CM Doc*, 3.

Gulland, J. A. (1968) The concept of the marginal yield from exploited fish stocks. *ICES Journal of Marine Science*, 32, 256.

Gulland, J. A. (1969) Manual of Methods for Fish Stock Assessment: Part 1. Fish population analysis. *FAO Manuals for Fishery Science*. Rome: FAO.

Gulland, J. A. (1983) *Fish Stock Assessment*. Chichester, UK: John Wiley.

Gulland, J. A. and Boerema, L. K. (1973) Scientific advice on catch levels. *Fishery Bulletin*, 71, 325–335.

Gulland, J. A. and Holt, S. J. (1959) Estimation of growth parameters for data at unequal time intervals. *ICES Journal of Marine Science*, 25, 47.

Gulland, J. A. and Rosenberg, A. A. (1992) A review of length-based approaches to assessing fish stocks. *FAO Fisheries Technical Paper*. Rome: FAO.

Hart, A. M. and Russ, G. R. (1996) Response of herbivorous fishes to crown-of-thorns starfish *Acanthaster planci* outbreaks. III. Age, growth, mortality and maturity indices of *Acanthurus nigrofuscus*. *Marine Ecology Progress Series*. Oldendorf, 136, 25–35.

Heincke, F. (1913) Investigations on the plaice. General Report. 1. The plaice fishery and protective measures. Preliminary brief summary of the most important points of the report. *Journal du Conseil International pour l'Exploration de la Mer*, 16, 1–67.

Hilborn, R. and Mangel, M. (1997) *The Ecological Detective: Confronting Models with Data*. Princeton, NJ: Princeton University Press.

Hilborn, R. and Walters, C. (1992) *Quantitative Fisheries Stock Assessment: Choice, Dynamics and Uncertainty*. New York, NY: Chapman and Hall.

Hjort, J. (1914) Fluctuations in the great fisheries of northern Europe, viewed in the light of biological research. *Rapport du Conseil International pour l'Exploration de la Mer*, 20, 228.

Hjort, J. (1926) Fluctuations in the year classes of important food fishes. *Journal du Conseil International pour l'Exploration de la Mer*, 1, 5–38.

Hjort, J., Jahn, G. and Ottestad, P. (1933) The optimum catch. *Hvalradets Skrifter*, 7, 92–127.

Hoenig, J. M. (1983) Empirical use of longevity data to estimate mortality rates. *Fisheries Bulletin*, 82, 898–903.

Hoffbauer, C. (1898) Die Alterbestimmung des Karpfens an seiner Schuppe. *Allegemeine Fischereizeitung*, 23, 19.

Hoggarth, D., Abeyasekera, S., Arthur, R., Beddington, J., Burn, R., Halls, A., Kirkwood, G., McAllister, M., Medley, P. and Mees, C. (2005) Stock Assessment for Fishery Management A Framework Guide to the use of the FMSP Fish Stock Assessment Tools. *FAO Fisheries Technical Paper*. Rome: FAO.

Isaac, V. J. (1990) The accuracy of some length-based methods for fish population studies. *ICLARM Technical Report*. Manila, Philippines: ICLARM.

Jennings, S., Grandcourt, E. M., and Polunin, N. C. V. (1995) The effects of fishing on the diversity, biomass and tropic structure of Seychelles' reef fish communities. *Coral Reefs*, 14, 225–235.

Jensen, A. L. (1996) Beverton and Holt life history invariants result from optimal trade-off of reproduction and survival. *Canadian Journal of Fisheries and Aquatic Sciences*, 53, 820–822.

Kahn, M. G., Alamgir, M. and Sada, M. N. (1997) The coastal fisheries of Bangladesh. In Silvestre, G. and Pauly, D., eds., *Status and Management of Tropical Coastal Fisheries in Asia. ICLARM Conference Proceedings*, **53**. Manila, Philippines: ICLARM, pp. 26–37.

Kleiber, P., Takeuchi, Y. and Nakano, H. (2001) Calculation of plausible maximum sustainable yield (MSY) for blue sharks (*Prionace glauca*) in the North Pacific. Administrative Report. Honolulu: Southwest Fisheries Science Center (NMFS).

Le Guen, J. C. (1971) Dynamique des populations de *Pseudotolithus* (*fonticulus*) *elongatus* (Bowd, 1825) Poissons-Sciaenidae. *Cahiers ORSTOM Série Océanographie*, 9, 3–84.

Lebeau, A. and Cueff, J. C. (1975) Biologie et peche du capitaine *Lethrinus enigmaticus* (Smith, 1959) du banc de Saya de Malha (Ocean Indien). *Revue des Travaux de l'Institut des Peches Maritimes*, 39, 415–422.

Loubens, G. (1978) Biologie de quelque especes de poisson du lagon Neo-Caledonien. I. Determination de l'age (otolithometrie). *Cahiers ORSTOM Série Océanographie*, 16, 263–283.

Loubens, G. (1980) Biologie de quelques espèces de poissons du lagon Néo-Calédonien. III. *Cahiers de l'Indo-Pacifique*, 2, 101–153.

Luckhurst, B. E., Dean, J. M. and Reichert, M. (2000) Age, growth and reproduction of the lane snapper *Lutjanus synagris* (Pisces: Lutjanidae) at Bermuda. *Marine Ecology Progress Series*, 203, 255–261.

McCormick, M. I. (1999) Delayed metamorphosis of a tropical reef fish (*Acanthurus triostegus*): a field experiment. *Marine Ecology Progress Series*, 176, 25–38.

Macdonald, P. D. M. and Pitcher, T. J. (1979) Age-groups from size-frequency data: a versatile and efficient method of analyzing distribution mixtures. *Journal of the Fisheries Research Board of Canada*, 36, 1001.

McManus, J. W., Nanola Jr., C. L., Reyes Jr., R. B. and Kesner, K. N. (1992) Resource ecology of the Bolinao tropical system. *ICLARM Studies and Reviews*, 22, 117 pp.

McPherson, G. R. and Squire, L. (1992) Age and growth of three dominant *Lutjanus* species of the Great Barrier Reef inter-reef fishery. *Asian Fisheries Science*, 5, 25–36.

Marriott, R. and Cappo, M. (2000) Comparative precision and bias of five different ageing methods for the large tropical snapper *Lutjanus johnii*. *Asian Fisheries Science*, 13, 149–160.

Morales-Nin, B. (1994) Growth of demersal fish species of the Mexican Pacific Ocean. *Marine Biology*, 121, 211–217.

Munro, J. L. (1974) The composition and magnitude of line catches in Jamaican waters. Part III of The Biology, Ecology, Exploitation and Management of Caribbean Reef Fishes: Scientific Report of the ODA/UWI Fisheries Ecology Research Project, 1969–1973: University of the West Indies, Jamaica. Second edn., 1983. Caribbean Coral Reef Fishery Resources. *ICLARM Studies and Reviews*. Manila, Philippines: ICLARM, pp. 26–37.

Munro, J. L. (1975) Assessment of the potential productivity of Jamaican fisheries. Part VI of The Biology, Ecology, Exploitation and Management of Caribbean Reef Fishes: Scientific Report of the ODA/UWI Fisheries Ecology Research Project, 1969–1973: University of the West Indies, Jamaica. Second edn., 1983. Caribbean Coral Reef Fishery Resources. *ICLARM Studies and Reviews*. Manila, Philippines: ICLARM.

Munro, J. L. (1982) Estimation of the parameters of the von Bertalanffy growth equation from recapture data at variable time intervals. *ICES Journal of Marine Science*, 40, 199.

Munro, J. L. (1983) Caribbean Coral Reef Fishery Resources: A second edition of The Biology, Ecology, Exploitation and Management of Caribbean Reef Fishes: Scientific Report of the ODA/UWI Fisheries Ecology Research Project, 1969–1973: University of the West Indies, Jamaica. *ICLARM Studies and Reviews*. Manila, Philippines: ICLARM.

Munro, J. L. (1999) Growth and mortality rates of tropical fish derived from mark-and-recapture and length-frequency data. Marine Protected Areas and the Management of Tropical Fisheries. ICLARM Technical Report to the Inter-American Development Bank. Manila, Philippines: ICLARM.

Munro, J. L. and Pauly, D. (1982) The ICLARM Network of Tropical Fisheries Scientists. *ICLARM Newsletter*. Manila, Philippines: ICLARM.

Munro, J. L., Sary, Z., and Gell, F. R. (2003) Escape gaps: an option for the management of Caribbean trap fisheries. *Proceedings of the Gulf and Caribbean Fisheries Institute*, 54, 28–40.

Munro, J. L. and Thompson, R. (1973) The Jamaican fishing industry. Part II of The Biology, Ecology, Exploitation and Management of Caribbean Reef Fishes: Scientific Report of the ODA/UWI Fisheries Ecology Research Project, 1969–1973: University of the West Indies, Jamaica. Second edition 1983. Caribbean Coral Reef Fishery Resources. *ICLARM Studies and Reviews*. Manila, Philippines: ICLARM.

Murawski, S. A. (1984) Mixed-species yield-per-recruitment analyses accounting for technological interactions. *Canadian Journal of Fisheries and Aquatic Sciences*, 41, 897–916.

Newman, S. J., Cappo, M. and Williams, D. M. B. (2000a) Age, growth and mortality of the stripy, *Lutjanus carponotatus* (Richardson) and the brown-stripe snapper, *L. vitta* (Quoy and Gaimard) from the central Great Barrier Reef, Australia. *Fisheries Research*, 48, 263–275.

Newman, S. J., Cappo, M. and Williams, D. M. B. (2000b) Age, growth, mortality rates and corresponding yield estimates using otoliths of the tropical red snappers, *Lutjanus erythropterus*, *L. malabaricus* and *L. sebae*, from the central Great Barrier Reef. *Fisheries Research*, 48, 1–14.

Newman, S. J. and Dunk, I. J. (2002) Growth, age validation, mortality, and other population characteristics of the red emperor snapper, *Lutjanus sebae*

(Cuvier, 1828), off the Kimberley coast of North-Western Australia. *Estuarine, Coastal and Shelf Science*, 55, 67–80.

Newman, S. J., Williams, D. M. B. and Russ, G. R. (1996) Age validation, growth and mortality rates of the tropical snappers (Pisces: Lutjanidae) *Lutjanus adetii* (Castelnau, 1873) and *L. quinquelineatus* (Bloch, 1790) from the central Great Barrier Reef, Australia. *Marine and Freshwater Research*, 47, 575–584.

Ntiba, M. J. and Jaccarini, V. (1988) Age and growth parameters of *Siganus sutor* in Kenyan marine inshore water, derived from numbers of otolith microbands and fish lengths. *Journal of Fish Biology*, 33, 465–470.

Pauly, D. (1980) On the interrelationships between natural mortality, growth parameters, and mean environmental temperature in 175 fish stocks. *ICES Journal of Marine Science*, 39, 175.

Pauly, D. (1984a) Fish population dynamics in tropical waters: a manual for use with programmable calculators. *ICLARM Studies and Reviews*. Manila, Philippines: ICLARM.

Pauly, D. (1984b) Length-converted catch curves: a powerful tool for fisheries research in the tropics (Part I). *Fishbyte*. Manila, Philippines: ICLARM.

Pauly, D. (1984c) Length-converted catch curves: a powerful tool for fisheries research in the tropics (Part II). *Fishbytes*. Manila, Philippines: ICLARM.

Pauly, D. (1984d) Length-converted catch curves: a powerful tool for fisheries research in the tropics (Part III: Conclusion). *Fishbyte*. Manila, Philippines: ICLARM.

Pauly, D. (1987) A review of the ELEFAN system for analysis of length-frequency data in fish and aquatic invertebrates. In Pauly, D. and Morgan, G. R., eds., *Length-based Methods in Fisheries Research. ICLARM Conference Proceedings*. Manila, Philippines: ICLARM.

Pauly, D. and Arreguin-Sanchez, F. (1995) Improving Shepherd's length composition analysis (SLCA) method for growth parameter estimations. *Naga*, 18, 30–33.

Pauly, D. and David, N. (1981) ELEFAN I, a BASIC program for the objective extraction of growth parameters from length-frequency data. *Meeresforsch*, 28, 205–211.

Pauly, D. and Martosubroto, P. (1980) The population dynamics of *Nemipterus marginatus* (Cuvier & Val.) off Western Kalimantan, South China Sea. *Journal of Fish Biology*, 17, 263–273.

Pauly, D. and Morgan, G. J. (1987) Theory and application of length-based methods for stock assessment. *ICLARM Conference Proceedings*. Manila, Philippines: ICLARM.

Pauly, D. and Munro, J. L. (1982) On the development and dissemination of new methodologies for tropical stock assessments. *Indo-Pacific Fishery Commission, Report of the Third Session of the Standing Committee on Resources Research and Development (Annex 3)*. Sydney, Australia: FAO Fisheries Department.

Pella, J. J. and Tomlinson, P. K. (1969) A generalized stock production model. *Bulletin of the Inter-American Tropical Tuna Commission*, 13, 419–496.

Petersen, C. G. J. (1892) Fiskerbiologiske forhold I Holbaek Fjord 1890–1891. *Beret. Danske Biol. Sta.1890–1891*, 1, 121–182.

Pilling, G. M., Grandcourt, E. M. and Kirkwood, G. P. (2003) The utility of otolith weight as a predictor of age in the emperor *Lethrinus mahsena* and other tropical fish species. *Fisheries Research*, 60, 493–506.

Pilling, G. M., Millner, R. S., Easey, M. W., Mees, C. C., Rathacharen, S. and Azemia, R. (2000) Validation of annual growth increments in the otoliths of the lethrinid *Lethrinus mahsena* and the lutjanid *Aprion virescens* from sites in the tropical Indian Ocean, with notes on the nature of growth increments in *Pristipomoides filamentosus*. *Fishery Bulletin*, 98, 600–611.

Polovina, J. J. (1984a) An overview of the ECOPATH model. *Fishbyte*. Manila, Philippines: ICLARM.

Polovina, J. J. (1984b) Model of a coral reef ecosystem. *Coral Reefs*, 3, 1–11.

Polovina, J. J. (1989) A system of simultaneous dynamic production and forecast models for multispecies or multiarea applications. *Canadian Journal of Fisheries and Aquatic Sciences*, 46, 961–963.

Pope, J. G. (1972) An investigation of the accuracy of virtual population analysis using cohort analysis. *Research Bulletin of the International Commission for Northwest Atlantic Fisheries*, 9, 65–74.

Pope, J. G. and Yang, J. (1987) Phalanx analysis: an extension of Jones' length cohort analysis to multispecies cohort analysis. In Pauly, D. and Morgan, G. J., eds., *Theory and application of length-based methods for stock assessment. ICLARM Conference Proceedings*. Manila, Philippines: ICLARM, pp. 177–192.

Punt, A. E. and R. Hilborn (2001) BAYES-SA: Bayesian stock assessment methods in fisheries. User's manual. *FAO Computerized Information Series (Fisheries)*, 12, 56 pp.

Quinn, T. J. and Deriso, R. B. (1999) *Quantitative Fisheries Dynamics*. Oxford, UK: Oxford University Press.

Ralston, S. (1987) Mortality rates of snappers and groupers. In Polovina, J. J. and Ralston, S., eds., *Tropical Snappers and Groupers: Biology and Fisheries Management*. Boulder, CO: Westview Press, pp. 375–404.

Ralston, S., Brothers, E. B., Roberts, D. A. and Sakuma, K. M. (1996) Accuracy of age estimates for larval *Sebastes jordani*. *Fishery Bulletin*, 94, 89–97.

Reibisch, J. (1899) Ueber die Eizahl bei Pleuronectes platessa und die Altersbestimmung dieser Form aus den Otolithen. *Wissenschaftliche Meeresuntersuchungen (Kiel)*, 4, 233–248.

Ricker, W. E. (1954) Stock and recruitment. *Journal of the Fisheries Research Board of Canada*, 11, 559–623.

Ricker, W. E. (1958a) Development of model reproduction curves on the basis of a theory of predation at random encounters. Appendix 1. In *Handbook of Computations for Biological Statistics of Fish Populations. Bulletin of the Fisheries Research Board of Canada*, 119, 263–270.

Ricker, W. E. (1958b) *Handbook of Computations for Biological Statistics of Fish Populations. Bulletin of the Fisheries Research Board of Canada*, 119, 1–300, (whole issue).

Ricker, W. E. (1975) Computation and interpretation of biological statistics of fish populations. *Bulletin of the Fisheries Research Board of Canada*, 191, 382.

Rikhter, V. A. and Efanov, V. N. (1976) On one of the approaches to estimation of natural mortality of fish populations. *ICNAF Research Documents*, 76, 1–12.

Robertson, D. R., Swearer, S. E., Kaufmann, K. and Brothers, E. B. (1999) Settlement versus environmental dynamics in a pelagic-spawning reef fish at Caribbean Panama. *Ecological Monographs*, 69, 195–218.

Russell, E. S. (1931) Some theoretical considerations on the "overfishing" problem. *ICES Journal of Marine Science*, 6, 3.

Sadovy, Y., Figuerola, M. and Roman, A. (1992) Age and growth of red hind, *Epinephelus guttatus*, in Puerto Rico and St. Thomas. *Fishery Bulletin*, 90, 516–528.

Sary, Z., Munro, J. L. and Woodley, J. D. (2003) Status report on a Jamaican reef fishery: current value and the costs of non-management. *Proceedings of the Gulf and Caribbean Fisheries Institute*, 54, 98–110.

Schaefer, M. B. (1954) Some aspects of the dynamics of populations important to the management of some commercial marine fisheries. *Bulletin of the Inter-American Tropical Tuna Commission*, 1, 25–56.

Schaefer, M. B. (1957) A study of the dynamics of the fishery for yellowfin tuna in the eastern tropical Pacific Ocean. *Bulletin of the Inter-American Tropical Tuna Commission*, 2, 245–285.

Schnute, J. and Fournier, D. (1980) A new approach to length-frequency analysis: growth structure. *Canadian Journal of Fisheries and Aquatic Sciences*, 37, 1337–1351.

Shepherd, J. G., Morgan, G. J. Gulland, J. A. and Matthews, C. P. (1987) Methods of analysis and assessment: report of working group II. In Pauly, D. and Morgan, G. J., eds., *Length-based Methods in Fisheries Research. ICLARM Conference Proceedings.* Manila, Philippines: ICLARM, pp. 353–362.

Silvestre, G. and Soriano, M. L. (1988) Effect of incorporating sigmoid selection on optimum mesh size estimation for the Samar Sea multi-species trawl fishery. *Contributions to Tropical Fisheries Biology. FAO Fisheries Report.* Rome: FAO.

Sparre, P. and Venema, S. C. (1992) Introduction to tropical fish stock assessment. Part 1. Manual. *FAO Fisheries Technical Paper.* Rome: FAO.

Sponaugle, S., Cowen, R. K., Shanks, A., Morgan, S. G., Leis, J. M., Pineda, J., Boehlert, G. W., Kingsford, M. J., Lindeman, K. C. and Grimes, C. (2002) Predicting self-recruitment in marine populations: biophysical correlates and mechanisms. *Bulletin of Marine Science*, 70, 341–375.

Strelcheck, A. J., Fitzhugh, G. R., Coleman, F. C. and Koenig, C. C. (2003) Otolith–fish size relationship in juvenile gag (*Mycteroperca microlepis*) of the eastern Gulf of Mexico: a comparison of growth rates between laboratory and field populations. *Fisheries Research*, 60, 255–265.

Szedlmayer, S. T. (1998) Comparison of growth rate and formation of otolith increments in age-0 red snapper. *Journal of Fish Biology*, 53, 58–65.

Templeman, W. and Squires, H. J. (1956) Relationship of otolith lengths and weights in the haddock *Melanogrammus aeglefinus* (L.) to the rate of growth of the fish. *Journal of the Fisheries Research Board of Canada*, 13, 467–487.

Terceiro, M., Fournier, D., and Sibert, J. R. (1992) Comparative performance of MULTIFAN and Shepherd's Length Composition Analysis (SRLCA) on simulated length-frequency distributions. *Transactions of the American Fisheries Society*, 121, 667–677.

Thompson, J. S. (1902) The periodic growth of scales in Gadidae and Pleuronectidae as an index of age. *Journal of the Marine Biological Association of the United Kingdom*, 6, 373–375.

Thompson, W. F. and Bell, F. H. (1934) Biological statistics of the Pacific halibut fishery. 2. Changes in yield of a standardized unit of gear. Report of the International Fisheries (Pacific Halibut) Commission.

Trinidad, A. C., Pomeroy, R. S., Corpuz, P. V. and Agüero, M. (1993) Bioeconomics of the Philippine small pelagics fishery. *ICLARM Technical Report*, 38, 74 pp.

Vakily, J. M., Palomares, M. L. and Pauly, D. (1986) Computer programs for fish stock assessment: Applications for the HP-41 CV calculator. *FAO Fisheries Technical Paper.* Rome: FAO.

Venema, S. C., Christensen, J. M. and Pauly, D. (1988) Training in tropical fish stock assessment: a narrative of experience. Rome: FAO Fisheries Department.

Von Bertalanffy, L. (1938) A quantitative theory of organic growth. *Human Biology*, 10, 181–213.

Walters, C., Christensen, V., and Pauly, D. (1997) Structuring dynamic modes of exploited ecosystems from trophic mass-balance assessments. *Reviews in Fish Biology and Fisheries*, 7, 139–172.

Walters, C., Pauly, D. and Christensen, V. (1999) Ecospace: prediction of meso-scale spatial patterns in trophic relationships of exploited ecosystems, with emphasis on the impacts of marine protected areas. *Ecosystems*, 2, 539–554.

Watson, M. and Munro, J. L. (2004) Settlement and recruitment of coral reef fishes in moderately exploited and overexploited Caribbean ecosystems: implications for marine protected areas. *Fisheries Research*, 69, 415–425.

Watson, M., Munro, J. L. and Gell, F. R. (2002) Settlement, movement and early juvenile mortality of the yellowtail snapper *Ocyurus chrysurus*. *Marine Ecology Progress Series*, 237, 247–256.

WILLIAM W. L. CHEUNG, JESSICA J. MEEUWIG,
AND VICKY W. Y. LAM

11

Ecosystem-based fisheries management in the face of climate change

INTRODUCTION

Climate change can have direct and indirect impacts on marine fisheries (Brander, 2007). Impacts of overfishing and other human factors, such as habitat destruction and pollution, on marine ecosystems and fisheries resources, are generally well known. Overfishing causes large-scale depletion of fish biomass in the ocean and structural changes in ecosystems (Pauly et al., 1998; Jackson et al., 2001; Pauly et al., 2002; Christensen et al., 2003; Myers and Worm, 2003). Simultaneously, other human activities disturb natural habitats and disrupt the ecology and biodiversity of marine ecosystems (Lotze et al., 2006; Worm et al., 2006; Halpern et al., 2008).

In contrast, impacts of global climate change on marine ecosystems are just starting to be recognized, lagging behind such recognition in terrestrial systems (Rosenzweig et al., 2008). Theory and empirical evidence show that climate change is an important factor affecting marine organisms, ecosystems, and the services they provide (Costanza et al., 1999; Roessig et al., 2004; Pörtner and Knust, 2007; Munday et al., 2008; Rosenzweig et al., 2008). For example, distributions of exploited marine fish and invertebrates have shifted as temperature and other ocean conditions change. Observations from the North Sea (Perry et al., 2005) and the Bering Sea (Mueter and Litzow, 2008) show that the average rate of latitudinal range shift has been around 30 km per decade over the last few decades. Fish assemblages in the North Sea are also found to have moved deeper at an average rate of 3.6 m per decade (Dulvy et al., 2008). These result in changes in species richness and composition (e.g., Hiddink and Hofstede, 2008). Moreover, the timing of peak abundance and migration of the pelagic community has shifted in response to climate changes, resulting in a mismatch in

Ecosystem Approaches to Fisheries: A Global Perspective, ed. V. Christensen and J. Maclean. Published by Cambridge University Press. © Cambridge University Press 2011.

seasonality between trophic and functional groups. Global warming increases the frequency and severity of coral bleaching events (e.g., Donner *et al.*, 2005), while ocean acidification affects the calcifying process of marine organisms (e.g., Orr *et al.*, 2005) and fertilization potential of broadcast spawners, with potential implications for recruitment of fisheries resources (Havenhand *et al.*, 2008).

Climate change affects fisheries management in terms of its capacity to achieve ecological, economic, and social objectives. Ecologically, changes in species distributions, productivity, and ecosystem structure affect patterns of biodiversity and may increase the extinction risk of vulnerable species, particularly as many populations are already at risk because of other human impacts (Dulvy *et al.*, 2003; Thomas *et al.*, 2004; Carpenter *et al.*, 2008). With regard to economics, changes in resource productivity and distribution affect fishing effort dynamics, and the cost and benefits of fishing activities (Harley *et al.*, 2006). Socially, climate change affects seafood supply and fisheries-related employment. Such social impacts will be most severe in socioeconomically vulnerable coastal communities (Brander, 2007; Allison *et al.*, 2009). Ecosystem-based fisheries management, which aims to balance diverse societal objectives by accounting for different components of ecosystems, including climate (Garcia and Cochrane, 2005), should address these potential ecological and socioeconomic implications of climate change.

As climate change covers multiple spatial and temporal scales across ecosystems, we propose that an important first step to incorporate climate change into ecosystem-based management is to understand the global pattern of its impacts on marine ecosystems and fisheries. A global picture allows scientists to identify the sensitivity of different species, regions, and fisheries to climate change impacts. It also raises public awareness effectively, facilitating consensus building and initiating actions among nations, societies, and stakeholders to address the problem. Results from global studies can then be applied on regional and local scales to improve understanding of potential impacts, help design management systems, and develop indicators and monitoring programs at finer spatial and temporal scales (Figure 11.1). Such an approach can ensure that root problems are consistently addressed across scales.

In this chapter, we provide examples of global studies on the potential impacts of climate change on marine ecosystems. These examples are drawn from ongoing projects and collaboration with the Sea Around Us project. We then discuss how global studies can

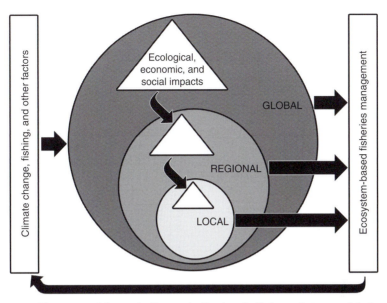

Figure 11.1 Schematic diagram indicating the linkages between global, regional, and local scale efforts in achieving ecosystem-based fisheries management.

help design ecosystem-based fisheries management at regional and local scales.

CLIMATE CHANGE EFFECTS ON MARINE FISHES AND INVERTEBRATES

Climate change effects on marine species are closely linked with environmental conditions and species' physiology and life history. Several decades ago, Pauly (1981, 1984) proposed that the aerobic capacity of fish is strongly related to metabolism, mortality, growth, and reproduction. Oxygen is fundamental to aerobic respiration, which drives routine body metabolism. The oxygen demand (D) and supply (S) of aquatic water-breathing ectotherms, including fishes and invertebrates, varies exponentially with body size (L), with $D \alpha L^a$ and $S \alpha L^b$ while $a > b$ and $a \approx 3$ (Figure 11.2a). In other words, as fish grow, their mass-specific aerobic capacity varies negatively with body mass while oxygen demand per unit mass remains relatively constant (Figure 11.2b). Thus, oxygen supply lags behind the increasing demand for routine body metabolism as fish increase in body size, providing a mechanistic explanation for the asymptotic growth pattern observed in fish and other water-breathing ectotherms (Pauly, 1998).

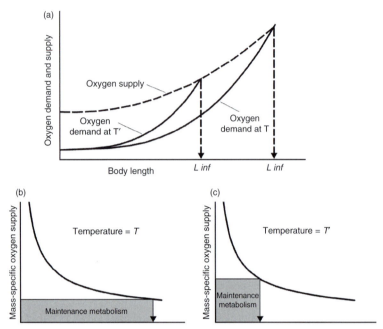

Figure 11.2 Oxygen demand and supply of water-breathing ectotherms generally vary exponentially with body length but the exponent for oxygen supply is less than that for oxygen demand. Thus, body size is limited by oxygen supply and remains smaller than asymptotic length (L inf) (a). For ectotherms, higher temperature (T' > T) increases metabolic rate and oxygen demand, reducing the mass at which oxygen supply becomes limiting to further growth and hence reduces asymptotic size (modified from Pauly, 1998). This can be illustrated by the "p-diagram" (b, c), which shows the relationship between mass-specific oxygen supply, body mass, and maintenance metabolism.

Pauly (1984) also proposed that limitation of oxygen supply relative to metabolic rates initiates sexual maturity in fish. He found that the ratio of metabolism at the size at first maturity to that at maximum size is approximately 1.4 across aquatic fish and invertebrates. Thus, size at maturity and maximum size decrease with decreasing ambient oxygen concentration (Kolding et al., 2008). Furthermore, compensatory responses of water-breathing ectotherms to increased oxygen demand are limited because oxygen supply is restricted by the available respiratory surface and other physiological constraints (Figure 11.2c). Thus, changes in temperature cause aerobic stress and affect the life history of these aquatic ectotherms.

The limitation of oxygen supply may also affect the movement, distribution, foraging behavior, and trophic interactions of marine animals (Bakun, this volume). For example, the increase in oxygen limitation following the growth of an animal can be mitigated by movement to deeper water where the cooler environment reduces metabolic rate and oxygen demand. The stronger limitation of oxygen supply for large predators relative to their smaller-bodied prey contributes to the restriction of their foraging effort (which is oxygen-demanding). The linkages between temperature, oxygen supply, life history, and ecology in fish and aquatic invertebrates have been demonstrated and elaborated by various theoretical and experimental studies (e.g., Pörtner and Knust, 2007; Kolding *et al.*, 2008).

A corollary of the above relationships is that climate change has predictable and ubiquitous impacts on aquatic ectotherms. The limitation of aerobic capacity of aquatic ectotherms creates a window of thermal tolerance, as physiological performance changes continuously from optimum level to beyond their thermal or aerobic tolerance limits (Pörtner *et al.*, 2001). The aerobic capacity of aquatic animals is also affected by other climate-induced biogeochemical changes, such as acidity and ion balances. In the ocean, climate change is likely to result in warming, increases in hypoxic zones, and acidification, among many other changes. As a result, mobile organisms may move to areas where environmental conditions are optimal for their growth. For example, as the water warms, fish may move poleward and to deeper waters and cooler habitats where their physiological performance (e.g., balance between oxygen supply and demand) remains optimal. For species with limited scope for movement and changes, such as those inhabiting semi-confined waters, survival may be most seriously affected (Pörtner and Knust, 2007; Cheung *et al.*, 2009).

The change in physiology and life history of marine species as a result of climate may affect their reproductive biology and trophic ecology. Recruitment of fish and invertebrates is closely linked to climate (e.g., Pörtner *et al.*, 2001; Drinkwater, 2005). Warmer temperatures can reduce body size and size at maturity of fish, potentially affecting fecundity and population growth rate. Reduction in body size may also affect community size-spectrums and energy flows along the food chain (Jennings *et al.*, 2008). Changing climate may affect food requirements, predation, and competition between and within species (Teal *et al.*, 2008). Overall, because organisms have different sensitivities to climate change, mismatches in their responses to this may potentially cause disruption to trophic interactions.

CLIMATE CHANGE AFFECTS GLOBAL MARINE BIODIVERSITY AND FISHERIES

Biodiversity is critical in maintaining ecosystem structure and functions (Naeem and Li, 1997; Worm and Duffy, 2003). Thus, it is important to understand how climate change affects the pattern of marine biodiversity and to identify areas with high sensitivity to climate impacts. The global pattern of marine biodiversity is determined by species distributions while the biogeography of marine species is strongly related to environmental factors, such as temperature (Macpherson, 2002). Observations and theory suggest that marine species respond to ocean warming by shifting their latitudinal range (Perry *et al.*, 2005; Hiddink and Hofstede, 2008; Mueter and Litzow, 2008) and depth range (Dulvy *et al.*, 2008). Changes in species' distributions under climate change lead to invasion and extirpation (local extinction) of species in an area, potentially disrupting its biodiversity and ecosystem structure (Rahel and Olden, 2008). Here, invasion refers to the expansion of a species into an area it has not previously occupied; extirpation refers to a species' ceasing to exist in an area although it may still exist elsewhere (Cheung *et al.*, 2009).

However, attempts to investigate climate change effects on marine species have dealt mostly with limited taxa and on specific regions. The analysis by Cheung *et al.* (2009) represents the first global projection of climate change impacts that encompasses a wide variety of marine animals (1066 species of marine fish and invertebrates). In this analysis, the global pattern of climate change impacts on marine biodiversity was predicted using a dynamic bioclimate envelope model (Cheung *et al.*, 2008b) with data obtained from global databases of marine animals, fisheries statistics, and climate projections, such as FishBase (www.FishBase.org; see Froese, this volume), SeaLifeBase (www.SeaLifeBase.org; see Palomares and Bailly, this volume), and the Sea Around Us database (www.seaaroundus.org; see Watson, Sumaila and Zeller, this volume).

The model of Cheung *et al.* (2008b) assumes that distributions of marine fish and invertebrates follow their temperature preferences and habitat requirements; assumptions that can be partly implied from the theory of oxygen limitation (Pauly, 1981, 1984). The distribution during 1980–2000 of 1066 species of abundant marine fish and invertebrates, expressed as relative abundance in a 0.5 degree cell grid of the world ocean, was predicted by an algorithm (Close *et al.*, 2006; www.seaaroundus.org) using information from FishBase and SeaLifeBase. The bioclimate envelope model infers preference profiles, defined as the suitability of different environmental variables for each species from its predicted current distribution. Future habitat suitability in each cell is projected to change under climate change scenarios. Changes in ocean conditions are projected from the global ocean–atmosphere coupled model (CM 2.1) developed by the US National Oceanic and Atmospheric Administration (NOAA) Geophysical Fluid Dynamics Laboratory (Delworth *et al.*, 2006). In addition, the degree of distribution shift is limited by migration of the studied animals. Migration consists of larval dispersal along ocean currents and adult migration, which is partly determined by ocean conditions and is explicitly represented in the model.

Cheung *et al.* (2009) predicted that the potential biodiversity impact will be highest in high latitudes – particularly the polar region – as well as the tropics and semi-enclosed seas (Figure 11.3). Such impact is expressed in terms of species turnover (i.e., sum of species invasions and extirpations). Specifically, invasion is most intense in the Arctic and the Southern Ocean, while extirpation is concentrated in the tropics, semi-enclosed seas, and subpolar regions. Moreover, the distribution ranges of fish and invertebrates are projected to shift typically by 45 to 59 km per decade, most of which will be in a polar direction (Cheung *et al.*, 2009).

Changes in species' distributions resulting from climate change affect the magnitude and distribution of catch. Using the predicted current species distribution (Close *et al.*, 2006) and the spatially explicit catch data maintained by the Sea Around Us project (Watson *et al.*, 2004; www.seaaroundus.org), Cheung *et al.* (2008a) developed an empirical equation that applies macroecological theory to predict the fisheries potential of exploited marine fishes and invertebrates. Given projected changes in species distribution (as described above) and primary productivity under climate change (e.g., Sarmiento *et al.*, 2004), this equation can be used to assess the effects of climate change on global catch potential (Cheung *et al.*, 2008a). Cheung *et al.* (2008a) applied the empirical model to project the change in magnitude and distribution of catch potential for small yellow croaker (*Larimichthys*

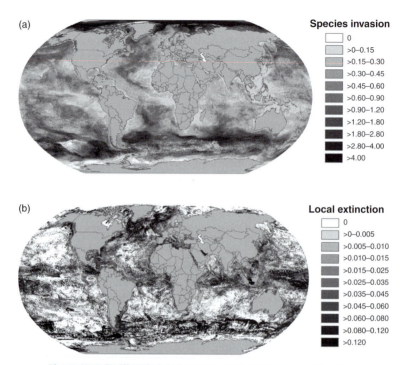

Figure 11.3 Predicted global pattern of species invasion (a) and extirpation (local extinction) (b) in 2050 due to range shifts in marine metazoans under a wide range of climate change scenarios. The values are expressed as proportion relative to the initial species richness in each 0.5 degree grid cell. This is based on an analysis of 1066 species of marine fish and invertebrates (redrawn from Cheung *et al.* 2009).

polyactis) under climate change scenarios. They identified the potential "winners" and "losers" in terms of gains and losses in catch potential of this species (Figure 11.4). By applying this approach to many of the exploited marine species around the world, the global pattern of climate change impacts on catch potential can be obtained (Cheung *et al.* 2010).

The changing catch potential has direct socioeconomic implications for fishing communities, other people depending on fish for food and income, and society as a whole. As many fisheries resources have already been fully exploited and/or overexploited, the socioeconomic impacts of such global changes will be exacerbated (Allison *et al.*, 2009). Impacts of climate change on the economics of fisheries worldwide can be quantified by comparing fisheries sector profits with and without

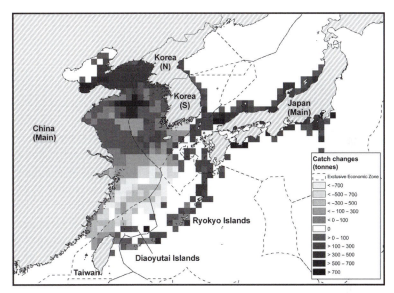

Figure 11.4 Projected changes in catch potential of the small yellow croaker (*Larimichthys polyactis*) under a 2.5°C increase in global ocean temperature (modified from Cheung *et al*., 2008a). Lighter shades represent decreases in catch potential ("losers") and darker shades represent increases ("winners").

climate change. Using global databases of fishing effort, price of fish, and cost of fishing (Watson, Sumaila and Zeller, this volume), the predicted net fishing profit under climate change can be computed. Socioeconomic factors, such as change in employment and food security, can be further analyzed based on changes in net profit from the fisheries sector. The results can also be combined with analysis of socioeconomic vulnerability of societies to climate change (e.g., Allison *et al*., 2009).

Despite numerous uncertainties associated with such global-scale projections, the general patterns revealed from such analyses, with support from empirical data, can provide guidance to design ecosystem-based fisheries management policy. The identified global patterns can provide null hypotheses of climate change impacts on marine ecosystems and fisheries, which can be tested with experiments and analyses at regional and local scales. The results can also help identify hotspots of impacts and help us understand the importance of large-scale dynamics and processes that are shaping marine ecosystems and fisheries.

APPLYING GLOBAL APPROACHES TO REGIONAL
STUDIES

Global-scale studies are powerful tools for examining general patterns of climate change impacts on the world's oceans. Although such studies may be too coarse for investigating details of regional or local impacts, the global patterns can provide a basis for developing analytical approaches that include finer-scale dynamics. In fact, such hierarchical approaches have been employed in climate modeling, in which regional- or local-scale projections rely on large-scale projections from global climate models (e.g., Wilby and Wigley, 1997; Solman and Nuñez, 1999).

Here, we describe an approach that applies the projections of global climate change impacts on marine biodiversity, fisheries, and socioeconomics to develop ecosystem-based fisheries management that is relevant to regional and local scales of management. This approach is being trialed in the west coast bioregion of Western Australia (Figure 11.5). Western Australia provides an interesting case study for regional applications of global approaches because its management jurisdiction extends from the tropics to temperate regions, providing a physical and administrative continuum along which species may redistribute. Fisheries resources along the west coast region are strongly influenced by the Leeuwin Current (Pearce and Phillips, 1988; Gaughan, 2007), a south flowing current that varies strongly with El Niño Southern Oscillation events and that is expected to reflect changes in climate (Pearce and Feng, 2007).

Global projections identify the sensitivity of broad areas, types of species, and fisheries to climate change impacts in the study region. These projections provide useful information to select samples of species that are representative of the ecosystem and fisheries. The next step is to collate local information on those species' historical distributions, life history, ecology, and fisheries. Species distribution maps that incorporate fine-scale habitat data allow more realistic projection of species distributions. Such data can be collated from the literature and contributions from local experts. Simultaneously, regional-scale climate projections, which capture fine-scale dynamics, such as eddies and mixing, can be used. The results can also be tested and validated with empirical data collected in the study area. The improved data inputs and understanding of the modeled processes can feed into a global-scale approach, further improving the large-scale projections.

The outcomes of this process are three-fold. First, predictions of regionally relevant locations where organisms are most sensitive to

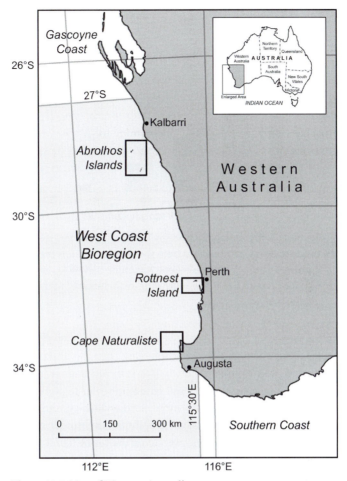

Figure 11.5 Map of Western Australia.

climate change can direct decisions with respect to the location of monitoring programs. Such locations should provide an early warning of changes in marine assemblages because, by incorporating a multi-species response, they should be the first locations to signal change in an otherwise complex environment. Establishing or using existing no-take marine reserves within these locations would further allow the disentanglement of the effects of climate change and fishing on marine communities.

Second, species that are predicted to be strongly responsive to climate change can be identified as key indicators for long-term monitoring across a range of sites. Predictions with regard to changes in

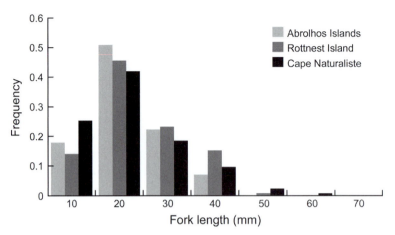

Figure 11.6 Size-frequency histogram for the lightly targeted western king wrasses (*Coris auricularis*) from the Abrolhos Islands (28°49'S), Rottnest Island (32°00'S), and Cape Naturaliste (33°35'S) showing increasing mean size to the south (Centre for Marine Futures, unpublished data).

relative abundance and distribution can then be linked to other regional and monitoring studies. In Western Australia, the identification of indicator species is linked to broad-scale, regional sampling programs based on the use of remote, stereo-video systems using bait (Harvey *et al.*, 2007). The stereo-video systems can provide estimates of relative abundance along with precise estimates of fish lengths. Such data are relevant to understanding shifts in abundance and size structure and can be compared against results from model projections. For instance, western king wrasse (*Coris auricularis*), a lightly exploited species, shows a latitudinal gradient of size distribution that may be attributed to the difference in water temperature rather than exploitation as the species is only very lightly targeted (Figure 11.6). Thus, the species is expected to respond strongly to climate change with respect to its size distribution; measuring changes in its mean size may help detect the impact of ocean warming on the species. Additionally, behavior measurements can be derived from video-based sampling. Such measures include time to arrival and time to respond to bait, which for ectotherms will be physiologically driven and reflect water temperature (see Bakun, this volume). Importantly, changes in feeding behavior, such as increased aggression of feeding, will also lead to increases in catchability, which, with increasing temperature, may mask real declines in catch (Stoner, 2004).

Third, projections of differential responses of a wide range of exploited species to climate change help determine directional changes of community-level indicators for fisheries management. Fisheries management increasingly relies on community-level indicators, such as the marine trophic index (Pauly and Watson, 2005) to monitor the status of ecosystems (e.g., Link *et al.*, 2002). However, climate change confounds the expected responses of these indicators to management or changes in fisheries. Projections of changes in relative abundance and distribution of species assemblages can be taken into account to improve the interpretation of these indicators in reflecting the status, pressure, and responses of ecosystems.

These three outcomes, by projecting changes in species distributions and fisheries under climate change, directly contribute to ecosystem-based management. For example, in Western Australia, fishing activity is controlled through two main mechanisms: zoning of the marine environment determines access for individual license holders and catch is controlled through either input or output controls (Fletcher and Santoro, 2007). Climate change will influence the distribution, abundance, and catchability of species across existing zoning and as such may significantly change the resources available to fishers in a given zone. Where input and output controls are adjusted on the basis of expected catches, such changes, if undetected, will distort the relationship between the amount of effort that can be supported by the resource (e.g., the demersal gillnet fishery) or the proportion of the resource allocated to quota (e.g., abalone). Effective ecosystem-based management of fisheries that recognizes climate change will require reconsideration of zoning and controls and will be partly dependent on the projected and observed responses of species to climate change.

TOWARD INTEGRATED ECOSYSTEM MODELING

Incorporating climate change factors into ecosystem simulation modeling is an important component of ecosystem-based fisheries management (Christensen and Walters, this volume). Particularly, it allows explicit assessment of the interactions between climate change and other human factors, such as fishing. Climate change is closely related to biogeochemical cycles of the ocean and ecophysiology of marine animals, strongly affecting ecosystem dynamics. These processes can be incorporated into an ecosystem model through detailed representation of the mechanism or the use of empirical relationships and forcing functions. The latter are especially useful to model climate change impacts on marine ecosystems at large spatial scales. For example, changes in primary productivity resulting from changes in physical conditions of the ocean can be predicted from empirical relationships (e.g., Sarmiento *et al.*, 2004). Changes in species distributions can be projected from the dynamic bioclimate envelope model described in this chapter. These can be used as forcing functions in ecosystem models to examine potential climate change impacts at the ecosystem level.

The availability of global databases on climate, biology, and fisheries, together with the development of database-driven model generation (Christensen *et al.*, 2009), makes the construction and application of ecosystem models to generate hypotheses of potential climate change impacts possible. At regional and local scales, again, the large-scale model can be used as a basis to incorporate more detailed dynamics that are important at these finer scales. In addition, such ecosystem models can be used to evaluate the performance of management systems at various scales (see Christensen and Walters, this volume).

REFERENCES

Allison, E., Perry, A., Badjeck, M. N., Adger, W., Brown, K., Conway, D., Halls, A., Pilling, G., Reynolds, J. and Andrew, N. (2009) Vulnerability of national economies to the impacts of climate change on fisheries. *Fish and Fisheries*, 10, 173–196.

Brander, K. M. (2007) Global fish production and climate change. *Proceedings of the National Academy of Sciences*, 105, 19709–19714.

Carpenter, K., Abrar, M., Aeby, G., Aronson, R., Banks, S., Bruckner, A., Chiriboga, A., Cortes, J., Delbeek, J. and Devantier, L. (2008) One-third of reef-building corals face elevated extinction risk from climate change and local impacts. *Science*, 321, 560.

Cheung, W. W. L., Close, C., Lam, V., Watson, R. and Pauly, D. (2008a) Application of macroecological theory to predict effects of climate change on global fisheries potential. *Marine Ecology Progress Series*, 365, 187–197.

Cheung, W. W. L., Lam, V. W. Y. and Pauly, D., eds. (2008b) *Modelling Present and Climate-Shifted Distribution of Marine Fishes and Invertebrates*. Fisheries Centre Research Reports 16 (3). Vancouver, Canada: Fisheries Centre, University of British Columbia.

Cheung, W. W. L., Lam, V. W. Y., Sarmiento, J. L., Kearney, K., Watson, R. and Pauly, D. (2009) Projecting global marine biodiversity impacts under climate change scenarios. *Fish and Fisheries*, 10, 235–251.

Cheung, W. W. L., Lam, V. W. Y., Sarmiento, J. L., Kearney, K., Watson, R., Zeller, D. and Pauly, D. (2010) Large-scale redistribution of maximum fisheries catch potential in the global ocean under climate change. *Global Change Biology*, 16(1), 24–35.

Christensen, V., Guénette, S., Heymans, J. J., Walters, C. J., Watson, R., Zeller, D. and Pauly, D. (2003) Hundred-year decline of North Atlantic predatory fishes. *Fish and Fisheries*, 4, 1–24.

Christensen, V., Walters, C. J., Ahrens, R., Alder, J., Buszowski, J., Christensen, L. B., Cheung, W. W. L., Dunne, J., Froese, R., Karpouzi, V., Kaschner, K., Kearney, K., Lai, S., Lam, V., Palomares, M. L. D., Peters-Mason, A., Piroddi, C., Sarmiento, J. L., Steenbeek, J., Sumaila, R., Watson, R., Zeller, D. and Pauly, D. (2009) Database-driven models of the world's large marine ecosystems. *Ecological Modelling*, 220, 1984–1996.

Close, C., Cheung, W. W. L., Hodgson, L., Lam, V. and Watson, R. (2006) Distribution ranges of commercial fishes and invertebrates. In Palomares, M. L. D., Stergiou, K. I. and Pauly, D., eds., *Fishes in Databases and Ecosystems*. Fisheries Centre Research Reports 14(4). Vancouver, Canada: Fisheries Centre, University of British Columbia, pp. 27–37.

Costanza, R., Andrade, F., Antunes, P., Van Den Belt, M., Boesch, D., Boersma, D., Caatarino, F., Hanna, S., Limburg, K., Low, B., Molitor, M., Pereira, J. G., Rayner, S., Santos, R. and Wilson, J. (1999) Ecological economics and sustainable governance of the oceans. *Ecological Economics*, 31, 171–187.

Delworth, T. L., Broccoli, A. J., Rosati, A., Stouffer, R. J., Balaji, V., Beesley, J. A., Cooke, W. F., Dixon, K. W., Dunne, J., Dunne, K. A., Durachta, J. W., Findell, K. L., Ginoux, P., Gnanadesikan, A., Gordon, C. T., Griffies, S. M., Gudgel, R., Harrison, M. J., Held, I. M., Hemler, R. S., Horowitz, L. W., Klein, S. A., Knutson, T. R., Kushner, P. J., Langenhorst, A. R., Lee, H. C., Lin, S. J., Lu, J., Malyshev, S. L., Milly, P. C. D., Ramaswamy, V., Russell, J., Schwarzkopf, M. D., Shevliakova, E., Sirutis, J. J., Spelman, M. J., Stern, W. F., Winton, M., Wittenberg, A. T., Wyman, B., Zeng, F. and Zhang, R. (2006) GFDL's CM2 global coupled climate models. Part I: formulation and simulation characteristics. *Journal of Climate*, 19, 643–674.

Donner, S. D., Skirving, W. J., Little, C. M., Oppenheimer, M. and Hoegh-Guldberg, O. (2005) Global assessment of coral bleaching and required rates of adaptation under climate change. *Global Change Biology*, 11, 2251–2265.

Drinkwater, K. F. (2005) The response of Atlantic cod (*Gadus morhua*) to future climate change. *ICES Journal of Marine Science*, 62, 1327–1337.

Dulvy, N. K., Rogers, S. I., Jennings, S., Dye, S. R. and Skjoldal, H. R. (2008) Climate change and deepening of the North Sea fish assemblage: a biotic indicator of warming seas. *Journal of Applied Ecology*, 45, 1029–1039.

Dulvy, N. K., Sadovy, Y. and Reynolds, J. D. (2003) Extinction vulnerability in marine populations. *Fish and Fisheries*, 4, 25–64.

Fletcher, W. J. and Santoro, K., eds. (2007) State of the Fisheries Report 2006/07, Western Australia: Department of Fisheries.

Garcia, S. and Cochrane, K. (2005) Ecosystem approach to fisheries: a review of implementation guidelines. *ICES Journal of Marine Science*, 62, 311.

Gaughan, D. J. (2007) Potential mechanisms of influence of the Leeuwin Current eddy system on teleost recruitment to the Western Australian continental shelf. *Deep Sea Research*, 54, 1129–1140.

Halpern, B. S., Walbridge, S., Selkoe, K. A., Kappel, C. V., Micheli, F., D'Agrosa, C., Bruno, J. F., Casey, K. S., Ebert, C., Fox, H. E., Fujita, R., Heinemann, D., Lenihan, H. S., Madin, E. M. P., Perry, M. T., Selig, E. R., Spalding, M.,

Steneck, R. and Watson, R. (2008) A global map of human impact on marine ecosystems. *Science*, 319, 948–952.

Harley, C., Hughes, A. R., Hultgren, K. M., Miner, B. G., Sorte, C. J. B., Thornber, C. S., Rodriguez, L. F., Tomanek, L. and Williams, S. L. (2006) The impacts of climate change in coastal marine systems. *Ecology Letters*, 9, 228–241.

Harvey, E. S., Cappo, M., Butler, J. J., Hall, N. and Kendrick, G. A. (2007) Bait attraction affects the performance of remote underwater video stations in assessment of demersal fish community structure. *Marine Ecology Progress Series*, 350, 245–254.

Havenhand, J. N., Buttler, F. R., Thorndyke, M. C. and Williamson, J. E. (2008) Near-future levels of ocean acidification reduce fertilization success in a sea urchin. *Current Biology*, 18, 651–652.

Hiddink, J. G. and Hofstede, R. T. (2008) Climate induced increases in species richness of marine fishes. *Global Change Biology*, 14, 453–460.

Jackson, J. B. C., Kirby, M. X., Berger, W. H., Bjorndal, K. A., Botsford, L. W., Bourque, B. J., Bradbury, R. H., Cooke, R., Erlandson, J., Estes, J. A., Hughes, T. P., Kidwell, S., Lange, C. B., Lenihan, H. S., Pandolfi, J. M., Peterson, C. H., Steneck, R. S., Tegner, M. J. and Warner, R. R. (2001) Historical overfishing and the recent collapse of coastal ecosystems. *Science*, 293, 629–638.

Jennings, S., Mélin, F., Blanchard, J. L., Forster, R. M., Dulvy, N. K. and Wilson, R. W. (2008) Global-scale predictions of community and ecosystem properties from simple ecological theory. *Proceedings of the Royal Society B, Biological Sciences*, 275, 1375–1383.

Kolding, J., Haug, L. and Stefansson, S. (2008) Effect of ambient oxygen on growth and reproduction in Nile tilapia (*Oreochromis niloticus*). *Canadian Journal of Fisheries and Aquatic Sciences*, 65, 1413–1424.

Link, J. S., Brodziak, J. K. T., Edwards, S. F., Overholtz, W. J., Mountain, D., Jossi, J. W., Smith, T. D. and Fogarty, M. J. (2002) Marine ecosystem assessment in a fisheries management context. *Canadian Journal of Fisheries and Aquatic Sciences*, 59, 1429–1440.

Lotze, H. K., Lenihan, H. S., Bourque, B. J., Bradbury, R. H., Cooke, R. G., Kay, M. C., Kidwell, S. M., Kirby, M. X., Peterson, C. H. and Jackson, J. B. C. (2006) Depletion, degradation, and recovery potential of estuaries and coastal seas. *Science*, 312, 1806–1809.

Macpherson, E. (2002) Large-scale species-richness gradients in the Atlantic Ocean. *Proceedings of the Royal Society B, Biological Sciences*, 269, 1715–1720.

Mueter, F. J. and Litzow, M. A. (2008) Sea ice retreat alters the biogeography of the Bering Sea continental shelf. *Ecological Applications*, 18, 309–320.

Munday, P. L., Jones, G. P., Pratchett, M. S. and Williams, A. J. (2008) Climate change and the future for coral reef fishes. *Fish and Fisheries*, 9, 261–285.

Myers, R. A. and Worm, B. (2003) Rapid worldwide depletion of predatory fish communities. *Nature*, 423, 280–283.

Naeem, S. and Li, S. (1997) Biodiversity enhances ecosystem reliability. *Nature*, 390, 507–509.

Orr, J. C., Fabry, V. J., Aumont, O., Bopp, L., Doney, S. C., Feely, R. A., Gnanadesikan, A., Gruber, N., Ishida, A., Joos, F., Key, R. M., Lindsay, K., Maier-Reimer, E., Matear, R., Monfray, P., Mouchet, A., Najjar, R. G., Plattner, G. K., Rodgers, K. B., Sabine, C. L., Sarmiento, J. L., Schlitzer, R., Slater, R. D., Totterdell, I. J., Weirig, M. F., Yamanaka, Y. and Yool, A. (2005) Anthropogenic ocean acidification over the twenty-first century and its impact on calcifying organisms. *Nature*, 437, 681–686.

Pauly, D. (1981) The relationships between gill surface area and growth performance in fish: a generalization of von Bertalanffy's theory of growth.
Meeresforschung, 28, 251–282.

Pauly, D. (1984) A mechanism for the juvenile-to-adult transition in fishes.
Journal du Conseil International pour l'Exploration de la Mer, 41, 280–284.

Pauly, D. (1998) Why squid, though not fish, may be better understood by
pretending they are. *South African Journal of Marine Science/Suid-Afrikaanse
Tydskrif vir Seewetenskap*, 20, 47–58.

Pauly, D., Christensen, V., Dalsgaard, J., Froese, R. and Torres, F. Jr. (1998) Fishing
down marine food webs. *Science*, 279, 860–863.

Pauly, D., Christensen, V., Guénette, S., Pitcher, T. J., Sumaila, U. R., Walters, C. J.,
Watson, R. and Zeller, D. (2002) Towards sustainability in world fisheries.
Nature, 418, 689–695.

Pauly, D. and Watson, R. (2005) Background and interpretation of the "Marine
Trophic Index" as a measure of biodiversity. *Philosophical Transactions of the
Royal Society, Biological Sciences*, 360, 415–423.

Pearce, A. and Feng, M. (2007) Observations of warming on the Western
Australian continental shelf. *Marine and Freshwater Research*, 58, 914–920.

Pearce, A. F. and Phillips, B. F. (1988) ENSO events, the Leeuwin Current, and
larval recruitment of the western rock lobster. *ICES Journal of Marine Science*,
45, 13–21.

Perry, A. L., Low, P. J. and Ellis, J. R. (2005) Climate change and distribution shifts
in marine fishes. *Science*, 308, 1912–1915.

Pörtner, H. O., Berdal, B., Blust, R., Brix, O., Colosimo, A., Wachter, B. D.,
Giuliani, A., Johansen, T., Fischer, T., Knust, R., Lannig, G., Naevdal, G.,
Nedenes, A., Nyhammer, G., Sartoris, F. J., Serendero, I., Sirabella, P.,
Thorkildsen, S. and Zakhartsev, M. (2001) Climate induced temperature
effects on growth performance, fecundity and recruitment in marine fish:
developing a hypothesis for cause and effect relationships in Atlantic cod
(*Gadus morhua*) and common eelpout (*Zoarces viviparous*). *Continental Shelf
Research*, 21, 1975–1997.

Pörtner, H. O. and Knust, R. C. (2007) Climate change affects marine fishes
through the oxygen limitation of thermal tolerance. *Science*, 315, 95–97.

Rahel, F. J. and Olden, J. D. (2008) Assessing the effects of climate change on
aquatic invasive species. *Conservation Biology*, 22, 521–533.

Roessig, J. M., Woodley, C. M., Cech, J. J. and Hansen, L. J. (2004) Effects of global
climate change on marine and estuarine fishes and fisheries. *Reviews in Fish
Biology and Fisheries*, 14, 251–275.

Rosenzweig, C., Karoly, D., Vicarelli, M., Neofotis, P., Wu, Q., Casassa, G.,
Menzel, A., Root, T. L., Estrella, N., Seguin, B., Tryjanowski, P., Liu, C.,
Rawlins, S. and Imeson, A. (2008) Attributing physical and biological
impacts to anthropogenic climate change. *Nature*, 453, 353–357.

Sarmiento, J. L., Slater, R., Barber, R., Bopp, L., Doney, S. C., Hirst, A. C.,
Kleypas, J., Matear, R., Mikolajewicz, U., Monfray, P., Soldatov, V.,
Spall, S. A. and Stouffer, R. (2004) Response of ocean ecosystems to climate
warming. *Global Biogeochemical Cycles*, 18, doi:1029/2003GB002134.

Solman, S. and Nuñez, M. N. (1999) Local estimates of global climate change: a
statistical downscaling approach. *International Journal of Climatology*, 19,
835–861.

Stoner, A. W. (2004) Effects of environmental variables on fish feeding ecology:
implications for the performance of baited fishing gear and stock assessment. *Journal of Fish Biology*, 65, 1445–1471.

Teal, L. R., De Leeuw, J. J., Van Der Veer, H. W. and Rijnsdorp, A. D. (2008) Effects of climate change on growth of 0-group sole and plaice. *Marine Ecology Progress Series*, 358, 219–230.

Thomas, C. D., Cameron, A., Green, R. E., Bakkenes, M., Beaumont, L. J., Collingham, Y. C., Erasmus, B. F. N., De Siqueira, M. F., Grainger, A., Hannah, L., Hughes, L., Huntley, B., Van Jaarsveld, A. S., Midgley, G. F., Miles, L., Ortega-Huerta, M. A., Townsend-Peterson, A., Phillips, O. L., and Williams, S. E. (2004) Extinction risk from climate change. *Nature*, 427, 145.

Watson, R., Kitchingman, A., Gelchu, A. and Pauly, D. (2004) Mapping global fisheries: sharpening our focus. *Fish And Fisheries*, 5, 168–177.

Wilby, R. L. and Wigley, T. M. L. (1997) Downscaling general circulation model output: a review of methods and limitations. *Progress in Physical Geography*, 21, 530–548.

Worm, B., Barbier, E. B., Beaumont, N., Duffy, J. E., Folke, C., Halpern, B. S., Jackson, J. B. C., Lotze, H. K., Micheli, F., Palumbi, S. R., Sala, E., Selkoe, K. A., Stachowicz, J. J. and Watson, R. (2006) Impacts of biodiversity loss on ocean ecosystem services. *Science*, 314, 787–790.

Worm, B. and Duffy, J. E. (2003) Biodiversity, productivity and stability in real food webs. *Trends in Ecology and Evolution*, 18, 628–632.

VILLY CHRISTENSEN AND CARL J. WALTERS

12

Progress in the use of ecosystem modeling for fisheries management

INTRODUCTION

We are moving toward ecosystem-based management of fisheries, and it is clear that ecosystem modeling is an important tool for evaluating scenarios and trade-offs as part of such a move. This chapter evaluates the extent of ecosystem modeling as an active research field, the potential usefulness of the models for fisheries management, and actual use of ecosystem models in fisheries management. In addition we present some recommendations for how the move toward ecosystem-based management can be supported through an adaptive environmental assessment and management process.

It is important at the outset to be careful about what it means to "use" a model in fisheries management. At one extreme, imagine taking model predictions at face value and applying them blindly in setting reference points and regulations; some managers seem to hope for or expect such models to appear, presumably as absolution or excuse for not making thoughtful choices in the face of uncertainty. No fisheries model, whether a highly "precise" single-species assessment or a crude ecosystem biomass flow scheme, will ever be reliable enough to use in such an uncritical way, if for no other reason than unpredictability in environmental conditions. At the opposite extreme, we can certainly use even very simple trophic interaction calculations to screen qualitative policy options and answer very basic questions raised in management settings (e.g., could predation rates by some particular predator that fishers do not like be high enough to ever justify a culling policy?). Between these extremes, to "use" a model in policy can mean a whole range of increasingly precise – and correspondingly more likely to be incorrect – qualitative and quantitative answers to queries by management stakeholders.

Ecosystem Approaches to Fisheries: A Global Perspective, ed. V. Christensen and J. Maclean. Published by Cambridge University Press. © Cambridge University Press 2011.

Development of ecosystem models would be largely a waste of time if their only intended use were to improve the predictions and prescriptions of single-species management, by accounting for some causes of variation in growth, natural mortality, and recruitment rates. Except in cases where we see persistent nonstationarity in such rates, or only have data for very limited ranges of abundance well after early stock declines due to fishing, existing single-species models based directly on measured rate data are quite adequate to define reference points and feedback policies for coping with unpredictable variation. Where ecosystem models become important, even logically necessary to compare policy options, is in situations where management objectives and policy options are broadened to include performance measures (e.g., diversity, abundance of nontarget species) and actions (e.g., habitat fertilization, protected areas) about which single-species models simply have nothing to say.

HOW ACTIVE IS THE FIELD OF ECOSYSTEM MODELING?

To gauge the activity in ecosystem modeling related to fisheries management, we here evaluate the trend in number of primary publications dealing with ecosystem approaches to fisheries and developing or applying ecosystem modeling.

We conducted an ISI Web of Knowledge[SM] search for the words (Ecosystem* + model* + fish*) as well as for (multispecies + fish*), where the wildcard (*) denotes any ending. We included results for the 20-year period from 1990–2009, and combined the results obtained using the two search terms. For each of the "hits" we examined the abstract (where available through Web of Knowledge[SM]), or title or paper copy (where not) to determine whether the publication actually developed, applied, or reviewed ecosystem modeling activities as opposed to only referring to it.

The search yielded 2785 ecosystem and multispecies modeling publications, of which 391 (or 14%) were publications developing, applying, or reviewing ecosystem modeling approaches (Figure 12.1). The results indicate an approximately 19% growth per year in the annual number of model publications since 1995. This indeed indicates that ecosystem modeling is an active field of research experiencing rapid growth.

More than half the modeling publications in the Web of Science[SM] search were related to the Ecopath with Ecosim (EwE)

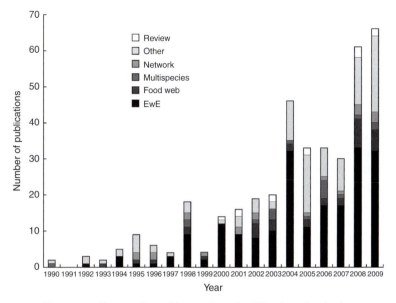

Figure 12.1 Temporal trend in number of publications developing or applying ecosystem modeling related to fisheries research. Results obtained from a Web of Science[SM] search for (Ecosystem* + model* + fish*) or (multispecies + fish*).

modeling approach (www.ecopath.org; described in Polovina, 1984; Christensen and Pauly, 1992; Walters *et al.*, 1997, 1999, 2000; Pauly *et al.*, 2000; Christensen and Walters, 2004). We assume that this dominance of EwE modeling is caused in part by the long history of the approach and its availability combined with the extended support for it over the time period examined (more than 30 training courses and workshops have been conducted throughout the world, with participation of more than 600 scientists).

Another factor is that the entry threshold for this kind of modeling is low; the starting point can be a descriptive model of what is known of the resources in an ecosystem, their state values and interactions. The end level is advanced, however, asking detailed questions of causes and effects over time, trade-offs, policy optimizations, and spatial design.

There are other modeling approaches and we strongly support that a diversity of models be used as we move toward ecosystem-based management of fisheries. Modeling should not be a "one fits all." It is important that models be built to address the policy questions at hand, rather than the opposite. We will, however, focus this overview on the use and capabilities of EwE because this is the area with which we are most familiar.

ARE ECOSYSTEM MODELS USEFUL FOR FISHERIES MANAGEMENT?

One of us did not think so just a decade ago: "We believe the food web modelling approach is hopeless as an aid to formulating management advice; the number of parameters and assumptions required are enormous" (Hilborn and Walters, 1992). While the statement serves to illustrate how careful one has to be with categorical statements (Walters and Martell, 2002), it is also clear that the author in question has changed his mind, noting that a substantial part of a textbook is dedicated to demonstrating how food web modeling can be of use for fisheries management (Walters and Martell, 2004). We will not seek to duplicate that effort here, but rather discuss the modeling procedure as well as illustrate the usefulness of ecosystem models for management based on experience obtained from a series of case studies where ecosystem models have been used to investigate questions of interest for ecosystem-based management of fisheries.

Indeed, we find that as fishery policy moves beyond the objectives in place for single-species management there is no choice but to adopt more elaborate ecosystem models. Policy choices for ecosystem-based fisheries management will necessarily involve predictions about the impact of nontraditional policy choices, and our abilities to and options for making such predictions are severely limited. In the past, we have based comparisons of ecosystem-related policy choices (i.e., predictions about the efficacy of the choices) on methods ranging from very simple risk avoidance models (e.g., don't harvest forage fishes at all because production of larger fish may be affected), to simple food chain or trophic cascade models (e.g., to evaluate policies related to fertilizing rivers to enhance salmon runs), to very complex food web models that attempt to explore possible reverberating effects going beyond direct predator–prey interactions (e.g., if species A is reduced by fishing, will species B increase, and will that increase in B cause a large change in abundance for species C, D, E, . . . ?). Much of the recent ecosystem modeling work has been aimed mainly at assessing risks of the more complex reverberating effects such as "cultivation-depensation" effects (Walters and Kitchell, 2001), on the assumption that complex interactions are likely to result in counter-intuitive responses (Pine *et al.*, 2009).

If ecosystem models are then to be of use in fisheries management it is necessary to demonstrate that the models can replicate historic trends in ecosystems, as a first step toward building some confidence that they can make plausible extrapolations to novel situations. Next, we examine this issue in more detail.

EVALUATING MODEL BEHAVIOR

The time-dynamic module Ecosim (Walters et al., 1997, 2000) of EwE, and the spatial-dynamic module Ecospace (Walters et al., 1999), are built on what has been termed "foraging arena theory" (Walters and Juanes, 1993; Walters and Martell, 2004). The basic assumption in this theory is that prey behavior limits predation rates, causing trophic interactions to be highly organized in time and space. When evaluating model behavior, it is necessary to "tune" the models so as to reflect the net effect of this organization on large-scale interaction rates. For Ecosim models, this mainly involves setting one parameter for each species, a vulnerability coefficient.

Vulnerabilities are factors describing how a change in a given predator biomass will affect predation mortality for a given prey. Low vulnerability factors imply that an increase in predator biomass will not cause any noticeable increase in the predation mortality that a predator will cause on a given prey. High vulnerability factors indicate that if the predator biomass is for instance doubled, it will cause close to a doubling in the predation mortality rate on a given prey. This then relates directly to assumptions about the carrying capacity for the predator in question.

If the predator is close to its carrying capacity, lowering its biomass (e.g., through pulse fishing) will be compensated for by an increase in the consumption/biomass ratio for the remaining individuals and increased surplus production will let the predator biomass return toward its carrying capacity. Thus, the population is stable when close to its carrying capacity. If, however, the predator is far from its carrying capacity, the individual predators will be very little affected by competition from peers; there is little surplus production. A change in its biomass (be it through pulse fishing, stock enhancement, or the appearance of a strong year class) will, due to the relative absence of compensation because of surplus production factors, lead to the directional change in biomass being maintained. Populations are unstable when far from their carrying capacities.

The settings for vulnerabilities, as described above, directly relate to assumptions about carrying capacities and, thus, have direct implications for an EwE model's ability to replicate historical time-series data. Were historic estimates of abundance available, we would in many cases have estimates for carrying capacity as well. Such cases are, however, rare. Usually, there is very little historical information about a given ecosystem. Typically, the available assessments go back only one or two decades, and assessments are only available for the most important commercial species. For evaluating ecosystem model behavior it is desirable to go further back in order to challenge the models with time-series trends and some contrasts in abundance estimates. Thus, when we talk about "historical" information, we typically consider a period beginning when industrialized fishing became a factor, typically the mid-1900s.

For many ecosystems, we have had to complement the available assessments with additional analyses for exploited species not covered by the single-species assessments conducted as part of the management process, e.g., for Chesapeake Bay (Christensen et al., 2009). For this, our choice of stock assessment method has most often been stock reduction analysis (Hilborn and Walters, 1992; Kimura et al., 1996; Walters and Martell, 2004) where abundance estimates are based on turning catch and productivity information to time-series trends or abundance data (Christensen and Martell, 2005; Christensen, 2006; Walters et al., 2006) with a deliberate aim to reach as far back in time as possible so as to estimate unfished "limits" for natural abundance.

HINDCASTING

The first criterion we set for using ecosystem models for fisheries management is whether they can replicate historic trends in ecosystems. We evaluate this by estimating the summed squared residuals between observations and ecosystem model predictions using log likelihood criteria (Figure 12.2). The "observations" include biomasses, mortality rates, average weights, diets and/or catches, and may be predictions from other models, e.g., virtual population analyses (VPAs) or stock synthesis models, which may be a cause for concern. It is indeed preferable to fit the ecosystem models to the data used in the stock assessments rather than the output from these assessments (FAO, 2008). This is, however, rarely possible due to data availability; yet it is a concern that should be taken seriously when the purpose of the analysis is not so much to compare single-species and ecosystem model predictions, but to use the ecosystem models as part of the management process.

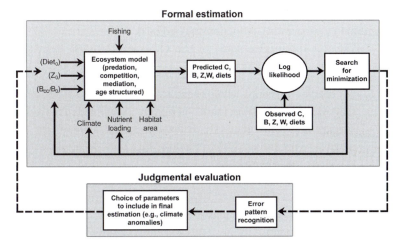

Figure 12.2 Overview of the EwE modeling process. Using log likelihood criteria, the input parameters or anomalies (e.g., climate) may be estimated based on a non-linear search routine. Prediction (fitting) failures after each estimation trial then inform judgmental changes in model structure and parameters. B is biomass, Z is total mortality, C is catch, W is average weight. Subscript 0 refers to the Ecopath model base year, and CC to carrying capacity.

We typically see that the summed squared residuals are reduced to around one third of initial values as part of the model fitting procedure (Figure 12.2). This procedure includes an iterative approach, with

(1)   iterations between the Ecopath and Ecosim modules of EwE to weed out obvious data errors (typically conversion mistakes or erroneous estimates of species productivity rates);

(2)   estimation of biomass accumulation rates (changes in biomass of a given species in the base Ecopath model year) to start the Ecosim simulations on the right tangent;

(3)   estimation of vulnerabilities, typically predator-specific rates, relating to assumptions of carrying capacities as discussed above. The estimation can be done using a nonlinear search routine, minimizing the summed squared residuals; and

(4)   estimation of system productivity rates over time. This estimation can also be through a nonlinear search routine, and is often combined with the search above.

Fitting the models to time-series data has been conducted for more than 30 ecosystems. It seems to be the rule rather than the exception that the models can be made to fit time-series data well (though "fit well" is not a strictly defined term; it is more a visual impression, albeit combined with a strong reduction in residuals).

We can summarize some of the experience gained from the model fitting.

- For species or groups where there are strong impacts from fisheries, the ecosystem models generally fit very well. This is not surprising because generally we are comparing results from single-species and ecosystem models, with both predominantly driven by fishing pressure.

- Where single-species and ecosystem model predictions diverge, the difference can often be explained by obvious model assumptions. An example is the Strait of Georgia where juvenile herring abundance in the 1960s was much higher in the VPA used for assessment than in the Ecosim model (Walters and Martell, 2002). The difference is attributed to juvenile herring having a much higher natural mortality due to higher predator abundance in the 1960s in the Ecosim simulations. Using the Ecosim model to obtain estimates for predation mortality (similar to how multispecies VPA is used at the International Council for Exploration of the Seas, ICES) would minimize the differences between model hindcasts.

- Ecosystem models may be accurate for some species, yet have problems with others. For example, Cox and Kitchell (2004) were able to simulate population trends for the some important species of whitefish (e.g., lake chub), but not for some of the other species (e.g., siskowet lake trout). Inability to fit the data for some species may well be due to lack of information about species-specific environmental drivers and their effects on such species. Indeed, we often find that adding more constraints (in the form of data) makes it possible to explain such exceptions rather than the opposite. The implication of the exceptions not invalidating other parts of the model is that ecosystem models can be used to address specific policy questions relating to part of the ecosystem only. We encourage this approach to modeling rather than an approach aimed at including and explaining everything simultaneously for all parts of an ecosystem.

- We observe impacts on forage species from changes in predator abundance, and occasionally vice versa, where changes in prey abundance affect predators, e.g., for striped bass and menhaden in Chesapeake Bay (Christensen *et al.*, 2009). In other studies, we have found that fishing mortality on a forage species may replace predation mortality, in essence that the fishery may outcompete the predators (Walters *et al.*, 2008). It is, however, often impossible to evaluate the credibility of the predicted trends for forage species due to a lack of time-series information as well as uncertainty about variation in productivity rates.

- We generally see very strong reactions throughout the ecosystem from changes in system productivity (e.g., Guénette *et al.*, 2006, 2008). Thus, it is usually necessary to incorporate or estimate overall system productivity over time in the form of nutrient availability or primary productivity. Indeed, the only ecosystem where we have been unable to find indications of changes in system productivity is the Gulf of Thailand (FAO/FISHCODE, 2001), where the fisheries effects are very strong while system productivity may be less variable.

Overall, we find that the ecosystem model applications demonstrate a capability for hindcasting ecosystem trends over the time periods where data are available. Given past experience with the chaotic nature of Lotka–Volterra type models, where population explosions and extinctions are extremely difficult to circumvent, we attribute the improved behavior of the Ecosim models (which are Lotka–Volterra derived) to the inclusion of prey behavior through the foraging arena theory as discussed above.

It is clear from the time-series fitting that this form of testing for ecosystem models is data demanding. However, the data required are generally accessible in any case and represent the ecosystem history: how we have exploited the ecosystem resources and what we know about population sizes over time. Nevertheless, the number of parameters to be estimated as part of the modeling process need not be very high (when fitting the model to historical data). Indeed, the number of parameters included in more "advanced" current single-species assessments in areas with fisheries management may well exceed the number of parameters used for ecosystem modeling of the same areas.

PREDICTIVE CAPABILITIES

Models are made for predictions, and the hindcasts discussed above, though they are model predictions, are not necessarily good examples of predictions. The next step is to evaluate if the ecosystem models can make plausible extrapolations to novel situations.

We emphasize that the predictive approaches are uncertain and that this uncertainty is largely caused by limited knowledge and data on states and processes. There is a clear lack of long-term monitoring data on nontarget species and life stages, and the concentration of interaction effects (trophic, habitat) that takes place in early life stages (recruitment) is difficult to monitor. Juvenile mortality rates are as a rule very high; this is thought to be mainly by predation, concentrated in short space–time windows, for instance marine mammal predation on juvenile salmon as they enter saltwater.

Contributing to the difficulty is that while we may fit the historical data well, it is far from certain that the fitting is good for the right reason (Essington, 2004). We typically evaluate fishery, environmental, and trophic effects in historical data, and seek to find simple explanations for often-confounded results. An example: the initial Ecosim run for the northwestern Hawaiian Islands indicated that a major decline in rock lobster abundance could be linked to fishing pressure and trophic inter-actions, and that this might have caused the endangered monk seal to decline; a simple parsimonious explanation. When, however, informa-tion that a subsequent stop to the rock lobster fisheries did not lead to a recovery of rock lobster (and subsequently of monk seals) was incorpo-rated, the story had to change. Satellite chlorophyll data indicated a persistent 40–50% decline in primary production at the time, and when this was incorporated, the combined effect "explained" both the continued monk seal decline and persistent low lobster abundance (Polovina, 2002). Can we ever be sure we have the right explanation? The general answer is no, but models are our best tool for choosing between alternative actions. As such they are useful – see the discussion about adaptive management below.

It is clear that we cannot resolve uncertainty about how ecosys-tems change based on models and time-series data only. As an example: salmon declines are often assumed to be linked to freshwater habitat loss, and we can make models that replicate trends in salmon runs by changing habitat parameters; but how do we know that ocean ecosys-tem changes (marine survival) are not more important factors (Bradford, 1999; Welch *et al.*, 2000; Melnychuk, 2009)?

Most of the predictive ecosystem management questions being asked today concern three issues: (1) "top-down effects," i.e., effects of harvesting top predators on species at lower trophic levels; (2) "bottom-up effects," i.e., effects of fisheries on species at intermediate trophic levels on the capacities of those species to provide "ecosystem support services" to species (harvested or not) at higher trophic levels; and

(3) effects of deliberate or inadvertent changes in habitat factors, e.g., through coastal nutrient loading, clearing mangrove for aquaculture, or removal of bottom structure through trawling.

Based on experience with a series of ecosystem model case studies, we have found the following.

(1)   *Top-down effects.* Models seem capable of predicting top-down effects, i.e., mortality of prey does seem to change with predator abundance. We have not observed in historical data sets used for model testing that predicted changes in mortality rates have somehow been cancelled out by abundance increases or switching behaviors of alternate predators. Hence, it appears that predation mortality rates in general are additive. An excellent example has been increases in shrimp stocks in the Atlantic in apparent response to reduced cod abundances (Worm and Myers, 2003). There is no clear indication (yet) that other species besides cod will replace the "natural" predation impact of cod so as to reduce shrimp production to its former, lower levels.

(2)   *Bottom-up effects.* We do not often see clear evidence of strong bottom-up effects; it appears that where forage species are reduced by fishing, the predatory fish may shift to other prey. There are exceptions though, e.g., very large effects of fishing have been observed on piscivorous birds in the Peru current (see Tovar *et al.*, 1987) and in parts of the Northeast Atlantic, but we have also found that it is very difficult to replace the dominant prey species, menhaden, in the diets of the common predator, striped bass, in Chesapeake Bay (Christensen *et al.*, 2009). Predictions of bottom-up effects are extremely difficult due to the potential for switching and appearance of alternate food organisms combined with complex effects of trophic ontogeny. As an example, herring reduction fisheries in the Strait of Georgia in the 1960s were expected have a clear negative impact on Chinook and coho salmon, which feed on herring. The opposite happened; the reduced herring abundance was associated with strong salmon runs. It may well be that herrings' influence as a competitor with juvenile salmon (both feed on copepods and euphausiids) outweighed its role as a prey for the older salmon.

(3)   *Essential habitats.* We have found it very troublesome to define the term "essential fish habitat" when working with ecosystem models. Most fish undergo complex trophic and habitat-use

ontogenies and some display considerable capabilities to use alternative habitats when preferred habitats are no longer available or overpopulated. Such adaptations and flexibilities are virtually impossible to predict without empirical, experimental experience.

While there are many reasons for uncertainty in making predictions about future ecosystem structure and the potential impact of management interventions, we really have no choice. Fortunately, there has been considerable progress in ecosystem modeling in recent years – some of it referred to in this chapter – and we conclude that it is becoming possible to develop useful predictive models for ecosystem management. We can with some credibility describe agents of mortality and trophic interdependencies, while evaluation of the relative impact of fisheries and environmental factors is progressing; we are at the "looking for correlation" stage. Overall, we can present our capabilities to use models to address ecosystem management questions in the form of a popularized report card (Table 12.1).

USE OF ECOSYSTEM MODELS AS PART OF THE FISHERIES MANAGEMENT PROCESS

If, as stated above, ecosystem models have reached a state where they can be of use to address fisheries policy questions, it may be worth examining the current state of affairs with respect to actually using such models as part of the fisheries management process.

While many scientists are working with ecosystem models throughout the world, and while many do so with the explicit intention of using the models to address policy questions, we have only been able to identify relatively few cases where the models have been incorporated as part of the management process. What we see are cautious attempts to incorporate the models in the following situations.

- Multispecies models
  - estimating predation mortality for use in stock assessment;
  - limiting harvest of prey species to meet predator demands;
  - impact of changing mesh size;
  - evaluating impact of top predators and impact of potential culling;
  - environmental impact assessments;
  - target species response to quotas.

Table 12.1 *A report card on the status quo of using models to address ecosystem management questions.*

Concern	Grade	Comment
Bycatch effects	A−	Prediction capabilities for direct effect of fishing in general is quite good
Top-down effects (e.g., of predator culling or protection)	C	Trophic effects of fishing can be classified as "top-down" or "bottom-up" with respect to where management controls are exerted
• on valued prey	B	Changes in natural mortality for prey species already subject to assessment can be handled quite well
• on "rare" prey	F	Prediction capability of outbreaks of previously rare species is wanting
Bottom-up effects (e.g., effects of prey harvesting on predator stocks)	C	There is uncertainty about flexibility of predators to find alternative food sources when prey are fished
Multiple stable states	B	"Cultivation-dispensation" mechanisms (Walters and Kitchell, 2001) may be the main cause of "flips"
Habitat damage	D	There is a lack of understanding about real habitat dependencies and bottlenecks
Selective fishing practices/ policies	F	We lack experience in this area
Production regime changes	B	Models look good when fitted to data, but have not stood the test of time
Regime shifts	C	Appropriate policy adjustments in response to ecosystem-scale productivity change are unclear

- EwE models
  - evaluating impact of shrimp trawling on bycatch species;
  - evaluating competitive and predatory impact of bycatch species;
  - evaluating impact of predators on target species;
  - demonstrating ecological role of species;
  - ecosystem impact of proposed fisheries interventions;

- environmental impact assessment of proposed fisheries interventions;
- environmental impact assessment of alternative quotas;
- target species' response to quotas;
- closed area sizing;
- valuation of top predator impact on target species.

We see the relatively few examples of the use of ecosystem models in the management process as indicative of (1) lack of experience with use of ecosystem models for predictive purposes and recognition that our capabilities to provide advice about large-scale dynamics are limited, and (2) software (like EwE) to make ecosystem data management relatively inexpensive having been available for a relatively short time.

Ecosystem modeling is designed to be of use for strategic management, i.e., to address questions of what fisheries impact is likely to be in the medium to long term. As such, modeling supplements the tactical single-species assessment that currently dominates the management process; it does not and will not replace it. The fisheries management process is indeed trapped in short-term tactical approaches with strategic decisions rarely being part of the agenda.

We argue that in the current situation where ecosystem manipulation is common, but based on a less than optimal set of decision tools (often being done accidentally in a totally opportunity-driven, ad-hoc manner), it is time to implement strategic considerations as part of the management process. Such strategic considerations cry out for incorporating ecosystem models into the management process.

We recognize that there has been much apparent distrust of multispecies and ecosystem models for fisheries policy analysis. At least some of this distrust is due to concern about the lack of adequate data to quantify the often complex predictions. Unfortunately, some of the objections also represent not real scientific concern but rather shortsighted assumptions about the objectives of management and unwillingness to take on a broader account of the impact of fishing, and a defensive approach by scientists who are comfortable with current management procedures and may lack the time, opportunity, and/or capability to master the more complex steps involved in developing ecosystem-scale assessment models. Adding to the latter problem have been severe difficulties in developing software for ecosystem modeling that is stable and flexible enough to be easily adopted and used by assessment scientists for whom time is at a premium due to the demands of maintaining existing assessment and management machinery.

ECOSYSTEM MODELS AS TOOLS IN ADAPTIVE POLICY DESIGN

All fisheries management policies are adaptive in the sense that when making policy choices we can never trust any single model prediction if for no other reason than the unpredictability of environmental effects. Instead, we use the models to guide initial choices, and we expect to have to monitor the fishery concerned over time in order to determine the impact of each choice. This requirement applies even more importantly to ecosystem management than it always has to single-species management. We are moving into new domains of policy choice involving new policy instruments, such as protected areas, predator culling, and other management choices, which go beyond simple harvest regulation. Here, it will be critical to treat every test of such choices as an adaptive management experiment, and to design "treatment" plans and monitoring programs using sound principles of experimental design as far as is practical (Walters, 1986). This may call for comparison of treatment of reference policies, and temporal and spatial replication, as well as monitoring for unexpected and expected treatment responses.

ACKNOWLEDGMENTS

This contribution is supported by the Sea Around Us project (www.seaaroundus.org), a scientific cooperation between the University of British Columbia and the Pew Environment Group. We acknowledge support from Canada's National Scientific and Engineering Research Council, and thank Daniel Pauly and Line Bang Christensen for discussions and suggestions on the draft.

REFERENCES

Bradford, M. J. (1999) Temporal and spatial trends in the abundance of coho salmon smolts from western North America. *Transactions of the American Fisheries Society*, 128, 840–846.

Christensen, L. B. (2006) *Reconstructing Historical Abundances of Exploited Marine Mammals at the Global Scale*. Vancouver, Fisheries Centre Research Reports 14 (9). Vancouver, Canada: Fisheries Centre, University of British Columbia.

Christensen, L. B. and Martell, S. J. D. (2005) A stochastic framework for reconstructing historical marine mammal abundance from catch records and sparse abundance information: application to the Antarctic blue whale and North Atlantic and Arctic fin whale. *ICES*, CM, R, 32.

Christensen, V., Beattie, A., Buchanan, C., Martell, S.J.D., Latour, R.J., Preikshot, D., Sigrist, M., Uphoff, J.H., Walters, C.J., Wood, R.J. and Townsend, H. (2009) Fisheries ecosystem model of the Chesapeake Bay: methodology, parameterization and model exploration. NOAA Technical Memorandum. Washington DC: NOAA.

Christensen, V. and Pauly, D. (1992) Ecopath II: a software for balancing steady-state ecosystem models and calculating network characteristics. *Ecological Modelling*, 61, 169–185.

Christensen, V. and Walters, C.J. (2004) Ecopath with Ecosim: methods, capabilities and limitations. *Ecological Modelling*, 172, 109–139.

Cox, S.P. and Kitchell, J.F. (2004) Lake Superior ecosystem, 1929–1998: simulating alternative hypotheses for recruitment failure of Lake herring (*Coregonus artedi*). *Bulletin of Marine Science*, 74, 671–683.

Essington, T.E. (2004) Getting the right answer from the wrong model: evaluating the sensitivity of multispecies fisheries advice to uncertain species interactions. *Bulletin of Marine Science*, 74, 563–581.

FAO (2008) Fisheries management. 2. The ecosystem approach to fisheries. 2.1 Best practices in ecosystem modelling for informing an ecosystem approach to fisheries. FAO Fisheries Technical Guidelines for Responsible Fisheries. No. 4, Suppl. 2, Add. 1. Rome: FAO.

FAO/Fishcode (2001) Report of a bio-economic modelling workshop and a policy dialogue meeting on the Thai demersal fisheries in the Gulf of Thailand held at Hua Hin, Thailand, May 31–June 9, 2000. FI: GCP/INT/648/NOR: Field Report F-16 (En). Rome: FAO.

Guénette, S., Christensen, V. and Pauly, D. (2008) Trophic modelling of the Peruvian upwelling ecosystem: towards reconciliation of multiple datasets. *Progress in Oceanography*, 79, 326–335.

Guénette, S., Heymans, J.J., Christensen, V. and Trites, A.W. (2006) Ecosystem models show combined effects of fishing, predation, competition, and ocean productivity on Steller sea lions (*Eumetopias jubatus*) in Alaska. *Canadian Journal of Fisheries and Aquatic Sciences*, 63, 2495–2517.

Hilborn, R. and Walters, C.J. (1992) *Quantitative Fisheries Stock Assessment: Choice, Dynamics and Uncertainty*. New York, NY: Chapman & Hall.

Kimura, D.K., Balsiger, J.W. and Ito, D.H. (1996) Kalman filtering the delay-difference equation: Practical approaches and simulations. *Fishery Bulletin*, 94, 678–691.

Melnychuk, M.C. (2009) Mortality of migrating Pacific salmon smolts in southern British Columbia, Canada. BSc Thesis, University of British Columbia, Vancouver, Canada.

Pauly, D., Christensen, V. and Walters, C. (2000) Ecopath, Ecosim, and Ecospace as tools for evaluating ecosystem impact of fisheries. *ICES Journal of Marine Science*, 57, 697–706.

Pine, W.E., Martell, S.J.D., Walters, C.J. and Kitchell, J.F. (2009) Counterintuitive responses of fish populations to management actions: some common causes and implications for predictions based on ecosystem modeling. *Fisheries*, 34, 165–180.

Polovina, J.J. (1984) Model of a coral reef ecosystem I. The ECOPATH model and its application to French frigate shoals. *Coral Reefs*, 3, 1–11.

Polovina, J.J. (2002) Application of Ecosim to investigate the impact of the lobster fishery on endangered monk seals in Hawaii. In Christensen, V., Reck, G. and Maclean, J.L., eds., *Proceedings of the INCO-DC Conference Placing Fisheries in their Ecosystem Context. Galápagos Islands, Ecuador, 4–8 December 2000.* Brussels: ACP-EU Fisheries Research Reports, 12, 30.

Tovar, H., Guillen, V. and Nakama, M. E. (1987) Monthly population sizes of three guano bird species off Peru, 1953–1982. In Pauly, D. and Tsukayama, I., eds., *The Peruvian Anchoveta and its Upwelling Ecosystem: Three Decades of Change. ICLARM Studies and Reviews,* 15, 208–218.

Walters, C. (1986) *Adaptive Management of Renewable Resources.* New York, NY: Macmillan.

Walters, C., Christensen, V. and Pauly, D. (1997) Structuring dynamic models of exploited ecosystems from trophic mass-balance assessments. *Reviews in Fish Biology and Fisheries,* 7, 139–172.

Walters, C. and Kitchell, J. F. (2001) Cultivation/depensation effects on juvenile survival and recruitment: implications for the theory of fishing. *Canadian Journal of Fisheries and Aquatic Sciences,* 58, 39–50.

Walters, C. and Martell, S. J. D. (2002) Stock assessment needs for sustainable fisheries management. *Bulletin of Marine Science,* 70, 629–638.

Walters, C., Martell, S. J. D., Christensen, V. and Mahmoudi, B. (2008) An Ecosim model for exploring ecosystem management options for the Gulf of Mexico: implications of including multistanza life history models for policy predictions. *Bulletin of Marine Science,* 83, 251–271.

Walters, C., Pauly, D. and Christensen, V. (1999) Ecospace: Prediction of meso-scale spatial patterns in trophic relationships of exploited ecosystems, with emphasis on the impacts of marine protected areas. *Ecosystems,* 2, 539–554.

Walters, C., Pauly, D., Christensen, V. and Kitchell, J. F. (2000) Representing density dependent consequences of life history strategies in aquatic ecosystems: EcoSim II. *Ecosystems,* 3, 70–83.

Walters, C. J. and Juanes, F. (1993) Recruitment limitation as a consequence of natural selection for use of restricted feeding habitats and predation risk-taking by juvenile fishes. *Canadian Journal of Fisheries and Aquatic Sciences,* 50, 2058–2070.

Walters, C. J. and Martell, S. J. D. (2004) *Fisheries Ecology and Management.* Princeton, NJ: Princeton University Press.

Walters, C. J., Martell, S. J. D. and Korman, J. (2006) A stochastic approach to stock reduction analysis. *Canadian Journal of Fisheries and Aquatic Sciences,* 63, 212–223.

Welch, D. W., Ward, B. R., Smith, B. D. and Eveson, J. P. (2000) Temporal and spatial responses of British Columbia steelhead (*Oncorhynchus mykiss*) populations to ocean climate shifts. *Fisheries Oceanography,* 9, 17–32.

Worm, B. and Myers, R. A. (2003) Meta-analysis of cod-shrimp interactions reveals top-down control in oceanic food webs. *Ecology,* 84, 162–173.

Section IV The human side

CORNELIA E. NAUEN AND GOTTHILF HEMPEL

13

Science and capacity building for sustainable development in fisheries

INTRODUCTION

Over the past 40 years we have witnessed a major shift in the way marine science and related capacity building have been understood and approached both in industrialized and developing countries. In the early post-colonial days, marine science centers and universities in tropical and subtropical countries were mostly remnants of the former colonial powers and were strongly influenced by a logic of industrialization of the production process, similar to the green revolution in agriculture. This needed underpinning by resource assessments to bolster the associated investments.

Before World War II, fishery biologists like Baranov (1918; see also Chuenpagdee, this volume), Bückmann (1938), and Graham and coworkers (1939, 1943) had already developed the concept of optimal fishing based on the growth curves of populations and of individual fish. In the 1950s, Beverton and Holt (1957) turned those approaches into a widely accepted model of growth overfishing and maximum sustainable yield (MSY) in fisheries for North Sea plaice and haddock. In those species the risk of recruitment overfishing did not seem likely. Since 1956, the Food and Agriculture Organization of the United Nations (FAO) has held training courses in various developing regions to spread the Beverton and Holt approach. However, the single-species stock assessment developed for long-lived fish with clear age readings did not prove applicable to short-lived tropical fish and multispecies fisheries. Daniel Pauly was one of the first to develop indirect methods for age determination and stock assessments for those fish and fisheries (see Munro, this volume).

In the spirit of assisting developing countries and in light of optimistic figures about the global expansion potential of fisheries,

Ecosystem Approaches to Fisheries: A Global Perspective, ed. V. Christensen and J. Maclean. Published by Cambridge University Press. © Cambridge University Press 2011.

(e.g., Moiseev, 1969; Gulland, 1971), national and international donors provided experts, equipment, research and fishing vessels, and also fellowships for overseas studies. Those efforts were meant to develop fisheries in tropical and subtropical regions in the image of temperate fisheries. They were only partially successful, though world production did increase according to world fisheries statistics maintained by the FAO and based on inputs from its member states. In 1979, at the United Nations Conference on Science and Technology for Development, developing countries demanded scientific cooperation for genuine solutions rather than simple technology transfer that was often poorly adapted to their conditions.

At about the same time, fisheries science in industrialized countries gradually moved away from the expansive approach of searching for new resources in the northern hemisphere and simply went further south and in deeper waters. Marked changes in the abundance and composition of fish populations in heavily exploited large ecosystems like the North Sea and Georges Bank as well as regime shifts in upwelling systems gave rise to the concepts of ecosystem overfishing and ecosystem restoration. In the management of individual species, precautionary regulations were introduced and the establishment of marine protected areas was advocated as a tool for the protection of marine biodiversity and as refuge for heavily exploited fish populations. Reduction of fishing effort was to be supported by phasing out fishing capacity-boosting subsidies and the creation of alternative employment outside the fisheries sector. Technologies were developed to replace destructive fishing methods and to reduce unwanted by-catch, though the widespread adoption of originally military technology in the fishing industry (such as sonar and global positioning systems) and of very heavy gear for fishing at great depths led to contradictory trends between industrial practice and conservationist advice.

In the general public, the rise, mostly in industrialized countries, of the political "green movement" in the late 1970s and through the 1980s also forced some change of attitude toward unsustainable harvesting practices of natural resources, including fisheries. In a report of the Study on International Fisheries Research (SIFR), jointly supported by the World Bank, United Nations Development Programme, African Development Bank, and European Commission (World Bank, 1990), Daniel Pauly and other experts cautioned against transferring costly research vessels to developing countries with weak institutional capabilities and research budgets because these sank scarce financial resources and skilled labor into inappropriate technology. They rather advocated compiling existing but scattered information (data "archeology") and spending resources on people to enable novel analyses as a more cost-effective and appropriate approach to the challenges in developing countries.

The 1992 Rio Earth Summit (UN Conference on Environment and Development) gave stronger currency to the term "sustainable development," first coined in the 1987 report of the World Commission on Environment and Development (Brundtland Commission) "Our Common Future." It also gave rise to the Convention on Biological Diversity, the international convention with the broadest based adhesion today (193 countries were parties to the Convention in 2010).

A parallel and overlapping series of events marked the gradual evolution of perceptions of trends in world fisheries and their increasing distance from sustainability. Preparing the Rio Summit was the Cancún (Mexico) International Conference on Responsible Fishing, which called on the FAO to develop a code for responsible fisheries. The growing fisheries crisis was first brought to wide public attention through a series of articles and reports in the general media in 1993 in many countries and several major languages. Going public in this way marked a stark deviation from dealing with the long-standing problems mostly in expert circles. The "Code of Conduct on Responsible Fisheries" was finally adopted in 1995 by the 28th Session of the FAO Conference. At the same time, fresh attempts were made to stamp out increasing illegal, unreported, and unregulated (IUU) fishing, on the one hand, and putting understanding of the effects of fishing into a wider context, on the other.

Stepping stones for this gradual process in the UN system, leading up to the World Summit on Sustainable Development in Johannesburg, 2002, were the 2001 Reykjavik Conference on Responsible Fisheries in the Marine Ecosystem (FAO, 2001) and the 2002 Dakar International Symposium on Marine Fisheries, Ecosystems, and Societies in West Africa: Half a Century of Change (Chavance *et al.*, 2004). In the Johannesburg Plan of Implementation, the resource conservation concept, which had become part of the political discourse since Rio, was officially interpreted as meaning ecosystem restoration from mostly grave fisheries-induced degradation as a pathway to sustainable development. Nowadays, large marine ecosystem (LME) projects, sponsored and administered by the Global Environment Facility and other United Nations (UN) organizations are based on the ecosystem approach to sustainable development.

In the following, we discuss how science and international scientific cooperation, often led by Daniel Pauly, have contributed directly and indirectly to this conceptual development and the changing perceptions of the public as to what sustainable development can mean in fisheries.

RESEARCH CHALLENGED CONVENTIONAL ANSWERS TO NEW AND OLD OVERFISHING PROBLEMS: AN ECOSYSTEM AND BIODIVERSITY APPROACH TO FISHERIES

In the run-up to the Rio Summit, it had already become clear that comprehensiveness in scientific documentation of life on Earth was a major requirement in order to identify and analyze gaps and set targets in cost-effective ways. Fishes accounted for more than 80% of world aquatic harvests. Thus, documenting all fish species known to science became necessary. Daniel Pauly, together with Rainer Froese, laid the foundations for this major achievement in the late 1980s, and received early support from the European Commission. The idea grew into a public web-based archive of scientifically validated information on all (more than 30 000) fish species in the world (www.fishbase.org), now led by an international consortium (see Palomares and Bailly, this volume). The staggered interface from the most simple to the highly sophisticated use represents a public knowledge good contributing to global capacity building and enabling many types of users and uses. It has been shown to contribute toward sustainability (Nauen, 2006).

Debunking a misconception about almost unlimited resources and light human impact on the oceans, Pauly and Christensen (1995) showed that the primary production necessary to support fisheries on coastal shelves – the most productive and most exploited parts of the world's oceans – was in the order of heavily exploited terrestrial ecosystems. This represented interesting linkages between previously disconnected work on ecology and ecosystems on the one hand and fisheries on the other. Since the ground-breaking work of MacArthur and Wilson (1967) on island biogeography and other seminal work, ecological concepts have caught on. Christensen, Pauly, and Walters progressively developed the Ecopath family of analytical tools (e.g., Christensen and Pauly, 1992; Walters and Maguire, 1996; Pauly et al., 2000). In terms of geographic delimitations of ecosystems, such modelling work often used the concept of Large Marine Ecosystems (LME), which was developed initially by Platt and Sathyendranath (1988) in terms of biogeographical provinces based on primary productivity patterns and by Sherman (1986) in terms of management units. The two LME approaches were reconciled by Watson *et al.* (2003) and Hempel and Pauly (2002); Hempel and Sherman brought the different strands together (see also Sherman and Hempel, 2008).

Some of the early ecosystem work already contained elements of historical perspective. Most importantly, Pauly (1995) pointed to the lack of documentation of past states of resource systems in association with the tendency of researchers to take their own professional experience as the reference framework for judging shifts in the states of resources. That led to what Pauly termed the "shifting baseline syndrome." Researchers (managers and others) were unwittingly presiding over creeping ecosystem degradation without the means to analyze it. This influential paper gave rise to many efforts in reconstructing past states of ecosystems before they were subjected to present-day fishing pressures (see Jackson and Jacquet, this volume). In the political arena, it took many additional steps of international negotiations and discourse development to recognize that sustainability under conditions of severe ecosystem degradation implied restoration, not simply conservation of the status quo.

These efforts were spearheaded by many researchers, foremost among them Pauly *et al.* (1998) with their article on "fishing down marine food webs," Hutchings (2000) with his analysis of collapse and (lack of) recovery of stocks of long-lived species overfished over extended periods, Jackson *et al.* (2001) with their analysis of long-term overfishing and the recent collapse of coastal ecosystems, Myers and Worm (2003) with their demonstration of the rapid depletion of predatory fish species, Christensen *et al.* (2003) with their analysis of 100 years of decline in North Atlantic predatory fishes, and Chavance *et al.* (2004) with their proceedings of the symposium on "Half a Century of Change in Ecosystems, Fisheries and Societies in West Africa."

The most comprehensive attempt to date to document the effects of fishing on global marine resources began in 1999 with the Sea Around Us project (www.seaaroundus.org), involving a massive "cleaning" and reinterpretation of official FAO fisheries statistics since 1950, and complemented with other data sets (Watson *et al.*, this volume). As a corollary of analyzing productivity of ecosystems across climatic and geographic boundaries, it also became clear that some of the catch reporting to the FAO was difficult, if not impossible, to reconcile with what was possible within documented primary and secondary productivity of ecosystems. Watson and Pauly (2001) revealed Chinese misreporting, by no means the only case, but particularly influential because of its scale effect on distorting world production trend data as reported by the FAO (see Baron, this volume).

These cumulative research efforts that digested much previous work enabled a new type of analysis, placing fisheries in their ecosystem context, resulted in new analytical frameworks, and pieced together the picture of severe ecosystem degradation at global scales. The implications of this notion are only very gradually being absorbed by specialists and the wider public, helped by the Millennium Ecosystem Assessment and Global International Waters Assessment (GIWA; 2005). Both paid particular attention to communicating the results and implications of those most ambitious analytical efforts so far.

SUSTAINABILITY MEANS MORE THAN THE STATE OF THE ENVIRONMENT AND ITS RESOURCES

That sustainable development cannot be equated to the environment alone needs underscoring. Indeed, humans are now affecting every part of the planet. Social and economic dimensions and the interaction between the three sustainability dimensions need to be considered concomitantly as these affect perceptions and decision making. In the marine domain, sustainability requires attention to marine resources in the ecosystem context, integrated with the best possible investigation and understanding of how societies appropriate marine ecosystems (notably the economic and social dimensions; see Ruddle, this volume, for the example of the South Pacific). Over the last decade, efforts have increased to ensure better coverage of the economic dimension of rehabilitation, resource use, and trade (e.g., Pauly *et al.*, 1999; Alder *et al.*, 2002; Sumaila, 2004). However, the social dimension of fishing is still only marginally investigated and integrated into the overall picture (Failler, 2002; Williams *et al.*, 2005; Collet, 2007). Because of their higher energy efficiency, selective gears, and social distribution mechanisms, small-scale fisheries are, in this context, explored as part of the solution rather than as part of the problem as suggested earlier (Pauly, 1997, 2006a, 2006b; see also Chuenpagdee, this volume).

The perceptions of the public tend to diverge from the fundamentals investigated by science and the same facts receive different interpretation depending on these perceptions. Therefore, it is unsafe to pretend that scientific findings of a disciplinary nature and their interpretations automatically translate into planning and decision making. Indeed, evidence about fisheries management in many parts of the world, including in the European Union, regularly diverges from one-to-one translation of available scientific advice. Often the recommendations by fisheries science are ignored altogether.

Technical knowledge about the three principal dimensions of sustainability – ecosystem/environmental knowledge, economics, and social concerns – must be integrated through governance and the political discourse in prevailing institutions (Gyawali et al., 2006) but, given the multiple dimensions, it is also clear that even a good disciplinary diagnosis cannot be expected to lead to effective action. This also provides an indication why isolated technical measures, such as mesh size regulations commonly proposed in response to observed overfishing, have not led to the expected results. Rather, in conjunction with economic incentives to cheat (overcapacity in catching and, in some areas, processing) and weak enforcement of rules, the technical measures have, at best, slowed ecosystem degradation and productivity losses. Moreover, enforcement is typically difficult and costly, particularly in the face of considerable fleet mobility and when social norms do not underpin technical measures effectively.

Whenever particular interests have much control over the resource allocation process, one dimension (e.g., short-term economics) may strongly prevail over all other considerations. Conversely, inclusiveness and participatory governance have more potential for a durable balance between social, environmental, and economic aspects of the resource system. Keeping in mind the shifting baseline syndrome, results in the scientific literature alone are not sufficient to influence the political process. "Translating" and communicating research results in easy-to-understand language and explaining what they mean for potential courses of action are critical preconditions for shortening the time between a scientific finding and the follow-up action taken to years rather than decades (European Environment Agency, 2001; Nauen et al., 2005; see also Baron, this volume; Reichert, this volume).

This confers a particularly important responsibility on publicly supported research to produce public knowledge goods on the basis of the resources and their ecosystem context, together with social and economic information. As is the case with a number of recent web-based archives, such as FishBase (Froese and Pauly, 2000) and SeaLifeBase (see Palomares and Bailly, this volume), such public goods should be easily and freely accessible to help create a level playing field (Pauly, 2001; Froese et al., 2003).

SUSTAINABILITY SCIENCE IS A NECESSARY BUT INSUFFICIENT CONDITION FOR MANAGEMENT FOR SUSTAINABILITY

The efforts to integrate different fields of scientific pursuit in a mutually compatible way have been conceptually spearheaded by Wilson with his demand for consilience (1999), or the "jumping together" of different strands of knowledge. This concerns first of all the natural sciences piecing together the environmental facts about human impact on ecosystems, their structure and dynamic change in response to anthropogenic and natural drivers. Here, the Ecopath family of modelling tools, among others, has created conditions for consilience between many disciplinary strands of investigation.

We now understand that the information provided by isolated disciplinary science is too limited to deal effectively with the loss of ecosystem productivity and biodiversity. This warrants education in transdisciplinary thinking oriented at understanding the links between nature and society. Furthermore, efforts are needed to speed up the – generally slow – transformation of complex multidisciplinary scientific knowledge into political action in its widest sense.

In line with the integrated approach to sustainability, the socioeconomic sciences need to develop in ways that build bridges to and are compatible with the study of nature. While the experimental and historical branches of the natural sciences search for overarching natural laws and principles, the social sciences are characterized by descriptive work at smaller scales because of the sheer diversity of social organization and local conditions.

A combination of global concepts and tailoring measures to site-specific conditions appears to be a promising general approach to finding sustainable solutions. There is so far relatively little precedent on how to achieve that, though combinations of global programs and regional (LMEs) and local projects represent potentially useful learning ground.

COMMUNICATING SCIENCE AND A NEW RELATIONSHIP WITH GLOBAL CITIZENS

Global public knowledge goods that help structure and retrieve accumulated knowledge in a manner accessible not only to specialists but to all citizens are important in this context. Formats, such as FishBase and even more so INCOFISH (www.incofish.org) are structured on global scientific principles and allow for local content beyond disciplinary boundaries. The organizational principles and easy public access improve integration and provide a support role to a wide range of uses of scientifically validated knowledge.

These valuable achievements notwithstanding, significant additional efforts are required to communicate research effectively to nonscientists, in particular to economic and political decision makers. The challenge is to develop narratives that connect to the perceptions of nonscientists given that the human brain seems to relate to such "stories" by default (Gerrig and Rapp, 2004). That may even make evolutionary sense, given that effort is required to be skeptical and validate such stories independently. Conversely, abstractions and de-contextualized results cannot be easily absorbed and even scientists themselves prefer a journalistic presentation of research results to the original in terms of readability (Whitfield, 2006; see also Baron, this volume). In the complicated arena of striking a balance between a technically desirable course of action and what is socially and politically feasible, scientific results have to be translated into more broadly accessible language and imagery, something Daniel Pauly has addressed throughout his career.

More importantly, today's world of cheap and easy-to-use communications, involving crowds of people in different locations with different backgrounds, opens entirely new avenues to knowledge accumulation and consolidation (Surowiecki, 2004). In a generic way, this is the underpinning principle of the public domain encyclopedia Wikipedia and other knowledge accumulation, validation, and sharing mechanisms essentially based on voluntary collaboration. That Wikipedia, which is free, should have a quality performance rivaling the long-established expert model Encyclopaedia Britannica (Giles, 2005b) is a case in point. It certainly does not make experts and scientists superfluous, but rather opens new perspectives on their roles (Giles, 2005a).

There is a notion of a global pool of information, some scientific, much not. All people contribute to it in one way or the other and use different pieces for their specific purposes. The construction of knowledge out of the pool of information is a social process, mediated through, e.g., culture, tradition, the media, formal education, research, and innovation. An anchovy may mean prey for predators, food for humans, fishmeal for aquaculture (see Pullin, this volume), a source of employment, a precious good of nature represented in ancient coastal cultures, an object of ecosystem research, including El Niño studies and ichthyology, as well as of speculations in the stock exchange, not to mention a proxy for paleoceanographers. It is all the same Peruvian anchovy (*Engraulis ringens*), but it has different meanings for different people.

The primary scientific products in the pool are data. But how can we facilitate the interpretation and use of such data for management in a broad sense? Capacity building in the sciences should now include training in communication skills. Young scientists anywhere in the world should learn as part of their regular education the basics of how the media work and how to convey in an easily understandable way what they research and why it is important for others, including nonscientists. We need more scientists everywhere who are able and willing to engage critically with citizens (see Baron, this volume) and policymakers (See Christensen and Lai, this volume). The idea is to bring down barriers between different types of knowledge and create a level playing field of scientifically validated information for all citizens, at least in principle. The more validated information is available for the public, the stronger will be sound, science-based pressure on managers and decision makers (see also Hirshfield, this volume; Reichert, this volume). Public awareness helps to control and engage politicians and it provides moral (and financial) support to further research and communication.

CAPACITY TO MAKE USE OF SCIENTIFIC KNOWLEDGE IS A PRECONDITION FOR SUSTAINABLE DEVELOPMENT

In the light of the new role of knowledge, it is also increasingly critical to develop scientific and technical capabilities to be able to actively participate in scientific research and in the absorption, adaptation, and use of its results (Fortes and Hempel, 2002). This is relevant in industrialized countries, but even more so in developing countries, which have much lower numbers of scientists per capita of economically active citizens. For comparison, the number of scientists and engineers per 1000 active inhabitants is approximately 18 in Finland, 8 in the United States, 7 in Germany, 1 in Brazil, and 0.5 in Mexico (De Brito Cruz and de Mello, 2006).

From the starting point of Beverton and Holt's single-species model from the temperate "north," the changes of perspective sketched out above make it all the more imperative that developing countries, many in the subtropics and tropics with highly varied multi-species ecosystems and fisheries, strengthen their own capabilities.

Some developing countries, including in Sub-Saharan Africa, derive significant foreign exchange income from international trade in fish and fisheries products and have positive balances of trade with the major importing blocks, Japan (22% of total imports in 2002), European Union (35%), and the United States (16%). Out of the 38% of internationally traded fishery commodities from capture and culture fisheries, more than half originate from developing countries. That represented US$18 billion export earning in 2002 for developing countries (out of a total of US$58.2 billion) and makes international trade in fishery products by far the most important for any food commodity – much more important than coffee, tea, rice, or cocoa (Lem, 2004). In the case of the modest African, Caribbean, and Pacific economies, the six countries earning most from fishery product exports to the EU in 2002 were Namibia (US$222 million), Seychelles (US$119 million), Senegal (US$192 million), Madagascar (US$160 million), Côte d'Ivoire (US$156 million), and Mauritania (US$126 million). Moreover, the fishery sector also plays a very important role in local employment (small-scale fisheries, postharvest activities, etc.) and food security (Lem, 2004).

It comes as little surprise that national or sector policymaking cannot rely only or primarily on external information and advice; thus, a shortage of science capacity represents a serious constraint. The evidence referred to above shows that the exploitation patterns underlying these economic gains are unsustainable, though decisions by managers and politicians regularly trade longer-term gains and sustainability for short-term gains. Shortage of human and institutional capacity to develop alternatives that would be socially and politically acceptable is the major factor in the persistence of the status quo.

International scientific cooperation, including North–South partnerships (Hempel, 2002), combining joint learning with capacity building, is the most promising approach to develop suitably contextualized knowledge about marine and freshwater ecosystems, their living resources and the socioeconomic conditions of their – hopefully – sustainable use. Mostly supported by public funding or foundations, international scientific exchange and cooperation has intensified over decades. It has taken the form of student exchange and joint research projects, much practiced by the University of British Columbia's Fisheries Centre. It was also a characteristic feature of work at the Institute of Marine Research in Kiel (now the Leibniz Institute for Marine Science – GEOMAR), the Centre for Tropical Ecology in

Bremen, and other institutions led by the second author. International scientific cooperation with particular emphasis on promoting sustainable use of aquatic systems is also the defining purpose of the program of the European Union in which the first author is active.

Empowerment of scientific capacity means primarily investing in people and institutions in developing regions, mostly in the tropical and subtropical parts of the world's oceans where biodiversity is greatest.

To a certain extent a fair division of research work between rich and poor countries might be envisaged. Rich countries have the capacity and hence the responsibility of advancing science in the broadest possible way – not only in natural and social sciences per se but also in theory and analysis of the interactions in the sustainability triangle. Those interactions differ in structure from region to region. Working in collaboration with colleagues and institutions worldwide, including developing countries with their rich and diverse perspectives, is a win–win situation.

Although international cooperation in marine science is stronger than in many other fields, the level of international cooperation is nowhere near adequate for the magnitude of the challenges (Hempel, 1999). The state of global aquatic ecosystems, the relatively underdeveloped state of social science research on how humans use these ecosystems, the still weak integration of knowledge, and the few scientists working on such challenges, particularly in developing countries, all represent a formidable challenge to moving toward sustainable resource use.

Conventional approaches will not be sufficient, particularly in the absence of adequately articulate and determined public-knowledge policies in developing countries. However, countries lacking the ability to develop their capabilities on all fronts at the same time still can gainfully invest in research and show tangible results, as illustrated in Cuba (Giles, 2005a). Despite the central policy setting, there may be more of a combination of top-down and bottom-up planning than meets the eye (Badgley et al., 2005).

Responses are most likely to be effective when concomitantly working on several fronts. Actions should incorporate and be inspired by the following principles:

- Adopt a partnership approach based on mutual respect, interest, and benefits.
- Help strengthen human and institutional capacity in each country to absorb, develop, and use scientific knowledge about its ecosystems.

- Promote integrated, interdisciplinary modes of pursuit of knowledge on aquatic ecosystems, their sustainability, and balancing drivers, such as international trade, local employment, food security, and wealth generation and distribution.
- Help develop and act on a new research agenda that connects fisheries research in its ecosystem and socioeconomic dimensions to the global political agenda of restoring degraded ecosystems and doing so, inter alia, through networks of marine protected areas (Johannesburg Plan of Implementation of 2002).
- Promote scientific excellence, transparency, and accountability.
- Promote social awareness, including gender, and responsibility, and connect research to education and social and technological innovation.
- Promote communication skills and novel ways of conducting research that connect social groups, including citizen organizations, with the research process, thus increasing mutual understanding and chances of uptake of research results.
- Promote working conditions that connect research to innovative action.
- Put emphasis on public knowledge goods.
- Use maximization and durability of social value as choice criteria for resource allocation.
- Promote policy dialogue among a wide range of actors to explore realistic transitions toward sustainable use and an enabling societal framework for science and general knowledge-intensive and locally contextualized approaches, including strengthening the capacity to take action.

CONCLUSION

The last 40 years have witnessed a considerable change in fisheries science from a predominantly single-species approach modeled on temperate industrial fisheries to ecosystem-based approaches to fisheries that additionally seek to integrate progressively the social and economic dimensions to fulfill sustainability requirements. Daniel Pauly has become one of the most prolific and influential promoters of these developments. Moreover, experience and research have shown that unless research is communicated in suitable narratives and engages with social actors, its impact on societal processes and resource governance takes decades.

Recent developments outside fisheries, particularly cheap communication technologies, have enabled two possibly converging trends that offer hope for some acceleration of more inclusive and participatory fishery governance: (1) the development of global public information systems structuring scientifically validated knowledge and bringing it potentially within reach of all citizens, not just an elite group of experts; and (2) the voluntary collaboration of large numbers of experts and non-experts in accumulating and validating information. In a "knowledge society," everybody may act at the same time as a user and contributor to a global endeavor to accumulate and validate knowledge, make it available free or quasi-free and, thus, combine global concepts with local knowledge and participation.

At the start of the new millennium, developing countries contributed over 50% of international trade in fisheries commodities. However, the majority of these fisheries are known to be unsustainable and often in decline. Scarce human and institutional capital is a key constraint. Innovative forms of international scientific cooperation promoting capacity building through partnerships offer greatest hope for increasing the contribution of research toward sustainable resource use. Finally, it is of utmost importance to link sustainability research concepts to education and innovation. Policy dialogue among a wide range of social actors can create the general context for building capacity to investigate and act on knowledge that enables legitimate and widely acceptable solutions.

REFERENCES

Alder, J., Pitcher, T., Zeller, D. and Sumaila, U. R. (2002) Economics of marine protected areas. *Coastal Management*, 30, 279–280.

Badgley, C., Perfecto, I., Wendl, M., Williams, N. and Lente, G. (2005) Cuban science democratic and not tied to profit. *Nature*, 437, 192.

Baranov, F. I. (1918) On the question of the biological basis of fisheries. *Nauchnyi issledovatelskii iktiolohisheskii institut, Izvestiia*, 1, 81–128.

Beverton, R. J. H. and Holt, S. J. (1957) *On the dynamics of exploited fish populations. Fisheries Investigations (Series II)*, 19, 533.

Bückmann, A. (1938) Über den Höchstertrag der Fischerei und die Gesetze organischen Wachstums [On the maximum yield in fisheries and the laws of organic growth]. *Berichte der Deutschen Wissenschaftlichen Kommission für Meeresforschung*, 9, 16–48.

Chavance, P., Bâ, M. and Gascuel, D. (2004) *Pêcheries maritimes, écosystèmes et sociétés en Afrique de l'Ouest: un demi-siècle de changement.* Des publications officielles des Communautés Europeennes et Paris. IRD Rapports de Recherche Halieutique ACP-EU, IS.

Christensen, V., Guénette, S., Heymans, J. J., Walters, C. J., Watson, R., Zeller, D. and Pauly, D. (2003) Hundred-year decline of North Atlantic predatory fishes. *Fish and Fisheries*, 4, 1–24.

Christensen, V. and Pauly, D. (1992) ECOPATH II – A software for balancing steady-state ecosystem models and calculating network characteristics. *Ecological Modelling*, 61, 169–185.

Collet, S. (2007) Pursuing the true value of people and the sea. Res halieutica: une ré-évaluation. *Social Science Information/Information sur les sciences sociales*. Special Issue, 46, 237.

De Brito Cruz, C. H. and De Mello, L. (2006) Boosting innovation performance in Brazil. OECD Economics Department Working Paper. Paris: OECD.

European Environment Agency (2001) *Late Lessons from Early Warnings 1896–2000*. Environmental Issue Report. Copenhagen: European Environment Agency.

Failler, P. (2002) Représentations, conceptions et appropriations de la nature; note synthétique et prolongement des textes de Catherine Larrère, Raphael Larrère et Serge Collet. La recherche halieutique et le développement durable des ressources naturelles marines en Afrique de l'Ouest, quels enjeux? Initiative de recherche halieutique ACP/UE. Rapport de Recherche Halieutique ACP-UE, EUR20188.

FAO (2001) *Report of the Eleventh Session of the Committee for Inland Fisheries of Africa*. FAO Fisheries Report. Rome: FAO.

Fortes, M. and Hempel, G. (2002) Capacity building. In Field, J. G., Hempel, G. and Summerhayes, C. P., eds., *Oceans 2020: Science, Trends, and the Search for Sustainability*. Washington DC: Island Press, pp. 283–308.

Froese, R., Lloris, D. and Opitz, S. (2003) Scientific data in the public domain. The need to make scientific data publicly available: concerns and possible solutions. In Palomares, M. L. D., Samb, B., Diouf, T., Vakily, J. M. and Pauly, D., eds., Fish Biodiversity: Local Studies as Basis for Global Inferences. ACP-EU Fisheries Research Report, 14, 267–271.

Froese, R. and Pauly, D. (2000) *FishBase 2000: Concepts, Designs and Data Sources*. Los Baños, Laguna, Philippines: ICLARM.

Gerrig, R. J. and Rapp, D. N. (2004) Psychological processes underlying literary impact. *Poetics Today*, 25, 265–281.

Giles, J. (2005a) Challenges of being a Wikipedian. *Nature*, 438, 901.

Giles, J. (2005b) Internet encyclopaedias go head to head. *Nature*, 438, 900–901.

Graham, M. (1939) The sigmoid curve and the overfishing problem. *Rapports Et Procès-Verbaux Des Réunions. Conseil International pour l'Exploration de la Mer*, 110, 15–20.

Graham, M., Corbet, S. A. and Disney, R. H. L. (1943) *The Fish Gate*. London: Faber & Faber.

Gulland, J. A. (1971) *The Fish Resources of the Ocean*. Farnham, UK: Fishing News Books.

Gyawali, D., Allan, J. A., Antunes, P., Dudeen, B. A., Laureano, P., Luiselli Fernández, C., Scheel Monteiro, P. M., Nguyen, H. K., Novácek, P. and Pahl-Wostl, C. (2006) EU INCO water research from FP4 to FP6 (1994–2006). A critical review. Luxembourg: Office for Official Publications of the European Communities.

Hempel, G. (1999) Reflections on international cooperation in oceanography. *Deep Sea Research II*, 46, 17–31.

Hempel, G. (2002) Capacity building in marine science: a review. In Wesnigk, J. and Rolston, S., eds., *The European Challenge: Proceedings, Pacem in Maribus 28, Hamburg (Germany), 3-6 December 2002*. Halifax: International Ocean Institute.

Hempel, G. and Pauly, D. (2002) Fisheries and fisheries science in their search for sustainability. In Field, J. G., Hempel, G. and Summerhayes, C. P., eds., *Oceans 2020: Science, Trends, and the Search for Sustainability*. Washington DC: Island Press, pp. 109–136.

Hutchings, J. A. (2000) Collapse and recovery of marine fishes. *Nature*, 406, 882–885.

Jackson, J. B. C., Kirby, M. X., Berger, W. H., Bjorndal, K. A., Botsford, L. W., Bourque, B. J., Bradbury, R. H., Cooke, R., Erlandson, J. and Estes, J. A. (2001) Historical overfishing and the recent collapse of coastal ecosystems. *Science*, 293, 629–637.

Lem, A. (2004) Fish Trade Issues in WTO and ACP-EU Negotiations. Globefish, available at http://www.globefish.org/index.php?id=2251.

MacArthur, R. H. and Wilson, E. O. (1967) *The Theory of Island Biogeography*. Princeton, NJ: Princeton University Press.

Millennium Ecosystem Assessment (2005) *Ecosystems and Human Well-being: Synthesis*. Washington DC: World Resources Institute.

Moiseev, P. A. (1969) The living resources of the world ocean. Israel Program for Scientific Translations; 1971 [available from the US Dept. of Commerce, National Technical Information Service, Springfield, VA].

Myers, R. A. and Worm, B. (2003) Rapid worldwide depletion of predatory fish communities. *Nature*, 423, 280–283.

Nauen, C. E. (2006) Implementing the WSSD decision of restoring marine ecosystems by 2015: scientific information support in the public domain. *Marine Policy*, 30, 455–461.

Nauen, C. E., Bogliotti, C., Fenzl, N., Francis, J., Kakule, J., Kastrissianakis, K., Michael, L., Reeve, N., Reyntjens, D., Shiva, V. and Spangenberg, J. H. (2005) *Increasing Impact of the EU's International S&T Cooperation for the Transition Towards Sustainable Development*. Luxembourg: Office for Official Publications of the European Communities.

Pauly, D. (1995) Anecdotes and the shifting baseline syndrome of fisheries. *Trends in Ecology & Evolution*, 10, 430.

Pauly, D. (1997) Small-scale fisheries in the tropics: marginality, marginalization and some implications for fisheries management. In Pikitch, E. K., Huppert, D. D. and Sissenwine, M. P., eds., *Global Trends: Fisheries Management*. Bethesda, MD: American Fisheries Society Symposium 20, 40–49.

Pauly, D. (2001) Importance of the historical dimension in policy and management of natural resource systems. In Feoli, E. and Nauen, C. E., eds., *Proceedings of the INCO-DEV International Workshop on Information Systems for Policy and Technical Support in Fisheries and Aquaculture*. ACP-EU Fisheries Research Report, 8, 5–10.

Pauly, D. (2006a) Major trends in small-scale marine fisheries, with emphasis on developing countries, and some implications for the social sciences. *Maritime Studies (MAST)*, 4, 7–22.

Pauly, D. (2006b) Rejoinder: towards consilience in small-scale fisheries research. *Maritime Studies (MAST)*, 4, 47–51.

Pauly, D. and Christensen, V. (1995) Primary production required to sustain global fisheries. *Nature*, 374, 255–257.

Pauly, D., Christensen, V. and Coelho, L., eds. (1999) *Proceedings of the '98 EXPO Conference on Ocean Food Webs and Economic Productivity*. Lisbon, Portugal, 1–3 July 1998. ACP-EU Fisheries Research Report 5.

Pauly, D., Christensen, V., Dalsgaard, J., Froese, R. and Torres Jr, F. (1998) Fishing down marine food webs. *Science*, 279, 860–863.

Pauly, D., Christensen, V. and Walters, C. (2000) Ecopath, Ecosim, and Ecospace as tools for evaluating ecosystem impact of fisheries. *ICES Journal of Marine Science*, 57, 697–706.

Platt, T. and Sathyendranath, S. (1988) Oceanic primary production: estimation by remote sensing at local and regional scales. *Science*, 241, 1613–1620.

Sherman, K. (1986) Introduction to parts one and two: Large Marine Ecosystems as tractable entities for measurement and management. In Sherman, K. and Alexander, L. M., eds., *Variability and Management of Large Marine Ecosystems*. AAAS Selected Symposia Series No. 99, pp. 3–7.

Sherman, K. and Hempel, G. (2008) *The UNEP Large Marine Ecosystem Report: a perspective on changing conditions in LMEs of the world's regional seas*. UNEP Regional Seas Report and Studies. Nairobi, Kenya: UNEP.

Sumaila, U. R. (2004) Intergenerational cost-benefit analysis and marine ecosystem restoration. *Fish and Fisheries*, 5, 329–343.

Surowiecki, J. (2004) *The Wisdom of Crowds: Why the Many are Smarter Than the Few and How Collective Wisdom Shapes Business, Economies, Societies, and Nations*. New York, NY: Doubleday Books.

Walters, C. and Maguire, J. J. (1996) Lessons for stock assessment from the northern cod collapse. *Reviews in Fish Biology and Fisheries*, 6, 125–137.

Watson, R. and Pauly, D. (2001) Systematic distortions in world fisheries catch trends. *Nature*, 414, 534–536.

Watson, R., Christensen, V., Froese, R., Longhurst, A., Platt, T., Sathyendranath, S., Sherman, K., O'Reilly, J., Celone, P. and Pauly, D. (2003) Mapping fisheries onto marine ecosystems for regional, oceanic and global integrations. In Hempel, G. and Sherman, K., eds., *Large Marine Ecosystems of the World 12: Change and Sustainability*. Amsterdam: Elsevier Science, pp. 375–395.

Whitfield, J. (2006) Science in the movies: From microscope to multiplex: an MRI scanner darkly. *Nature*, 441, 922–924.

Williams, S. B., Hochet-Kibongui, A. M. and Nauen, C. E. (2005) *Gender, fisheries and aquaculture: Social capital and knowledge for the transition towards sustainable use of aquatic ecosystems*. ACP-EU Fisheries Research Reports. Brussels: EU.

Wilson, E. O. (1999) *Consilience: The Unity of Knowledge*. New York: Vintage Books.

World Bank (1990) Study on International Fisheries Research. World Bank Policy & Research Series 19. Washington DC: World Bank, UNDP, African Development Bank and European Commission.

14

Thinking big on small-scale fisheries

INTRODUCTION

In one of his seminal papers, Daniel Pauly directed our attention to the marginality of small-scale fisheries and related this marginalization to their physical, socioeconomic, political, and cultural remoteness from urban centers (Pauly, 1997). The often remote setting of many small-scale fishing communities around the world puts them at a disadvantage for infrastructure and market support. For example, landing facilities and road systems may not be well developed, restricting direct access to markets and consequently minimizing their bargaining power. Further, when compared with large-scale industrialized fisheries, the small-scale fishing subsector generally receives far less financial support (e.g., subsidies) from government (Jacquet and Pauly, 2008; Sumaila *et al.*, this volume). With their small income on a per caput basis and low economic status, small-scale fishers lack political power to put their concerns on the government agenda.

Is marginalization of small-scale fisheries caused by the lack of appreciation for the importance of this sector? Several studies and reports emphasize the significant contribution of small-scale fisheries to food security, sustainable livelihoods, and poverty alleviation (Kurien, 1998; Berkes *et al.*, 2001; Béné, 2003; FAO, 2004). Small-scale fisheries have comparative advantages over industrial fisheries, including greater economic and fuel efficiency (lower capital costs and fuel consumption), better social justice (e.g., less use of catches for fish reduction), and fewer negative environmental impacts (e.g., fewer discards; FAO, 2005; Pauly, 2006). Based on the above, small-scale fisheries deserve to be at the center of fisheries research and policy discussion.

The importance of small-scale fisheries is well recognized, but does not prevent implementation of policies that promote large-scale

Ecosystem Approaches to Fisheries: A Global Perspective, ed. V. Christensen and J. Maclean. Published by Cambridge University Press. © Cambridge University Press 2011.

fisheries, often at the expense of small-scale fisheries (FAO/RAP/FIPL, 2004) and which results in declining fisheries resources (Pauly and Maclean, 2003). Small-scale fisheries in some instances are also capable of overexploiting their resource base through destructive fishing methods or by adopting modern technologies (Butcher, 2004). Economic hardship and social ramifications from stock collapses and ecosystem degradation fall heaviest on small-scale fishers and their families, who rely greatly on fisheries for food and livelihoods, and whose alternative employment options are limited.

In addition to marginalization due to physical, socioeconomic, and political remoteness, are small-scale fisheries also marginalized when the distinction between them and the large-scale fisheries sector is not explicitly stated in research and policy discussion and in the search for pragmatic solutions? Or is it because such distinction be easily made due to the lack of comparable information on the two subsectors? The FAO publishes fisheries statistics, such as landings from capture fisheries by species groups, from member countries on an annual basis. These data mainly concern large-scale fisheries, while catches from small-scale fisheries are likely ignored (Zeller *et al.*, 2006).

This chapter focuses on an initiative by the Sea Around Us project (www.seaaroundus.org) to provide systematic and broad-based information about small-scale fisheries through the development of a global database of small-scale fisheries. This database is one means to overcome the marginalization problem of small-scale fisheries. The more is known about this sector, the less it can be ignored. The chapter first examines, from research and policy perspectives, whether marginalization of small-scale fisheries is still an issue. Next, the structure of the database is presented with a summary of the key findings and suggestions on how to improve the database (and hence, estimates based on it). Contributions of women in fisheries are also highlighted.

MARGINALIZATION OF SMALL-SCALE FISHERIES

In 1994, Pauly noted the proliferation of journal articles that extensively discussed the declining state of fisheries resources without due emphasis on small-scale fisheries, notwithstanding their recognized importance in most developing countries and some developed countries (Pauly, 1997). A decade later, the Fourth World Fisheries Congress was held in Vancouver, Canada, to focus on reconciling fisheries with conservation. An assessment of 223 papers presented at the Congress

Table 14.1 *Distribution of papers at the Fourth World Fisheries Congress by type of fisheries and study areas. The papers total more than 223 because some papers were in more than one category. Source: Chuenpagdee et al. (2005).*

	Type of fisheries				
Study area	Aboriginal	Recreational	Subsistence	Small-scale	Industrial
Developed	15	28	5	37	52
Developing	3	4	9	19	11
Global	0	0	1	3	4
Not identified	1	3	4	12	29
Total	19	35	19	71	96
% Total	8	15	8	30	40

showed two encouraging signs. First, about 60% of the papers addressed subsistence and small-scale fisheries as well as aboriginal and recreational fisheries, which may also be considered small-scale (Table 14.1). Of these, about 60% were related to fisheries in developed countries, which was likely due to the congress venue in North America. Yet, the coverage in developing countries, particularly of subsistence and small-scale fisheries, was remarkably high.

Second, about 60% of the papers were of multidisciplinary nature, addressing combinations of issues related to natural systems, social issues, economics, and policy (Chuenpagdee *et al.*, 2005). Further examination of the papers that focused on social dimensions showed that such topics as resource allocation, stakeholder conflicts, management impacts, justice and equity, property rights, local knowledge, and stakeholder values dominated the discussion (Liguori *et al.*, 2005). These issues are pertinent to small-scale fisheries, suggesting that current fisheries research does address the marginalization of this sector.

A policy focus on small-scale fisheries is evident in several Food and Agriculture Organization of the United Nations (FAO) initiatives. In the Code of Conduct for Responsible Fisheries developed by the FAO, several articles endorse the contribution of small-scale fisheries to generate local knowledge bases and participatory decision making in aquatic ecosystem management (FAO, 1995). Such measures as marine protected areas (MPAs), co-management, and community-based management, proposed in the Code of Conduct and other conventions and agreements as responses to global fisheries crises, validate the critical roles of small-scale fisheries to enable their implementation. Success stories in applications of these management schemes are often associated with small, well-defined coastal communities that rely mainly on fishing but with alternative livelihood options (Pollnac *et al.*, 2001), where social integration exists among resource users and within local communities (Jentoft, 2000), and where participation of stakeholders and communities is meaningful (White *et al.*, 2002).

A series of recent meetings marked an important attention shift toward small-scale fisheries. Held under the auspices of the FAO, the fourth session of the Advisory Committee on Fisheries Research in December 2002 highlighted the lack of attention that this sector received. At its 25th session in February 2003, the Committee on Fisheries agreed that small-scale fisheries should be treated as a stand-alone agenda item; and later that year, a Working Party on Small-scale Fisheries was convened to evaluate the role and importance of small-scale fisheries and to elaborate a research agenda for this sector.

Two related publications arose from these efforts: a research agenda for small-scale fisheries (FAO/RAP/FIPL, 2004) and the technical guidelines for responsible fisheries, developed as part of the implementation strategy (FAO, 2005). On the whole, a new vision for small-scale fisheries has developed to recognize, value, and enhance their contribution to national economies, poverty alleviation, and food security. It is a vision that directly addresses the marginalization of small-scale fisheries, and the case for small-scale fisheries made by Pauly (1997) is reiterated in these two FAO documents.

Several research agenda and institutional changes required to enhance the visibility of small-scale fisheries in policy dialogue are proposed in the "Research Agenda for Small-Scale Fisheries" (FAO/RAP/FIPL, 2004). One suggestion emphasizes the urgency in obtaining better estimates of the various contributions of small-scale fisheries and corresponds well with the initiative undertaken by the Sea Around Us project to develop a global database of small-scale fisheries described here. Small-scale fisheries are now receiving research and policy attention, although it remains uncertain how proposed changes will be realized and whether they result in desirable outcomes.

GLOBAL DATABASE OF SMALL-SCALE FISHERIES

The Sea Around Us project's small-scale fisheries database is the first major effort to systematically document information about this sector in all countries of the world. As described in the report "Bottom-Up, Global Estimates of Small-Scale Marine Fisheries Catches"

(Chuenpagdee *et al.*, 2006), the current database contains fields for definitions and characteristics of small-scale fisheries, reported or estimated number of fishers, boats, and catches, and other key features, including information about gender.

DEFINING SMALL-SCALE FISHERIES

In addition to providing systematic documentation of key features about small-scale fisheries in all countries around the world, one main objective in developing the database is to enable comparisons of this sector, in terms of estimated numbers of fishers and catches, between regions and with large-scale fisheries. These estimates are made based on the premise that there is a certain degree of commonality among small-scale fisheries, despite their diversity and dynamics. Most development and government agencies as well as research communities (e.g., World Bank, 1991; Kurien, 1998; FAO, 2005) are generally reluctant to formulate a universally accepted definition for small-scale fisheries because each and every small-scale fishery should be explicitly acknowledged for its uniqueness (Kurien, 1998). Instead of defining small-scale fisheries, they are characterized as follows:

> Small-scale fisheries can be broadly characterized as a dynamic and evolving sub-sector of fisheries employing labour-intensive harvesting, processing and distribution technologies to exploit marine and inland water fishery resources. The activities of this sub-sector, conducted full-time or part-time, or just seasonally, are often targeted on supplying fish and fishery products to local and domestic markets, and for subsistence consumption. Export-oriented production, however, has increased in many small-scale fisheries during the last one to two decades because of greater market integration and globalization. While typically men are engaged in fishing and women in fish processing and marketing, women are also known to engage in near shore harvesting activities and men are known to engage in fish marketing and distribution. Other ancillary activities such as net-making, boat-building, engine repair and maintenance, etc. can provide additional fishery-related employment and income opportunities in marine and inland fishing communities. Small-scale fisheries operate at widely differing organizational levels ranging from self-employed single operators through informal micro-enterprises to formal sector businesses. This sub-sector, therefore, is not homogenous within and across countries and regions and attention to this fact is warranted when formulating strategies and policies for enhancing its contribution to food security and poverty alleviation. (FAO, 2005)

This characterization of small-scale fisheries is so general that most of it can also be applied to large-scale fisheries. The most distinct feature of small-scale fisheries is related to harvesting (e.g., size, power, and ownership of boats and gears, time spent, duration of trip, number of fishers, utilization of catches, and involvement of women). The distinction is less clear in the post-harvest area, with globalization affecting both small and large scale.

For management and regulation purposes, government agencies in each country do have certain definitions for what they consider small-scale as opposed to large-scale. Of the 140 countries included in the database (US Alaska, US Hawai'i, American Samoa, and Guam are distinguished in this database due to their markedly different characteristics), 70% provide definitions or characterizations of their small-scale fisheries that are surprisingly similar. For example, about 65% of them use boat size as a key factor and the common range of small-scale fisheries boats is either less than 10, 12, or 15 m, or 5–7 m in length (Table 14.2). Some countries use gross registered tonnage and/or engine size as key characteristics while others describe small-scale fisheries by type of gear used. To a lesser extent, small-scale fisheries are defined by

Table 14.2 *Summary of common definitions of small-scale fisheries indicated by 140 countries. GRT = gross registered tonnage, HP = horsepower. Source: Chuenpagdee* et al. *(2006).*

Key features	Common definition (range)
Boat size	5–7 m; less than 10, 12, or 15 m (2–24 m)
Boat GRT	Less than 10 GRT (3–50 GRT)
Size of engine	Less than 60 HP; between 40 and 75 HP (15–400 HP)
Boat type	Canoe, dinghy, non-motorized boat, wooden boat, boat with no deck, traditional boat
Gear type	Coastal gathering, fishing on foot, beach seining, small ring net, handlining, diving, trapping
Distance from shore	5–9 km; within 13 km; up to 22 km
Water depth	Less than 10, 50, or 100 m depth
Nature of activity	Subsistence, ethnic group, traditional, local, artisanal
Number of crew	2–3; 5–6
Travel time	2–3 hours from landing site

distance or depth where fishing takes place. Only a few countries refer to small-scale fisheries by nature of activity, such as subsistence, traditional, ethnic, etc. Often, these measures are given together to characterize small-scale fisheries. The overall consistency found in the definitions and characterizations of small-scale fisheries implies that there are sufficient commonalities among small-scale fisheries in most countries to enable a generalized approach where data for missing countries can be estimated based on countries that have data.

GLOBAL ESTIMATES OF SMALL-SCALE FISHERIES

The database on small-scale fisheries is developed using a comparable format with that of large-scale fisheries. In addition to definitions, information about target species, gears used, and any special features of small-scale fisheries, particularly about roles of women and children, are documented. Three sets of quantitative data are included in the database, namely numbers of fishers and vessels, and catches. A major source of data was the set of FAO fisheries country profiles (http://www.fao.org/fi/fcp/fcp.asp), which contain standardized information about the small-scale fisheries of most countries, mostly from the late 1990s to early 2000s. Other sources are used where available to replace FAO data. The current estimates are based on data from 86 countries.

Countries are categorized into three groups by the Human Development Index (HDI)[1] developed by the United Nations Development Programme (UNDP, 2000). Grouping of countries by HDI allows for statistical improvement of the global estimates, as available data are averaged within groups of countries ("strata"); computation for missing values (i.e., their replacement by within-stratum averages) is performed for countries in the same HDI categories. In total, there are 43 countries of high HDI, 76 of medium HDI, and 21 of low HDI. On average, based on combined sources, data are available for about half of the countries, with the highest percentage of data availability in low HDI countries, followed by medium and high HDI. Also, there are more data on number of fishers and catches than of vessels. Thus, only estimations of number of fishers and catches are attempted.

---

[1] HDI measures a country's status in terms of life expectancy, educational attainment of its citizens, and adjusted real income, and is considered more appropriate for small-scale fisheries estimates than gross domestic product (GDP), often used for ranking and grouping countries and their national fisheries.

Given that inshore fishing area (IFA) can be estimated for all countries (through the Sea Around Us project's database), it is used as a reference for the estimation. IFA is defined as the shelf area ranging from shoreline to 50 km offshore or to 200 m depth, whichever is less. The first limit is based on the assumption that small-scale fishers usually perform day trips (a few hours sailing, a few hours fishing, and a few hours sailing back), and hence the limit in distance from shore that they can reach in a day. The latter is assumed because small-scale fishers generally do not fish in deep waters, except in areas where the shelf is very narrow (e.g., around oceanic islands).

The procedure used to obtain global estimates of numbers of fishers is as follows. First, mean number of fishers per km^2 of IFA is estimated for each HDI stratum using available reported data. These means are then used to estimate numbers of fishers in countries with no data. The final estimate for each stratum is an aggregation of both reported and estimated number of fishers across countries. The same procedure is performed for catch estimation. As shown in Table 14.3, these estimates are based on 61% and 54% of available data for fishers and catches, respectively, enabling the assumption that underestimates in certain countries will compensate for overestimates in others (Sokal and Rohlf, 1995).

About 75% of fishers are in medium HDI countries, contributing about 58% of the total small-scale fisheries catches (Table 14.3). The densities of fishers and catches in low HDI countries are consistently higher than those in other countries. Yet, fishers in high HDI countries are proportionately better off in terms of catch per fisher. Globally, the

Table 14.3 *Estimates of small-scale fishers and their catches by Human Development Index category and globally. HDI = Human Development Index. Source: Chuenpagdee* et al. *(2006).*

	High HDI	Medium HDI	Low HDI	Global
Number of countries	43	76	21	140
Mean fisher density (no. km^{-2})	0.15	1.02	2.50	
Estimated no. of fishers (10^6)	1.1	8.7	1.8	11.6
Countries with fisher data	19	51	16	86
Mean catch density (t. km^{-2})	0.77	1.26	2.93	
Estimated catch (10^6 t)	7.2	12.1	1.5	20.8
Countries with catch data	18	38	19	75

Table 14.4 *Estimated number of fishers and catches in medium Human Development Index countries by region. Source: Chuenpagdee* et al. *(2006).*

Region	No. fishers (10^6)	Catches (10^6 t)	No. countries
Africa	0.59	1.44	20
America/Caribbean	1.02	1.95	22
Asia/Pacific	4.81	5.64	17
Europe/West Asia	2.30	3.07	17
Total	8.72	12.10	76

number of fishers is estimated at 12 million with a total annual catch of about 21 million tonnes.

At the regional level, medium HDI category countries in Asia-Pacific dominate both numbers of fishers and catches: 55% and 47%, respectively, of the total in this category (Table 14.4). The traditional and cultural importance of fish and fisheries for these fish-eating nations is recognized in the Regional Guidelines for Responsible Fisheries in Southeast Asia (SEAFDEC, 2003), along with an acknowledgment that fisheries structure in the region is different from those in developed countries. The guidelines include social and economic aspects of small-scale, coastal, and subsistence fisheries, as well as the many species and fishing gears characteristic of their fisheries.

IMPROVING THE ESTIMATES

Similar to large-scale fisheries, estimates of small-scale fisheries are likely to be conservative, although for different reasons. Commercial catches based on FAO data are likely underestimated due to illegal landings and discards and underreported catches (Pauly *et al.*, 2002; Zeller *et al.*, 2007; Zeller and Pauly, 2007). For small-scale fisheries, official records often do not include seasonal and migrant fishers, who could contribute significant effort in small-scale fisheries in many countries, particularly in Africa. Some portions of catches from this sector are not recorded because they are directly consumed in households or they are not of high commercial value. Another key factor contributing to underreporting of small-scale fisheries catches is the involvement of women who collect fish and shellfish in intertidal zones or in mangrove areas.

Estimates reported here are very preliminary and can be improved. First, effort must be made to obtain information on the 40% of countries for which currently no information is available as well as to replace FAO data with local sources to the extent possible. These data should be checked, verified, and regularly updated to provide better estimates, as part of the auto-calculation routine in the Sea Around Us project database. With more data points, different assumptions can be used to obtain estimates instead of categorization of countries by HDI or estimation of catches and fishers based on density in the IFA.

Next, corrections must be made to account for seasonal and migrant fishers and to incorporate catches from women and children, based on both qualitative and quantitative information. Published sources, particularly in social science studies of small-scale fisheries, can be used to fill the gaps. Ultimately, improvement can be made in the way data for official statistical records at the national level are collected and reported to the FAO, especially in countries with high contributions from small-scale fisheries.

For such improvement to occur, the relative importance of small-scale fisheries in comparison to large-scale fisheries has to be demonstrated. Pauly (2006) pointed out that small-scale fisheries employ more people than large-scale fisheries (12 million as estimated here versus about 0.5 million, respectively) to produce about the same annual catches. Further, costs associated with small-scale fisheries are a lot lower in terms of capital cost and environmental and social cost. Social cost is expressed as amount of fishmeal and oil reduction from fisheries, which is almost zero in small-scale fisheries but 20–30 million tonnes in large-scale fisheries (Alder *et al.*, 2008). Fishmeal production is considered a social cost in view of the current food security problem faced in many countries (Alder *et al.*, 2008). Environmentally, discards from small-scale fisheries are very small compared to those from large-scale fisheries (Pauly, 2006).

WOMEN IN SMALL-SCALE FISHERIES

The role of women in fisheries has long been documented. The *ICLARM Quarterly* April 1989 issue is an example of early attention paid to this subject. More recently, several forums were created specifically to address women in fisheries issues, including the International Symposium on Women in Asian Fisheries in 1998 and the Global Symposium on Women in Fisheries in 2001.

Catch contributions of women and children come from such activities as reef gleaning in Southeast Asia and the Pacific (Chapman, 1987), and gathering of estuarine bivalves and other invertebrates in West and East Africa (Williams, 2001) and in South and Central America (Gammage, 2004). These contributions are substantial, as in Papua New Guinea where catches from female fishers account for 25–50% of total yield (Kronen, 2002), and in Samoa, where women provide 20% of the per capita seafood consumption (Lambeth, 2001). Commonly, in many countries worldwide, women also take part in the processing and marketing of fish and fishery products.

Women's participation in the harvest and post-harvest sectors gives them the opportunity to influence fisheries operation and management. For example, female traders and processors in West Africa provide a very reliable funding system, giving them an important position in the decision making process (ICSF, 2002b). In Argentina (Elías et al., 2010), Brazil (Diegues, 2002), and Ecuador (ICSF, 2002a), women are active members in fishers' associations and cooperatives and in some cases hold high positions in these organizations.

Despite the recognition women enjoy in some countries, there are other cases where their contributions cannot be officially acknowledged. For example, women involved in the bait fishery for octopus in San Felipe, Mexico, although members of a women's fishing cooperative, are not eligible for government assistance (such as funding to repair gear or boats destroyed in a hurricane) as are male fishers. This is because their primary target species is listed as a "community" resource, not designated for commercialization outside the port (Gavaldon and Berdugo, 2004). In another case, shellfish collectors in Spain are not well served by official definitions of fishing because they operate on foot along the foreshore, and their practice does not fit either of the two categories, i.e., fisheries and aquaculture, recognized at the European level (European Commission, 2003).

Failure to acknowledge women's involvement in fisheries has other negative consequences. In Tonga, female reef gleaners smash corals (with knives, iron poles, and hammers) to find shells and use poisons from sea cucumbers and plants to stun fish. In Fiji, women pour bleach, pesticides, and fertilizers into streams to catch freshwater prawns (Matthews, 2002). These practices may remain undocumented because women's needs and harvest activities are usually the focus of separate offices and agencies, not integrated into overall fisheries development programs. Research about the changing roles of women in fisheries globally, and communication of research results to policymakers, must be expanded in order to fully acknowledge their contributions and to address their needs.

CONCLUSION

Collecting and making available information about small-scale fisheries, and enabling cross-sector comparison, as attempted through this database, are important steps toward de-marginalization of the small-scale sector. The importance of small-scale fisheries to ecosystem health, sustainable livelihoods, poverty reduction, and food security can be exemplified by the much larger number of persons involved than in the large-scale sector, especially when the contributions from women and children are included. Although the current database does not enable a proper analysis of the extent of small-scale fisheries in the national picture, some possible scenarios can be explored (Chuenpagdee *et al.*, 2006). If all small-scale fisheries catches estimated in this database were included in national statistics, small-scale fisheries would contribute 38% of the catches. Thus, the sector needs differential treatment in management and policies.

Understanding small-scale fisheries per se, and in the context of large-scale fisheries, offers helpful insights and alternative views to address current problems in fisheries. Differentiating fisheries into large- and small-scale sectors enables proper analysis of problems and solutions. Such issues as resource overexploitation, unsustainability, and over-capacity play out differently in countries where fisheries are dominated by the large-scale sector and require different solutions. Instead of broad-based prescriptions and applications of overall management strategies and policies, different formulae may be needed for countries dominated by small-scale fisheries.

Improvement of the database to enhance its coverage and to increase its usefulness and the accuracy of the estimates is an ongoing effort. The uploading of the database on to the Sea Around Us project makes frequent updates easy and will encourage data sharing and knowledge building about small-scale fisheries worldwide.

ACKNOWLEDGMENTS

This chapter was based largely on a global database on small-scale fisheries project, developed through the Sea Around Us project, a scientific cooperation between the Pew Environment Group and the University of British Columbia, and with support from a European Union-funded

INCOFISH project on "Integrating multiple demands in coastal zones, with an emphasis on fisheries and aquatic resources" (Project # INCO 003739). I would like to acknowledge the important contributions from Lisa Liguori, who worked with me throughout this project, and Dr. Maria Lourdes (Deng) Palomares for her help with database development and analysis. Most importantly, I thank Daniel Pauly for the inspiration, direction, and encouragement, as well as for his trust and friendship all through my time at the University of British Columbia and beyond.

REFERENCES

Alder, J., Campbell, B., Karpouzi, V., Kaschner, K. and Pauly, D. (2008) Forage fish: from ecosystems to markets. *Annual Review of Environment and Resources*, 33, 153–166.

Béné, C. (2003) When fishery rhymes with poverty: a first step beyond the old paradigm on poverty in small-scale fisheries. *World Development*, 31 (6), 949–975.

Berkes, F., Mahon, R., McConney, P., Pollnac, R. and Pomeroy, R. (2001) *Managing Small-Scale Fisheries: Alternative Directions and Methods*. Ottawa: IDRC.

Butcher, J.G. (2004) *The Closing of the Frontier: A History of the Marine Fisheries of Southeast Asia c. 1850–2000*. Singapore: Institute of Southeast Asian Studies.

Chapman, M.D. (1987) Women's fishing in Oceania. *Human Ecology*, 15, 267–288.

Chuenpagdee, R., Bundy, A., Ainsworth, C., Buchary, E.A., Cheung, W.L., Dingerson, L., Ferris, B., Freire, K.M.F., Giannico, G., Holt, C., Lambert, D., Liguori, L., Liu, Y., Nandakumar, D., Poon, A., Salas, S., Salomon, A., Simms, J., Turnipseed, M. and Ware, C. (2005) Reconciling Fisheries with Conservation: Overview of Papers Presented at the 4th World Fisheries Congress. Innovation and Outlook in Fisheries: An Assessment of Research Presented at the 4th World Fisheries Congress. Fisheries Centre Research Report, 13 (2). Vancouver, Canada: Fisheries Centre, University of British Columbia.

Chuenpagdee, R., Liguori, L., Palomares, M.L.D. and Pauly, D. (2006) Bottom-up, global estimates of small-scale marine fisheries catches. Fisheries Centre Research Report. Vancouver, Canada: Fisheries Centre, University of British Columbia.

Diegues, A.C. (2002) Sea tenure, traditional knowledge and management among brazilian artisanal fishermen. São Paulo, Brazil: NUPAUB, Universidade de São Paulo.

Elías, I., Carozza, C., Di Giácomo, E.E., Isla, M.S., Orensanz, J.M., Parma, A.M., Pereiro, R.C., Perier, M.R., Perrotta, R.G., Ré, M.E. and Ruarte, C. (2010) Profile of coastal fisheries from Latin American and the Caribbean: Argentina. In Salas, S., Cabrera, M.A., Sánchez, J., Ramos, J. and Flores, D., eds., *Coastal Fisheries of Latin America and the Caribbean. COASTFISH Conference Proceedings*, pp. 13–48.

European Commission (2003) Women in fisheries: an unnoticed role. Fishing in Europe. Brussels: Directorate-General for Fisheries of the European Commission.

FAO (1995) Code of conduct for responsible fisheries. Rome: FAO.

FAO (2005) Increasing the contribution of small-scale fisheries to poverty allevi-ation and food security. FAO Technical Guidelines for Responsible Fisheries. Rome: FAO.

FAO/RAP/FIPL (2004) A research agenda for small-scale fisheries. Bangkok, Thailand: FAO Regional Office for Asia and the Pacific.

Gammage, S. (2004) The tattered net of statistics. *Gender Agenda – Women in Fisheries: A Collection of Articles from SAMUDRA Report.* International Collective in Support of Fishworkers (ICSF). India, pp. 36–40.

Gavaldon, A. and Berdugo, J. (2004) Gender relations in a coastal village of Yucatan, Mexico. Paper presented at the International Congress Society for Human Ecology: Tourism, Travel and Transport. Session: Gender and fisheries within livelihoods, towards sustainability. Cozumel, Mexico, February 18–24, 2004.

ICSF (2002a) *Gender and Coastal Fishing Communities in Latin America.* Prainha do Canto Verde, Ceara, Brazil. Chennai, India: International Collective in Support of Fishworkers.

ICSF (2002b) Report of the study on problems and prospects of artisanal fish trade in West Africa. Centre Social, Derklé, Dakar, Sénégal: International Collective in Support of Fishworkers; Collectif National des Pecheurs Arti-sanaux du Senegal (CNPS); Centre de Recherches pour le Developpment des Technologies Intermediairies de Pêche (CREDETIP).

Jacquet, J. L. and Pauly, D. (2008) Trade secrets: renaming and mislabeling of seafood. *Marine Policy*, 32, 309–318.

Jentoft, S. (2000) The community: a missing link of fisheries management. *Marine Policy*, 24, 53–60.

Kronen, M. (2002) Socioeconomic status of fisherwomen. *Secretariat of Pacific Communities Women in Fisheries Bulletin*, 11, 17–22.

Kurien, J. (1998) Small-scale fisheries in the context of globalisation. In *The Ninth Biennial Conference of International Institute of Fisheries Economics and Trade.* Tromso, Norway: Institute for Development Studies, pp. 1–46.

Lambeth, L. (2001) News from the Community Fisheries Section. *Secretariat of the Pacific Communities Women in Fisheries Information Bulletin*, 8, 2–8.

Liguori, L., Freire, K. M. F., Lambert, D. and Poon, A. (2005) How Are We Performing in the Social Aspects of Fisheries Science? Innovation and Outlook in Fisheries: An Assessment of Research Presented at the 4th World Fisheries Congress. Fisheries Centre Research Report, 13 (2). Vancouver, Canada: Fisheries Centre, University of British Columbia.

Matthews, E. (2002) Integrating women's subsistence fishing into Pacific fish-eries and conservation programmes. *Secretariat of Pacific Communities Women in Fisheries Bulletin*, 11, 13–14.

Pauly, D. (1997) Small-scale fisheries in the tropics: marginality, marginalization and some implications for fisheries management. In Pikitch, E. K., Huppert, D. D. and Sissenwine, M. P., eds., *Global Trends: Fisheries Management.* Bethesda, MD: American Fisheries Society Symposium 20, pp. 40–49.

Pauly, D. (2006) Major trends in small-scale marine fisheries, with emphasis on developing countries, and some implications for the social sciences. *Maritime Studies (MAST)*, 4, 7–22.

Pauly, D., Christensen, V., Guénette, S., Pitcher, T. J., Sumaila, U. R., Walters, C. J., Watson, R. and Zeller, D. (2002) Towards sustainability in world fisheries. *Nature*, 418, 689–695.

Pauly, D. and Maclean, J. L. (2003) *In A Perfect Ocean: The State of Fisheries and Ecosystems in the North Atlantic Ocean.* Washington DC: Island Press.

Pollnac, R. B., Crawford, B. R. and Gorospe, M. L. G. (2001) Discovering factors that influence the success of community-based marine protected areas in the Visayas, Philippines. *Ocean & Coastal Management*, 44, 683–710.

SEAFDEC (2003) Regional guidelines for responsible fisheries in Southeast Asia: responsible fisheries management. Malaysia: Southeast Asian Fisheries Development Center.

Sokal, R. R. and Rohlf, F. J. (1995) *Biometry: The Principles and Practice of Statistics in Biological Research.* New York, NY: W.H. Freeman.

UNDP (2000). *Human Development Report (2000).* New York, NY: United Nations Development Programme.

White, A. T., Courtney, C. A. and Salamanca, A. (2002) Experience with marine protected area planning and management in the Philippines. *Coastal Management*, 30, 1–26.

Williams, S. B. (2001) Making each and every African fisher count: women do fish. In Williams, M. J., Chao, H. N., Choo, P. S., Matics, K., Nandeesha, M. C., Shariff, M., Siason, I., Tech, E. and Wong, J. M. C., eds., *Global Symposium on Women in Fisheries Sixth Asian Fisheries Forum Kaohsiung*, Taiwan, November 29, 2001. The WorldFish Centre, Penang, Malaysia: ICLARM, pp. 145–154.

World Bank (1991) Small-scale fisheries: research needs. World Bank Technical Paper Number 152, Fisheries Series, Washington DC: World Bank.

Zeller, D., Booth, S., Craig, P. and Pauly, D. (2006) Reconstruction of coral reef fisheries catches in American Samoa, 1950–2002. *Coral Reefs*, 25, 144–152.

Zeller, D., Booth, S., Davis, G. and Pauly, D. (2007) Re-estimation of small-scale fishery catches for US flag-associated island areas in the western Pacific: the last 50 years. *Fisheries Bulletin*, 105, 266–277.

Zeller, D. and Pauly, D., eds. (2007) Reconstruction of marine fisheries catches for key countries and regions (1950–2005). Fisheries Centre Research Report, 15 (2). Vancouver, Canada: Fisheries Centre, University of British Columbia.

15

Coastal-marine resource use in human ecological context: the scale and modes of integration

INTRODUCTION

Here I examine some ideas based on Daniel Pauly's various forays into coastal zone resources use, and, in particular, Malthusian overfishing, a contribution that will probably always be a work in progress. Ignoring the admonition "Here be Dragons," Daniel Pauly sowed the seed, and then essentially left it to others to take it from there. Much of the later discussion about Malthusian overfishing has been rather narrowly focused. But in this chapter, I will elaborate on aspects of integrated resource use and management. This is both explicit and implicit through much of the work of Daniel Pauly. And by design it often leads us far from the ocean and seas, where his main work lies, into the linked hinterlands of mountains and farming, and down the corridors of ministries, fisheries departments, development agencies, and donors.

The basic characteristics of Malthusian overfishing were described by Pauly (1988, 1994a, 2006) as occurring where (1) a relatively large agricultural sector releases excess labor because of both population growth and land "reform," which (2) then migrates to urban, upland, coastal, or other areas. In coastal areas (3) under this influx, traditional arrangements preventing open access to the fisheries gradually collapse, which then (4) leads to excessive fishing pressure, that itself is (5) exacerbated by inshore industrial fishing, by new recruits to fishing as the male children of fishers pick up their fathers' trade, and by the contribution of many young people who leave to work in urban areas or overseas, providing a subsidy for men to continue to fish, even when resources are depleted. At the same time, (6) migrants to upland areas accelerate and/or complete the deforestation initiated

Ecosystem Approaches to Fisheries: A Global Perspective, ed. V. Christensen and J. Maclean. Published by Cambridge University Press. © Cambridge University Press 2011.

by logging companies, which leads to siltation of rivers and streams, and, in turn, (7) eventually to the smothering of coral reefs and other coastal habitats, further reducing coastal fisheries yields.

It is essential to understand that Malthusian overfishing is the effect on coastal fisheries and fishing communities of unsustainable development in an entire national economy. Thus, it is but a subset of a Malthusian overexploitation of all resources in all of the primary sectors of an economy. As such, it can be alleviated only through balanced sustainable development of an entire national economy, and, ultimately, by checking population growth.

At first glance, overcoming Malthusian overfishing is conceptually simple. But when seen in the context of an entire national economy it becomes complex and interlinked, such that separate remedies for it become notoriously oversimplified, and plans for development and management of the fisheries sector alone dangerously naïve. All this was noted by Daniel Pauly in his original exposition. A fundamental part of any remedy is to empower women in all rural communities to limit their desired number of children. This is still an enormously difficult task in many places, where the powerful forces of religion, politics, local culture, and family often combine to stifle basic human rights for women. Pauly further observed that mitigation of Malthusian overfishing would require the creation of land-based alternative employment opportunities for ill-trained young fishers, but that this was another tall order. And then with pressures on the resource reduced, a "rollback" strategy becomes thinkable in which devolution of state authority to local fisher communities would lead to a rebuilding of "traditional" management mechanisms limiting entry, complemented with "modern" measures, such as gear restrictions, and the establishment of sanctuaries. All noble thoughts.

The essential weakness of the original concept was the linearity of its postulated linkages among population, production, and resource condition, with the implicit assumption that either the resource would be operated under open access or that limited access would be overwhelmed by the volume of in-migration. The reality is not so simple, as various studies have demonstrated that, more than the fish or other resources, it is the local institutions and power structure that control access to that resource and its redistribution – if such occurs (Ruddle et al., 1992; Ruddle, 1987, 1989a, 1994, 1998). This was recently noted by Béné (2003) in terms of poverty within the fisheries sector. Of course, this applies equally to other resources, such as upland farming, and not just to fisheries.

The many interlinked global crises of ecosystem degradation and destruction, pollution loading, persistent poverty, and food insecurity, all exacerbated by extremes of weather that may be precursors of dangerous climatic change, come together in the tropical coastal zones, the world's richest and most abused ecosystems. Much of the blame for this can be traced to sectoral economic development strategies, and the narrow boundaries of scientific disciplines that have informed them. Whereas economies and disciplines are sectoralized, the resultant problems are clearly integrated, as therefore so must be the solutions to them. This much is now understood, as demonstrated by broad global frameworks like the Millennium Development Goals or the Johannesburg Plan of Implementation, and international arrangements for regional collective action. But these then need to be complemented by more spatially restricted local action, for which concrete plans can be drawn up and implemented, such that all stakeholders can witness the rapid emergence of local benefits. That requires a different level of understanding and skills.

In this chapter, I examine the topic in the context of integration of fishing communities into their rural context, and linked with adjacent ecosystems. It is always important to recall that the problems of marine environments and fisheries, together with their solutions, not uncommonly reside outside the fisheries sector. It is equally important never to forget that the entire issue is highly politicized and donor driven, with sensible and direct solutions often hampered by the requirement to fulfill objectives that are not perceived as directly relevant to local issues.

FOCI AND TRENDS OF RURAL DEVELOPMENT POLICIES: 1950S TO THE PRESENT

Greatly simplified, the main emphases in rural development theory and practice over the last 60 years began in the 1950s, focusing mainly on community development. The 1960s was a period of modernization led by small farm growth, followed by state intervention and integrated rural development with small farm development within that framework during the 1970s. The 1980s was a period of market liberalization that was also characterized by participation, empowerment, and the recognition of multiple actors and perspectives in development. That continued into the 1990s, when the emphasis switched to sustainable livelihoods as an integrating framework. From 2000, rural development has been given prominence in strategies to reduce poverty. These were broad trends only. For example, although the "sustainable livelihoods approach," currently especially popular in the United Kingdom, was first outlined in the 1980s and developed in the 1990s, only from the beginning of the twenty-first century did it enter the mainstream of rural development theory and practice.

Inevitably, there has been a substantial element of older approaches continuing throughout these six decades. There have been several key foci and main points of change during the evolution of rural development thinking. Above all, the focus on the small farm and an increase in its efficiency has been a predominant and enduring paradigm since the beginning of the 1960s. This can be traced to the works of Johnston and Mellor (1961) and Mellor (1966), and, in particular, to *Transforming Traditional Agriculture*, the seminal 1964 book by Theodore Schulz that saw in the rational allocation of resources by small farmers a potential future engine to power rural development.

In the 1980s and 1990s, the focus of overall development approaches switched from a national level policy based on external technologies, or a top-down approach, to the bottom–up or grass-roots approach, whereby empowered rural populations participated in, or even controlled, the processes of their own development. Rapidly increasing research in and exposure to the realities of rural conditions in poorer areas, combined with disenchantment at the inability of big government to deliver rural development infrastructure and services during earlier decades, led to new concepts and approaches. The most important were farming systems research, the use of local knowledge, through which rural people could contribute to solving their own problems, and the use of participatory rural survey methods, which began in the 1980s with rapid rural appraisal (RAA), and evolved into participatory rural appraisal (PRA) and participatory learning and action (PLA) during the 1990s. As a consequence, grand theories as a guide to action fell out of vogue, and were replaced by an emphasis on the unique quality of all local areas and the experiences of their inhabitants.

Small-scale farmers were seen as rational economic decision makers, and as being more efficient than larger ones in combining abundant family labor with small farm size and scarce capital. A major advantage of the small over the large farm is that land productivity is often twice that of the largest ones. This results mostly from high cropping intensity; "usually, small farmers' advantages are due less to high yields of the same crop than to a higher value crop mix, more double-cropping and inter-cropping, and less fallowing" (IFAD, 2001, p. 79). This is underpinned by important ecological principles.

FACTORS CAUSING CHANGE IN RURAL DEVELOPMENT STRATEGIES

Rural development has always been much broader than a concern with just small-scale farmers, infrastructure development, and economic growth. Implicit in all of these activities have been concerns with health, education, participation in the political process, reduction of poverty, and protection of vulnerable groups. The poverty agenda articulated by the World Bank in 2000 provides a resharpened focus to guide rural development activities (World Bank, 2000). That, together with ongoing trends and changes in rural areas, has altered the nature of the debate about rural development.

Similarly, rural economies have never been just about farming, as has been well known from case studies long before the advent of the "livelihoods approach," or the sustainable livelihoods framework, which asserts that rural households depend on sets of capital assets that include natural, physical, human, financial, and social capital. Food security, rural development, and poverty reduction are closely linked. In the next 30 years, expanding populations and changing eating habits will require a doubling of food production. Since it is argued that local food demand should be met mostly by local food production, a prosperous small farm sector must be a key component of any strategy to reduce poverty and hunger (FAO, 2000). Similarly, poverty cannot be understood in sectoral terms, since the rural poor usually have a broader range of livelihood strategies as a buffer against their inherent insecurity. Equally, there are varied strategies that may be employed by rural households to escape from poverty. These include intensification, diversification, increased asset base, increased off-farm income, and exit from agriculture. Based on a study of 70 farming systems around the world, Dixon et al. (2001) observed that diversification was the best approach to reducing rural farm poverty. Livelihood diversification is now a central issue for both national governments and major donors. In this approach, it is imperative to understand that the core focus is not small farm households, but all rural households.

The "livelihoods approach" is excellent as just another tool in the kit. But it should not replace other approaches. The small farm should still remain a major and co-equal focus and efforts within that should highlight on-farm income diversification. One of the repeated errors of the "development business" is that each new generation – quite naturally, in the spirit of innovation and the advancement of science – is apt to discard its predecessors' approaches, and develop its own new directions.

For example, the sustainable livelihoods approach, which began to emerge in the 1990s, is simply recognition of the long-known fact that many rural households secure their livelihoods from a variety of economic activities, and not just farming. Proponents of the approach claim that it must become the cornerstone of policy if rural development effort is to reduce rural poverty effectively, since a focus on small farms alone is totally unrealistic. Nevertheless, agricultural development remains the center of official development policy and the major single recipient of public funding within the rural development sector (IFAD, 2001). This is unequivocally set forth in the report of the International Conference on Agrarian Reform and Rural Development (ICARRD) (FAO, 2006), in which the member states "strongly believe in the essential role of agrarian reform and rural development to promote sustainable development, which includes, inter alia, the realization of human rights, food security, poverty eradication, and the strengthening of social justice, on the basis of the democratic rule of law" (first paragraph). Later (paragraph 11) they reiterate "the importance of traditional and family agriculture, and other smallholder production as well as the roles of traditional rural communities and indigenous groups in contributing to food security and the eradication of poverty."

THE ISSUE OF INTEGRATION

Integration based on ecosystem approaches is now a fashionable topic in Western academic and donor circles. However, it is certainly nothing more than commonplace and routine to most rural people in the tropical world. As part of the temperate bias in science, few people have thought to consider the value of pre-existing systems of integrated resource management that have long been widespread in tropical regions. Hence the now fashionable "ecosystem approach," for example, was promulgated without reference to pre-existing and time-tested alternatives (Ruddle and Hickey, 2008).

The ecosystem approach was adopted in 2000 by the Convention on Biological Diversity (CBD, 2000). It contains nothing new or startling, since it is a straightforward interdisciplinary methodology for environmental research, planning, and management. All the basic ideas are inherent in most pre-existing tropical systems of management that acknowledge ecological relationships. Indeed, one need look no further than various places in the South Pacific, where the "ecosystem approach" was expressed traditionally in the concept of "corporate estate," a territory held jointly by a kinship-based group to whom it both provided a collection of rights and imposed duties. On high islands in the Pacific, "estates" are usually wedge-shaped, extending from a central watershed along lateral ridges into inshore marine waters. These are or were self-contained units that include a complete set of the resource areas and habitats required to provision the society that inhabited them. It remains a widespread integrated management strategy, as Ruddle (1994) noted. Examples include the Hawaiian *ahupua'a* (Meller and Horowitz, 1987), the Yap *tabinau* (Lingenfelter, 1975; Schneider, 1984), the Fijian *vanua* (Ravuvu, 1983), the Marovo (Solomon Islands) *puava* (Hviding, 1996), the Cook Islands *tapere* (Crocombe, 1967), and the estate of the Yolngu aboriginals of North Australia (Davis, 1985). Examples also occur in Africa and other areas (Manshard, 1974; Ruttenberg, 1980), and South America (Ruddle and Chesterfield, 1977).

The ecosystem approach is a strategy for promoting the integrated management of environments and natural resources to ensure their conservation and sustainable use in an equitable way. It focuses on the biological organization, structure, processes, functions of and interactions among organisms and their environment, and recognizes that humans, with their cultural diversity, are an integral component of many ecosystems. The approach requires that the organizations formed by human settlements to carry out essential political, economic, and social processes are synchronized with the systemic structures of the natural ecosystems that make up the local habitats. It demands adaptive management to deal with the complex and dynamic nature of ecosystems in the absence of complete knowledge or understanding of their functioning. Because there is no one "correct" way to implement the ecosystem approach, which depends on local, provincial, national, regional, or global conditions, it seeks to integrate various approaches and methodologies (e.g., biosphere reserves, protected areas, and single-species conservation programs, among others), and not replace them.

Among the main limitations to the ecosystems approach are that it is a political and societal concept rather than one solely grounded in science. Further, concrete rules for action cannot be provided because there is no single correct way to achieve an ecosystem approach to management. A major weakness is that "societal choice" and "decentralization" imply a degree of democracy that is not always present in many societies. More, implementation depends entirely on national policy choices regarding poverty reduction and national development, and the resilience of various vested interests, as well as on the cultural perceptions governing environments and resources.

A constraint on adopting an ecosystem approach is the weakness of the different concepts being applied by international agencies. Some have even apparently failed to realize that ecosystems themselves cannot be managed, and that management can be applied only to human activities!

INTEGRATION AT THE HOUSEHOLD LEVEL

Since one of the main points proposed for the "Operational Guidance for the Ecosystems Approach" is to manage at an appropriate scale and decentralize to the lowest possible level, it is logical to begin the examination of integration at the smallest scale, that of the individual household.

The ecological rationale of household crop integration

The integration of renewable natural resource use, as exemplified by such farming systems as shifting cultivation or irrigated rice farming, is an ancient practice in tropical regions. Most ecologically sound farming systems have traditionally had a multispecies focus, thereby mimicking the surrounding (or formerly surrounding) natural environment into which they have been projected (Geertz, 1963; Ruddle, 1989b). Among the most complex of purely agricultural variants of such mimetic systems are house or "dooryard" gardens, and areas under shifting cultivation. In wetland environments, more sophisticated and more highly mimetic of the natural system are the widespread integrated ricefield fisheries and the complex, and less commonplace, integrated systems of aquaculture–agriculture (Ruddle, 1980, 1982; Ruddle and Zhong, 1988; Ruddle, 1989b).

The principal ecological (and, by extension, economic) attributes of integrated "mimetic systems" have been summarized as follows (Ruddle, 1989b): (1) a polycultural mimicry of a natural state with a variety of intercropped species represented by a small number of individuals;

(2) the maintenance of the structure of the natural ecological system into which the agro-ecosystem is projected; (3) the maintenance of the gross pattern of the natural community; (4) the recycling and minimizing of losses of energy and materials by using wastes and products of decay as raw materials, largely in the biotic community; (5) the structural congruence of the multilayered natural system and the cultural system, which reduces the requirement for energy subsidies and labor inputs; and (6) integration of components that permit a fuller utilization of heat, light, moisture, and nutrients by species with different habits and nutritional requirements than is possible in unintegrated systems.

Rural households are generally classified by the dominant visible economic activity or activities. This notion is oversimplified, and when the total household economy is substituted for the farming system per se as the unit of classification, most tropical small-scale farm households clearly have integrated and diversified economic systems, only a part of which is farming. Most rural households exploit diverse yet complementary resources to secure at least their basal subsistence. In humid tropical Asia, small-scale farm units are commonly characterized by several components of varying importance: irrigated rice cultivation (usually the principal activity); multiple cropping of other annual crops with the rice; permanent cropping of perennial (tree) and subperennial (root and tuber) crops, either adjacent to the ricefield or on unirrigated upland sites; dooryard garden cultivation of a complex plant assemblage for food, condimental, medicinal, and magicoreligious purposes; and livestock, such as cattle or buffalo for draft, and poultry, pigs, or goats that act as scavengers (Ruddle, 1991).

As a result, imputing a single motive to such household economic behavior as expressed in the cropping patterns of a farming system is fallacious; it might express ecological sensitivity, or maybe economic rationality. But certainly it represents an attempt to secure a livelihood, which includes risk spreading. Generally, a consciously integrated combination of motives underlies household economics. This, in turn, implies that realistic management and social and economic accounting systems cannot be abstracted from either the total household economic situation or the regional economic context, of which farming forms but a part (Ruddle, 1991).

The household benefits of on-farm integration

In integrated farming systems an underlying concept is that many outputs (sometimes called "wastes" or "by-products") of subsystems become basic inputs for other subsystems, rather than just additive components of the overall farm economy. A synergism is thereby created such that the total productivity of the system exceeds the sum of the individual subsystems. This results in higher yields for all commodities produced and a wider range of products than could otherwise be obtained per unit area. Under such systems, the economic results from any one component are less important than is maximizing the returns from the whole.

There are three main ways via which household economics can be enhanced by farm system integration. First, because energy and materials (e.g., feeds and fertilizers) are produced within the system, there can be increased production for either household subsistence or market sales. This can augment the household economy of the small-scale farm by reducing actual or potential expenditures on externally sourced farm inputs while at the same time increasing productivity. Thus, any system design must seek to produce on-farm, as much as possible, the biological and labor inputs required to intensify production. Moreover, the uncertainties of supply commonly associated with the use of commercially produced feeds and inorganic fertilizers in developing countries are almost eliminated. Second, the sale off-farm of agricultural wastes for industrial or other use provides another potential source of cash income for farm households. And third, household incomes will increase as more "downstream" jobs are created with the diffusion of innovations that raise productivity, and thus either directly or indirectly increase local labor demand, especially for the harvesting and processing of products as well as for distribution and marketing channels. Increased household incomes lead to an increased demand for a wider variety of goods and services than before. This translates into off-farm employment and economic opportunities (Ruddle, 1991).

The integration of farming systems is also beneficial to regional ecological systems because the nonpolluting recycling of wastes within farming systems, or their external absorption by new industries, reduces their potential for environmental pollution, and inputs to the system generated within the system reduce demands for external sourcing as well as pressures caused by over-exploitation on the general environment. Further, integrated farming systems are energy efficient, principally because production of inputs within the system saves energy on external production and transport, and biological and chemical energy within the system is more efficiently utilized by integrated farming.

Apart from increased yields resulting from the intensification of existing activities, significant increases in productivity and the farm-based component of household incomes could result from farming systems that integrate crop cultivation with both conventional live-stock husbandry and/or aquaculture. Although aquaculture is locally important in many parts of the world, its potential for contributing to rural development was not widely appreciated until relatively recently. In contrast, agriculture is widely believed to be the main means of reducing poverty and hunger and ensuring food security (FAO, 2000). As was demonstrated by the comprehensive research and other output of the former International Center for Living Aquatic Resources Management (ICLARM), to which Daniel Pauly also made significant contributions (Dizon and Sadorra, 1995; Pullin, this volume), integrated agriculture–aquaculture systems (IAAS) could become important in rural livelihoods and general rural development by improving nutri-tion and health, by improving incomes and generating employment and thereby contributing to increased farm sustainability and reduced vulnerability of the farm family. A particularly important aspect of IAAS is their contribution to increased farm efficiency and sustainabil-ity, when agricultural by-products, such as manure from livestock and crop residues, provide fertilizer and feed inputs for small-scale and commercial aquaculture, and nutrient-rich pond mud and pond waters become a valuable fertilizer substitute on farm crops and a nutrient rich source of irrigation water for them. Ponds are important sources of water for crops and livestock. An earlier mistake was to regard farm ponds just as "fish ponds" and not as "multi-functional ponds" (Ruddle, 1996, 1997; Ruddle and Prein, 1997). The improved efficiency of water use has been taken up by the Food and Agriculture Organization of the United Nations (FAO) (e.g., FAO, 1999, 2001).

LARGE-SCALE INTEGRATION: THE QUESTION OF LINKED ECOSYSTEMS

Malthusian overfishing is but a subset of a Malthusian overexploitation of all primary resource sectors of an economy that can be alleviated only through a thorough understanding of the issues involved, and then planning for an integrated and sustainable development to overcome them. This is well illustrated in coral reef fisheries, coastal wetlands, and the problems of highland zones, the interconnectedness of which is illustrated in the photo series of this chapter (Figures 15.1 to 15.8).

Figure 15.1 Moorea, Society Islands, Polynesia. Pre-existing institutions in many Pacific island nations managed resource use and biodiversity conservation in an integrated manner, from the volcanic peaks downslope to the outer reef slope. All the ecosystems and the marine and terrestrial habitats depicted in this photograph would have been included within such a management system. Photo: Kenneth Ruddle, 1972.

Coral reef fisheries

Coral reef fisheries are affected by three basic categories of activity that cause a reduction of fishery yields: (1) deleterious small-scale fishery activities within the reef ecosystem, (2) external industrial offshore fisheries, and (3) non-fishery activities both within the reef ecosystem and in linked ecosystems. All such activities are now familiar through various bodies of literature. The reduction of fishery yields by fishery activities, is, of course, the immediate "usual" suspect, and includes such diverse activities as fishing with poisons or explosives, the deliberate breaking of coral to drive fish, capture for the live fish trade and for the ornamental coral and aquarium fish trade, and shell gathering for collectors and for small-scale industry like handicrafts, fashion accessories, and button-making. Were it not for poverty and the difficulty of providing alternative sources of income – admittedly impossible conditions to satisfy – small-scale fishery activities are relatively easy to manage. Similarly, the problem of external industrial fisheries impinging in nearshore waters is theoretically easy to control using

Figure 15.2 Palawan Island, Philippines. Forested watersheds require protection and management for sustainable use of their various resources. However, as over much of the tropical world, in the Philippines they are cleared and burned either by shifting cultivators or to clear land for sedentary agriculture. Regardless of the motive, soils become depauperate and are eventually lost, and hydrological systems irrevocably altered (Figure 15.3). Weakened soils are washed downslope in the rainy season, and become deposited on the adjacent coral reefs (Figure 15.6). Photo: Kenneth Ruddle, 1977.

such spatial restrictions as zoning. However, enforcement and limiting the powers of vested interests are other matters entirely.

In contrast it is less easy to comprehend, measure, and plan to overcome the third type of activity – fish yield reduction caused by non-fishery activities. This includes such slippery issues as increased sedimentation on reef flats, a problem essentially traceable to human population growth where soil is loosened and easily flows away because of poor farm and forest management, and especially farming on steep hillsides. The construction of buildings, roads, other changes in land use, particularly land reclamation for building sites, and mining and the dumping of mine tailings, are also important, if generally localized, culprits. Coral reef fisheries are also damaged by fertilizer residues from the agriculture sector, and pesticide residues from both the agriculture and public health sectors, as well as by industrial, domestic, and untreated human wastes. Those issues can be effectively handled through comprehensive areal planning and management,

Figure 15.3 Palawan Island, Philippines. Upland forest clearance results in severely disrupted hydrological systems, especially during the rainy season. In addition to loss of water supply and creation of an ideal environment for waterborne disease vectors, this also alters the regime of freshwater inputs to downslope aquatic environments, with impacts on the resources and inhabitants. Photo: Kenneth Ruddle, 1977.

Figure 15.4 Near Korovisilou, on the southern coast of Viti Levu, Fiji. Poor farming practices and poorly planned infrastructural development commonly lead to major landslides, with associated loss of forest and soil, which ends up on the adjacent reef (Figure 15.6). Photo: Kenneth Ruddle, 1986.

Figure 15.5 Near Korovisilou, on the southern coast of Viti Levu, Fiji. The soil ends up here, as attested to by the woman gleaning the reef. Photo: Kenneth Ruddle, 1986.

Figure 15.6 The seashore of the Citarum Delta, Karawang Regency, West Java, Indonesia. Forest clearance and poor farming practices upslope in the nearby mountainous center of Java result in deposition along the Java Sea coast, and in a rapid progradation of the coastline. This negative impact on linked ecosystems can also provide new environments with new economic opportunities (Figures 15.7 and 15.8). Photo: Kenneth Ruddle, 1978.

Figure 15.7 A *surjan* integrated farming system on the coast of Karawang Regency, West Java, Indonesia. Rapid deposition along the Java Sea coast, and the fast progradation of the coastline provides an ideal environment in which to develop integrated farming systems (*surjan*) that combine agriculture and aquaculture. In addition to fish, these yield rice and a wide range of dryland crops both for a balanced household subsistence food supply and a marketable surplus. Photo: Kenneth Ruddle, 1978.

from the adjacent watersheds through to the seashore. Various approaches need consideration, including the examples provided by pre-existing systems, like those in the Pacific Islands.

Tropical wetlands

Tropical wetlands suffer from a somewhat different set of problems that have an impact on linked ecosystems. Ecologically sound policy and planning require that tropical wetlands always be understood and exploited as multiple-use environments, as they historically have been in many widely separated parts of the world (Ruddle, 1989b). However, modern policymakers and planners have lost that concept. Historically, economic uses of tropical wetlands, mainly capture fisheries, aquaculture, agriculture – that included mostly irrigated rice-fields, often with fish culture – animal husbandry, collecting forest products, and hunting animals and gathering plants, could function without impeding the major natural functions of coastal wetlands. These functions are of major economic and ecological importance,

Figure 15.8 A complex integrated aquaculture–agriculture system in the Zhujiang Delta, Guangdong Province, China. Beginning two millennia ago, the system was used to reclaim coastal swamps along the seaward edge of the Zhujiang Delta, in Guangdong Province of South China. With intense polyculture of carps and crops on the intervening dikes, this system was a rational way of reclaiming rapidly prograding coastal lands. Photo: Kenneth Ruddle, 1981.

and include, mainly, a large production and large export of energy and matter to other linked ecosystems, a buffering of extreme changes of nutrient levels, a major role in biogeochemical cycles of nitrogen and sulfur, the storage of water for dry season release, providing a nursery habitat for fish and other animals, and the natural treatment of organic wastes and some chemical pollutants. But these have been destroyed and are everywhere threatened by local deforestation in wetlands (which damages soils, water patterns, vegetation, and microclimates), the use of resources upstream, wetland reclamation projects, the over-use of wetland resources, the increased intrusion of seawater because freshwater flow from land has been disrupted by users and/or dams, and by pollutants entering from land via rivers and from the sea.

Perhaps the major threat to tropical wetlands is lack of information, knowledge, and scientific "know how" for making ecologically and socially good policies for their use (e.g., Ruddle *et al.*, 1978). Again, a major asset that we can draw on to help overcome this problem is an understanding of pre-existing wetland management systems and their knowledge base for using acid peat soils productively, such as exist in large areas of eastern Sumatra and Borneo in southeast Asia (Ruddle *et al.*, 1978; Ruddle, 1989b).

Upland areas

Upland watersheds are critical areas, both internally and for the adjacent downslope ecological zones with which they are tightly linked via the hydrological system. The ecological "condition" of upland zones is a major determinant of the quality of coastal marine waters and their fisheries, and thus of the economic, nutritional, and health conditions of the human populations dependent on them. Both the causes of and solutions to problems in upland watershed areas are numerous, complex, and interlocking (Figure 15.9). As a result, there are many complementary facets to any successful development program implemented in such regions. All facets require careful consideration and coordination to ensure their appropriateness and synchronization.

The main underlying cause of environmental problems in upland watershed areas is usually an increasing human population pressure and associated rapid rates of growth. This has an immediate impact on the environment, as deforestation occurs to make space for agriculture and to provide timber for domestic fuel and construction. Since flat land is rare in uplands, the space cleared for farming invariably means that steep slopes have to be cultivated, which, in the absence of terracing, quickly results in overexploitation of fragile and impoverished soils.

Water and soil environmental problems then occur rapidly. The destruction of upland watersheds quickly results in soil erosion and landslides, followed in both uplands and the adjacent lowlands by catastrophic floods, reduced water supply, and sedimentation of rivers and reservoirs.

In turn, this results in human and economic problems in upland watershed areas. Stagnant or declining agricultural production occurs quickly after deforestation, and this eventually causes local food shortages. Seasonal and eventually permanent human migrations then begin to other upland areas, where the cycle is repeated, or to the adjacent lowlands, in search of better opportunities. Eventually, land and human settlements are abandoned in the uplands.

Such problems are individually complex, but as a group they become interlocking, mutually reinforcing and daunting. As a result, the management tasks in upland watershed areas are complex, and

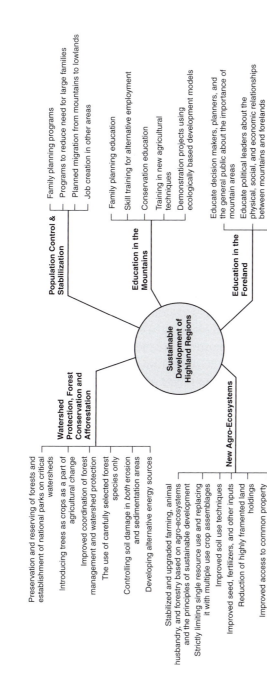

Figure 15.9 Requirements for sustainable development and integrated management of environments and resources in upland regions.

there are no easy solutions. Moreover, because all the problems are urgent, it becomes difficult for decision makers to agree on priorities.

Solutions require a consideration of multiple factors, the principal of which are social, cultural, educational, technological, biological, and physical factors that involve forelands (the lowland areas adjacent to the uplands) as well as mountain environments and societies. Successful management, development, and ecological conservation in upland watershed areas require development programs that are multisectoral, interregional, and integrated in space and time.

Two key factors must usually share top priority. These are that (1) the human population problem that is the root cause of all upland watershed area problems requires control measures; and (2) the destruction of watersheds is the principal problem resulting from (1), and which finds its basic solution in forest protection and rehabilitation.

PROMOTING INTEGRATION

It is clear that simplistic policies, epitomized by the sectoral approach, have failed to solve the problems of the world's tropical nearshore fisheries. And it is equally apparent and increasingly widely recognized that a management approach based on an integration of activities both within ecosystems and among linked ecosystems is an indispensable route toward a solution. Yet there will be impediments as vested interests battle vigorously to preserve a little modified status quo.

Only a few of the more important problems can be addressed here. Fundamental yet sensitive problems that are usually avoided in "polite discourse" include the inappropriate approaches and models of scientists and donors, the problems that weak local government would cause for integration, and the reorganization of government fisheries departments to suit integrated resource management.

INAPPROPRIATE APPROACH AND MODELS OF SCIENTISTS AND DONORS

The underlying reason for the failure of management in tropical nearshore fisheries is the implementation of policies and programs based on Western models and approaches, coupled with an inability and/or unwillingness to consider non-Western alternatives of empirically proven value (Ruddle and Hickey, 2008). This attitude is embedded in donor and development agency behavior. It is strongly manifested in a relative lack of understanding of tropical milieux and a persistence of various prejudices, in particular a temperate bias in conventional approaches to fisheries education and management.

Further, despite a relatively belated recognition of the importance of small-scale capture and culture fisheries, a focus on industrial fisheries has been the long-standing policy of all international agencies and most national fisheries services. And notwithstanding a rise in the study of small-scale fisheries since the mid-1970s, they are still not well understood. Policy, administration, and management have tended to focus on making small-scale fisheries more economically efficient while conserving fish stocks. Programs have been based on a sectoral approach, and it was not widely appreciated that fisheries are but one of a range of economic activities that occur in coastal zones. Also detrimental to small-scale fisheries is that they have not been included in the general framework of rural development programs during the last half-century, when, as demonstrated above, activities have focused on small-scale farm development and related infrastructure and institutions (Ruddle and Hickey, 2008).

Ironically, and with an astounding level of arrogance, all that has taken place in the context of a relative lack of knowledge on tropical nearshore fish and fisheries. The fisheries biologists and social scientists who advise them often have only limited or sometimes no experience in the tropical milieux. Further, there is an extremely negative connotation to the term "tropics" among fisheries scientists based in the temperate latitudes. Daniel Pauly (1994b) summarized the prevailing attitude together with its pernicious implications in a concise and insightful essay, inspired by a peer review that he received and which in its entirety read "Rubbish, may apply in the tropics – but not here." Not surprisingly, fisheries scientists commonly fail to appreciate differences between the temperate zone industrial fisheries with which they are familiar from their own training and research experience, and tropical nearshore fisheries. This means that erroneous interpretations are passed to those who fund and make development policies and programs.

Fisheries management in industrialized countries is mostly top-down, centralized, science-based, and bureaucratic, and, like in most natural resource and environmental management, states exercise special claims to control common pool resources. This model has mostly been perceived as a failure, as evidenced by the collapse of fisheries under this management approach, and replaced by models based on decentralization and approaches that emphasize participatory management and co-management.

Another major example of exasperating wrong-headedness is the donor-driven agenda that sees marine protected areas (MPAs) as a global panacea for the conservation of natural resources and protection of biodiversity. This seemingly single-minded and universal drive has promoted MPA establishment targets ranging from 10% to 30% of national areas, with high levels of Global Environment Facility (GEF) support and funding by major foundations. The MPA model is increasingly seen as culturally and socially flawed (Christie, 2004; Dowie, 2005), and proliferation of the Western ideal of a "protected area" seems foreign and counter-intuitive to indigenous peoples, who have been providing environmental stewardship and protection of these areas for centuries, if not millennia. A particularly unpleasant consequence is the estimated millions of "conservation refugees" (Dowie, 2005).

The goal in promoting biodiversity conservation should be to promote an overall sustainable approach to resource management and development, as has inherently been practiced traditionally by a great many societies, including those in the Pacific Islands. This would mean appreciating and incorporating the concepts and methods of indigenous people to sustainably manage resources using a balanced, holistic approach to resource utilization, not locking them out of their ancestral lands and marginalizing them. Nevertheless, today an increasingly single-minded Western strategy to create more MPAs in the Pacific overshadows support for the broad range of pre-existing resource management strategies available, primarily because of the seductive power of the relatively huge amount of money being expended. Although MPAs are but one tool available, they consume the bulk of the funding to support resource management. Although the ultimate objective is laudable, the approach and methodology used need a major overhaul. Again, a compromise is required, and should be sought in one based on hybrid non-Western and Western approaches.

POLITICS AND LOCAL GOVERNMENT: WEAKEST LINKS OR ACHILLES' HEELS IN INTEGRATION?

Although it was not mentioned explicitly as part of the original formulation of Malthusian overfishing, one of the biggest obstacles to the design and implementation of remedial measures is the crucial weakness of various levels of government and the organization of ministries and departments within them. Local administrative capacity is probably the most critical input needed to make policy operational, and expansion of local, district, and provincial government capacity to support it is the major bottleneck to implementing any strategy of integrated resource and ecosystems management.

Local political leaders and elites must be committed to the goals of sustainable development. Indeed, sustainable development projects should focus directly on building the capacity of governments and private institutions to sustain rural development, since the success of even those rural development projects with strong political and administrative support at the national level depends in large measure on the support of local public and private organizations in rural areas, and particularly on politically responsible and socially conscious bureaucracies in rural areas. But, in few nations do local governments perform these functions effectively. In many, local government is the least capable organization in the national institutional structure, ignored by central government and local populations alike. Its effectiveness varies directly with the financial and administrative skills of local officials and with the degree of political support received from the national government. This cannot be overcome by a simple but ineffective formal delegation of functions. Local governments in developing nations often lack even the basic skills to support rural development; officials are poorly trained with little knowledge of budgeting, record keeping, planning, or service delivery. Many local officials are appointed by the central government, usually to reward political loyalty rather than on administrative ability and experience. Political appointees then usually appoint cronies to lower-level administrative positions (Rondinelli and Ruddle, 1978).

Further, ministry and state officials are often reluctant to delegate real responsibility for planning and resource decision making to local officials. In some countries, moreover, local people simply do not trust the central government and their skepticism concerning the authenticity of decentralized power and responsibility raises a barrier to cooperation. Attitudes of local officials often are not considered conducive to long-range planning and analysis: feelings of helplessness concerning their ability to solve local problems through deliberate action, an acceptance of

> fate rather than a belief in their ability to control their environment, and a disinterest in problems beyond those exerting immediate pressures or

> the boundaries of their local jurisdiction. Moreover, the scarcity of information and reliable records at the local level with which to formulate plans and programs or to allocate resources is compounded by the limited staff in central ministries to provide the technical assistance, guidance, or close supervision of local administrative units needed to make decentralization work. Local political conflicts and squabbles among contending factions over the allocation of government funds often result in domination by local traditional elites who may be insensitive to the needs of rural people and unsympathetic to central government redistribution policies. (Rondinelli and Ruddle, 1978, p. 29)

However, the situation is quite different where pre-existing or traditional local organization and institutions remain strong and functional. For example, such strategies now promoted by Western scientists to manage marine resources as closed areas, species, and seasons, limited access, and gear restrictions have been practiced in the Pacific for centuries (Johannes, 1978; Hickey, 2006). In the South Pacific, increasing recognition and support for pre-existing or traditional marine resource management strategies and tenure systems, and their underlying knowledge base, have resulted in a renaissance of pre-existing systems, and modern management based on them is emerging widely, as in Vanuatu (Johannes and Hickey, 2004; Hickey, 2006), Samoa (Fa'asili and Kelekolo, 1999), Fiji (Veitayaki, 2002), and the Cook Islands (Tiraa, 2006), among other nations (Johannes, 2002).

Overcoming the weaknesses that constrain the ability of communities to manage themselves and their resource endowment in an integrated manner is key to local development; not some elaborate plan devised from afar. Unfortunately, many donor-designed projects simply take too long, their design is too elaborate, they involve too many actors and levels, and there is far too much scope for sabotage. In contrast, many of the earlier studies on non-Western management systems, (e.g., Johannes, 1977, 1978) proposed using pre-existing local systems for a modern purpose in precisely those locations (e.g., Samoa, Vanuatu, Solomon Islands) where traditional systems remained either still functional or well remembered, as had been done effectively long ago in Japan (Ruddle, 1987).

FISHERIES DEPARTMENTS IN RURAL COASTAL DEVELOPMENT

The ecosystem approach to fisheries is essentially an extension of the conventional principles for sustainable fisheries development and management to deal explicitly with such ecosystem issues as resources conservation, habitat protection, and fishery and nonfishery impacts, among other things (Garcia *et al.*, 2003). But what nowhere seems to have been appreciated is that adoption of the ecosystem management concept is a major paradigm shift that would demand a fundamental change of the Western-style fisheries management institutions. Although still not fully thought out as either a concept or in operational definition, the ecosystem approach requires the phasing out of sectoral policies for the marine environment and resources. Fisheries management would become part of a broader ecosystem management strategy with new and longer-term time horizons, and so would cease to be based on a sectoral policy. Present organizational structures and the institutional inertia behind them would be unlikely to cope with such changes. Fisheries co-management would also either fall by the wayside or be incorporated into the new paradigm.

But it is self-evident that given the complexity of the integrated resources management together with the grossly inadequate state of local management in most countries, there is an urgent need to reconsider the role and status of fisheries departments as administrative units. Apart from the major fishing nations and those archipelagic nations, composed mostly of atolls, like Kiribati or the Maldives, where fish are the principal natural resource and terrestrial resources are extremely limited, fisheries departments in most countries are relatively young and small entities, which reflects the comparative lack of importance of fisheries (Marriott, 1990). Further, they generally have little clout in political circles, where their interests are usually subordinated to more important sectors of the economy. Reflecting their low overall status, administration is often not of a high standard in most national fisheries departments, staff morale often is low, and turnover rates relatively high (Everett, 1983). Further, fisheries departments do not generally attract the ablest recruits to administration, whose career aspirations are better served in more important ministries. None of these factors bodes well for the effective management of either coastal or high seas fisheries, particularly now that problems and conflicts have become intractable.

Since fisheries are often small, the departments are commonly linked with agricultural, forestry, and other natural resources within a single ministry. Most fisheries departments have a dual focus, one on fisheries management and the other on general rural development and welfare issues. Whereas the relative importance of these two main trusts varies depending on country and situation, in general the latter is becoming more important. Marriott (1997) observed that fisheries institutions tend to be practical rather than analytical and theoretical, with policy failures as a result of this tendency. Reform has focused mostly on such "practical" and administrative aspects as organization, training, funding, and the like, with little consideration of the purpose of the institution.

International fisheries relationships and general affairs are another important aspect of the work of many fisheries departments, regardless of their perceived status within a nation's administrative framework. This is usually highly political in nature, and generally beyond the competence of fisheries technical specialists, since it involves diplomacy, international law and treaties, and financing. As such it is best left to ministries of foreign affairs, to which deep- and distant-water fisheries specialists should be permanently reassigned.

Indeed, there is precious little logic in retaining old-style, comprehensive fisheries departments in their existing structure. So a radical restructuring of fishery policy, administration, and management is urgently required. Deep- and distant-water fisheries should be separated from coastal and small-scale fisheries, with the former being allocated to the control of a specialized national fisheries agency working in close coordination with an international coordinating agency. Small-scale capture and culture fisheries should be removed from national fisheries departments and reassigned to a national organization responsible for all rural development. As is well recognized, aquaculture is "farming" and not "fishing." And it is imperative to recognize that small-scale capture fishing is just another activity that rural households can opt to engage in, and that not all fishers are professionals who live in highly specialized communities. In other words, there is a large range of combinations in which small-scale fishers are or can be involved and combined with other activities.

CONCLUSION

Daniel Pauly with his attempt to address the issue of fisheries management via Malthusian overfishing started us all thinking. Of course, his concept does not go far enough. That was the idea; to get others to think and contribute to it. Malthusian overfishing needs to be expanded in terms of a fisheries human ecology that puts "fisheries in context" outside the "fisheries envelope." The concept needs to be further developed to address in an *integrated* or human ecological manner the study of all the resources and income opportunities used by "fisheries" communities and households. To be put to practical use in policy and program design for solving routine problems in the "real world," that approach should be based on *quantitative* data developed by *detailed fieldwork* at least for harvest rates of *all* resources used and not just of fish, energy flows, time allocation by *age* and gender (and not just time spent working), and labor demand and supply by and to the various resource systems used by a community.

In a rethinking such is suggested in this essay, it is important to interweave new components into time-tested management designs, to adapt the latter to the various conditions that have altered over time. Although it is almost a cliché to argue that development strategies should be based on a thorough understanding of existing conditions, emerging needs, and local cultural traditions, this basic principle is often lost in the urgency to activate development plans and programs. But one of the enduring lessons of development experience is that the most pervasive and lasting changes can often be attained by using and transforming existing resources and by promoting institutional change by building on culturally embedded arrangements and practices. Community social and economic institutions, no matter how inadequate they may be for modernization, survive because they perform necessary functions. They are often adapted to cultural peculiarities and satisfy local needs. Understanding their operation is crucial to designing new organizations or strategies for community-centered resources management. The adaptation and use of existing and culturally embedded arrangements can often be more effective and less costly than introducing new systems from scratch.

There is an urgent and immediate need to devise a radically different approach to fisheries management within a human ecological context, to provide alternatives to the sectoralized Western models that have been inappropriately used in tropical waters for so long. For that we need to accept that there exist in many tropical developing countries, such as in many Pacific Island nations, pre-existing and time-tested systems for managing coastal-marine resources that provide proven alternative approaches to management and which provide blueprints for the design of new systems, since they are already pre-adapted to the characteristics of tropical nearshore fisheries and cultural milieux.

There is a need to finally bite the bullet on this issue and implement radical reforms. Past attempts have been too piecemeal and avoided central issues in attempting to compromise and obtain conference documents or inter-ministerial plans of action that satisfy all disparate interests. They do that so well; but central issues are never addressed and real problems never tackled. Instead, the problems fester and become eventually much worse and less tractable. Bureaucratic inertia is the final nail in the coffin in which any hope of progress is usually buried.

ACKNOWLEDGMENTS

With this contribution, I wish to express my gratitude to Daniel Pauly for nearly three decades of friendship. Elsewhere I have acknowledged the fundamental contribution he made to my understanding of the physical and biological oceanographic aspects of monsoon seasonality in Southeast Asian coastal waters, which helped me explain the biological basis of marine fish supply to the fermentation industry (Ruddle, 2005; Ruddle and Ishige, 2005). I derived much pleasure from sharing ideas on our commitment to tropical regions, to interdisciplinary approaches that combine biological, physical, and sociocultural factors, and to objectively evaluating alternative and often unconventional potential solutions to various problems.

REFERENCES

Béné, C. (2003) When fishery rhymes with poverty: a first step beyond the old paradigm on poverty in small-scale fisheries. *World Development*, 31, 949–976.
CBD (2000) Decisions Adopted by the Conference of the Parties to the Convention on Biological Diversity at its Fifth Meeting. Nairobi: UNEP.
Christie, P. (2004) Marine protected areas as biological successes and social failures in Southeast Asia. *American Fisheries Society Symposium*, 42, 155–164.
Crocombe, R. G. (1967) From ascendancy to dependency: the politics of Atiu. *Journal of Pacific History*, 2, 97–112.
Davis, S. (1985) Traditional management of the littoral zone among the Yolngu of North Australia. In Ruddle, K. and Johannes, R. E., eds., *The Traditional Knowledge and Management of Coastal Systems in Asia and the Pacific*. Jakarta: UNESCO-ROSTSEA pp. 101–124.
Dixon, J., Gulliver, A. and Gibbon, D. (2001) *Global Farming Systems Study: Challenges and priorities to 2030*. Rome: FAO and World Bank.
Dizon, L. B. and Sadorra, M. S. M. (1995) Patterns of publication by the staff of an international fisheries research center. *Scientometrics*, 32, 67–75.
Dowie, M. (2005) Conservation refugees. *Orion*, 24, 16–27.
Everett, G. W. (1983) *Conflicts, Compatibility and Constraints in Determining Fishery Development Objectives. Case Studies and Working Papers Presented at the Expert Consultation on Strategies for Fisheries Development*. Rome: FAO.
Fa'asili, U. and Kelekolo, I. (1999) The use of village by-laws in marine conservation and fisheries management. *SPC Traditional Marine Resource Management and Knowledge Information Bulletin*, 11, 7–10.

FAO (1999) Report of the ad hoc working group of experts in rural aquaculture, Bangkok, Thailand. FAO Fisheries Report. Rome: FAO.

FAO (2000) State of Food Insecurity Report. Rome: FAO.

FAO (2001) Report of the Eleventh Session of the Committee for Inland Fisheries of Africa. FAO Fisheries Report. Rome: FAO.

FAO (2006) Appendix G, Conference Declaration: Report of the International Conference on Agrarian Reform and Rural Development, Porto Alegre, Brazil. Rome: FAO.

Garcia, S. M., Zerbi, A., Aliaume, C., Chi, T. and Lasserre, G. (2003) The ecosystem approach to fisheries: issues, terminology, principles, institutional foundations, implementation and outlook. FAO Fisheries Technical Paper. Rome: FAO.

Geertz, C. (1963) *Agricultural Involution: the Processes of Ecological Change in Indonesia.* Berkeley, CA: University of California Press.

Hickey, F. R. (2006) Traditional marine resource management in Vanuatu: acknowledging, supporting and strengthening indigenous management systems. *SPC Traditional Marine Resource Management and Knowledge Information Bulletin*, 20, 11–23.

Hviding, E. (1996) *Guardians of Marovo Lagoon.* Honolulu: University of Hawaii Press.

IFAD (2001) *Rural Policy Report 2001: The Challenge of Ending Rural Poverty.* Oxford, UK: Oxford University Press.

Johannes, R. E. (1977) Traditional law of the sea in Micronesia. *Micronesica*, 13, 121–127.

Johannes, R. E. (1978) Traditional marine conservation methods in Oceania and their demise. *Annual Review of Ecology and Systematics*, 9, 349–364.

Johannes, R. E. (2002) The renaissance of community based marine resource management in Oceania. *Annual Review of Ecology and Systematics*, 33, 317–340.

Johannes, R. E. and Hickey, F. R. (2004) Evolution of village-based marine resource management in Vanuatu between 1993 and 2001. *Coastal Region and Small Island Papers*, 15.

Johnston, B. and Mellor, J. (1961) The role of agriculture in economic development. *The American Economic Review*, 51, 566–593.

Lingenfelter, S. G. (1975) *Yap: Political Leadership and Culture Change in an Island Society.* Honolulu: University of Hawaii Press.

Manshard, W. (1974) *Tropical Agriculture: A Geographical Introduction and Appraisal.* London: Longman.

Marriott, A. (1990) Third World fisheries departments. *Marine Policy*, 14, 453–454.

Marriott, S. P. (1997) Fisheries institutional reform in developing countries. *Marine Policy*, 21, 435–444.

Meller, N. and Horowitz, R. H. (1987) Hawaii: themes in land monopoly. In Crocombe, R., ed., *Land Tenure in the Pacific*. Suva, Fiji: University of the South Pacific.

Mellor, J. W. (1966) *The Economics of Agricultural Development.* Ithaca, NY: Cornell University Press.

Pauly, D. (1988) Some definitions of overfishing relevant to coastal zone management in Southeast Asia. *Tropical Coastal Area Management*, 3, 14–15.

Pauly, D. (1994a) From growth to Malthusian overfishing: stages of fisheries resources misuse. *Traditional Marine Resource Management and Knowledge Information Bulletin*, 3, 7–14.

Pauly, D. (1994b) May apply in the tropics – but not here! In *On the Sex of Fish and the Gender of Scientists: Essays in Fisheries Science*. London: Chapman & Hall, pp. 1–4.

Pauly, D. (2006) Major trends in small-scale marine fisheries, with emphasis on developing countries, and some implications for the social sciences. *Maritime Studies (MAST)*, 4, 7–22.

Ravuvu, A. D. (1983) *The Fijian Way of Life*. Suva, Fiji: Institute of Pacific Studies.

Rondinelli, D. A. and Ruddle, K. (1978) Urbanization and rural development: A spatial policy for equitable growth. New York, NY: Praeger Publishers.

Ruddle, K. (1980) A preliminary survey of fish cultivation in ricefields, with special reference to West Java, Indonesia. *Bulletin of the National Museum of Ethnology*, 3, 801–822.

Ruddle, K. (1982) Traditional integrated farming systems and rural development: the example of ricefield fisheries in Southeast Asia. *Agricultural Administration*, 10, 1–11.

Ruddle, K. (1987) Administration and conflict management in Japanese coastal fisheries. Rome: FAO Fisheries Department.

Ruddle, K. (1989a) Social principles underlying traditional inshore fishery management systems in the Pacific Basin. *Marine Resource Economics*, 5, 231–243.

Ruddle, K. (1989b) Some adaptive strategies and natural resource uses in tropical wetlands. In Patten, B. C., ed., *Wetlands and Shallow Continental Water Bodies*. The Hague: SPB Academic Publishing.

Ruddle, K. (1991) Integrated farming systems and future directions for Asian farming systems research and extension. *Journal of the Asian Farming Systems Association*, 1, 91–99.

Ruddle, K. (1994) A guide to the literature on traditional community-based fishery management in the Asia-Pacific tropics. Fisheries Circular, FIPP/C869. Rome: FAO.

Ruddle, K. (1996) The potential role of integrated management of natural resources in improving the nutritional and economic status of resource-poor farm households in Ghana. In Prein, M., Ofori, J. K. and Lightfoot, C., eds., *Research for the Future Development of Aquaculture in Ghana*. Manila, Philippines: ICLARM.

Ruddle, K. (1997) A potential nutritional and household economic role for integrated agriculture-aquaculture in rural Africa: the case of Ghana. *Journal of Policy Studies*, 3, 55–78.

Ruddle, K. (1998) Traditional community-based coastal marine fisheries management in Viet Nam. *Ocean and Coastal Management*, 40, 1–22.

Ruddle, K. (2005) The use and management of small clupeoids in Viet Nam. *Senri Ethnological Studies*, 67, 215–236.

Ruddle, K. and Chesterfield, R. A. (1977) Education for traditional food procurement in the Orinoco Delta. *Iberoamericana*, 53 Berkeley and Los Angeles: University of California Press.

Ruddle, K. and Hickey, F. (2008) Accounting for the mismanagement of tropical nearshore fisheries. *Environment, Development and Sustainability*, 10, 565–589.

Ruddle, K., Hviding, E. and Johannes, R. E. (1992) Marine resources management in the context of customary tenure. *Marine Resource Economics*, 7, 249–273.

Ruddle, K. and Ishige, N. (2005) Fermented fish products in East Asia. Hong Kong: SAR, International Resources Management Institute.

Ruddle, K., Johnson, D. V., Townsend, M. and Rees, J. D. (1978) *Palm Sago: A Tropical Starch from Marginal Lands*. Honolulu: University Press of Hawai'i.

Ruddle, K. and Prein, M. (1997) Assessing potential nutritional and household economic benefits of developing integrated farming systems. In Mathias, J. A., Charles, A. T. and Hu, B., eds., *Integrated Fish Farming*. Boca Raton and New York: CRC Press, pp. 112–121.

Ruddle, K. and Zhong, G. F. (1988) *Integrated Agriculture Aquaculture in South China: The Dike Pond System of the Zhujiang Delta.* Cambridge, UK: Cambridge University Press.

Ruttenberg, H. (1980) *Farming Systems in the Tropics.* Oxford, UK: Clarendon House.

Schneider, D. M. (1984) *A Critique of the Study of Kinship.* Ann Arbor, MI: University of Michigan Press.

Tiraa, A. (2006) Ra'ui in the Cook Islands – today's context in Rarotonga. *SPC Traditional Marine Resource Management and Knowledge Information Bulletin*, 19, 11–15.

Veitayaki, J. (2002) Customary marine tenure and the empowerment of resource owners in Fiji. In South, G. R., Cleave, G. and Skelton, P. A., eds., *Oceans in the New Millennium: Challenges and Opportunities for the Islands.* Bucharest: Dada, pp. 148–150.

World Bank (2000) World Development Report 2000/2001: attacking poverty. New York, NY: Oxford University Press.

U. RASHID SUMAILA, ANDREW J. DYCK, ANDRÉS
M. CISNEROS-MONTEMAYOR, AND REG WATSON

16

Global fisheries economic analysis

INTRODUCTION

The starting point for global fisheries economics work in the Sea Around Us project at the University of British Columbia Fisheries Centre is the creation of global databases. Over the last few years, we have created and/or compiled global databases on ex-vessel fish prices, subsidies, recreational fisheries, social discount rates, and consumer price indices. We are currently developing two additional global databases: cost of fishing and fisheries employment. This information, combined with other project databases, provides remarkable opportunities for conducting global-scale fisheries analyses.

This chapter summarizes the results reported by Sumaila et al. (2010), which provide estimates of global fisheries subsidies; and Cisneros-Montemayor and Sumaila (2010) and Dyck and Sumaila (2010), which estimate the contribution of ecosystem-based marine recreation and ocean fish populations to the global economy, respectively.

FISHERIES SUBSIDIES WORLDWIDE

Fisheries subsidies are defined as financial transfers, direct or indirect, from public entities to the fishing sector, which help the sector make more profit than it would otherwise (Sumaila et al., 2008). Such transfers are often designed to either reduce the costs of production or increase revenues. In addition, they may also include indirect payments that benefit fishers, such as management and decommissioning programs.

Subsidies have gained worldwide attention because of their complex relationship with trade, ecological sustainability, and

Ecosystem Approaches to Fisheries: A Global Perspective, ed. V. Christensen and J. Maclean. Published by Cambridge University Press. © Cambridge University Press 2011.

socioeconomic development. It is widely acknowledged that global fisheries are overcapitalized, resulting in the depletion of fishery resources (Hatcher and Robinson, 1999; Munro and Sumaila, 2002). Although many reasons have been ascribed to the decline of fishery resources, the contribution of subsidies to the expansion of capacity and overfishing cannot be sufficiently emphasized (WWF, 2001). Subsidies that enhance revenues or reduce fishing costs lead to a marginal increase in profit, thereby increasing participation and fishing effort (Sumaila, 2003). Subsidies that promote fishery resource conservation and management are, however, regarded as beneficial and necessary (Milazzo, 1998).

Sumaila *et al.* (2010) set out to estimate the amount and extent of several different subsidy types nationally, regionally, and globally in order to determine the proportion of the estimated subsidies that contribute to increased fishing capacity.

Previous estimates of annual global fishery subsidies have included US$14–20 billion (Milazzo, 1998) and US$54 billion (FAO, 1992). The Organisation for Economic Co-operation and Development (OECD), WWF, Asia-Pacific Economic Cooperation (APEC), and United Nations Environment Programme (UNEP) have also produced significant data on fisheries subsidies. Regional annual subsidy estimates are about US$12 billion for the Asia-Pacific rim (APEC, 2000) and about US$2.5 billion for the North Atlantic (Munro and Sumaila, 2002).

A more recent estimate of global fisheries subsidies is US$30–34 billion for the year 2000 (Sumaila and Pauly, 2006). Sumaila *et al.* (2010) built on these estimates by collecting more recent data and improving the methodology for estimating missing data.

Khan *et al.* (2006) classified subsidies into three categories: the "good," the "bad," and the "ugly." The basis for this classification is the potential impact of given subsidy types on the sustainability of the fishery resource. "Good" subsidies enhance the conservation of fish stocks over time, e.g., subsidies that fund fisheries management. A new addition to good subsidies is spending by governments to establish and operate marine protected areas (Cullis-Suzuki and Pauly, 2008). "Bad" subsidies lead to overcapacity and overexploitation, e.g., fuel subsidies. "Ugly" subsidies can lead to either the conservation or overfishing of a given fish stock, e.g., buyback subsidies, which, if not properly designed, can lead to overcapacity.

After updating the database reported in Sumaila and Pauly (2006), the information therein was used to estimate and analyze subsidies paid by governments of maritime countries throughout the world in 2003.

Table 16.1 *Fisheries subsidies by category, US$ billion.*

Category	World total
Good	8.0
Bad	16.2
Ugly	3.0
Total	27.2

Sumaila *et al.* (2010) estimated the total magnitude of fishery subsidies in marine capture fisheries, summarized by category in Table 16.1, at US$27 billion per year. Subsidies in the "bad" category are the highest, totaling about US$16 billion, with about 70% of this total provided in developed countries. Good subsidies, which are also mostly provided in developed nations, are the next highest in total (US$8 billion). Subsidies categorized as "ugly" contribute the least amount to the global total (US$3 billion), with more than 90% again provided in developed countries.

ECOSYSTEM-BASED MARINE RECREATIONAL VALUES

Marine recreation activities (MRAs) such as recreational fishing, whale watching, and diving have recently come to the forefront of discussion and research regarding their ecological, economic, and social impacts and importance (e.g., Hoyt, 2001; Pitcher and Hollingworth, 2002; Aas, 2008). Although often labeled as "ecotourism," there is much debate on when or whether such activities can be considered as such (Holland *et al.*, 1998), so we prefer the term "ecosystem-based" MRAs.

To estimate the value of MRAs, Cisneros-Montemayor and Sumaila (2010) first identified three indicators of socioeconomic value in ecosystem-based marine recreational activities: (1) level of participation, (2) total employment in the sector, and (3) sum of direct expenditure by users. A database of reported expenditure on MRAs was then compiled for 144 coastal countries. Using this database, a meta-analysis was performed to calculate the yearly global value for MRAs in terms of expenditure, participation, and employment.

Cisneros-Montemayor and Sumaila (2010) found that recreational fishing takes place in 118 maritime countries around the world; country-level data on expenditure, participation, and employment are available for 38 of these countries (32% of the total). The authors estimated that in 2003, nearly 60 million recreational anglers around the world generated a total of about US$40 billion in expenditure, supporting over 950 000 jobs. In their analysis, countries with data accounted for almost 95% of estimated total expenditures and 87% of participation. Thus, the authors argued that this estimate likely provides a close approximation to actual global recreational fishing effort and expenditure.

Data on whale watching were found for a total of 93 countries and territories (70 countries), mostly during 1994–2006 (Hoyt, 2001; Hoyt and Iñiguez, 2008). It is estimated that over 13 million people worldwide participated in whale watching in 2003. The estimated total expenditure by these participants was US$1.6 billion for that year (Cisneros-Montemayor and Sumaila, 2010). Based on available data, it is estimated that 18 000 jobs worldwide are supported by this industry. These numbers are only an indication of the potential economic contribution that can be expected from whale watching, given that marine mammals are found in all of the world's oceans (Kaschner *et al.*, 2006) and currently only a few countries have well-established whale watching industries.

There are limited national data on recreational diving outside the United States, Australia, and to some extent, Canada and the Caribbean region. Using market surveys and other data on active divers (Cesar *et al.*, 2003), it is estimated that 10 million active recreational divers and 40 million snorkelers around the world generate annually more than US$5.5 billion (2003) in direct expenditure, supporting 113 000 jobs.

In total, Cisneros-Montemayor and Sumaila (2010) estimate that 121 million MRA participants generate US$47 billion in expenditures annually and support more than one million jobs (Table 16.2).

OCEAN FISH POPULATIONS'CONTRIBUTION
TO THE WORLD ECONOMY

Estimates of gross revenues from capture fisheries suggest that this sector directly contributes US$85 billion to world output annually (Sumaila *et al.*, 2007). This amount is by no means the total contribution from ocean fish populations. As a primary industry, vast numbers of secondary economic activities from boat building to international transport are supported by world fisheries (Pontecorvo *et al.*, 1980).

When fisheries output is combined with other sectors dependent on ocean resources, its contribution to the economy is much greater (Pontecorvo *et al.*, 1980). Hence, although the national contribution of

Table 16.2 *Estimated global participation, expenditure, and employment in ecosystem-based marine recreational activities in 2003.*

	Total	Recreational fishing	Diving and snorkeling	Whale watching
Participation (million)	123	60	50	13
Expenditure (US$ billion)	47.1	40	5.5	1.6
Employment (thousand)	1081	950	113	18

fisheries in many countries ranges between 0.5% and 2.5% of the gross domestic product, the industry supports more output throughout the national economy by way of "trickle-up" linkages (Béné et al., 2007). These linkages are referred to in the literature as "multipliers" – factors by which we can multiply the value of an economic activity's output to obtain its total contribution to the economy, including activities directly and indirectly dependent on it.

The economic multiplier is used in fisheries research to emphasize that the industry has many linkages throughout the economy. The importance of this industry to the economy is understated when considering only the direct values obtained through the usual method of national accounting. The total value of fisheries sector catch (referred to as "landed value," Sumaila et al., 2007) is the value of fish when they change hands for the first time after leaving the boat. In input–output analysis, this is considered to be the direct economic value of fisheries sector output and is just one part of the total economic impact of this industry.

Dyck and Sumaila (2010) applied an input–output approach to estimate the total of direct, indirect, and induced economic effects arising from ocean fish populations in the world economy. Their results suggested that there is a great deal of variation in fishing output multipliers between regions and countries. However, when the authors applied the output multipliers to the capture fisheries sector at the global scale, they found that due to significant indirect and induced effects (Table 16.3), the contribution of this sector to world output was more than three times larger than the value of fish at first sale – about US$240 billion per year.

Table 16.3 *World fisheries sector output by region, US$ billion.*

Continent	Landed value	Economic impact	Average multiplier
Africa	2.10	5.46	2.59
Asia	49.89	133.31	2.67
Europe	11.45	35.78	3.12
Latin America and Caribbean	7.20	14.78	2.05
North America	8.23	28.92	3.52
Oceania	5.22	17.06	3.27
World total	84.10	235.31	2.80

CONCLUDING REMARKS

The contributions reported in this chapter continue to impact policymakers at the highest levels. The influence of these works is exemplified by invitations to many prestigious institutions, including the Canadian parliament, US White House, US Congress, British House of Lords, World Trade Organization, World Bank, and United Nations.

ACKNOWLEDGMENTS

We thank members of the Fisheries Economics Research Unit and the Sea Around Us project at the Fisheries Centre of the University of British Columbia (UBC) for their input to this study. Thanks also to Sylvie Guénette and Patrizia Abdallah for translations from French and Spanish, respectively, and to Andrew Sharpless of Oceana, for access to various information sources. A. Khan is indebted to the World University Service of Canada, UBC Chapter, for financial support during his study at UBC. We also thank the Pew Charitable Trusts of Philadelphia for financial support through the Sea Around Us project, a scientific cooperation between the Pew Environment Group and the University of British Columbia. We are also grateful to the participants of the World Bank seminar on subsidies on October 30, 2006; particularly Bill Shrank and Matteo Milazzo. This chapter is a product of the Global Ocean Economics

Project at the UBC Fisheries Centre, which is funded by the Pew Charitable Trusts.

REFERENCES

Aas, O. (2008) *Global Challenges in Recreational Fisheries*. Singapore: Blackwell Publishing.

APEC (2000) Study into the nature and extent of subsidies in the fisheries sector of APEC member economies. PricewaterhouseCoopers Report. APEC.

Béné, C., MacFadyen, G. and Allison, E. H. (2007) Increasing the contribution of small-scale fisheries to poverty alleviation and food security. FAO Fisheries Technical Paper. Rome: FAO.

Cesar, H., Burke, L. and Pet-Soede, L. (2003) *The Economics of Worldwide Coral Degradation*. Amsterdam: Cesar Environmental Economics Consulting.

Cisneros-Montemayor, A. M. and Sumaila, U. R. (2010) A global valuation of ecosystem-based marine recreation. *Journal of Bioeconomics*, 12 (3), 245–268.

Cullis-Suzuki, S. and Pauly, D. (2008) Preliminary estimates of national and global costs of marine protected areas. Fisheries Centre Research Report, 16 (7). Vancouver, Canada: Fisheries Centre, University of British Columbia.

Dyck, A. J. and Sumaila, U. R. (2010) Contribution of ocean fish populations to the world economy. *Journal of Bioeconomics*, 12 (3), 227–243.

FAO (1992) Marine fisheries and the law of the sea: a decade of change. FAO Fisheries Circular. Rome: FAO.

Hatcher, A. and Robinson, K., eds. (1999) *Overcapacity, Overcapitalization and Subsidies in European Fisheries*. Portsmouth: CEMARE, University of Portsmouth.

Holland, S. M., Ditton, R. B. and Graefe, A. R. (1998) An ecotourism perspective on billfish fisheries. *Journal of Sustainable Tourism*, 6, 97–116.

Hoyt, E. (2001) *Whale Watching 2001: Worldwide Tourism Numbers, Expenditures, and Expanding Socioeconomic Benefits*. Yarmouth Port, MA: International Fund for Animal Welfare.

Hoyt, E. and Iñiguez, M. (2008) *The State of Whale Watching in Latin America*. Yarmouth Port, MA: International Fund for Animal Welfare, Global Ocean, WDCS.

Kaschner, K., Watson, R., Trites, A. W. and Pauly, D. (2006) Mapping world-wide distributions of marine mammal species using a relative environmental suitability (RES) model. *Marine Ecology Progress Series*, 316, 285–310.

Khan, A., Sumaila, U. R., Watson, R., Munro, G. and Pauly, D. (2006) The nature and magnitude of global non-fuel fisheries subsidies. In Sumaila, U. R. and Pauly, D., eds., *Catching More Bait: a Bottom-up Re-estimation of Global Fisheries Subsidies*. Fisheries Centre Research Report, 14 (6). Vancouver, Canada: Fisheries Centre, University of British Columbia.

Milazzo, M. (1998) Subsidies in world fisheries: a re-examination. World Bank Technical Paper. Washington DC: The World Bank.

Munro, G. and Sumaila, U. R. (2002) The impact of subsidies upon fisheries management and sustainability: the case of the North Atlantic. *Fish and Fisheries*, 3, 233–250.

Pitcher, T. J. and Hollingworth, C. E. (2002) *Recreational Fisheries: Ecological, Economic, and Social Evaluation*. Oxford, UK: Blackwell Science.

Pontecorvo, G., Wilkinson, M., Anderson, R. and Holdowsky, M. (1980) Contribution of the ocean sector to the United States economy. *Science*, 208, 1000–1006.

Sumaila, U. R. (2003) A fish called subsidies. *Down to Earth*, 12 (12), 55.

Sumaila, U. R., Khan, A., Dyck, A., Watson, R., Munro, G., Tydemers, P. and Pauly, D. (2010) A bottom-up re-estimation of global fisheries subsidies. *Journal of Bioeconomics*, 12 (3), 201–225.

Sumaila, U. R., Marsden, A. D., Watson, R. and Pauly, D. (2007) Global ex-vessel fish price database: construction and applications. *Journal of Bioeconomics*, 9, 39–51.

Sumaila, U. R. and Pauly, D. (2006) Catching more bait: a bottom-up re-estimation of global fisheries subsidies. Fisheries Centre Research Report, 14 (6). Vancouver, Canada: Fisheries Centre, University of British Columbia.

Sumaila, U. R., Teh, L., Watson, R., Tyedmers, P. and Pauly, D. (2008) Fuel price increase, subsidies, overcapacity, and resource sustainability. *ICES Journal of Marine Science*, 65, 832.

WWF (2001) Hard facts, hidden problems: a review of current data on fishing subsidies. Washington DC: WWF.

Section V Impacting policy

JOSHUA S. REICHERT

17

Linking conservation policy and science

For much of human history, people have waged war on nature, taming and transforming wild landscapes in ways that were perceived to benefit society. It is only rather recently that we have become aware that the domestication of wild places, and the commoditization of wild things, may ultimately do the human race great harm. Not only do wilderness systems and the life they contain provide us with a wide array of previously underappreciated services, but also we are rapidly running out of both. Unfortunately, we are coming to this realization somewhat late and, even then, awareness of the problem is far from uniform.

For thousands of years, the evolving conflict between human society and the natural world has been conspicuous mainly on land, because that is where most of it has occurred. Similarly, scientists who have devoted attention to chronicling and understanding the impact of human activity on nature have focused primarily on terrestrial systems. Relatively little emphasis has been placed on changes taking place in the sea because much of it has remained inaccessible for so long. Indeed, for most of the human experience, the world's oceans appeared so vast and limitless as to be impervious to the efforts of people who were barely able to navigate their outer edges, much less observe what was happening beneath the surface. With the exception of those areas along the shoreline that were readily accessible and, therefore, vulnerable to human exploitation, this was generally the case. It is not anymore. We know now that human activity is taking a massive toll on life in the world's oceans, as it has on land.

The detrimental impacts of human society on the Earth's natural systems – on land, in the ocean, and most recently on the global atmosphere – have increasingly been brought to light by scientists. At the same time, as concern mounts over the fate of the Earth's

Ecosystem Approaches to Fisheries: A Global Perspective, ed. V. Christensen and J. Maclean. Published by Cambridge University Press. © Cambridge University Press 2011.

environment, scientists have been drawn into the public debate over the scope and severity of these problems and how they should be addressed. Scientists – prompted by divergent interests to communicate their findings beyond the boundaries of their respective disciplines to the media, policymakers, and resource management agencies – are increasingly encouraged to take a public position on how these resources should be managed. Often, this is unfamiliar or uncomfortable ground for scientists, because it is fraught with political controversy and subject to pressures from constituencies motivated by economic, social, and ethical concerns.

The growing perception that the global environment is in crisis is influencing the way in which some scientists view their disciplines and their roles. Indeed, within such fields as fishery and forestry science, there is mounting pressure to shift away from the traditional emphasis on resource extraction to a focus on maintaining the integrity of ecosystems and ensuring that the life they contain is adequately protected. Managers and scientists in these hard-pressed areas are struggling to redefine their professional roles and responsibilities.

Most scientists would prefer to do their work in less stressful circumstances than those imposed by a global crisis. Sadly, that luxury no longer exists. The crisis is upon us. The potential effects of climate change on the biology of the planet are daunting and open up an entirely new and destructive dimension in the relationship between people and nature. Moreover, just as the world's forests and the millions of species they harbor are rapidly disappearing – for the first time in human history – we are facing the prospect of a relatively lifeless sea, devoid of the vast majority of fish that populated it not so long ago, along with a great many other creatures that inhabit the Earth's marine environment and are important to its well being. And while experts differ over the gravity of the problems we face, few, if any, knowledgeable professionals deny they exist.

Ultimately, the major decisions affecting the global environment will be made by politicians. These decisions will, however, be influenced by scientists. The extent of that influence will depend on the willingness of scientists to engage in the public debate over how best to manage the interaction between people and nature in ways that are beneficial to the former without being lethal to the latter.

Scientists can either embrace the role of helping to inform and shape management decisions and practices, or choose to avoid becoming involved and "let the data speak for itself." Historically, most scientists have opted to focus on the work of science rather than the application of science to the design and implementation of policy. Increasingly, that is a perilous road to travel – not so much for science, although there is the risk that scientists will become the equivalent of Nero fiddling while Rome burns. Rather, it is natural resource policy that is likely to suffer. For in the highly charged debate over what actions need to be taken to preserve and protect nature, scientists generally have the greatest credibility. If they choose to remain silent, their views will go unheeded.

There is no inherent contradiction between having a point of view and doing good science, particularly when the former is based on the latter. Scientists can uphold the highest standards of objectivity in relationship to their work and still be active participants in the debate over conservation policy. In a world where nature is increasingly imperiled by human activity, conservation is a moral imperative. In this regard, neutrality in the public debate over protecting the Earth's basic natural systems is certainly an option – but it is by no means a virtue.

So what does it mean for scientists to become more involved in the formulation and implementation of resource management policy? How can scientists continue to be scientists and also contribute to the broader debate about how society should manage its interaction with nature without compromising their professional credibility? In short, how can scientists also be engaged citizens?

It is unrealistic to suggest that scientists can set the course of national or international environmental policy. The major decisions regarding how countries manage their own environment, as well as that of the global commons (the atmosphere and that part of the oceans that lies beyond the territorial boundaries of individual nations), are complicated, subject to many competing interests, and will inevitably be made by governments. But scientists have an important role to play, for they are in a unique position to inform policymakers on how human society is affecting the global environment; what the consequences of that impact are likely to be for plants, animals, and human life alike; and how we might best manage these resources in ways that will have minimum impact. Whether policymakers heed the advice of scientists is an open question, but they should at least have the opportunity to hear what scientists have to say.

Nor is it only politicians and government officials who should be the beneficiaries of this information. The public needs it as well, because the resources that lie at the heart of the environmental crisis are part of the Earth's great patrimony and must be managed properly for society as a whole. Moreover, in democracies, citizens can, if they choose, wield power through the ballot box. To reach the public, however, or those segments of the public that exert influence on environmental decision making, scientists must be able to communicate to a broader audience than simply their academic peers. To do that, they must learn to use mainstream media, such as newspapers, radio, television, and the Internet.

COMMUNICATION WITH THE PUBLIC

Few scientists communicate their views beyond the books and technical articles they write for specialized audiences and the university classes they teach. Nor does their training prepare them to reach out to broader audiences. This needs to change. Scientists, as part of their professional training, should learn to write and speak to nontechnical audiences. They should be trained to do radio, television, and print interviews, to write opinion editorials for newspapers, to communicate via the Internet, and to speak in public settings outside the lecture hall.

They should also learn how to take advantage of and encourage journalists' interest in their work and to collaborate with conservation and public health organizations with which they share common concerns and goals.

It is not difficult to add training to these skills to the course curriculum of budding scientists, or to ensure that media proficiency is part of their formal training through other types of activities. Ultimately, well-developed communication skills may be as important to their careers as any preparation in biology, ecology, or taxonomy, because such skills will best prepare them to effectively communicate the results of their research to lay people and to inform and shape conservation policy that is grounded in science. Not all scientists will be interested in participating in the environmental policy debate, preferring to focus all their time and attention on the traditional work of science. That is a decision that each individual must make. However, lack of preparation should not be an obstacle for those scientists who want to assume an active public role.

INTERACTION WITH PUBLIC OFFICIALS

In democracies, government decisions regarding the management of natural resources and broad environmental policy are rarely made in a vacuum. People have numerous opportunities to express their concerns and share their perspective with opinion makers and resource managers. These include written, electronic, and spoken communication with public officials and their staff; testimony at formal public hearings and participation in community forums; and collaboration with nongovernmental organizations seeking to influence the design and implementation of environmental policy. Scientists have important roles to play in all these activities and should be equipped to pursue them. Even though many scientists should avoid endorsing one policy over another, at a minimum they may be prepared and encouraged to communicate their research findings and the implications of those findings to lawmakers and their staffs. But to facilitate such interaction, universities, nonprofit organizations, government institutions, and scientists themselves need to establish working relationships and create opportunities that can lead to this kind of interchange.

REMOVING THE BARRIERS TO EXERCISING A PUBLIC VOICE

For many years, the norm within the scientific community has been that its members should refrain from taking public positions on an issue if they might be perceived as jeopardizing the professional objectivity with which they approach their work. More often than not, this has encompassed issues that are contentious and involve factors that have little or nothing to do with science per se, such as job loss and restriction of certain types of commercial and recreational activity on public land.

Unfortunately, when it comes to conservation, most policy debates are contentious and do involve factors that lie beyond the realm of science. For example: Should we reintroduce wolves into areas where they were systematically killed off, despite the objections of livestock owners that the wolves will prey on their cattle or sheep? Should we further restrict quotas in particular fisheries in order to increase their health and that of the broader ecosystem of which they form a part – even though it may cost fishing jobs and income in the short to medium term? Should we ban the use of off-road vehicles in ecologically sensitive areas, although they are popular with recreation enthusiasts? The list goes on. All of these involve ethical, political, and/or economic decisions. So too do some of the most pressing and well known conservation challenges, such as whether we should try to save some of the world's most charismatic species like the mountain gorilla or the Siberian tiger from extinction. Fundamentally, the question of whether we should or should not is not a scientific issue. It is a moral one.

Numerous scientists – Rachel Carson being perhaps the best known – have bucked the norm and adopted strong public positions on controversial conservation issues. Most, however, have tried to side-step taking sides. Quite understandably, scientists typically prefer to avoid this kind of situation. The fear of losing research money, of jeopardizing advancement opportunities, and of being labeled as advocates rather than "objective observers" has discouraged many scientists, particularly those still seeking university tenure and stability, from engaging in the public debate over the environment. There are signs that this is beginning to change, as prominent scientists, both old and young, have adopted wider public roles on some of the world's most serious environmental problems, such as climate change, collapse of marine fisheries, and rampant destruction of forests and other critical wildlife habitats. But the number of scientists who have ventured into the public square remains quite small.

To break down these barriers more rapidly, scientists could receive incentives to communicate their knowledge – and the perspectives gleaned from that knowledge – to the public and to policymakers. Just as scientists accrue "career rewards" for publishing and, in some cases, for excellent teaching, they should also be rewarded for communicating their work via articles in newspapers or magazines, radio and television commentary, and public testimony in legislative forums, among other venues. Universities and research institutions ought to formally acknowledge the contributions of faculty when they contribute to the public debate and exercise their responsibilities as both public citizens and experts in the formulation of policies that are of major consequence to the societies in which they live.

In my view, encouraging scientists to become more involved in conservation policy decisions will help improve those decisions. Admittedly, it is unlikely to quell the debate in the scientific community over whether it is appropriate for scientists to be public advocates. In fact, it may actually exacerbate that debate, bringing it more into the open rather than letting it haunt the corridors of academia. Opponents will argue that advocates of policy remedies that are deemed foolish, unpopular with certain groups, or proved to be unsound not only will discredit themselves but will damage the credibility of all scientists. Or, in cases where the fundamental issue is less a question of science than of ethics, economics, or other factors, critics will assert that scientists have no greater ability or expertise to opine on these topics than anyone else and should avoid such debates because their position as scientists gives them a false veneer of credibility.

There are undoubtedly cases where this will be true. Still, I would assert that the opposite course – that of noninvolvement – is worse. For it denies society the voice of some of our most knowledgeable and thoughtful individuals in the debate over how our environment should be managed, the consequences of which will have enormous implications for the future of life on Earth.

Scientists may not be better equipped than nonscientists to express reasoned opinions over the fundamental moral and ethical issues that often lie at the heart of conservation policy. But they are highly knowledgeable about the causes and consequences of, and often the solutions to, many of the environmental problems we face. They are also particularly well positioned to analyze the trade-offs inherent in the choice of one policy option over another, and to assess the cost to the natural world and ultimately to the human race of doing nothing. To the extent that this information is accompanied by a personal opinion regarding the most advisable course of action to pursue, we should welcome it.

18

Using the science

This chapter outlines my perspective on the scientist not at as a communicator or advocate but as an academic, and how the products of the academic scientist are used in conservation advocacy and by organizations like ours.

I was trained as a true academic. In those days, the rule was that you were not allowed to work on anything in your own backyard – it had to be very far away from where you work if you are going to study it – and it couldn't be of any use to humanity. We were all guilty of the shifting baseline syndrome (Pauly, 1995; Jackson and Jacquet, this volume); wherever we went, we considered the area pristine, or close to it, especially if it was in the tropics. So the academic stereotype is an individual who is not really connected to the real world – in fact, someone who could not be further from the real world. We are blessed in our current state of ocean conservation advocacy that there are scientists, indeed real academic scientists, with respected careers at universities, who are willing to put their work to use.

By conservation advocacy, I mean the work of organizations interested in change, such as Oceana and the Natural Resources Defense Council. These organizations are interested in social change, whether by changing behaviors of fishers or polluters. One of the critical first steps, the truism of social change, is that if we want change to happen, we have to have to first make people dissatisfied with the status quo. This is very obvious, but not necessarily easy to accomplish.

Another relevant aspect of change was articulated by Niccolò Machiavelli (1469–1527). He said in effect that anyone who wants to make change will have a very difficult time because everyone who benefits from the status quo is against it. And there will be only tentative weak support from those who might benefit from the change. Thus, those in favor of change will make enemies. I do believe you can

Ecosystem Approaches to Fisheries: A Global Perspective, ed. V. Christensen and J. Maclean. Published by Cambridge University Press. © Cambridge University Press 2011.

truly know people by their enemies. As an example, I will describe a study by the Natural Research Council of the US Academy of Science commissioned by the National Marine Fisheries Service (Magnuson *et al.*, 2006). It was commissioned by the US Government seemingly to discredit the science done by scientists like Daniel Pauly.

In part, the Government charged that "Several conclusions from these studies have received considerable media coverage and raised public concern and controversy over the effects of fishing on marine ecosystems." A National Academy of Sciences panel was reviewing research because the public was concerned. This was remarkable. It meant that the status quo – in this case represented by the Government – was threatened by the work produced by these individuals. Talk about impact! A study that results in a counter-attack is evidence of success. I find it very encouraging that people are not just ignoring the work of academics.

Some examples are the Myers and Worm (2003) study on decline of large fish species, fishing down food webs (Pauly *et al.*, 1998; Stergiou and Christensen, this volume), and shifting baselines (Pauly, 1995) – all big ideas. They are threatening because they change our view of the status quo. Our vision of the status quo really includes our perspective on where we've been. It informs our perspective on the present, and it incorporates our expectations of future trends. The result of the work of Daniel Pauly and others has been our improved understanding of the true state of the oceans, getting us away from the beautiful pictures in Blue Planet, to something that is a better approximation of reality.

Having both a picture of what things were like in the past, an accurate picture of today, and scenarios going into the future, we should heed the old saying, "If we don't change the direction where we're heading, we're going to end up where we're going." The work of Daniel Pauly and others has shown us the fiction of easy recovery from overfishing.

As mentioned, advocacy organizations like Oceana could not work if they did not allow us to make people unhappy with the status quo. And they could not succeed in this if we did not have the facts. However, the facts are not sufficient, we need the perspective that we get from academic scientists.

Scientists have also given the conservation advocacy community big ideas. They have given us ways of organizing our work, given us ways of talking about how the world should be viewed, and how oceans should be managed. There is no question that the ecosystem approach comes from the scientific community, and fisheries concepts like "keep the big old females from getting slaughtered" are part of the basis for our work on the ecosystem approach.

Scientists are showing that fishing gear matters, and that allows people to think about the oceans as more than just a catch curve. There is collateral damage depending on how we fish. Concepts like marine protected areas as a management tool have also come from the academic community. All of these drive the agendas of conservation advocacy organizations.

Academic scientists also give us ammunition. I use the term deliberately because it is an apt metaphor for many advocacy organizations: they have guns, they have them aimed, but they need ammunition. This ammunition very often comes from specific incidents in the oceans that we think require action in response. We may not know about them adequately – or would have no credibility if we talked about them – if it were not for the work of credible academic scientists.

For example, Barbara Block's paper reporting on bluefin tuna spawning in the Gulf of Mexico (Block et al., 2005) led almost immediately to a petition fronted by several organizations, including Carl Safina's Blue Ocean Institute and Oceana, to protect critical breeding areas in the Gulf from destruction by longliners. The story of the leatherback turtle (Safina, 2006) has led to a tremendous amount of work by conservation organizations to save them. The Atlantic cod, of course, has been a spectacular shifting baseline story – with recovery taking decades. Similarly, the decline of sharks has been well described by Baum and Myers (2004), and the spectacular decline of table fish in the North Atlantic over the last century (Christensen et al., 2003). Another is the damage caused by bottom trawling to deep sea corals – unknown to conservation groups before the work of scientists, first documented in Norway (Fosså et al., 2002). Yet another example is the barndoor skate, which was petitioned to be on the endangered species list following publication about its near extinction (Casey and Myers, 1998).

So our world view, the context that advocacy organizations work in, comes from academic scientists. Yet there are some who say, "What more can I do? What more can I give you?". And after being asked questions, some of them difficult, even seeming impossible to answer initially, Daniel Pauly took on the assignment of providing answers – answers to questions that we did not even know we had in some cases. The Sea Around Us project, which he leads, is a wonderful resource for conservation organizations. You can find out what is being caught in a country's exclusive economic zone (EEZ); where a species is being caught and who's catching it; and what is happening on the high seas. And you can now find out the size of the ecological footprint of countries all over the world. Thus, you can learn not only what a country is doing in its own EEZ but also what it is doing in the EEZs of other countries or on the high seas.

There are many academics who might, by chance, produce information that is useful in conservation or they may be interested in conservation, but do not want to get too closely connected to advocacy organizations because of the potential loss of credibility that may result. And while those scientists are certainly very useful to us in our advocacy role, it is very rare – and Daniel Pauly is one of those very rare scientists – that they will actually ask, "what will be useful?". I know this is the case because following a lecture at Oceana recently, Pauly said "here are all the things that the Sea Around Us project is doing and is planning to do in the future. What else would you like us to do?". I responded by asking for an ecological footprint map. At the time, Daniel was a little evasive, not knowing the degree of difficulty. But now it is done, and I can assure you that it is already of use and will continue to be of use to conservation organizations. Thank you, Daniel, for all that you have done, continue to do, and will do in the future, and thank you to all the other academics who are willing to think about the use to which their work can and should be put. We look forward to working closely with you for many, many years to come.

REFERENCES

Baum, J. K. and Myers, R. A. (2004) Shifting baselines and the decline of pelagic sharks in the Gulf of Mexico. *Ecology Letters*, 7, 135–145.

Block, B., Teo, S., Walli, A., Boustany, A., Stokesbury, M., Farwell, C., Weng, K., Dewar, H. and Williams, T. (2005) Electronic tagging and population structure of Atlantic bluefin tuna. *Nature*, 434, 1121–1127.

Casey, J. M. and Myers, R. A. (1998) Near extinction of a large, widely distributed fish. *Science*, 281, 690–692.

Christensen, V., Guenette, S., Heymans, J. J., Walters, C. J., Watson, R., Zeller, D. and Pauly, D. (2003) Hundred-year decline of North Atlantic predatory fishes. *Fish and Fisheries*, 4, 1–24.

Fosså, J., Mortensen, P. and Furevik, D. (2002) The deep-water coral *Lophelia pertusa* in Norwegian waters: distribution and fishery impacts. *Hydrobiologia*, 471, 1–12.

Magnuson, J., Cowan Jr, L., Crowder, L., Dallmeyer, D., Deriso, R., Paine, R., Parma, A., Rosenberg, A. and Wilen, J. (2006) *Dynamic Changes in Marine Ecosystems: Fishing, Food Webs, and Future Options*. Washington, DC: National Academy Press.

Myers, R. A. and Worm, B. (2003) Rapid worldwide depletion of predatory fish communities. *Nature*, 423, 280–283.

Pauly, D. (1995) Anecdotes and the shifting baseline syndrome of fisheries. *Trends in Ecology & Evolution*, 10, 430.

Pauly, D., Christensen, V., Dalsgaard, J., Froese, R. and Torres, F. (1998) Fishing down marine food webs. *Science*, 279, 860–863.

Safina, C. (2006) *Voyage of the Turtle: In Pursuit of the Earth's Last Dinosaur*. New York: Henry Holt.

19

The scientist as communicator

As the state of scientific knowledge has advanced and scientists have peered into the ocean and seen its future more clearly, many have realized that it is not enough to publish their findings in academic journals. They have come to understand that the role of scientists has to change with times now dominated by industrial lobbyists, influence peddlers, spin-doctors, and professional contrarians. Fisheries ministers, for the most part, do not read peer-reviewed journals, and so if scientists are to share their wisdom with the wider world, they have to come out of their ivory towers to take to the public podium, return news reporters' calls, testify before policymakers, and let their knowledge be heard – or cede the debate to those who at best know far less, and at worst arrive with an agenda.

A call to arms of sorts came in a paper published in *Science* in 1998 and written by Jane Lubchenco, who was then president of the American Association for the Advancement of Science (and now Under Secretary of Commerce and Administrator of NOAA). She proposed a new social contract that would have scientists "communicate their knowledge and understanding widely in order to inform decisions of individuals and institutions." She suggested her colleagues invoke "the full power of the scientific enterprise in discovering new knowledge, in communicating existing and new understanding to the public and to policymakers and in helping society move towards sustainability through a better understanding of the consequences of policy actions – or inaction."

Traditionally, scientists have viewed their role in science more narrowly: ask questions that would advance the state of knowledge and then go out and find those answers. Successful publication in a peer-reviewed journal was the end game, the final act in a long and difficult process. Today, more and more scientists recognize the limits of this

Ecosystem Approaches to Fisheries: A Global Perspective, ed. V. Christensen and J. Maclean. Published by Cambridge University Press. © Cambridge University Press 2011.

tradition and are moving beyond publication to communicate their results to the wider world.

Inadequate and antiquated policies as well as the unraveling of previously established protections are among the reasons that scientists feel they must become involved in communicating what they know. Universities, fellowship programs, and individual scientists are beginning to acknowledge the importance of communicating science. Historically however, scientists were often penalized rather than rewarded by their peers for going beyond publication to the communication of their results to media, policymakers, and the public. Thus, the decision to get involved is usually not an easy one.

Daniel Pauly is among those at the forefront in this shifting culture of science. His sphere of influence goes far beyond his reams of publications in scientific literature. Indeed, he has a knack for broad-based statistical analyses that have upended fisheries dogma and shown leadership that has shaken up fisheries management circles. Equal to his scientific record is his reach around the globe, alerting journalists, the public, and policymakers to the problems facing the world's future fish supplies. When it comes to fisheries, Pauly is one of the most effective science communicators of his time, at a time when such communication is urgently needed.

As a young researcher, Pauly thought strategically about his career and followed the counsel of Peter Medawar (1979), in his book *Advice to a Young Scientist*: "Any scientist who wants to make important discoveries must study an important problem."

From his earliest days as a scientist, Pauly was concerned with poverty, food security, and solving management issues where data were sparse. He designed new ways to problem solve and shared his approaches with the scientific community. Today, he is also sharing his discoveries with the wider world. Pauly, along with a growing number of other researchers, believes academic scientists have an obligation to make themselves heard when science is not put to use for the public good, especially since scientists who work for governments are often censored and silenced.

In recent years, Pauly and a handful of others have brought fisheries and the problems facing oceans into the mainstream. Pauly (2005) believes that "scientists should be able to articulate the political implications of their science – this is not something that should be reserved for policymakers who are often very far removed from the science itself."

Pauly's common sense ability to explain complexity has played a major role in bringing a new awareness to unsustainable ways of conducting fisheries – a topic of global concern that until fairly recently had only echoed in the mazes of government bureaucracies and ivory towers of academia. His outspokenness has raised the ire of some other scientists, while his ability to call it like he sees it – often before anyone else – has sometimes been called egoism. But Pauly's ability to ask big questions and then, with the help of his team, to reveal the answers, has repeatedly proven him right.

Reflecting on how science advances, cancer researcher Judah Folkman was quoted as saying "You have to think ahead. Science goes where you imagine it" (Kalb, 2008). While visionaries may see things before others, they cannot always find their way alone. In fisheries science, Pauly is often the front man, venturing out on a tightrope across the abyss of the unknown. He and his skillful team of colleagues design the meta-analyses and models to test his ideas – much of which Pauly freely admits is beyond his own technical know-how. Once, in an interview with *Nature* (Anon., 2003), he summarized himself in the form of a title of a paper: "Longitudinal single case study documents instance of a scientist 'making it' notwithstanding apparent lack of key skills." Pauly's collaboration with his teammates in the Sea Around Us project at the University of British Columbia's Fisheries Centre has produced a series of highly cited papers published in top tier journals. Yet these papers alone would not have garnered as much attention without Pauly's commitment to communicating their results. This is what sets him apart.

While his ability to ask original and penetrating questions about "The Sea Around Us" leads to the "big" science that is his trademark, his talent as a communicator lies in his original forms of expression. He is a storyteller, and the business of journalism is based on stories. He is a master of metaphor, who invites audiences to envision memorable comparisons to understand what is going on in global fisheries. His comparisons are sometimes startling, which grabs the attention of journalists, policymakers, and the public alike.

Asked to explain his success as a communicator Pauly replies, "Compelling graphics have helped me immensely to get the message across. As well, my public lectures tend to combine a 'heavy' message with some levity in the form of the presentation, and this somehow seems just right to get the message across" (Anon., 2003). Journalists know that they can always count on Daniel for a pithy sound bite that is catchy, clever, and directly on point.

In the interview with *Nature* (Anon., 2003) he was asked, "How would you like to be remembered?" His reply: "As the one who showed that the effect of fisheries on marine life is equivalent to that of a large meteor strike on terrestrial life."

Here are some examples of Pauly's science and how he translates it to audiences outside academia.

FISHING DOWN MARINE FOOD WEBS

Pauly is perhaps best known for his description and documentation with his colleagues of the "fishing down marine food webs" concept (Pauly *et al.*, 1998; see Stergiou and Christensen, this volume). While this paper is considered a classic amongst marine ecologists and fisheries scientists, what is more remarkable is that the concept has become widely cited by journalists and policymakers. The reason is that Pauly summed up years of work and mountains of data into a simple graphic that is now used far and wide, and a few oft-repeated catch phrases. "Fishing down marine food webs" has become part of the vernacular in some circles.

Then he spices it up for general audiences with a hint of humor, "Having systematically stripped the oceans of the top predators, we are now eating bait, and we're headed for jellyfish ... my children will tell their children, 'eat your jellyfish soup'" (Baron, 1998).

MARINE RESERVES

When Pauly ticks off problems that face the ocean, he often points to the need for large no-take marine reserves as part of the solution, given their present tiny proportion of the world's oceans (0.8%) and the slow growth of this coverage (Wood *et al.*, 2008). Pauly invests a great deal of time giving public lectures on the importance of marine reserves which have been vigorously resisted by those who baulk at the idea of further restrictions on industrial or recreational fishing. But Pauly can diffuse hostility with humor. His talks frequently begin with a map of the global ocean painted red. The slide reads, "All the areas in green are protected in marine reserves." It takes a moment for the audience to realize there is no green on the map. This quietens his detractors and softens the crowd. "If you want to keep a population going, you have to limit the area where it interfaces with death so there will be some that can live their whole life cycle and reproduce," says Pauly. "This is why we need marine reserves. Yet, fish, until recently, had marine protected areas. They were the places that the fish could hide. But technology has stripped them all away. We add vitamins to food because they have been lost through technology. A marine protected area replaces a natural refuge that technology has made us lose" (Baron, 1998). Again Pauly uses metaphor and common sense examples.

THE DECLINE IN GLOBAL FISHERIES

Pauly has created a niche for his team as global auditors who design meta-analyses to test the accepted state of fisheries. They have been a thorn in the sides of government organizations that downplay the problems and cling to the status quo.

In 2001, Reg Watson and Daniel Pauly (2001) challenged the very basis of international fisheries management: the data reported to the Food and Agriculture Organization (FAO) of the United Nations, the only institution that keeps official global fisheries statistics. As a United Nations organization, the FAO collects but is usually not able to verify or correct the statistics reported by member countries, even when they are suspected of being wrong. Reg Watson and Daniel Pauly resolved to do a forensic audit of these official reports.

Using the FAO's catch data and a massive statistical analysis that compared the predicted fisheries catch against those reported, they revealed errors in the official fishery statistics. Their study, published in *Nature*, showed that China had vastly over-reported their fisheries catch. These inflated numbers, combined with the large and wildly fluctuating catch of a small fish (the Peruvian anchoveta) painted a false picture of the health of the oceans: they masked an actual decline in global fisheries that started in the late 1980s, giving the impression that "business as usual" was sustainable. "I have been troubled a long time by the mismatch between what we know is the case for various fisheries – that they are going downhill – and the triumphalist reports of a global catch that continues to increase," said Daniel Pauly. "This study reconciles what we see at the local level – failing fisheries – with what is happening at the global level – falling catches."

To clarify the message, Pauly, with the assistance of SeaWeb worked on a press release that would not only present the science but answer the question "So what? Why does this matter to me?" Pauly realized that the public would not relate to the graphs in the actual paper as the public and journalists generally cannot read graphs. At least, not unless the graphs are very simple. Reg Watson translated the original graph: "What does this mean in terms of the availability of seafood for each of us – over the years?" This got people's attention.

When the study hit the news, the media ripples went straight to China. As Daniel told the story in an interview with National Public Radio, "China's over-reporting stuck out like a sore thumb. ... It's like a monstrous storm on the weather map." The response to the Associated Press by a Chinese official was, "well, we don't do that anymore." China later retracted this admission but the word was out. The message of the paper opaquely titled in *Nature* as "Systematic Distortions in World Fisheries" became clear. Time and time again the headlines read "Something's Fishy in Global Fisheries." While the FAO was initially upset, this subsequently led to improved attention to this problem; also the FAO now reports global fisheries statistics with and without China, thus implicitly endorsing the Watson and Pauly (2001) study.

THIRD PARTY COMMENTATOR

Many journalists turn to Pauly for comments, not only on his own work, but also on that of others. Not only does he have credibility, he can also be relied upon to describe a paper succinctly in a way that helps journalists as well as their public audiences grasp the significance of a study. The cover story of the 15 May 2003 issue of *Nature* revealed that we have only 10% of all large predatory fish – both open ocean species including tuna, swordfish, marlin, and large ground fish, such as cod, halibut, skate, and flounder – left in the sea (Myers and Worm, 2003). Most strikingly, the study showed that industrial fisheries took only 10–15 years to grind any newly exploited fishery to one tenth of what it was before.

Journalists turned to Pauly for his interpretation. "The longlining data tell a story we have not heard before," he said. "It shows how Japanese longlining has expanded globally. It is like a hole burning through paper. As the hole expands, the edge is where the fisheries concentrate until there is nowhere left to go."

This quote appeared time and time again in the wave of media awareness generated by the study. There are many other examples of Pauly offering a third party perspective on a paper in which he was not directly involved. While some scientists may not consider it worth their time to talk to journalists about other scientists' papers, this can be time well spent as it builds credibility and often leads to the journalist returning time and time again to trusted sources and experts. Journalists are always looking for someone to help put science in perspective. Hence scientists do public service by taking the time and trouble to comment on topics they understand.

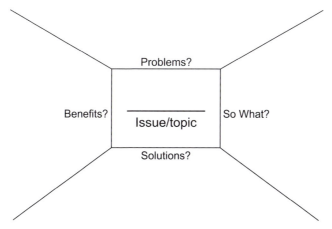

Figure 19.1 Message box developed by SeaWeb, a multimedia public education project, for communication by scientists to journalists.

THE OVERFISHING STORY

Journalists are always looking for stories. Yet "thinking story" like a journalist is very different from the way scientists describe their work. The trick is for scientists to learn how to take that scientific methodology that's so deeply ingrained, and tell a story that explains "what's the problem, so what, what are the solutions, and what would be the benefits."

Figure 19.1 presents a "message box," a tool that scientists can use to translate their scientific studies into a story format. Pauly intuitively follows the principles of storytelling, remembering to explain why it matters and what are the solutions.

The issue is overfishing: Pauly can be blunt when he speaks about the abuse of ocean ecosystems due to overfishing, but he tells the story in ways that people can understand.

What is the problem? In Daniel's words: "The industry has acted like a terrible tenant who trashes their rental."

So what? "As a society, we don't have to do everything we *can* do. We don't allow people to drive over the speed limit to get somewhere faster, we don't allow machine guns to hunt deer, and we need not allow destruction of our marine resources."

What are the solutions? "This is why we need marine reserves. You need fish to make fish." What are the benefits? "A future with fish and food security."

A HIPPOCRATIC OATH FOR THE SEAS

In 2005, Pauly won the International Cosmos Prize from the Expo '90 Foundation in Japan for both his scientific and communications work. In his acceptance speech, he came out with a strong message addressing the most sensitive question in the minds of most scientists: should scientists be advocates for their work and at what point do they cross the line and lose their scientific credibility?

Pauly likens the role of ecological scientists to that of physicians for the planet. In his view, many scientists working on environment related issues have been too meek when managers, lobbyists, and politicians have challenged or contorted the results of their work. In his acceptance speech Pauly (2005) declared, "The main tool they have used to silence us is the notion that an engagement of the environment would compromise our scientific objectivity. Yet this argument is never invoked in medicine. Indeed passionate engagement for the patients against disease causing agents is not only the norm, but an essential element of doctors' professional ethics."

What Pauly is saying is that environmental scientists should have a Hippocratic oath that dictates: "First do no harm." If a scientist knows that a course of action by managers or policymakers will result in environmental harm, they have a professional and ethical obligation to stand up and be heard, and to speak up on behalf of "the patient" – in his case the ocean and fisheries.

> We must learn to combine scientific integrity with taking firm positions, not only on the conservation of the plants and animals about which we have expertise, but also for the continued existence of the ecosystems of which they are parts … we can secure continued (ecosystem) services only if we give them the space they need and the time they need … It is the job of scientists working on ecosystems and on wild flora and fauna to remind politicians and the public of that, and being silent when this is not taken into account is unethical.

In his own career and in his encouragement of his scientific colleagues, Pauly both embodies and instills these ethics. As Principal Investigator of the Sea Around Us project, Pauly leads a flourishing cadre of top fisheries scientists to produce groundbreaking new research, but equally important, he teaches young scientists that doing world-class science is not enough. The need for science to inform policy and management decisions is emerging as one of the critical needs of society. Even when choices facing society are moral and ethical, science can help people understand the consequences of different choices.

"We came here to make a difference," said Dr. Jackie Alder, then a research fellow at the Fisheries Centre (now with the United Nations Environment Programme in Nairobi) in a profile of Pauly published in the New York Times (Yoon, 2003). "If you want to stir the pot, he'll hand you the spoon."

REFERENCES

Anon. (2003) Lifelines: Daniel Pauly. *Nature*, 421, 23.
Baron, N. (1998) The Straits of Georgia. *Georgia Straight*, 22, 1602.
Kalb, C. (2008) A quiet hero in the cancer war. Dr. Judah Folkman, in memoriam. *Newsweek*, January 28.
Lubchenco, J. (1998) Entering the century of the environment: a new social contract for science. *Science*, 279, 491.
Medawar, P. B. (1979) *Advice to a Young Scientist*. New York, NY: Basic Books.
Myers, R. A. and Worm, B. (2003) Rapid worldwide depletion of predatory fish communities. *Nature*, 423, 280–283.
Pauly, D. (2005) An ethic for marine science: thoughts on receiving the International Cosmos Prize. *Sea Around Us Newsletter*, 32, November/ December 2005.
Pauly, D., Christensen, V., Dalsgaard, J., Froese, R. and Torres, F., Jr. (1998) Fishing down marine food webs. *Science*, 279, 860–863.
Watson, R. and Pauly, D. (2001) Systematic distortions in world fisheries catch trends. *Nature*, 414, 534–536.
Wood, L., Fish, L., Laughren, J. and Pauly, D. (2008) Assessing progress towards global marine protection targets: shortfalls in information and action. *Oryx*, 42, 340–351.
Yoon, C. K. (2003) Scientist at work: Daniel Pauly; iconoclast looks for fish and finds disaster. *New York Times*. January, 21.

20

Scenario development for decision making

Turning the tide is easy. Tides are after all very predictable; just wait for the right moment before pushing the water back. When it comes to re-directing a current it is far more difficult – it takes climate change to shift the Gulf Stream.

What is happening to the world's fisheries, at the local, regional, or global scale appears to be more like a one-way current than a tide with ups and downs (Pauly *et al.*, 2003). Strong enforcement of effort restrictions may bring a relief in the parts of the world where strong governance is in place (Worm *et al.*, 2009), while most of the world's marine ecosystems continue to be overexploited. We are gradually eroding many of the ecosystems on which our food supply from the oceans relies, even if we may not notice it as individuals (Pauly, 1995). What can we do to curb the direction of widespread degradation? It is a daunting task to embark on – one where we cannot explicitly express how we will go about solving the problem. We do, however, have an idea of, and experience with, techniques and materials we can use to deliver a small contribution toward the solution.

What is clear is that if we as scientists are to make such contributions we must speak up and seek to be heard (Baron, this volume). We must convey the best available scientific information to decision and policymakers (Reichert, this volume). But, how may we go about explaining this to, for instance, politicians who may have very little background and knowledge about ocean resources, yet be tasked with overseeing it?

We take as a starting point that few ministers of fisheries actually have a clear picture of what it is they are managing; they don't go to sea. Their agricultural colleagues appear in the evening news when there is a crisis, kicking the soil and handling the grain. How do you take a minister of fisheries on a field trip? And how can we show the minister

Ecosystem Approaches to Fisheries: A Global Perspective, ed. V. Christensen and J. Maclean. Published by Cambridge University Press. © Cambridge University Press 2011.

the impact we have had on ocean resources, and those our future actions will have? We can get underwater video showing how things look now, but not how they were before industrialized fisheries became the rule, and we certainly cannot show how things will look in the future based on video footage.

Can our ecosystem models then be used to create a credible virtual reality, credible enough to convince a politician that what s/he is watching is real? To answer the question, we need to consider at least two aspects; one relates to whether the ecosystem models are up to the task, the second whether we can link the models to a photorealistic-style 3D-visualization in such a way as to create an underwater make-believe world.

A necessary factor for us to even consider an approach as outlined above is that ecosystem modeling has taken some major steps in recent years linked to the incorporation of foraging arena considerations (Walters and Martell, 2004; Walters and Christensen, 2007), and making us quite capable of reproducing the known history of exploited populations in a large range of marine ecosystems (Christensen and Walters, this volume). We are learning in the process that to explain historic trends we must, as a rule, include fisheries as well as environmental factors (e.g., Guénette *et al.*, 2006). This provides an important component of the techniques we need to set up realistic, virtual field trips. As for materials, we have at hand a suite of global, spatial databases that can be used for database-driven model generation (see Christensen, this volume), which when combined with local information can be used to parameterize the ecosystem models needed for the field-trip simulations.

Adding to this is progress in gaming-theoretical approaches needed to set up a realistic framework for the future scenario simulations. Going back to the "fish wars" approach of Levhari and Mirman (1980), the games of Carl Walters and colleagues (Walters, 1994), the work of Clark *et al.* (2005), and the recent integration of economic value chain and ecosystem modeling (Christensen, 2010; Christensen *et al.*, 2010) we now have a well-developed portfolio for including economic aspects, while the human behavior aspects still need improvement. Adding to this is research in human–computer interactions aimed at improving such interactions in environmental group decision-support systems (Lai, 2008).

A major component to be added is visualization. We are, as scientists, inclined to communicate with other scientists. Our tools are designed to that end, and presenting figures in PowerPoint and tables in papers may well be the right media for such purposes. If we examine the world where decisions about ecosystem management are made, it is, however, one dominated by people with very diverse backgrounds and experience. We therefore need to consider means of communication going beyond our usual repertoire. Visualizations can provide powerful messages, and, if built on the best available science, the messages may also be convincing and enabling. The behavior of a flight simulator is trusted by the professional pilots who train on it. Can we develop something corresponding for environmental decision making? That is what we are doing.

We have entered in partnership with the Lenfest Ocean Program (www.lenfestocean.org) to develop a methodology for "Ocean Summits" ambitiously aimed at shifting the current (www.lenfest oceanfutures.org). We intend to bring together decision makers for a couple of days' deliberations about the management of specific ecosystems. We will work for months prior to each summit with scientists from the given area to produce an ecosystem model describing the known history of exploitation, as well as to describe the social and economical aspects for the system utilization. At the summits we will run through the ecosystem history visualized in 3D, above and below the surface, and emphasize ecological, economic, and social impacts of our exploitation. This will set the stage for forward-looking scenarios aimed at quickly exploring how ecosystem and society are likely to react to management interactions and resulting fishing pressure. The people at the table will represent all aspects of the management process, including wide stakeholder-representation. For this, we are developing software for environmental group decision support that incorporates multiple objectives and management options, all as part of a theoretical gaming approach.

Building a decision support system for decision makers such as politicians is more complex than building systems for golfers, who may just want to know if it is going to rain or not. We will need to develop, explore, and present a series of alternative options and highlight trade-offs, but yet simplify the output of the complex simulation, in order to focus the attention. Just as an airplane instrument panel only presents the key information to the pilot, while the flight engineer and ground staff access the more technical information needed to ensure a safe flight, we need to present the key indicators to the managers, while the details of the data gathering and analysis are left to the care of the scientists. There are many aspects to consider when building a system of this ambition, and our focus is on four components, the hardware, software, procedure, and people (DeSanctis and Gallupe, 1987).

The hardware plays a critical role in building group decision systems. The type, location, and size of hardware have the capacity to significantly alter the flow during the decision process. Computers have to be responsive, notably fast enough to not impede the decision-making processes. As an example, scenario exploration cannot be done if a scenario run takes three hours, not to talk of three weeks as is common for many fine-scale models.

Computers with high-end video cards are needed to output real-time 3D photo-realistic visualizations as are intended for the summits, yet the capabilities called for are not beyond what are currently available. The use of displays also needs to be carefully considered. Displays have to be closely tied to the spatial arrangement as decision room based systems, e.g., with the table shaped like a horse shoe with a central display (DeSanctis and Gallupe, 1987), or a legislative session type arrangement for a larger group, or possibly systems where participants are attending remotely; all would play a significant role in the design of a decision support system. The size and resolution (Ni *et al.*, 2006) can affect navigation tasks, and location can impede on privacy issues if not carefully considered (Shoemaker and Inkpen, 2001). The privacy issues relate to how information is shared on common displays or is restricted to private displays. It has been demonstrated that the question of shared versus private displays may be especially important for the communication processes during summits when participants have hidden agendas (Lai, 2008).

How one interacts with the decision system is also important. People who are not "natural" mouse and keyboard users may have to use cognitive resources to point and click to navigate the system for information (Buxton, 1983), instead of focusing on the discussion at hand. More universal access forms (Holzinger, 2003), such as touch and gesture based displays (Forlines *et al.*, 2007), could minimize the use of the cognitive resources, and all should be considered when designing summit procedures.

Software also plays an important role in designing successful summits. The interface of the software can greatly support or impede the flow of the process. The underlying scientific modeling software outputs a large diversity of results. The gaming interface, which communicates with the underlying scientific software, needs to be designed to quickly browse key indicators selected from the results, and to compare indicators between different scenario runs.

The indicators may have to be aggregated to summarize each scenario, but aggregation, in turn, requires weighting of indicators. This is problematic, as summit participants will allocate different importance to the various indicators based on their interests.

The procedure of the summit must be closely considered. The procedure is important to keep the participants informed, integrated, and collaborative during the process. Pre-summit procedures to build the ecosystem model and other models and data ahead of time are required to ensure participants know that the scenarios are realistic and built on the best available science, enabling suspension of disbelief while exploring scenarios during the summits.

The Aspen Institute Congressional Program (Paarlberg, 2001) provides a good example where the program enforces strong procedures to enforce policy neutrality, internal privacy where what happens within the summit is not exposed to the general public, and detachment from representations such as political parties or viewpoints. These procedures aim at building an environment conducive to collaboration.

Lastly, when building a group decision support system, one has to consider who the participants will be, their knowledge of the topic, and the problems faced. One must consider the participants' ability to read graphs and charts, their trust in the model software, and their trust of the other participants in the summit. Participants will rarely be expert users capable of aggregating memory (Ericsson and Kintsch, 1995). In general the cognitive short-term memory capacity of most humans is limited to approximately seven units (Miller, 2003). Overloading participants with the diversity of available simulation data, graphs, and tables, will entice the users to dwell in details, and move the discussion away from the higher-level issues at hand. Further, understanding problems related to task switching (Norman and Shallice, 2000), such as using the computer to navigate from one indicator to another, should be minimized to enable smooth discussions.

There is a need for a facilitator to enable the use of the group decision process (DeSanctis and Gallupe, 1987). A facilitator can act in three different modes; the first is user-driven, where participants receive some initial training, then fully use the system as they wish (Gallupe et al., 1988), the second is facilitator-driven, where a non-group member directs the participants as to what features to use and when to use them (McCartt and Rohrbaugh, 1989). The last is the chauffeur-driven system where a non-group member, who knows the technical aspects of the system, acts at the direction of the participants, but does not direct or advise the group during the process (Jarvenpaa *et al.*, 1988).

All of the four components discussed above interact and play an important role for the design of a successful summit. While the visualizations and the underlying modeling approach are important for conveying impact, they will only set the stage for the negotiations at the table. The aim is to enable discussions and display results, notably of trade-offs resulting from alternative management decisions. It is not intended to point to "best solutions" to be obtained, e.g., through optimizations (though such optimizations are indeed feasible and will be used to provide reference points). We hope there will be win–win scenarios emerging (shifting the current, remember?) but realize that there are serious trade-off issues to be dealt with in a world of "real-politik" that may limit the feasible options (Walters and Coleman, 2004).

Constructing the software for the Ocean Summits has involved a total redesign and reprogramming of the underlying Ecopath with Ecosim (EwE) software system (Christensen and Pauly, 1992; Pauly *et al.*, 2000; Christensen and Walters, 2004); a new version was required in order to link EwE to the visualization software.

We have linked the Ecosim model of EwE directly to a 3D-gaming engine, the open-source Blender, in such a way as to render real-time visualizations of how many fish of different species appear over time as the simulations unfold (Figure 20.1). This may well be the first time that a gaming engine has been used for real-time visualizations of scientific data, controlled by a scientific model.

By linking the ecosystem model to the gaming engine we have made it possible to visualize in real-time how management may impact ecosystem resources through interventions. We do so by designing a decision support system, which assumes that (1) the models represent the best available science, and (2) it should be possible to explore alternative scenarios, without having the scientists behind the model doing the scenario evaluations. Instead we leave this to the summit participants; they are in control. This represents a break with how management councils typically operate – an expert is commissioned to explore some alternatives, and s/he shows up at the requested time to give a presentation, hand over a report, and answer questions. The models and software are as a rule expert systems that hardly ever can be operated by more than the few experts who developed them. We break with this, by constructing alternative interfaces for the decision support systems, and while the underlying scientific models are the same, the simplified interface for the Ocean Summits allows decision

Figure 20.1 Scene from underwater visualization developed by the Lenfest Ocean Futures project using the Blender 3D-gaming engine. Visualization: Mike Pan and Dalai Felinto.

makers to explore scenarios, with themselves in the driving seat, developing and deciding on the scenario explorations. What would happen if we placed a protected area here? Or, could we open a new fishery for this prey species without jeopardizing the livelihood for those who rely on harvesting its predators?

We present the outcome of the simulations in different ways. The field-trip visualizations are important to give a visual impression of a large set of complex abundance estimates and resulting exploitation patterns. Try to visualize how life on the Grand Banks off the Canadian east coast has changed over the last several hundred years. Explorers described how they could tell they were on the banks from the large numbers of birds living off the abundant resources, and some describe how the cod were so abundant as to stop the boats. We do not have any footage from that time, but we can generate it virtually. Fast forward to modern times, where we can visualize how the cod stocks have plummeted, harvesting shooting up, only to land us in a seemingly new permanent state where the ecosystem is dominated by invertebrates, sculpins, seals, etc., and cod is just a factor in old peoples' memories.

We can replicate this history with ecosystem modeling based on historic information, be it from scientific data or traditional knowledge. The coupling of the scientific model and the gaming engine gives us the capability to not just imagine in our heads how life in the ecosystem and among fishers of the Grand Banks has changed but also to show it using virtual reality.

Figure 20.2 Scene from the animated documentary "Life in Chesapeake Bay" co-produced by NOAA Chesapeake Bay and the Lenfest Ocean Futures Project. Developed using the Blender 3D-gaming engine. Visualization: Mike Pan and Dalai Felinto.

Another of the thousands of potential cases is Chesapeake Bay, which used to be dominated by vast banks of oysters. They are gone now, and may never return. Here, we have used visualizations to describe key aspects of the history and ecology of the Chesapeake Bay in a six-minute animated documentary (Lai and Christensen, 2009; http://ecopath.org/LifeInTheChesapeakeBay/) in the process further developing the visualization techniques (Figure 20.2).

We are, for the development of the Ocean Summits methodology, relying heavily on the scenario laboratory at the UBC Fisheries Centre, even though we do not anticipate that more than a few of the anticipated summits will be held there. The scenario laboratory is designed with the defined intention of enabling the form of cooperation and visualization that is needed for the Ocean Summits – almost with "war-room" functionality (Figure 20.3). Technically, this is achieved with focus on enabling discussions around a high-tech super-ellipse table, while allowing all participants a sense of immersion through large wall flat screens, and a sense of control through direct access to information and management controls via the built-in workstations as well as to the resulting impacts.

Both the modeling and visualizations represent clear challenges, but they are challenges we are fairly certain we can meet, making it a technical and scientific challenge, rather than an art form. Where the

Figure 20.3 The Scenario Laboratory at the UBC Fisheries Centre is constructed for use as a decision support facility and is a highly interactive facility designed to facilitate scenario development and exploration. Underwater visualizations play an important part for communicating ecosystem effects of management interventions. Photo: Sherman Lai.

art comes in is in getting the summit participants to actually explore and eventually adopt ecosystem-based management options that will change the direction we have taken in most of the world's ecosystems – in shifting the current.

REFERENCES

Buxton, W. (1983) Lexical and pragmatic considerations of input structures. *ACM SIGGRAPH Computer Graphics*, 17, 31–37.

Christensen, V. (2010) MEY = MSY. *Fish and Fisheries*, 11, 105–110.

Christensen, V. and Pauly, D. (1992) Ecopath II: a software for balancing steady-state ecosystem models and calculating network characteristics. *Ecological Modelling*, 61, 169–185.

Christensen, V., Steenbeek, J. and Failler, P. (2010) A combined ecosystem and value chain modeling approach for evaluating societal cost and benefit of fishing. Working paper # 2010-06. Vancouver, Canada: Fisheries Centre, University of British Columbia.

Christensen, V. and Walters, C. J. (2004) Ecopath with Ecosim: methods, capabilities and limitations. *Ecological Modelling*, 172, 109–139.

Clark, C. W., Munro, G. R. and Sumaila, U. R. (2005) Subsidies, buybacks, and sustainable fisheries. *Journal of Environmental Economics and Management*, 50, 47–58.

DeSanctis, G. and Gallupe, R. B. (1987) A foundation for the study of group decision support systems. *Management Science*, 33, 589–609.

Ericsson, K. and Kintsch, W. (1995) Long-term working memory. *Psychological Review*, 102, 211–244.

Forlines, C., Wigdor, D., Shen, C. and Balakrishnan, R. (2007) *Direct-touch Versus Mouse Input for Tabletop Displays*. New York, NY: ACM, pp. 647–656.

Gallupe, R. B., DeSanctis, G. and Dickson, G. W. (1988) Computer-based support for group problem-finding: an experimental investigation. *MIS Quarterly*, 12, 277–296.

Guénette, S., Heymans, J. J., Christensen, V. and Trites, A. W. (2006) Ecosystem models show combined effects of fishing, predation, competition, and ocean productivity on Steller sea lions (*Eumetopias jubatus*) in Alaska. *Canadian Journal of Fisheries and Aquatic Sciences*, 63, 2495–2517.

Holzinger, A. (2003) Finger instead of mouse: touch screens as a means of enhancing universal access. In *Lecture Notes in Computer Science*. Heidelberg, Germany: Springer, pp. 387–397.

Jarvenpaa, S. L., Rao, V. S. and Huber, G. P. (1988) Computer support for meetings of groups working on unstructured problems: a field experiment. *MIS Quarterly*, 12, 645–666.

Lai, S. (2008) Shared Displays to Support Collaborative Exploration of Ocean Summits. MSc thesis, University of British Columbia, Vancouver, Canada.

Lai, S. and Christensen, V. (2009) *Life in the Chesapeake Bay*. Canada, 6 min, available at http://ecopath.org/LifeInTheChesapeakeBay/.

Levhari, D. and Mirman, L. J. (1980) The great fish war: an example using a dynamic Cournot-Nash solution. *The Bell Journal of Economics*, 11, 322–334.

McCartt, A. T. and Rohrbaugh, J. (1989) Evaluating group decision support system effectiveness: A performance study of decision conferencing. *Decision Support Systems*, 5, 243–253.

Miller, G. A. (2003) The magical number seven, plus or minus two: some limits on our capacity for processing information. *Psychological Review*, 63, 81–97.

Ni, T., Bowman, D. and Chen, J. (2006) *Increased Display Size and Resolution Improve Task Performance in Information-Rich Virtual Environments*. Toronto: Canadian Information Processing Society, pp. 139–146.

Norman, D. and Shallice, T. (2000) Attention to action: willed and automatic control of behavior. In Gazzaniga, M. S., ed., *Cognitive Neuroscience: A Reader*. Oxford, UK: Blackwell Publishers Ltd., pp. 376–390.

Paarlberg, R. L. (2001) Environmentally sustainable agriculture in the 21st century. *Aspen Institute Congressional Program*, 29, 29–36.

Pauly, D. (1995) Anecdotes and the shifting baseline syndrome of fisheries. *Trends in Ecology & Evolution*, 10, 430.

Pauly, D., Alder, J., Bennett, E., et al. (2003) The future for fisheries. *Science*, 302, 1359–1361.

Pauly, D., Christensen, V. and Walters, C. (2000) Ecopath, Ecosim, and Ecospace as tools for evaluating ecosystem impact of fisheries. *ICES Journal of Marine Science*, 57, 697–706.

Shoemaker, G. and Inkpen, K. (2001) Single display privacyware: augmenting public displays with private information. New York, NY: ACM, pp. 522–529.

Walters, C. (1994) Use of gaming procedures in evaluation of management experiments. *Canadian Journal of Fisheries and Aquatic Sciences*, 51, 2705–2714.

Walters, C. and Christensen, V. (2007) Adding realism to foraging arena predictions of trophic flow rates in Ecosim ecosystem models: shared foraging arenas and bout feeding. *Ecological Modelling*, 209, 342–350.

Walters, C. J. and Coleman, F. C. (2004) Proceedings of the fourth William R. and Lenore Mote international symposium in fisheries ecology, November 5–7, 2002, Sarasota, Florida: Confronting trade-offs in the ecosystem approach to fisheries management. Preface. *Bulletin of Marine Science*, 74: 489–490.

Walters, C. J. and Martell, S. J. D. (2004) *Fisheries Ecology and Management*. Princeton, NJ: Princeton University Press.

Worm, B., Hilborn, R., Baum, J., Branch, T., Collie, J., Costello, C., Fogarty, M., Fulton, E., Hutchings, J., Jennings, S., Jensen, O. P., Lotze, H. K., Mace, P. M., McClanahan, T. R., Minto, C., Palumbi, S. R., Parma, A. M., Ricard, D., Rosenberg, A. A., Watson, R. and Zeller, D. (2009) Rebuilding global fisheries. *Science*, 325: 578.

21

The relationship between science and ocean policy

Science and policy share a dynamic relationship, at times shunning one another, at times bound in uneasy co-dependency, or enjoying mutual cooperation. The tone of the relationship determines reality: sustainable fisheries or decimated populations, protected coastlines or overrun beaches. Like it or not, scientists have the opportunity, and responsibility, to influence the outcome. Our choices help determine which histories will repeat.

Policy needs science in order to meet its mandates effectively. The goal is not to return nature to a pre-human, pristine state. Instead, it is to achieve sustainable use of our natural resources so that our children, the unborn, and we are able to benefit from them. Whether we use nature for commerce, recreation, appreciation, or evolution, all of these values are better served by abundance than by scarcity. Science does not determine or set these values, society does. But science can inform these values so society's policy goals are fulfilled.

WHEN SCIENCE IS IGNORED OR DISMISSED

When science is ignored or dismissed to support industry ideologies, it often results in the loss of a once plentiful resource. One of the most well-documented and still unresolved examples is the case of the Atlantic bluefin tuna (*Thunnus thynnus*). These fish are truly giants of the sea, growing to over 700 kg, swimming at up to 80 km per hour, and traversing ocean basins. Their speed, agility, and power have inspired art and legend. Their unique circulatory and fine-tuned navigation systems have amazed scientists. And their tender flesh has tempted many a sushi aficionado.

For thousands of years, these silver beasts were revered and slaughtered in the elaborate nets ("almadraba" and "tonnara") of

Ecosystem Approaches to Fisheries: A Global Perspective, ed. V. Christensen and J. Maclean. Published by Cambridge University Press. © Cambridge University Press 2011.

Mediterranean fishers (Maggio, 2000). On the western and northern shores of the Atlantic, however, they were considered worthless, nuisances, or at most, a challenge on the line (Pauly, 1995). But no longer. Bluefin tuna is the most expensive fish flesh in the world. It is tragically ironic that demand for the raw, deep red meat – the very product of the bluefin's vitality, speed, and endurance – is driving the species toward the point from which it may never swim again.

The current status of Atlantic bluefin is characterized by a 90% reduction in the western population and at least a 50% reduction in the eastern population since the 1970s. That happened not due to a lack of science but to dismissal of scientific findings.

The International Commission for the Conservation of Atlantic Tuna (ICCAT, hereafter known as "the Commission"), formed in 1966, was formally designated as the scientific and management authority for Atlantic tuna and other large predatory species. After over a decade of a steadily declining western bluefin population, the Standing Committee on Research and Statistics (the scientific arm of the Commission) recommended that the catch of western bluefin be "reduced to as near zero as feasible" (Safina, 1993). At this stage, it seemed as though science was at least partially embraced, for the Commission set a quota of 1160 tonnes, ostensibly for scientific monitoring.

Unfortunately, the effect of this quota was never tested, as the following year, under pressure from fisheries lobbyists, the Commission more than doubled the quota to 2660 tonnes. It remained at that level through the 1980s although catches continued to plummet. Despite consistent predictions of further decline from its own scientists, the Commission failed to implement any changes in the quota. And it continues to do so. In November 2009, despite a strong recommendation by scientists for a complete moratorium, the Commission passed a 13 500 tonnes quota for 2010. By ignoring the science, the very institution that is charged with maintaining the stock instead has had a play-by-play, front row view of the fishery's slow and steady demise. What they witness from their inaction is not a sudden and surprising population collapse. It is a gradual and unwavering march toward extinction propelled by their own negligence.

The imminent total collapse of the Atlantic bluefin tuna is slowly gaining attention, however. The scientific committee of ICCAT (long ignored by the Commission) has shown that as of 2009, the species meets the criteria for a ban on international trade. In support of such action, a United Nations Food and Agriculture Organization (FAO) expert panel concluded that the Atlantic bluefin tuna meets the requirements for Appendix I listing under the Convention on International Trade in Endangered Species of Wild Fauna and Flora (CITES). The FAO expert panel has a strong influence on how countries vote at the CITES annual meetings, and a listing under Appendix 1 would lead to a ban on international trade of Atlantic bluefin tuna, and with it a likely closure of the fishery.

Such an example shows that when science is ignored, a centuries-old fishery may be brought to collapse. When the science is manipulated or abused so as to obscure the reality of a situation, even more harm may result.

WHEN SCIENCE IS CORRUPTED

The case of the bluefin tuna is also a striking example of the devastation caused by purposeful manipulation of the data and shows how a situation can go from bad to worse. While the population of bluefin tuna continued to decline and the Commission's own scientists were calling for reduced quotas, the Commission decided to disregard data from the 1960s and 1970s that showed a clear positive relationship between the biomass of the stock and the level of recruitment. By amputating the dataset, the Commission effectively removed any link between the current biomass of the stock and the future of the stock, and claimed recovery was independent of the stock biomass. This rationale was not only irrational but also fictitious; nevertheless, it was long used to argue for maintaining the exceedingly high quota levels. In the years leading up to the potential CITES listing, that quota no longer carried any significance, as the entire fishing fleet could only catch one tenth of the quota due to the extremely reduced population size of the western stock. The population has finally collapsed under the weight of decades of cynical inaction propelled by greed.

To avoid such corruption of the data, scientists must take an active role in not only presenting the data as fact, but also defending it. We are the experts, the ones who understand the nuances and implications of the data we provide. It is, therefore, our responsibility to make sure that the consequences of policy decisions are clearly and loudly defined.

WHEN SCIENCE IS SCORNED

In no situation is it more important for scientists to defend the facts than in the current struggle to implement effective climate change policy. Here, scientists face not just dismissal of the science, but an active campaign to discredit it. Our data may be imperfect, but applying imperfect new knowledge is almost always better than business as usual, especially when the problems are so apparent. For example, while it is understandable that people construct seawalls to defend coastal homes, it is inexcusable for development to continue on the unstable environments of the shore. Scientists must make these catastrophic consequences known.

Science is the discipline of discovery, of exposing what is going on out there in the wild. To be a scientist, therefore, requires a solemn obligation to keep the focus on what really is happening in nature. It is important that we stick to the facts and refrain from exaggeration or dramatization. But it is imperative that we never abandon the facts to simply drift in the current of public opinion or be carried away by the winds of the political atmosphere. Providing information is not enough; advocacy is required for the facts to hold their value.

WHEN SCIENCE IS MADE TO OBSCURE THE FACTS

Many cases of misuse of science are not as blatantly obvious as data manipulation or active attack. Science is sometimes used to obscure the underlying problems in an effort to promote special interests. Pacific salmon in the Columbia River were victims of such a campaign and serve as a clear example of what happens when science is used to distract attention from environmental crises. Populations of salmon have been reduced in large part due to the changes in river water quality associated with the massive deforestation of the ancient forests (over 95% have been cut down in the United States) as well as construction of insurmountable dams, jointly creating a new environment with evolutionary challenges for survival (Waples *et al.*, 2008). Hatcheries were propounded as the way to allow dams and deforestation to go forward. The slogan was "Salmon without rivers" (Lichatowich, 2001). Here, the science of aquaculture was used not to address the environmental problem so much as to enable and abet it. The result was continued decline in salmon populations.

WHEN SCIENCE IS HEEDED

When scientific findings are properly applied, positive change can result. Sound science and its continued application led to understanding the declines and formulating recovery plans for such coastal species as striped bass and many New England groundfish, with reasonable success to date (Safina *et al.*, 2005). The good news is that recovery can occur even when science is applied late in the game.

The case of the Atlantic swordfish is an interesting example of what can happen when science is first ignored, but then applied rigorously. In this instance, negligent management policies were reversed by consumer pressure and lawsuits based upon scientific findings.

The catch of swordfish in the first half of the twentieth century was mostly by harpoon fishers, and was relatively stable. Longlining began in 1962 and was immediately followed by declines in the population. Regulations on mercury levels caused slight fluctuations in the abundance of swordfish, with stricter limits set in the early 1970s resulting in a small increase in the population. In the late 1970s, the limits were relaxed and the population responded with a steep decline through the late 1990s. It was at this time that boycotts and lawsuits were filed, bringing the attention of the declines to a wider public audience (Jacquet *et al.*, 2009). The science was clear: the stock was on the verge of collapse. The response was also clear: policy changes based on the science should take the form of closures and reduced quotas. In this case, applying science resulted in a long-term recovery trend.

While there is still a ways to go for this population to be really recovered, the population is currently recovering (Williamson, 2008). The message here is that human activities directly affect wild populations, a concept that is often questioned because of the difficulty in observing nature beneath the waves. Scientific data are the eyes with which to "see" into this blue realm. Scientists are the ones who can explain the link between how we act and how nature responds.

WHEN SCIENCE IS APPLIED ON MULTIPLE FRONTS

Science can succeed in mediating between even the most complex problems of human demands and nature's requirements. Seabirds and turtles provide encouraging examples of once critically threatened populations that are now showing signs of recovery.

For albatross, foraging migrations can be tremendously taxing, with adults enduring 12 000 km trips between the tropics and the unforgiving northern climes of the Aleutian Islands (Safina, 2002). The additional mortality due to bycatch on longlines of these giant winged wanderers has proved unsustainable to many species. But the longline fishery is an entrenched economic and social enterprise in this region and closing the fishery is not an option. Instead, science has been used to determine what inexpensive but effective changes can be made to reduce the unwanted catch of seabirds in this industry. As it turns out, simple changes in fishing techniques – setting lines from the sides of boats instead of the rear, or running extra lines and buoys to frighten birds out of the danger zone – are very effective at reducing bycatch. These modifications are increasingly used and provide hope for dwindling albatross populations.

For sea turtles, mortality due to human activities occurs through-out their life: adult turtles fall prey to hunters on the beach while laying eggs or drown in trawl nets or on longlines; hatchlings are given the additional, often insurmountable challenge to find the water's edge among the barrage of artificial lights that obscure the horizon's subtle glow (Safina, 2006). However, in some regions, such as the southern United States, statistics on declining turtle populations (as well as the more obvious declines in nesters observed on the beaches) have resulted in policy decisions that have led to recent increases in population size for some species. Turtle exclusion devices have reduced bycatch in trawl fisheries, and new data on the foraging/diving patterns of loggerheads have helped define less risky depths in which to set longlines. Campaigns on beaches to turn off lights during the breeding season have proved successful in encouraging more females to come ashore and lay eggs and causing less confusion among hatchlings crawling toward the sea. Green turtle populations in Florida are increasing, as are loggerheads. These efforts need now to expand to the international arena.

THE ROLE OF SCIENTISTS

The state of the world's oceans and its inhabitants is at best alarming, and at worst, depressing. Despite decades of scientific research, we have yet to achieve sustainable management or proper stewardship of our ocean resources. But the failure is not due to a lack of science. Rather, this reality persists as a consequence of the interaction between science and policy. History shows us that science may be scorned, ignored, acknowledged, or sometimes, fully incorporated into policy, with drastically different consequences for the planet's ecosystems as a result. The conflicts are never really between conser-vation and future use, because conservation ensures future use. Rather, most environmental conflicts are the result of short- versus long-term thinking, the difference between selfishness and wisdom. It is a question of values and the greater good that illuminates what is the "right" decision. How can science take part in such a socially driven issue? Science cannot tell us what to do, but it can tell us what things to do to successfully achieve stated value-driven goals.

The role of science is clear: to inform decision makers of the consequences of their decisions and not let anyone lose sight of the implications (Reichert, this volume). This is particularly important with regard to the oceans because science is the only pathway by which information is carried from that obscure, submerged world to our terrestrial reality. Scientists are the conveyors of this knowledge. We must produce useful data, advocate their appropriate application, and also safeguard the data against both corruption and dismissal (Hirshfield, this volume). Only then will we effectively avoid shifted baselines and empty oceans.

REFERENCES

Jacquet, J., Hocevar, J., Lai, S., Majluf, P., Pelletier, N., Pitcher, T., Sala, E., Sumaila, R. and Pauly, D. (2009) Conserving wild fish in a sea of market-based efforts. *Oryx*, 44, 45–56.

Lichatowich, J. (2001) *Salmon Without Rivers: A History of the Pacific Salmon Crisis.* Washington DC: Island Press.

Maggio, T. (2000) *Mattanza: Love and Death in the Sea of Sicily.* Cambridge, MA: Perseus.

Pauly, D. (1995) Anecdotes and the shifting baseline syndrome of fisheries. *Trends in Ecology & Evolution*, 10, 430.

Safina, C. (1993) Bluefin tuna in the west Atlantic: negligent management and the making of an endangered species. *Conservation Biology*, 7, 229–234.

Safina, C. (2002) *Eye of the Albatross: Visions of Hope and Survival.* New York, NY: Henry Holt and Co.

Safina, C. (2006) *Voyage of the Turtle: In Pursuit of the Earth's Last Dinosaur.* New York, NY: Henry Holt and Co.

Safina, C., Rosenberg, A., Myers, R., Terrance Quinn, I. and Collie, J. (2005) US ocean fish recovery: staying the course. *Science*, 5735, 707–708.

Waples, R., Zabel, R., Scheuerell, M. and Sanderson, B. (2008) Evolutionary responses by native species to major anthropogenic changes to their eco-systems: Pacific salmon in the Columbia River hydropower system. *Molecular Ecology*, 17, 84–96.

Williamson, G. (2008) Tail of hope: Canada's north Atlantic straddling and highly migratory fish stocks, and the Prince of Darkness, a note. *University of Miami Inter-American Law Review*, 40, 383–412.

Index